Exploring Translation and Multilingual Text Production:
Beyond Content

Text, Translation, Computational Processing

3

Editors
Annely Rothkegel
John Laffling

Mouton de Gruyter
Berlin · New York

Exploring Translation and Multilingual Text Production: Beyond Content

Edited by
Erich Steiner
Colin Yallop

Mouton de Gruyter
Berlin · New York   2001

Mouton de Gruyter (formerly Mouton, The Hague)
is a Division of Walter de Gruyter GmbH & Co. KG, Berlin.

♾ Printed on acid-free paper which falls within the guidelines
of the ANSI to ensure permanence and durability.

Library of Congress Cataloging-in-Publication Data

> Exploring translation and multilingual text production : beyond
> content / edited by Erich Steiner, Colin Yallop.
>   p. cm. − (Text, translation, computational processing ; 3)
>   Includes bibliographical references and index.
>   ISBN 3 11 016792 1 (cloth : alk. paper)
>   1. Translating and interpreting. 2. Discourse analysis. I.
> Steiner, Erich. II. Yallop, Colin. III. Series.
> P306.E93 2001
> 418′.02−dc21
>   2001030324

Die Deutsche Bibliothek − Cataloging-in-Publication Data

> Exploring translation and multilingual text production: beyond
> content / ed. by Erich Steiner ; Colin Yallop. − Berlin ; New
> York : Mouton de Gruyter, 2001
>   (Text, translation, computational processing ; 3)
>   ISBN 3-11-016792-1

© Copyright 2001 by Walter de Gruyter GmbH & Co. KG, D-10785 Berlin.
All rights reserved, including those of translation into foreign languages. No part of
this book may be reproduced or transmitted in any form or by any means, electronic or
mechanical, including photocopy, recording, or any information storage and retrieval
system, without permission in writing from the publisher.
Printing: WB-Druck, Rieden/Allgäu. − Binding: Lüderitz & Bauer-GmbH, Berlin.
Printed in Germany.

Contents

Part I
Theoretical Orientation

Introduction
Erich Steiner and Colin Yallop 3

Towards a theory of good translation
M.A.K. Halliday 13

What can linguistics learn from translation?
Michael Gregory 19

The environments of translation
Christian M.I.M. Matthiessen 41

Part II
Modeling translation

How do we know when a translation is good?
Juliane House 127

Intralingual and interlingual versions of a text — how specific is the notion of *translation*?
Erich Steiner 161

Towards a model for the description of cross-linguistic divergence and commonality in translation
Elke Teich 191

The construction of equivalence
Colin Yallop 229

Part III
Working with translation and multilingual texts: computational and didactic projects

Teaching translation
Susanna Shore 249

Computer assisted text analysis and translation: a functional approach in the analysis and translation of advertising texts
Chris Taylor and Anthony Baldry 277

Translation, controlled languages, generation
Anthony Hartley and Cécile Paris 307

Author Index 327

Subject Index 331

Part I
Theoretical Orientation

Introduction

Erich Steiner and Colin Yallop

The purpose of this introduction is to explain some general features of this book (1.1), to give a brief summary of the chapters within it (1.2) and to make some suggestions about how the book might be used (1.3). We hope that our remarks here will not only introduce the book but also make it clear why we believe it to be well placed in the series *Text, Translation, Computational Processing*.

1. What kind of book is this?

As the sub-title of the book implies, one of our aims is to move beyond the notion of *content* in thinking about language and translation. The book is an attempt to face the demands of translation and multilingual text production by modeling texts as configurations of multidimensional meanings, rather than as containers of *content*. A common conception of translating is that it is a process of transferring content from (texts in) a source language to (texts in) a target language. From that kind of perspective, multilingual text production — if it is seen as a textual operation in its own right at all — is simply the expression of some (usually pre-existing) content in several languages. This book sets out to challenge such folk notions, as well as their more technical variants in logic-oriented approaches to language. It will be a recurrent argument in this book that unstructured and one-dimensional notions of *content* are insufficient for an understanding of the processes involved in translation and multilingual text production. Even more refined variants of such notions in logic-oriented semantics suffer at least from the privileging of one dimension of meaning. Rather than using the assumption of some stable, unchanged *content* in modeling the processes in focus here — an assumption which is rarely if ever equal to the day-to-day reality of work in translation and text generation — we rely on the notion of *meaning*, a concept that allows us to recognize multidimensionality and internal stratification into levels. For the processes in focus are complex, and we need to do justice to them.

Thus we do not apologize for problematizing simplistic notions of content. Beyond that, we hope to demonstrate how more complex and more flexible notions of meaning can lead directly to a better understanding and to enhanced professional practice. The various contributions to this volume take up relevant research questions, problematize existing answers to them, and either show the way towards or provide new answers. In some cases these answers take the form of computational and methodological tools for analysing and producing texts in multilingual settings.

Seen against this background, our book establishes a middle ground between a conventional text book and a collection of research papers. The readers we hope to address are advanced students rather than beginners; experienced students and translators who are interested in opening up and engaging with questions of research; teachers who are interested in ways of helping their students to become independent reflective professionals, with an eye on research and development not only in translating and interpreting but also in multilingual text production, including machine translation and multilingual text generation; and the research community in general.

We hope that the frequent use of specific textual examples — and substantial use of major portions of real texts — will help to provide ways of entry into the more technical areas addressed in our chapters. We hope also that those who teach translation studies or train translators and interpreters will appreciate both the engagement with texts and the specific comments on possible improvements in teaching methods. Given the increasing intermingling of translation tasks and work in multilingual text processing, teachers may also find value in the scope and perspectives of this book. And, while the contributions to this book do have an orientation towards long-term and fundamental questions, more so than is perhaps usual in the research literature, the book is intended to be at least thought-provoking to researchers.

Naturally enough, the authors of the different chapters adopt slightly different stances towards their topics and their audience, depending on their particular focus within the general field. All of the chapters try to explore key concepts and to provide arguments for the proposed approach or solution, and all of them should therefore be seen as contributions to a modeling of translation and multilingual text production, beyond the specific problems addressed in each case. Chapters by House, Steiner, Teich and Yallop are perhaps the clearest demonstrations of this. In some places we find, in addition, an explicit attention to pedagogy, notably in Shore's and Taylor and Baldry's contributions. In others, we see the technical expert explaining and arguing for specific technological solutions to problems of translation and multilingual text production (e.g. Hartley and Paris, Taylor and Baldry, Teich). Some of the chapters have a decidedly theoretical orientation (e.g. Gregory, Halliday, Matthiessen) but there is nowhere in this book a categorial and strict separation of theory and application.

The contributors bring to their work a range of expertise — in linguistics, translation studies (including interpreting), language teaching, lexicography and computer science, and this variety of educational and professional background is one of the factors which give us hope that we can provide some new insights into the complex phenomena addressed here. The authors collectively exemplify interdisciplinarity, and perhaps even transdisciplinarity, in the sense that at least some of us would not feel too happy about being assigned exclusively to any one of the traditional disciplines. But there is another sense in which this group of authors represents transdisciplinarity: while our initial disciplinary backgrounds are diverse (linguistics, translation studies, literary studies, computer science), all of us have at some point come into contact with a particular functional theory of language, Systemic Functional Linguistics. And it is our particular pleasure to have Michael Halliday, the central figure of this school, as one of the contributing authors. While several of us would hesitate, for one reason or another, to call ourselves "systemicists", all of us have had extended working contact with the theory, which supports a certain terminological and conceptual coherence in the book. An important side effect of this is that notions from Systemic Functional Linguistics are explored and tested critically for their suitability in the modeling of translation and multilingual text production.

Despite this unifying backdrop of Systemic Functional Linguistics, the book does not assume thorough familiarity with the theory. While the authors have some shared background — we all work, broadly speaking, in intercultural and multilingual communication, and we all have some acquaintance with SFL — we do not assume that our readers will also share that background. As contributors we have therefore taken care to explain terms more often than we might have chosen to do in a research paper, and to make contact terminologically with other approaches to the field. We thus hope that this book will be accessible to interested audiences beyond those who come to the book with similar backgrounds to our own. On the other hand, the book does not claim to be a beginner's introduction to translation or multilingual text production from scratch, and we do assume some knowledge of the field.

One more feature of this book will, we hope, contribute to its coherence and make it appealing to the reader. All of the chapters in this book were written for the book: this is not a relatively loose collection of conference papers, nor a gathering of previously published work, but a focussed work. Indeed, the idea for this book arose from a workshop on translation studies in Sydney in 1996, and the idea was further developed and tested in an all-day workshop in Cardiff in 1998, attended by all but one of the authors. Between these two events there was considerable exchange of electronic mail, and at the Cardiff workshop authors presented a preliminary version of their chapter for the benefit and reactions of the other members of the group. Finally, the editors were able to consult intensively, when one of us (Erich Steiner) was visiting Sydney for three months.

In the next section of this introduction we give more detail of each chapter. But we hope that what we have said so far has made it clear why we believe the series *Text, Translation, Computational Processing* provides a very fitting environment for our book. The approaches advocated here are firmly grounded in models of language in use, that is in text and discourse, rather than in models of an assumed language system dissociated from its use. Furthermore, the emphasis is on textual operations across languages, contexts and cultures, on translations or other forms of multilingual information sharing. Finally, the computational systems whose architectures are discussed here are typical of recent developments, focussing on support for multilingual experts, rather than aiming to replace them in the style of many of the older machine translation systems. Finally, it is an overall assumption of the contributions presented here that intercultural and interlingual communication is best conceptualized not as some kind of transfer of *content*, but rather as transfer and interaction of textual features along a whole series of dimensions.

2. The contributions to this book

The chapters following this introduction are grouped under three broad headings, namely (1) Theoretical Orientation; (2) Modeling Translation; (3) Working with Translation and Multilingual Texts: Computational and Didactic Projects. As will be clear from the brief summaries of the chapters, none of these three headings is to be interpreted too rigidly: chapters that are theoretically oriented, for example, do not neglect practical application and illustration, and chapters that focus more obviously on models and projects do not exclude theoretical discussion and implications.

The Theoretical Orientation opens with a chapter by Michael Halliday, who asks a fundamental question: what is a theory of good translation? And he begins by contrasting the linguist's interest in a translation theory which studies "how things are" and a translator's interest in a theory which studies "how things ought to be". His chapter proceeds by refining these questions and setting them in a wide context of reflection on language — for example by characterizing theories as "indicative" or "imperative", and by drawing analogies between translation studies and textual analysis. He offers some thought-provoking comments on system, equivalence and value, and his chapter serves both to provide a significant theoretical introduction to the book, and to establish a style of theorizing which makes constant contact with important practical issues such as why some texts are much more highly valued than others, and how it is that a translation can be judged good.

By asking the question "what can linguistics learn from translation?", Michael Gregory seems to be approaching translation studies from the opposite direction to Halliday. Gregory comments on the long history of translating as a human activity and suggests that "as well as diversity there is also a commonality of human social experience" which makes translation possible. While valuing functional theories of language, Gregory also gives a sympathetic hearing to formal and cognitivist theorizing, and argues for a "socio-cognitive linguistics that attempts to combine systemic-functional insights and Chomskyan perspectives…" Gregory also digs deeply into Bible translation, not only commenting on various kinds of English translations of the Bible ("formal equivalence" versions, "paraphrases", and so on) but also using a short extract from the New Testament to illustrate and evaluate different translations into English. He shows how contextual factors, like assumptions about how a translation is to be used and "self-consciousness" about theological affiliation, find their consequences in the wording, in nuances of meaning. He concludes his chapter by noting trends in Bible translation and presenting them as food for thought for linguists.

Christian Matthiessen sets out to "locate" translation and translation theory. He investigates translation as a process, as a process of transformation and a process of creation; and translation as product, as the concrete outcome of transformation or creation. He then develops the notion that translation can be understood as a multilingual potential. With the help of a "map" he relates translation to other areas of multilingual interest in linguistics and shows how these different multingual concerns can inform one another.

The four chapters making up the section on Modeling Translation begin with one by Juliane House. House takes up one of Halliday's questions: "how do we know when a translation is good?" She gives a detailed and useful review of the highly diverse ways of understanding and approaching this question, and outlines her own functional approach (which is "mainly based on systemic-functional theory" but also "draws eclectically on Prague school ideas, speech act theory and discourse analysis"). She demonstrates her approach by testing it on a German translation of an English children's book.

Erich Steiner explores the notion of translation by a detailed examination of "intralingual" and "interlingual" versions of a text. He begins with a discussion of the important notion of "register" and then proceeds to deal with a set of closely related texts. All of these texts are excerpts from advertisements for Rolex Oyster watches, some in English, some in German, published in magazines such as *Newsweek*, *Time International* and

Der Spiegel. Steiner combines the broad perspective of register and variation with careful attention to the details of wording, from the "sheer ability" of a Rolex Oyster to keep going, to the Oyster case "sculptured" (or is it "hewn" or "produced"?) from a solid block of metal. This detailed textual analysis leads to some theorizing about relationships among texts and about the nature of translation, including some reasons why translated texts are systematically different from other types of text and might be considered to constitute a register on their own

Elke Teich offers a model of the contrastive-linguistic resources involved in translation. She provides a review of categories of linguistic description in Systemic Functional Linguistics and discusses the ways in which languages tend to differ from each other — "the dimensions of contrastive-linguistic description". She grounds her discussion in an examination of some differences between English and German, using as a specific text an extract from an article on *The hidden strength of hydrogen*. Teich compares the English text, as published in *Scientific American*, with the German translation that appeared in *Spektrum der Wissenschaft*, and there is added interest for the reader in her use of the SYSTRAN system to generate an English back translation of the German text. Teich's chapter concludes with some perceptive remarks about translation strategies, translation types and translation procedures, viewed within the model she has developed.

Colin Yallop's chapter begins with what may seem like a philosophical discussion of uniqueness and similarity: indeed, everything in the world is unique and changeable. This introduces both a discussion of how it is that we can judge things to be "the same" or "equivalent" and an examination of a text which many might think wildly adventurous, namely a translation of Lewis Carroll's *Alice's Adventures in Wonderland* into the Australian Aboriginal language Pitjantjatjara. Or is it a translation? With the help of a back translation of the Pitjantjatjara (printed beside the Pitjantjatjara in the published book), Yallop is able to show that there are points of anchorage, similarities between Carroll's original and the Pitjantjatjara version, as well as points of (radical) departure, which will leave many readers wanting to call the Pitjantjatjara text an adaptation rather than a translation (and the published book, *Alitji in the Dreamtime*, does in fact describe itself as having been "adapted and translated" from *Alice in Wonderland*.).

The final section of the book consists of three chapters, each focussing on a relatively concrete demonstration of computational and didactic projects in translation studies and multilingual text generation. Susanna Shore's chapter turns our attention particularly to pedagogy. After some brief comments on conventional translation exercises in schools and universities and a review of basic concepts, Shore tackles the practicalities of teaching translation in the classroom. Her discussion includes, for example, classroom attention to the commissioning of translations. It may be possible for teachers in schools and universities to give their students translation assignments that have no obvious customer or audience — but in real life, translators get their jobs from people who often have very definite ideas about why and how and for whom this text is to be translated. A professional teacher should ensure that students are prepared for this reality. In keeping with the spirit of this book, Shore's chapter is not only practical advice but also a demonstration of principles on a specific text, in this case two excerpts from a catalogue of Finnish children's literature, accompanied by a (published) translation into English.

Chris Taylor and Anthony Baldry are, like Shore, involved and interested in pedagogy. Their chapter introduces computer assisted text analysis and translation, and outlines a specific project on which they themselves have been working in Italy. They have developed an interactive computer application which has been programmed with textual analyses. This allows the translation student to view a text, to go to various modules which assist in relevant analysis of the text (for example, cohesion or thematic structure) and then to type in a translation and get feedback about the adequacy of the translation. Readers should not only appreciate the careful explanation of how this application works but also enjoy the linguistic details that are revealed in the text (which is a light-hearted television advertisement for the Mitsubishi Pajero).

Tony Hartley and Cecile Paris have extensive experience of working on multilingual documentation and "controlled languages" – varieties of language in which there are restrictions on grammatical patterns and on choice of vocabulary in order to create a less ambiguous, more consistent language for such purposes as writing technical manuals. Hartley and Paris carefully and helpfully explain the nature and role of controlled languages and multilingual text generation in commercial settings, highlighting some of the problems, giving concrete textual illustration, and showing how research is contributing to the development of useful tools.

3. How this book might be used

The contributors to this book, each in their own way, are exploring concepts and relationships among concepts, and arguing for or against certain types of modeling. In a general sense, therefore, the book may serve as text book for advanced and postgraduate seminars and working groups in education, research and development settings. Most chapters could serve as topics for further general discussion, but perhaps most notably those by Halliday, with its accessible exposition of Systemic Functional perspectives, and by Gregory, with its inclusion of Chomskyan as well as Systemic Functional insights. House's chapter is a solid general introduction to the topic of translation evaluation as well as an outline of her own approach; while Matthiessen's will be useful to those wishing to pursue discussion of the relationship of translation to comparative linguistics and typology in a broad multilingual framework.

More specifically, some chapters can serve as starting points for particular discussions or projects: for example, Hartley and Paris's chapter may form the basis for a discussion of multilingual documentation and its increasing relevance to the work of commercial translators; or Shore's practical suggestions may provide the material for a discussion of how to apply or adapt her ideas to improve the teaching of translation in local settings; or Taylor and Baldry's chapter might be studied to see whether the kinds of textual analysis being offered to students could be used in the context of other languages and other institutions.

Given that particular care has been taken to provide textual exemplification of arguments, the book incorporates a wide variety of examples of real translation tasks, supported by detailed attention to the wording of the texts. Steiner's chapter includes some detailed examination of similar advertisements in English and German, and Teich's a similarly useful examination of differences between English and German versions of popular scientific writing. Such studies might provide examples to inspire further attention to textual detail, whether in English and German or in other languages. Yallop's chapter may be helpful to those interested in literary or "creative" translation (although this book should make it clear that there is no simple dichotomy of factual commercial or scientific translation and literary or creative translation) and may suggest comparable exercises in examining portions of translated imaginative works.

None of these suggestions is of course intended to imply that the chapters can be used *only* in the ways mentioned, and we hope that the book will, beyond functioning as an advanced textbook, also offer strategies and concepts for research and development teams in the area of multilingual technologies and perhaps also make some contribution towards providing a common language for discussing phenomena in translation and multilingual text production — a common language which is urgently needed.

We acknowledge that what we are offering here is, of course, a traditional written book — with all the attendant advantages and disadvantages. But it may be helpful to point out that some of the contributions and some of the specific technologies described here are also accessible electronically. Various text and translation corpora are also mentioned in the book, and these resources are becoming indispensable in modern translation studies. Where it is not already stated within this book how to access such tools and resources (e.g. via an internet address), we recommend that interested readers make contact with the individual authors to obtain advice about access and availability.

Finally, we hope readers will find the book in itself enjoyable as well as useful. All of us who have contributed to the book have put considerable effort into making this a coherent collection. We hope that we have managed to realize our aims in a readable text and that the book is a faithful and worthy translation.

Towards a theory of good translation
M.A.K. Halliday

We all indulge in theorizing when we have to: we become medical advisers when someone we know is ill, and we are always ready with theories about translation, when faced with quaint or impenetrable instructions on some gadget imported from overseas. Among scholars in science and the humanities are many with a serious interest in the practice and theory of translation as it impinges on their own disciplines; writers and literary scholars have probably contributed the most to exploring the translation process and the relation between a translated text and its original. But there are two groups of professionals who theorize about translation in its entirety: the translators themselves, and the linguists. Both these groups are concerned with a general theory of translation; but they interpret this in rather different ways. For a linguist, translation theory is the study of how things are: what is the nature of the translation process and the relation between texts in translation. For a translator, translation theory is the study of how things ought to be: what constitutes good or effective translation and what can help to achieve a better or more effective product (cf. Bell 1991: ch.1).[1]

Of course, in putting it in these personalized terms I am consciously being schematic. Some translators are interested in the nature of their undertaking from the point of view of linguistic theory; and some linguists engage in improving the quality of translations and in training translators. It is entirely possible for the same person to adopt both these theoretical perspectives. Nevertheless they do raise different issues. To express it in grammatical terms: the linguist's theory of translation is a declarative theory (or better, indicative, since a theory of this kind is as much interrogative as declarative), whereas the translator's theory of translation is an imperative theory. Each is, obviously, an important and productive enterprise. What concerns me here is the relationship between the two.

Let me recall here something I have said at times with respect to text analysis. When we analyze a text linguistically, we usually have one of two possible goals. One is to explain why the text means what it does: why it is understood the way it is — by the analyst, or by anyone else. That is the lower of the two goals, the one that is easier to attain. The higher goal is to explain why the text is valued as it is — again, by anyone who may be evaluating it: this might be, in the case of a literary or religious text, by a general consensus within the culture. This second goal is more difficult to attain, if only because it includes the first one: to be able to explain why a text is more, or perhaps less, effective in its context one must first be able to explain why it means what it is understood to mean. I am using "meaning" here in a broad, Firthian sense: a text has meaning at all linguistic strata, those of expression as well as those of content. The rhyme scheme of a poem is part of its phonological meaning.

How does this relate to the theory of translation? Let me approach this in two steps. First: suppose we are considering two texts, in different languages, the one said to be a translation of the other. The questions that arise are: is this text a translation of the other, or is it not? and if it is, is it a good translation? Of course, all such categories are fuzzy; but since they are all equally fuzzy, this does not affect the point. With the first question, we are considering what the text means; with the second, we are considering whether it is effective — and again, the second appears as the harder one to answer, since it is dependent on the first: we cannot judge whether a text is effective unless we know what it means.

With the second step, we ask two questions that are analogous to my questions regarding text analysis: why is this text a translation of the other? and why is it, or is it not, a good translation? In other words: how do we know? But in order to take this second step, we have to shift our stance. As long as we are asking only whether the two texts have these particular properties, we are simply observing instances: the two are being compared directly one with the other. Once we start asking why, our stance shifts and we are now observing systems: the systems of the two languages that lie behind the texts being compared. Just as the exercises in text analysis involve the theory of descriptive linguistics, so these exercises in translation analysis involve the theory of comparative descriptive linguistics (cf. Ellis 1966).

The problem of reconciling the two concepts of a theory of translation is that they make different assumptions about the stance of the observer. What I have called the linguist's perspective is systemic: it assumes that you can theorize the relationship of translation only by referring to language as system (or of course to other, non-linguistic features of the culture; but here also, to culture as system). The translator's perspective, on the other hand, is more likely to be instantial: it assumes that to theorize about how to improve a translation you have to engage with language as text. So, for example, in modeling functional variation in language the translator is more likely to think of "a register" as a text type, whereas the linguist will think of "a register" as a sub-system. The major difference between the indicative and the imperative perspectives seems to be that people tend to look at "translation" systemically, whereas they look at "good translation" instantially.

It is notoriously difficult to say why, or even whether, something is a good translation, since this must depend on a complex variety of different factors that are constantly shifting in their relationship one to another.

The central organizing concept is presumably that of "equivalence"; but equivalence with respect to what? It seems that one might need some kind of typology of equivalences, which could be assigned differential values according to the specific conditions attaching to a particular instance of translation. Is there such a typology ready to hand?

One likely source will be found in the parameters of language itself. If we construe these in terms of systemic functional theory there are three vectors which are probably the most relevant: stratification, metafunction and rank. Stratification is the organization of language in ordered strata: phonetic, phonological, lexicogrammatical and semantic — and one or more contextual strata outside of language proper. Metafunction is the organization of the content strata (lexicogrammar and semantics) in functional components: ideational, interpersonal and textual — roughly, the parts of the system that have to do with construing human experience, enacting social relationships, and creating discourse. Rank is the organization of the formal strata (phonology and lexicogrammar) in a compositional hierarchy: for example, in the grammar of English, clause complexes, clauses, phrases, groups, words and morphemes. All of these have been used in models of translation, and I will refer to each of them in turn.

In his book *A Linguistic Theory of Translation* (1965), Catford defined equivalence explicitly by reference to the different strata in language. The sense in which "translation equivalence" is most typically understood would be that of equivalence at the semantic stratum; but Catford recognizes equivalence at all the other strata, not only those of content but also those of expression (phonology and phonetics — and also, since he is taking account of the written medium, the analogous strata of "graphology" and "graphetics"). There could be purely graphic equivalence between symbols that resembled each other visually, even if they were functionally quite distinct. This kind of equivalence does not usually carry much value — though I used to play a game of multilingual Scrabble in which the roman letters also stood for their nearest graphic equivalents in Cyrillic: *w* for Russian *ш* and so on; and there are certainly contexts in which phonic equivalence may be valued rather highly. But the point I want to make here is the general one: that equivalence at different strata carries differential values; that in most cases the value that is placed on it goes up the higher the stratum — semantic equivalence is valued more highly than lexicogrammatical, and contextual equivalence perhaps most highly of all; but that these relative values can always be varied, and in any given instance of translation one can reassess them in the light of the task.

Catford's theory was entirely "indicative" in approach. In 1962 I wrote an article on translation in which (since it was offering a model for machine translation) I took a more "imperative" approach, adopting the notion that Ellis subsequently called "translation at ranks". This operated at the stratum of lexicogrammar, and the idea was to list a set of equivalents at the lowest rank, that of the morpheme, ranged in order of probability; and then to modify the choice of equivalent in a stepwise move up the rank scale, each step locating the item in the context of the next higher unit — first the word, then the group an so on. So for example the Russian morpheme *общ* might have as its most likely equivalent the English *socio-;* but in the context of the word *общий* it becomes *general*; when this word, in turn, occurs in the group *общая длина (obščaja dlina)*, this gets translated as *the overall length* (not *the general length*), the criterion being 'if the noun functioning as Thing is a measure of quantity'. This has never been adopted as far as I know as a strategy for machine translation — but it defines translation equivalence with respect to rank. Here again we can observe that equivalence at different ranks carries differential values; and that, again, the value tends to go up the higher the rank — clause complex (sentence) equivalence is valued more highly than clausal, clausal than phrasal and so on; but, again, there may always be particular circumstances in which equivalence at a lower rank acquires a relatively higher value.

The third vector in respect of which equivalence may be defined is that of metafunction. This is different from the other two discussed in that there is no ordering among the different metafunctions — no ordering, that is, in the system of language, although they are typically ordered in the value that is assigned to them in translation, with the ideational carrying by far the highest value overall. It is not hard to see the reason for this. As a general rule, "translation equivalence" is defined in ideational terms; if a text does not match its source text ideationally, it does not qualify as a translation, so the question whether it is a good translation does not arise. For precisely this reason, one of the commonest criticisms made of translated texts is that, while they are equivalent ideationally, they are not equivalent in respect of the other metafunctions — interpersonally, or textually, or both. To express this in analogous contextual terms, the field of discourse has been adequately construed in the target language but the tenor, or else the mode, has not. We cannot here assign a typical scale of values; but there can be considerable variation in the value that is accorded to equivalence in the non-ideational metafunctions. In some contexts, matching the relations of power and distance, and the patterns of evaluation and appraisal, set up in the original text may be very highly valued in the translation, to such an extent as even to override the demand for exact ideational equivalence.

This situation typically arises where the highest value, in stratal terms, is being placed on contextual equivalence, overriding the requirement for equivalence at the semantic stratum. In such cases what is being expected of the translator is a text which would have equivalent function to the original in the context of situation. This is analogous to what Hasan (1996: ch.5) describes as "semantic variation" between different coding orientations within one language (for example, where different mothers use different semantic strategies in giving reasons for regulating their child's behavior). And the analogy with the concept of variation provides another way of looking at the phenomenon of "equivalence value" that I have been discussing. If, for example, value is given to equivalence at some higher rank, the implication is that features at lower ranks are allowed to vary: provided the clauses are equivalent, the words and phrases need not be. The common motif, which permits us to look at translation as a kind of variation, is that of variation against some higher-level constant. This is a strategy that the translator has recourse to all the time.

To summarize the discussion of "equivalence value": in any particular instance of translation, value may be attached to equivalence at different ranks, different strata, different metafunctions. In rank, it is usually at the higher lexicogrammatical units that equivalence is most highly valued; lower units are then exempted (e.g. words can vary provided the clauses are kept constant). In strata, likewise, equivalence is typically most valued at the highest stratum within language itself, that of semantics (where again the lower strata may be allowed to vary); value may also attach explicitly to the level of context, especially when equivalence at lower strata is problematic. In metafunction, high value may be accorded to equivalence in the interpersonal or textual realms — but usually only when the ideational equivalence can be taken for granted (it is interesting to speculate on why this should be so).

If we now return to the two interpretations of "theory of translation" with which I started, these may seem a little less incommensurable. Let me express this as a characterization of the target language text (it could alternatively be expressed as a characteristic of the text pair). A "good" translation is a text which is a translation (i.e. is equivalent) in respect of those linguistic features which are most valued in the given translation context.

What this problematizes, of course, is the notion of value itself. I have been talking of the relative value that is accorded to translation equivalence at the various strata, ranks or metafunctions as outlined above. What I have left out of consideration is the value accorded to the (source language) text as a whole. Should a "great lyric poem" in the source language become a "great lyric poem" in the target? — in other words, what value is being assigned to the perceived quality of the original text? This is a question of the value that is being placed on value itself. And this constitutes one further variable for the translator, which we might need to add to the definition: ... and perhaps also in respect of the value which is assigned to the original (source language) text.

It also raises once more the second part of my analytic inquiry: why is the text evaluated as it is? If we can answer this, it may help us to decide, when translating it, how much value to place on the factor of equivalence in value.

Notes

1. For a fuller exploration of "equivalence of contextual function", and related issues, see the chapters in the present volume by Erich Steiner and by Colin Yallop. Steiner draws on the notion of variation in explaining "identity" of texts in translation, and suggests that "For something to count as a translation, it need not have the same register features as its source text, but register features which function similarly to those of the original in their context of culture". Yallop defines equivalence as constructed out of "a rich diversity of similarities", and discusses the metaphors with which the concept of equivalence has been embellished. He stresses that there may in fact be no equivalence at the level of cultural context — a situation familiar to Bible translators, which Yallop illustrates by reference to the "translation" of *Alice in Wonderland* into Pitjantjatjara.

References

Bell, Roger T.
    1991   *Translation and Translating: theory and practice*. London: Longman (Applied Linguistics and Language Study).

Catford, J.C.
    1965   *A Linguistic Theory of Translation*. London: Oxford University Press (Language and Language Learning 8).

Ellis, J.
    1966   *Towards a General Comparative Linguistics*. The Hague: Mouton (Janua Linguarum Series Minor).

Halliday, M.A.K.
    1962   Linguistics and machine translation. Zeitschrift für Phonetik, Sprachwissenschaft und Kommunikationsforschung 15.i/ii. Reprinted in Angus McIntosh & M.A.K. Halliday, 1966 *Patterns of Language: papers in general, descriptive and applied linguistics*, London: Longmans' Linguistics Library.

Hasan, Ruqaiya
    1996   *Ways of Saying: Ways of Meaning*, edited by Carmel Cloran, David Butt & Geoff Williams. London: Cassell (Open Linguistics Series).

Steiner, Erich
    (this volume) Intralingual and interlingual versions of a text — how specific is the notion of "translation"?

Yallop, Colin
    (this volume) The construction of equivalence.

What can linguistics learn from translation?

Michael Gregory

1. Prologue

I began the last, and only previous, piece I have written on translation, and that was nineteen years ago, with the disclaimer that I was not a translator, nor an expert on translation, but "a linguist, a philologist whose specialties are the description of present-day English, sociolinguistics and stylistics" (Gregory 1980: 45). That remains true today with the proviso that I have taught and written increasingly about linguistic theory since then. In that paper I was concerned with what help linguistics in the Firthian tradition might be in the practice and study of translation. So I started with some of Firth's own insights: that "the whole problem of translation is in the field of semantics" (Firth 1957: 32), and for Firth semantics was what linguistics was all about: "the disciplines and techniques of linguistics are directed to assist us in making statements of meaning" (Firth 1957: 191). He saw these statements as being dispersed throughout the different *modes* of description: the phonetic (including the phonoaesthetic), the phonological, the morphological, the syntactic, the collocational (or lexical) and the situational, and recognized that with some modes we might be facing meanings that are untranslatable (Firth 1957: 193). He also pointed out that it would pay to distinguish the kind of translation that is being called for, in his words "creative translations" (literary translations that aim to be works of art in the target language), "official" translation and machine translation; he saw a need for "the restriction of research in translation to the circumscribed fields of restricted languages" (Palmer ed. 1968: 91). Firth was at that time ahead of his time when, as regards machine translation his hunch was that the best progress would be made by the study of long units rather than the minimal segments favored by his transatlantic colleagues, and also by the examination of the mutual expectancy of words in cliches and high frequency collocations, particularly within restricted languages.

From Firth it was not too long a step to J. C. Catford's (1965) concise and lucid *A Linguistic Theory of Translation*, and his development of Firthian ideas on translation within the framework of scale and category linguistics and, very importantly, what is now called dialect and register (or diatype) theory, itself a sophistication and extension in many ways of Firth's concept of restricted language. So I spent much of the paper summarizing Catford's articulation of the concept of *translation equivalence* within the parameters of language variation (see Halliday, Matthiessen, and Steiner in this volume).

There was little originality in my paper and I have always been agreeably, if a little shamefacedly, surprised that so many real translators and genuine experts have, over the years, expressed their appreciation of it. I was, indeed, serious in my disclaimer of translation experience. However, as an undergraduate at Oxford in the middle to late 'fifties, pursuing studies in the Honour School of English, I was, of course, faced with the expectation that one should be able to translate, with extensive "gobbet" commentary Greek (Aristotle, Sophocles, Euripides, Aeschlyus), Latin (Vergil), French (Boileau, Racine, Corneille) and Anglo-Saxon: all this for "Prelims" at the end of the first two terms. After that there was *Beowulf* and, if you wanted it, some Old Norse and Old and Middle High German, and so on. At Oxford in those days "they", with the exception of Nevill Coghill, did not think Middle English needed much translation but there was extensive linguistic commentary to be done on the texts. I imagine things have changed, even at Oxford, over the last forty years. Some of you, perhaps, will know the nature of the translating in which we were involved: heavily literal, morpheme by morpheme, and some will remember the inestimable value of "cribs" and the surreptitious homage paid to Loeb.

However, even in the light of this limited and narrowly focussed experience, I have always been impressed by the very facts of translation: the fact that it has long been a constant human activity (to it we owe our first dictionaries in the West, bilingual and then "hard" or "foreign word" glossaries); the fact that translation is clearly seen throughout the world as socially and culturally necessary and useful; and the fact that whatever problems it faces, translation overcomes enough of them to be acknowledged as worthwhile, successful enough to earn a great investment of time, energy, and human and material resources.

One can, then, surely assume that it has proven, and does prove, its worth as one of humanity's answers to Babel. Another answer is the learning of foreign languages, itself necessarily implicated in the act and art of translation; and foreign language teaching and learning has contributed much to linguistics, particularly to that of the descriptive, tagmemic, Firthian and Hallidayan traditions (as, for example, in the work of C. C. Fries and of Halliday, McIntosh, and Strevens 1964). Perhaps it is now translation's turn, and it is appropriate that we reflect on what linguistics might learn about what it studies from the facts, processes and consequences of translation.

The omnipresence and long history of translation has, to my mind, two important theoretical implications. The first is one that should give encouragement to functional theorists of language. The relative success of translation suggests that as well as diversity there is also a commonality of human social experience and, in significant measure, of the linguistic representation and processing of experience amongst different cultures living through different languages. Otherwise translation would be well nigh impossible. Now it is true that translation of the documents of another culture does not usually begin in the absence of some considerable degree of cultural contact by way of trade, war, imperialism, religious missions, migrations and so on. But once there is contact, translation of one sort of another commences. That translation might at first be the sort of inter-actional, inter-linguistic negotiations that leads eventually to pidgins and then later, possibly to creoles. This begins with human social interchanges which are rooted in the activities in which language can operate with what Bernstein (1976, 1972, 1974) called a *restricted code*. In other words there is something concretely "going on" between the participants which is meaningful in itself to both sides and to which language is a communicative support rather than the major mode of meaning: the exchange of beads or gems (or for that matter, traveller's cheques) for water, food, and shelter requires a minimum of linguistic interchange as do the "meanings" of friendliness, hostility, or guarded neutrality. But we do make noises with our faces in order to live, in Firth's idiom, and sooner rather than later there is the attempt to match the different noises with the different acts and experiences of living. Small wonder, then, that of all the kinds of translation, one of the first in a new contact between cultures and languages is, ironically, an attempt at one of the most difficult in some respects, simultaneous interpretation. I became aware of the pidiginization and language borrowing aspects of simultaneous interpretation, even of a most sophisticated kind, in the early nineteen sixties as a Scottish delegate at the Council of Europe's *Seminarium Erasmianum* on the relationships between what, in those politically not so correct days, were called developed and underdeveloped countries. Here were a group of scholars from each European country, and guests from the sub-continent, Africa and Asia: economists, sociologists, political scientists, linguists and anthropologists, all having their say in their own professional, restricted languages and interpreters working in English or Dutch or French having to cope. They did a marvelous job. When one of the French or Dutch or Belgian economists was holding forth on *plannification* I would put on the headset and listen to how the interpreters were getting on. There were some extraordinary sentences of a polyglot nature gallantly produced in the heat of the moment but they did their job in the exchange of meanings.

Once cultural contact is instituted and maintained on a basis usually of some kind and degree of equality, elaborated code translations follow, particularly if the cultures are literate. And they too have their measure of success.

So the functional theorist can take comfort. Cultural relativity, cultural diversity there most certainly is, but we are, in many important ways, potentially "all members, one of another". We share a common human experience as Shakespeare's Shylock put it so succinctly:

> I am a Jew. Hath not a Jew eyes? Hath not a Jew hands, organs, dimensions, senses, affections, passions, fed with the same food, hurt with the same weapons, subject to the same diseases, heal'd by the same means, warmed and cooled by the same winter and summer as a Christian is? If you prick us do we not bleed: If you tickle us do we not laugh? If you poison us do we not die? ...
>
> (*Merchant of Venice* III i 48–56)

And that speech of Shylock's, like most of Shakespeare, has been translated into over a hundred languages effectively enough for it to have been estimated that a Shakespeare play is being performed in one language or another somewhere in the world every hour of every day.

However, the most translated body of writings in the world is almost certainly that collection known as the Bible: the Hebrew and Christian scriptures written in Hebrew over many centuries and first and, possibly second century, Greek, with a touch of Aramaic; and these writings are myths, legends, poems, songs, legal documents, chronicles, narratives and letters. And all or part of these writings have been, according to the United Bible Societies *1997 Scripture Language Report*, translated into two thousand, one hundred and ninety seven languages. These languages have a re-presentation of the original text's representation of the meanings of the cultures in which they originated.

So the functional linguist is emboldened to postulate general theories of grammar for the description of particular languages and their texts: for example, that they can be described in terms of unit, structure, class and system along scales of rank, delicacy and exponence (Halliday 1961), or units-in-hierarchy and context which can be approached from particle, field and wave perspectives (Pike 1967, Pike and Pike 1982). We set up and test functional roles such as Actor, Process and Goal (Halliday (1967) or Actor, Undergoer and Scope (Pike and Pike 1982), or Agent, Patient, Recipient, Processor (Gregory 1982) or Agent, Affected, Carrier (Fawcett 1980). We do this to capture, among other things, the "languaging" of roles played by participants in the material and mental events of human lives. There is confidence, too, that in all languages there are formal resources which enable speakers to assert what they believe to be facts of human experience, or question them, or direct the behaviour of others; there is confidence that there are also resources to indicate the inter-connectedness of what we say in texts and to point out the degrees of importance of different parts of the message we make with language (Halliday and Hasan 1976, Halliday 1967).

The fact of translatability, however that might be a matter of degree, has led translation scholars such as Beekman, Callow and Kopesec (Beekman and Callow 1974; Beekman, Callow and Kopesec 1981), influenced by functional theories of language, to see value in recognizing *concept* as a theoretical postulate, that is to recognize that our cognitive segmentations of experience that are lexicalised in a particular language as individual lexical items do not limit the linguistic expression of other segmentations of experience which are so lexicalised in another language but not in that particular language. The speaker of one language can use phrases (including clauses) to catch the nuances the speaker of another language may, as we say, "have a word for".

Indeed the distinguishing of translations as "literal" or "free", of having formal or dynamic equivalence, of being paraphrases or adaptations speaks to this challenge. One interesting example: in the fourth chapter of the letter to the Ephesians, traditionally attributed to Paul of Tarsus, there is a passage in which the task of Christian leaders is seen to be, in the recent but, in many respects, conservative, translation of the New Revised Standard Version, "to equip the saints for the work of ministry, for building up the Body of Christ" (v. 11–12). Now, the Greek word translated as "equip", *katartizo*, was originally a medical term, describing the treatment of dislocations and fractures. It is "a word Paul's companion, Dr. Luke, would have used to describe what he had to do quite often and what a chiropractor does today, that pulling and twisting about of limbs the practitioner euphemistically calls 'adjusting'" (Bowen 1998: 4); In other words, the Greek word is itself consonant with the metaphor of the church as the Body of Christ, whereas "equip" would fit better with one of the Pauline military, rather than corporeal, metaphors for the church.

I have always thought that if F. R. Palmer, in his brisk and not very well argued dismissal of the value of concept in his book, *Semantics* (1981: 24–29), had thoroughly considered the process of translation he might have had second thoughts. Culturally specific cognitive and linguistic segmentations of experience might present the translator problems in searching for the "right word" but there may be combinations of words which will suffice. Seeking to isolate the conceptual properties of the source language word can help in finding the appropriate word or words in the target language. Translation does indeed draw attention to the lexicality of language as the rich dictionary proposals of Mel'cuk (Steele ed. 1990; Mel'cuk and Pertsov 1987) and Fleming (1988) attest. The Collins Cobuild projects have a most important contribution to make in this area.

The second implication of what I have called the "fact" of translation should be an encouragement to formal and cognitivist theorists of language. Despite the apparently widely different uses made of syntactic, morphologic, and phono/graphologic resources in different languages, the utilitarian success of translation as well as the fact of language learning suggest that there must be a significant measure of *"universality"* in human grammars that involves, even if it is not just a matter of, a common innate *linguistic competence* (see, for example, Chomsky (1986: 17–29, 37–40, 145–152)). Chomsky's question as to how it is that, from scraps and shreds of evidence, we learn our first language so quickly is a legitimate and central one that linguistics has to ask of its phenomenon and seek to answer, particularly if one realizes that the question is not about learning social and cultural meanings, which are over-determined, but about learning principles of structuration. A capacity for language, not a language, is our genetic gift. Research into principles of human grammatical organization and the distinguishing of parameter settings for individual languages and groups of languages is an endeavour of the greatest importance in addressing language as *process, program* (see Fawcett 1992, Gregory 1998) as well as of potential value in the theory and practice of translation. So long as functional and formal schools of linguistics exist in an *apartheid* relationship, just so long are we open to the accusation that we prefer the securities of tunnel vision and collegial comfort to the full range of intellectual challenges set by the phenomena.

That is why I maintain that to separate in any absolute way a theory of form (or structure) from a theory of function (or usage), to privilege the one activity over the other, is profoundly to misinterpret the essential nature of any language as an open, dynamic system, one in which what we call form and function are in a productive, symbiotic relationship. The grammar of a language (its form) allows the speaker to do what the speaker wants (function) but insists on how the speaker does it (symbiosis), which means that ultimately the grammar is functionally predictable and interpretable even though it is not functionally determined in any absolute way which would prohibit its ability to respond to and create new meanings (Gregory 1995b: 434). The fact of translation witnesses to this symbiotic process.

This is also why Elissa Asp and I are working to develop a socio-cognitive linguistics that attempts to combine systemic-functional insights and Chomskyan perspectives with some important influences from Richard Hudson's *Word Grammar* (1984), particularly as regards the multiple inheritance of properties by the instance from models and the priority of the instance over any models (see Asp (1992, 1995, 1998a, 1998b, in press), Gregory (1995a, 1995b, 1998a, 1998b)): key factors in translation.

In the next section of this article we will look, from the point of view of this kind of linguistics, at a group of texts which are all English translations of a particular New Testament Greek text. The translations present themselves variously as being "formal equivalence", "dynamic equivalence", and "paraphrase" versions and the Canadian Bible Society regards them as having "distinctive features" and "theological affiliations". We shall see how far we can go in discovering the functional and formal models from which they inherit properties and what light this brief and largely informal comparative analysis throws on the question of the relationship between translation and linguistics.

Among the resources for this part of the paper are biblical concordances, dictionaries, expository dictionaries, a grammar of New Testament Greek and that monument of philological scholarship, Alfred Marshall's *Nestlé Text Inter-Linear Greek-English New Testament* (1958); so perhaps, forty years on, I am returning, at least in some respects to an activity that was resented by many but prescribed by Oxford philologists. Now I hope I can recognize that there are limits to our objectifying of the subjective, and generalizing the specific, but that there is knowledge to be gained by trying.

2. Texts

In 1997, two American professors of religion, Steven M. Sheeley and Robert N. Nash Jr. published their book *The Bible in English Translation: An Essential Guide*, henceforth Sheeley and Nash, and in the same year the Canadian Bible Society distributed to members and churches *Our Bible: How it came to us*, henceforth *Our Bible*.

Sheeley and Nash is a hundred and sixteen page book written by two teaching scholars for a general audience, and *Our Bible* is a twenty-four page public relations and informational booklet. Both have, however, the following in common: they survey the origin of that collection of writings known to Christians as the Holy Bible, the history of its translation into English, the large and increasing number of twentieth century English translations, and offer information and advice to help what might be termed consumers choose one or more translations for use in private devotions, study, and/or public worship. Use will be made of both of them here as a gnostological resource, an indication of what knowledge about the Bible and its current English translations is widely available to the communicating community context of literate North Americans at the end of the twentieth century.

Our Bible presents a chart which categorizes twelve available translations: five as having *formal equivalence*: The King James Version (KJV), The New King James Version (NKJV), the New American Standard Bible (NASB), the New American Bible (NAB) and the New Revised Standard Version (NRSV); five as having *dynamic equivalence*: the Contemporary English Version (CEV), the New International Version (NIV), Today's English Version also known as the Good News Bible (TEV/ GNB), God's Word (GW) and the New Century Version (NCV); and two as being *paraphrases*: the Living Bible (LB) and The Message (TM). Each version is given a *reading level* using Dale-Chall, Fry, Raygor and Spache Formulas, a short statement of *distinctive features* such as for the NRSV, "published 1990 as a revision of the RSV. Gender inclusive language when supported by the original language" and a *theological affiliation* such as for the NIV: "Transnational, transdenominational team of scholars. Conservative, evangelical". The full chart is appended.

Sheeley and Nash also comment in more detail, and frequently in a more critical vein, on all the above with the exception of GW which has the lowest reading level of all: 4.3, compared with 12.0 for the KJV and 11 for the NASB. They do, however, comment extensively on five other modern translations: the Jerusalem Bible (JB), the New Jerusalem Bible (NJB), the New English Bible (NEB), the Revised English Bible (REB) and the New Living Translation (NLT). They use similar translation categories to *Our Bible* but, rather unhappily, have *verbal* for *formal* equivalence. With some reservations they place the NIV in that category whereas *Our Bible* has it in the dynamic category. Sheeley and Nash subdivide the dynamic into general idiomatic translations (JB, NEB, REB, NCV, NLT) and common language versions (TEV/GNB, CEV). They point out that

> ... the dynamic equivalence theory was first proposed by Eugene Nida as an approach to biblical translation that might assist Bible translators in various cultural contexts ... a general idiomatic approach was launched by translators like James Moffat, Edgar Goodspeed, J. B. Phillips and Ronald Knox who viewed their translations as phrase-for-phrase efforts to reproduce the meaning of the text in modern English. In the words of Phillips their goal was to make their translation 'not sound like a translation at all' (62).

They then indicate that "a second movement among dynamic translators, known as the *common language approach*, emerged later as a result of efforts by the American Bible Society to use linguistic analysis to translate Bibles in international mission contexts ... Extensive linguistic analyses and theories about the communication of meaning from one language to another provided the theoretical foundation for these common language translations" (63).

Sheeley and Nash also express an awareness of the fuzziness at the edges of such categories. Discussing the debate over the value of paraphrased versions they write: "In many ways all translations are paraphrases of the Bible, because no translation can ever capture the exact meaning of the original language ...... Perhaps the whole debate is simply a matter of degree" (87). *Our Bible*, however, distinguishes paraphrase from translation as including "built-in personal commentary" (24).

In another section *Our Bible* presents four types of translation: "a) literal (formal equivalent); b) idiomatic equivalent; c) functional (dynamic) equivalent, d) free (added commentary) paraphrase." (4).

It is clear, throughout both Sheeley and Nash and *Our Bible*, that their authors would ultimately, if pressed, agree with Eugene Van Ness Goetchius that "generally speaking, *no* Greek word has an exact 'literal' equivalent in English which may be used to render it in every context" (Goetchius 1965: XV). In other words, there is a reasonable amount of linguistic sophistication in both these popular publications.

Our Bible gives in its chart a passage comparison for each of its categorized versions. The passage is 2 Timothy 3: 16–17. Here is a transliterated Greek version from the Nestlé Greek text with Alfred Marshall's interlinear English translation (1958).

V.16 *pasa graphe theopneustos kai ophelimes*
Every scripture [is] God-breathed and profitable
pros didaskalian, pros elegmon, pros epanarthoain,
for teaching, for reproof, for correction,
pros paideian ten en dikaiooune
for instruction — in righteousness,
V.17 *hina artios e o tou theou anthropos,*
in order that [5]fitted [4]may [1]the [3]of God [2]man, be
pros pan ergon agathon exerpromenos
for every work good *having been* furnished

It is somewhat remarkable how close the five formal equivalence translations (KJV (1611), NKJV (1982), NASB (1971/95), NAB (1986), NRSV (1989)) of this passage are despite their temporal, geographical and theological contexts.

"Scripture" however is initially capitalized only in the NKJV and the NASB, two professedly evangelical and conservative translations. It is not so in the Roman Catholic NAB (the formal version in 1986 of the 1970 dynamic translation) nor in the "mainline and inter-confessional" NRSV, and interestingly, not in the generic model for both the NKJV and the NASB, the KJV, also known as the Authorized Version (that is authorized to be read in Church of England churches) and a translation still praised and reverenced by contemporary self-styled conservatives and evangelicals for its literalness. Indeed, the addition of "conservative and evangelical" to "Church of England" in the theological affiliation for the KJV is a very modern and American appellation and would have meant something rather different in the seventeenth century. There is, of course, no initial capitalization in the Greek text.

In interpreting *pasa graphe* the translator has available a co-textual collocation and colligation in the preceeding verse (15): *hiera grammata*, literally 'sacred letters', translated as 'holy scriptures' in the KJV and 'sacred writings' in the NASB and NRSV. As Craig S. Keener has pointed out, *hi-*

era grammata "was also used for pagan religious writing (e.g. in the cult of Isis) but is attested in Greek speaking Jewish sources as a name for the Bible that then existed", i.e. the Hebrew scriptures (Keener 1993: 630). It is doubtful as to whether the author of 2 Timothy is referring to anything else despite the LB version of this noun phrase as "the whole Bible".

The item *pasa* is regularly glossed in New Testament Greek-English lexicons (see e.g. Vine's (1996), Strong's (1996), Bauer, Arndt and Gingrich (1979)) as 'all', 'every' or 'any'. Marshall chooses the simple universal reference deictic 'every' which concords with singular heads; the five formally equivalent translations in the chart choose the inclusive reference deictic 'all' which concords with plural and non-count heads which suggests that scripture (with or without an initial capital) is interpreted as a non-count noun.

Marshall's morphologically accurate translation of *theopneustos* as 'God-breathed' stands in contrast to the five formally equivalent translations' use of a form of 'inspire' and the agentive 'by God'. This latter translation is in the tradition of Wycliffe (1384), Tyndale (1526), Coverdale (1535) and the Greek Bible (1539). Interestingly the NIV, categorized in the chart as dynamically equivalent but as 'verbal' equivalent by Sheeley and Nash, uses the literal 'God-breathed'. This raises the question of items which, by way of long respected translations such as the KVJ which have the status of generic models, have become terms in the field of discourse of Anglophone theology. This passage has several of them: 'inspiration', 'doctrine' and 'righteousness' which are key terms in systematic theology and often the centres for controversy, and 'reproof', 'correction' and 'instruction' which have their place in pastoral theology. So there is a strong tendency, as one contemporary translator said to me, to stick with the "golden oldies"; they are lexical models of which the Bible translator is very aware.

Ophelimos from a form of *ophelos*, literally to 'heap up' and by extension, 'accumulate', 'benefit' or 'gain' is translated by Marshall, KJV, NKJV and NASB as 'profitable'. The KJV as a model and a capitalist cultural heritage which gives value to anything to do with 'profit' might well be behind this selection. The other contemporary formally equivalent translations and all the dynamically equivalent translations and the paraphrases avoid 'profitable' and select the culturally more neutral 'useful'.

The other terms in this verse, translated by the KJV as 'doctrine', 'reproof', 'correction' and 'instruction' are all, as Keener points out (1993: 630), standard terms from ancient, particularly Greek education, no matter how severe they seem interactionally to us now. The abstract noun, *didaskalia* was derived from the agentive noun *didaskosos*, an 'instructor' or 'teacher', itself derived from *didasko*, a causative form of the primary verb *dao* 'to learn'. So 'doctrine' (KJV, NKJV) and 'teaching' (Marshall, and all the other formally and the dynamically equivalent translations) are both candidates. The modern and contemporary preference for 'teaching' may be because it is perceived as being more dynamic and open-ended than 'doctrine' now is, and can, for those translators who do not feel the need to be too literal, project a noun phrase or clausal complement as in 'teaching the truth' (TEV/GNB) and 'teach us what is true' (LB). 'Reproof' (*pros elegmon*) central to the practice of Judaism and of early Jewish Christians (as Paul's letters and *Acts* attest) was usually done privately and gently at first, and only publicly when that failed. *Pros epanarthoain*, literally 'for correction', etymologically derived from *epi*, a primary preposition, and *anothro*, 'to straighten up', and in many contexts translatable as 'rectification' provides the purpose and consequence for the 'rebuke', 'reproof' or 'admonishment' of the previous phrase. Neither 'rebuke' or 'correction' are in the forefront of contemporary educational theory and practice and so dynamic/functional and paraphrase versions which are usually not accompanied by explanatory footnotes (as are the Study Bible versions of formal equivalence translations such as the NRSV, the REB and the NIV, borderline dynamic/formal), seem to recognize a need for the expansion here, making use of the complement possibilities of English -ing forms, so we have:

'helping people and converting them' (CEV),
'rebuking error, correcting faults' (TEV/GNB),
'pointing out errors, correcting people' (GW),
'for showing people what is wrong in their lives, for correcting faults' (NCV),
'to make us realize what is wrong in our lives, it straightens us out' [re-etymologizing at work here?] (LB),
'exposing our rebellion, correcting our mistakes' (TM).

Several preachers from a range of denominations (Roman Catholic, Anglican, United Church of Canada, Presbyterian and Baptist) have told me that they prefer to use these more clausal translations in sermons or homilies because they are more "dynamic" and "concrete" (in the sense of particularizing relevance) than the literal/formal equivalent translations with their noun phrases, which they consider "static" and "abstract".

The final phrase of verse 16: *pros paideian ten en dikaiooune*, is translated identically by Marshall, the KVJ and NKJV but the other formal translations have 'training' for 'instruction', and with the exception of the TEV/GNB ('giving instruction') the dynamic translations also prefer 'training' or 'train'. Significantly the Greek *paideia* (noun) and *paideuo* (verb) are both frequently used in collocations and contexts which suggest that the 'tutelage', 'instruction', 'education' is accompanied by discipline or chastening (see Strong (1996: 672–673), Vine (1996: 328)). Clearly contemporary translations have not allowed this to influence their choices.

As noted above, 'righteousness' has become the term for a complex and controversial concept in theology and has remained in the modern formal translations. In the article on righteousness in the *Oxford Companion to the Bible*, John Zeisler (1993: 656) points out that "it has been maintained that Paul consistently uses 'justify' (*dikaioo*) for the restoration and maintenance of the relationship with God and 'righteousness' (*dikaiosune*) for the consequent life of his people, with both justification and righteousness being by faith. But there is disagreement about the exact meaning of most of the relevant passages.". Given this kind of a problematic, and scholarly doubt about Paul's authorship of the Letters to Timothy compounding the matter, it is perhaps understandable that relatively conservative contemporary formal translations such as NASB, NAB and NRSV stay with the "authorized" KJV model of 'righteousness' in this passage. However, with the exception of the NIV, the dynamic translations and the paraphrases do not hesitate to "unpack the meaning", and they do so in one direction. We are presented with 'showing them how to live' (CEV), 'giving instruction for right living' (TEV/GNB), 'training them for a life that has God's approval' (GW), 'teaching how to live right' (NCV), 'helps us to do what is right' (LB), 'training us to live God's way' (TM), and one notes here again a preference for English clausal and transitivity possibilities.

Verse 17 reminds the translator and the linguist that the parameter settings of Greek and English are not identical and that word-by-word translation can produce non-English; form insists on how we say what we mean and Marshall's word-by-word translation has to make use of ordering numerals:

"In order that [5]fitted [4]may be [1]the [3]of God [2]man"

It also raises the question of inclusive language. For the seventeenth century translators of the KJV and for Marshall in (1958) 'man of God' for *theou anthropos* might be considered a generic use of 'man', but it is somewhat surprising to see this translation maintained in the NKJV (1982/83), the NASB (1971/1995 update) particularly as Greek has the word *aner* to mean, specifically, a male. The expression the New Testament writer worded as *theou anthropos* has a long history: the ancient Hittites used it to describe religious figures, and the Hebrew scriptures used it for those commissioned by God to be spokepersons. This lies behind the inclusive translations such as 'God's servants' (CEV, GW, 'the person who serves God' (TEV/GNB/NEV). The NAB and NRSV use the somewhat more formal translation reflecting the possessive genitive: 'one who belongs to God', and 'everyone who belongs to God' respectively.

3. Epilogue

In this brief look at excerpts of Bible translation we have seen that the contextual parameters in which they occur have a perceivable significance and are reflected in nuances of experiential, interactional and organizational meaning. Purposes and preoccupations about the use of the translation (private devotions, public worship, study and evangelism) play their part as does self-consciousness about theological affiliation (conservative, evangelical, mainstream, Roman Catholic) and all these are open to use in market exploitation. Small wonder, then, that there is also, to a considerable extent, an institutionalizing of different views of equivalence: formal/literal, dynamic/functional and free paraphrase.

Two trends seem to be emerging and both should give food for thought to the linguist. The first trend is towards revising functional translations in a more formal direction. This has been the case in the 1985 New Jerusalem Bible version of the 1966 Jerusalem Bible and the 1989 Revised English Bible version of the 1970 New English Bible. The motivations for this move may be rather complex: it is probably, and partially, a response to some of the scholarly criticisms and reservations as regards accuracy and fidelity to the originals that were expressed about the earlier versions despite their considerable success; it may also have been motivated by a desire to compete for recommendation in official lectionaries which are increasingly in use in so called main-line denominations; and, finally, these revisions may be aiming for the theological college and seminary market. Both these translations are competitors in the Study Bible market with the NRSV, and the increasing optionality of Hebrew and Greek for candidates for ministry has meant that professors of scripture are more and more anxious that their students should be using translations that preserve the original word order and sentence structure as much as possible, and which also provide detailed notes: historical, linguistic, and interpretive for hermeneutic and exegetical purposes. In this they belong to a very long history of interpretation which is to some extent responsible for the very nature of the Biblical texts which are being translated, as Kugel (1947) has so cogently argued at length. One might call this trend the "philological" trend and the linguist as philologist should take note of it.

The second trend might be called the "linguistic" trend and is contained in the replacement of the free paraphrase *Living Bible* of 1971 with the functionally equivalent *New Living Translation* of 1996. The LB was an immense success both in sales and influence but many critics felt that the rigidly evangelical stance of its progenitor, a seminary trained publisher, Kenneth N. Taylor led to some distorting paraphrases. Taylor did, however, set up a missionary foundation to receive the royalties from the LB and the success of that paraphrase enabled him to establish Tyndale House Publishing which has produced the NLT 1996, not a paraphrase but a version which probably most reflects the postulates on translation of linguists in the Catford, Nida, and Summer Institute of Linguistics traditions. Its translation seems free of any partisan distortions and for this reader the volume was only marred by the inclusion of a *Tyndale Verse Finder* which smacks of a "proof-text" view of scripture, a nod perhaps to the theological inclinations of the founder of the publishing house. In their introduction (XII) the Bible Translation Committee of the NLT give a succinct account of functional equivalence. They write: "the goal of this translation theory is to produce in the receptor language the closest natural equivalent of the message expressed by the original language text—both in meaning and style. Such a translation attempts to have the same impact on modern readers as the original had on its audience." These two trends, what I have called the "philological" and the "linguistic" are, of course, ultimately not contradictory; like "formal" and "functional" as regards translation equivalence, they mark different positions on a cline or continuum in this case of linguistic scholarship, and they help translations of complex and culturally significant documents such as the Bible serve different but related purposes. There is a need, irrespective of market considerations, both for translations of the Bible which give a more or less literal rendering of the Greek and Hebrew texts and translations which express the Greek and Hebrew in the natural language of today. And linguistics has important roles to play in both of these activities. In fulfilling those roles the linguist can be forced to pay increased attention to the inheritance of properties from diverse but appropriate models: generic, syntactic and lexical; and to recognize that the form of a particular language is a particular setting of a universal capacity for language, a setting which will allow you to do what you want to do but, in the end, will insist on how you do it. This symbiosis of form and function means that the translator has to have an ultimate fidelity to messages rather than morphemes but also recognize that morphemes make messages; it also means that the linguist must surely question any theoretically rigid distinction between a theory of structure and a theory of usage, between linguistics and philology, if her or his work is to be socially and culturally useful, usable, and accountable.

Our short, informal look at different English translations of the same *Koine* Greek passage in section 2 indicated, I suggest, that translators do manage to realize much of the experiential, interactional and organizational meanings of the original even if the formal resources of the target and source language differ: for example, predicating verb followed by complement/argument organizes for textual prominence differently than do Greek nominalizations of processes, but 'pointing out errors, correcting people' may well be as appropriate for the late twentieth century English reader as *pros elegmon, pros epanarthoain* was for the first century user of Greek. There are limits to translatability as there are limits to our ability to characterize linguistic universals but both endeavours are surely well worthwhile and mutually enriching.

34 Michael Gregory

Appendix

Table 1. Translations of the Bible

	TRANS-LATION	READING LEVEL*	DISTINCTIVE FEATURES	PASSAGE COMPARISON	THEOLOGICAL AFFILIATION
Formal Equivalence — Seeks to transmit in English the literal words and structure of the original language	King James Version	12.0	Poetic literary style using Elizabethan English. Most universally accepted translation for centuries. Considered the most difficult to read.	All scripture is given by inspiration of God, and is profitable for doctrine, for reproof, for correction, for instruction in righteousness: that the man of God may be perfect, throughly furnished unto all good works.	Church of England, conservative and evangelical
	New King James Version	8.0	Modern language in the elegant style of the KJV but much easier to read and understand. Word-for-word accuracy.	All Scripture is given by inspiration of God, and is profitable for doctrine, for reproof, for correction, for instruction in righteousness, that the man of God may be complete, thoroughly equipped for every good work.	Transnational, trans-denominational team of scholars. Conservative, evangelical.
	New American Standard Bible	11.0	A revision of the 1901 American Standard Version into modern language. An accurate translation at the word-for-word level.	All Scripture is inspired by God and profitable for teaching, for reproof, for correction, for training in righteousness; that the man of God may be adequate, equipped for every good work.	Conservative and evangelical.
	New American Bible	6.6	Official translation of the Roman Catholic Church.	All scripture is inspired by God and is useful for teaching, for refutation, for correction, and for training in righteousness, so that one who belongs to God may be competent, equipped for every good work.	Roman Catholic.

What can linguistics learn from translation? 35

Table 1. Translations of the Bible (Continued)

	TRANSLATION	READING LEVEL*	DISTINCTIVE FEATURES	PASSAGE COMPARISON	THEOLOGICAL AFFILIATION
	New Revised Standard Version	8.1	Published in 1990 as a revision of the RSV. Gender inclusive language when supported by the original language.	All scripture is inspired by God and is useful for teaching, for reproof, for correction, and for training in righteousness, so that everyone who belongs to God may be proficient, equipped for every good work.	Mainline and interconfessional.
Dynamic Equivalence Seeks to transmit in modern English words and style the meaning of the original language	Contemporary English Version	5.4	Natural, uncomplicated English for use by the entire family. Appropriate for new Bible readers and youth. Gender inclusive language when supported by the original language.	Everything in the Scriptures is God's Word. All of it is useful for teaching and helping people and for correcting them and showing them how to live. The Scriptures train God's servants to do all kinds of good deeds.	Conservative, evangelical and mainline.
	New International Version	7.8	Popular modern-language translation used by a number of conservative denominations. Attempts to balance literal and dynamic translation methods.	All Scripture is God-breathed and is useful for teaching, rebuking, correcting and training in righteousness, so that the man of God may be thoroughly equipped for every good work.	Transnational, trans-denominational team of scholars. Conservative, evangelical.
	Today's English Version	7.3	Also known as the Good News Bible. Praised for its freshness of language. Appropriate for those for whom English is a second language.	All Scripture is inspired by God and is useful for teaching the truth, rebuking error, correcting faults, and giving instruction for right living, so that the person who serves God may be fully qualified and equipped to do every kind of good deed.	Evangelical and interconfessional.

Table 1. Translations of the Bible (Continued)

TRANSLATION	READING LEVEL*	DISTINCTIVE FEATURES	PASSAGE COMPARISON	THEOLOGICAL AFFILIATION
God's Word	4.3	A meaning-for-meaning translation.	Every Scripture passage is inspired by God. All of them are useful for teaching, pointing out errors, correcting people, and training them for a life that has God's approval. They equip God's servants so that they are completely prepared to do good things.	Lutheran/evangelical.
New Century Version	5.6	Puts biblical concepts into natural terms. Vocabulary choice is based on *The Living Word Vocabulary*, by Dr. Edgar Dale and Dr. Joseph O'Rourke.	All Scripture is given by God and is useful for teaching, for showing people what is wrong in their lives, for correcting faults, and for teaching how to live right. Using the Scriptures, the person who serves God will be capable, having all that is needed to do every good work.	Conservative and evangelical
The Living Bible	8.3	A popular, readable paraphrase. Used by many for easy personal reading.	The whole Bible was given to us by inspiration from God and is useful to teach us what is true and to make us realize what is wrong in our lives; it straightens us out and helps us do what is right. It is God's way of making us well prepared at every point, fully equipped to do good to everyone.	Conservative and evangelical.

Paraphrase
Includes built-in personal commentary

Table 1. Translations of the Bible (Continued)

TRANS-LATION	READING LEVEL*	DISTINCTIVE FEATURES	PASSAGE COMPARISON	THEOLOGICAL AFFILIATION
The Message	4.8**	A free paraphrase that seeks to recapture the expressiveness of the original languages.	Every part of Scripture is God-breathed and useful one way or another — showing us truth, exposing our rebellion, correcting our mistakes, training us to live God's way. Through the Word we are put together and shaped up for the tasks God has for us.	Evangelical.

* The relative difficulty or grade level on which the text is written. Using Dale-Chall, Fry, Raygor, and Spache Formulas.
** Based on New Testament text samples. Adapted from a chart by Thomas Nelson Publishers.
Reprinted from *Our Bible, How It Came To Us*. Canadian Bible Society, 1997

References

Asp, Elissa D.
 1992 Natural language and human semiosis: a socio-cognitive account of metaphor. Ph.D. dissertation. York University, Toronto.
 1995 Knowledge and laughter: an approach to a socio-cognitive linguistics. In: Peter Fries and Michael Gregory eds., 141–158.
 1998a On the paradigmatic functions of syntagmata. Paper to the 25th International Systemic Functional Congress, Cardiff University, Cardiff, U.K. (mimeo).
 1998b Praying for a crowd: John Donne's 'The Language of God' as interaction. Paper to the 10th Euro-international Systemic Functional Workshop, Liverpool University, Liverpool, U.K. (mimeo).
 in press How to do things with words: some observations on speech acts in relation to a socio-cognitive grammar for English. In: Jessica De Villiers and Robert Stainton, *Communication in Linguistics*. Toronto: Alan Bordeaux.

Bauer, W., W. F. Arndt and F. W. Gingrich
 1979 *A Greek-English Lexicon of the New Testament and Other Early Christian Literature*. Chicago: University of Chicago Press.

Beekman, John and John Callow
 1974 *Translating the Word of God*. Grand Rapids, MI: Zondervan.

Beekman, John, John Callow and Mark Kopesec
 1981 *The Semantic Structure of Written Communication*. Dallas, Texas: Summer Institute of Linguistics.

Bernstein, Basil
 1971 *Class, Codes and Control, Vol. 1: Theoretical Studies Towards a Sociology of Language*. London: Routledge & Kegan Paul.

Bernstein, Basil (ed.)
 1973 *Class, Codes and Control, Vol. 2: Applied Studies Towards a Sociology of Language*. London: Routledge & Kegan Paul.

Bernstein, Basil
 1974 Introduction to *Class, Codes and Control, Vol. 3: Towards a Theory of Educational Transmissions*. London: Routledge & Kegan Paul.

Bowen, John
 1998 Getting in shape. In: *Good Idea* Vol. 5, No. 2. Toronto: Wycliffe College.

Canadian Bible Society
 1997 *Our Bible: How It Came to Us*. Toronto: CBS.

Catford, J. C.
 1965 *A Linguistic Theory of Translation*. London: Oxford University Press.

Cha, Jin Soon (ed.)
 1995 *Before and Towards Communication Linguistics: Essays by Michael Gregory and Associates*. Seoul: Sookmyung Women's University.

Chomsky, Noam
 1986 *Knowledge of Language: its Nature, Origin and Use*. New York: Praegor.

Fawcett, Robin
   1980   *Cognitive Linguistics and Social Interation: Towards an Integrated Model of a Systemic Functional Grammar and the Other Components of a Communicating Mind.* Heidelberg: Julian Groos Verlag.
   1992   Language as program: a reassessment of the nature of descriptive linguistics. *Language Sciences*, Vol. 14, No. 4, 623–657.

Firth, John. Rupert.
   1957   *Papers in Linguistics 1934–1951*, London: Oxford University Press.

Fleming, Ilah
   1988   *Communication Analysis.* Vol. 2. Dallas: Summer Institute of Linguistics.

Fries, Peter and Michael Gregory (eds.)
   1995   *Discourse in Society: Systemic Functional Perspectives.* Norwood, New Jersey: Ablex.

Goetchius, Eugene Van Ness
   1965   *The Language of the New Testament.* New York: Scribner's Sons.

Gregory, Michael
   1980   Perspectives on translation from the Firthian tradition. *Meta* Vol. 25, No. 4, 455–466. Montreal: University of Montreal Press.
   1982   *Notes on Communication Linguistics.* Toronto: Glendon College of York University.
   1995a   Remarks on a theory of grammar for a socio-cognitive linguistics. In: Jin Soon Cha (ed.), 413–433.
   1995b   Arguments, roles, relations, prepositions and case: proposals within a socio-cognitive grammar of English. In: Jin Soon Cha (ed.), 434–476.
   1998a   Systemic functional linguistics and other schools: retrospectives and prospectives. Plenary paper to the 25th International Systemic Functional Congress, University of Cardiff, Cardiff, U.K. (mimeo).
   1998b   The grammar of interaction: interpersonality and intertextuality in John Donne's *The Bait*. Paper to the 10th Euro-international Systemic Functional Workshop, University of Liverpool, Liverpool, U.K. (mimeo).

Halliday, M. A. K.
   1961   Categories of the theory of grammar. *Word*, No. 17, 241–292.
   1967   Notes on transitivity and theme in English. *Journal of Linguistics*, No. 3, Part 1, 37–81, Part 2, 199–244.

Halliday, M. A. K. and Ruqaiya, Hasan
   1976   *Cohesion in English.* London: Longman.

Hudson, Richard
   1984   *Word Grammar.* London: Blackwell.

Keener, Craig S.
   1993   *The IVP Bible Background Commentary: New Testament.* Downers Grove, Ill: Inter Varsity Press.

Kugel, James L.
   1997   *The Bible As It Was.* Cambridge, Mass: The Belknap Press of Harvard University Press.

Marshall, Alfred
    1958   *The Interlinear Greek-English New Testament*. London: Samuel Bagster and Sons.

McIntosh, Angus, M. A. K. Halliday and Peter Strevens
    1964   *The Linguistic Sciences and Language Teaching*. London: Longman.

Mel'cuk, Igor and Nikolaj Pertsov
    1987   *Surface Syntax of English: a Formal Model within the Meaning-text Framework*. Philadelphia: John Benjamins.

Metzger, Bruce M. and Michael D. Coogan (eds.)
    1993   *The Oxford Companion to the Bible*. New York: Oxford University Press.

Palmer, Frank R. (ed.)
    1968   *Selected Papers of J. R. Firth, 1952–59*. London: Longman.

Palmer, Frank R.
    1981   *Semantics*. Cambridge: Cambridge University Press.

Pike, Kenneth L.
    1967   *Language in Relation to a Unified Theory of the Structure of Human Behaviour*. The Hague: Mouton.

Pike, Kenneth L. and Evelyn G. Pike
    1982   *Grammatical Analysis*. Dallas, Texas: Summer Institute of Linguistics and the University of Texas at Arlington.

Sheeley, Steven M. and Robert W. Nash, Jr.
    1997   *The Bible in English Translation*. Nashville: Abingdon Press.

Steele, James (ed.)
    1990   *Meaning-text Theory: Linguistics, Lexicography, and Implications*. Ottawa: University of Ottawa Press.

Strong, James
    1996   *The New Strong's Complete Dictionary of Bible Words*. Nashville: Thomas Nelson.

Vine, W. E., Merrill F. Unger and William White, Jr.
    1996   *Vine's Complete Expository Dictionary of Old and New Testament Words*. Nashville: Thomas Nelson.

Zeisler, John
    1993   Righteousness. In: Metzger and Coogan (eds.).

The environments of translation[1]
Christian M.I.M. Matthiessen

1. Introduction

In this chapter, I shall take an "outsider's" look at translation: I shall approach translation as a functional linguist — more specifically, a systemic functional one — with an interest in issues relating to multilinguality. I am not a translation theorist; my experience is with description of various languages, language typology and with multilingual (as well as multimodal) text generation. Nor am I a professional translation practitioner. But our family covers three languages (Swedish, German and English). I grew up in Swedish with translation by my mother as the only early mode of access to German- and English-speaking family members; and I have had innumerable opportunities to practice translation myself since the "translation method" was, fortunately, still favoured by the teachers who tried to teach me English, German, French and Arabic. Further my brother and sister-in-law, Tryggve and Ingrid Emond, and one of their daughters, Vibeke Emond, do translation on a professional basis from various languages spoken in Europe and from Japanese into Swedish and I have benefited from listening to their experiences. So translation is in a sense part of daily life for me — a situation which is actually very common, even typical, in families around the world.

1.1. Value of contextualizing "translation"

My main concern in this chapter is to "locate" translation along the dimensions that organize the semiotic complex of language in context — both as a phenomenon in its own right and also as one multilingual concern in relation to other multilingual concerns — in particular language comparison and typology. My impression is that it is helpful to try to contextualize translation in this way, since as an "outsider" looking at recent accounts of translation I am struck by the degree to which these accounts tend to insulate translation from other at least potentially relevant concerns:

- "translation theory" and "science of translation" seem to be reserved for translation of texts by human translators: the development since the 1950s of translation by computers — *machine translation* (MT) — does not seem to have contributed to these fields; and they do not theorize the complementarity of human translation and MT. By the same token, MT does not make much reference to translation theory and the science of translation.

- accounts of translation do not on the whole refer to multilingual research within *comparative and contrastive linguistics* and within *typological linguistics.*[2] By the same token, typological linguistics does not have translation on its research agenda — neither as a phenomenon nor as a methodology.
- accounts of translation do not on the whole refer to research into *multilingual communication*, as in multilingual and bilingual contexts and in multilingual generation within computational linguistics.
- accounts of translation seem to be confined to translation between languages rather than translation between semiotic systems in general (a task made relevant by current developments under the headings of *multimodality* and *multimedia*).
- accounts of translation may make reference to general *theories of language* (as in Eugene Nida's reference to early Chomskyan concepts such as the distinction between deep structure and surface structure (Gentzler 1993: Ch. 3) or in the translation studies drawing on the Prague School (Gentzler 1993: Ch. 4)); but translation theory seems to exist fairly independently of current general theories of language. By the same token, current general theories of language do not seem to have "translation" on their agendas and as Michael Gregory (in this volume) has pointed out, linguistics can learn a good deal from translation.

Perhaps the most surprising tendency in accounts of translation is the omission of MT. For example, among recent books, neither the historical accounts produced by Gentzler (1993) and Venuti (1995) nor the more practical text book by Baker (1992) deal with it. MT is mentioned only in passing by Bell (1991) — although the model of translation he proposes in fact looks very similar to the kind of accounts given by researchers working on MT within computational linguistics. However, Hatim & Mason (1990: 22–25) discuss the role of machine translation and refer to it in other contexts as well.

To the extent that my impressions reflect the general tendency in the field of translation, they are not of course in themselves indicative of a problem. It may be that as a phenomenon manual translation needs to be given a special and distinct status. However, I believe that we can only gain further linguistic insight into translation by contextualizing it rather than by insulating it. This will mean among other things exploring where the outer limits of translation as a phenomenon lie — where translation ceases to be re-construal of meaning and shades into first-time construal of meaning, where translation as a phenomenon is located in a typology of systems, and where translation as a field of study is located relative to other fields concerned with multilinguality — comparative linguistics, contrastive analysis and typological linguistics. In a way, Catford (1965) does all these things: his linguistic theory of translation is a wonderfully rich contribution; he develops a very comprehensive picture of translation by systematically examining it in the light of a general theory of language and it can serve as a basis for similar efforts now. The central theoretical task is to expand his account in the light of new theoretical developments and descriptive findings.

In this chapter, I will contextualize translation — starting with the widest environment possible and then gradually narrowing the focus. The reason for this approach will become clear along the way — particularly in Section 3. But before I start, I would like to explore the conception of translation embodied in the lexicogrammar of English in order to bring out certain key issues in the modelling of translation. The first step in my contextualization is thus to contextualize it in the lexicogrammar of English.

1.2. The context of "translation" in English lexicogrammar

To explore this conception of translation, I extracted all the occurrences of "transl*" in LOB (the Lancaster-Oslo/Bergen Corpus), the one-million word corpus of British English created as a British counterpart to the Brown corpus. I filtered out lexemes unrelated to translation, such as *translucent;* but I retained all the forms of the verb *translate* and the nouns *translation* and *translator.* I then analysed the clauses and nominal groups containing these words, selecting those instances where the sense of translation is "semiotic" (which corresponds to entry II.1 in *The Shorter Oxford English Dictionary:* "to turn from one language into another; 'to change into another language retaining the sense' (J. [= Johnson's Dictionary])", except that semiotic systems other than languages may be involved and different subsenses need to be recognized, as noted below) and filtering out those instances where it has a different (though possibly related) sense (as in *In 1910 Dr. Talbot was translated to Winchester, and Dr. Hubert Burge became Bishop of Southwark.*) There is a total of 28 clauses with *translate* as Process and 40 nominal groups with *translation* or *translator* as Thing in LOB; the distribution across the crude genre categories recognized in LOB is quite uneven, as shown in Table 1. People write about translation in certain registers, such as that of religious discourse, but not at all in others (fiction and humour). (The results are very clear even though the different text types are not represented by samples of the same size in LOB.)

Clauses with *translate* as Process were analysed for VOICE and PROCESS TYPE. The voice analysis is straightforward: the clause is either 'operative' (Process realized by an active verbal group) or 'receptive' (Process realized by a passive verbal group); if it is 'receptive', it is either 'agentive' (the Agent is present, realized by a *by*-phrase) or 'non-agentive' (the Agent is absent). In English in general, the 'operative' option is unmarked and the 'receptive' one is marked; but the marking is quite strikingly reversed in the small sample of clauses from LOB: 23 out of 28 clauses are 'receptive' and only 5 are 'operative'. The vast majority of the 'receptive' clauses are 'non-agentive' (21 out of 23). This means that translator is very clearly backgrounded in the lexicogrammatical construction of translation — a striking confirmation of Venuti's (1995) notion of the invisibility of the translator.

Table 1. The distribution of senses of *transl** in LOB

"Genre" category	# of occurrences of "transl*" in semiotic sense [clauses + nominal groups]	PROCESS TYPE [clause]		VOICE [clause]		
		material clause	relational clause	operative clause	receptive: agentive clause	receptive: non-agentive clause
Category A (Press: reportage)	1	0	0			
Category B (Press: editorial)	0	0	0			
Category C (Press: reviews)	11	3	2			
Category D (Religion)	15	1	6			
Category E (Skills, trades and hobbies)	2	2	0			
Category F (Popular lore)	2	1	1			
Category G (Belles lettres, biography, essays)	24	10	0			
Category H (Miscellaneous, mainly Government documents)	1	0	0			

Table 1. The distribution of senses of *transl** in LOB (Continued)

"Genre" category	# of occurrences of "transl*" in semiotic sense [clauses + nominal groups]	PROCESS TYPE [clause]		VOICE [clause]		
		material clause	relational clause	operative clause	receptive: agentive clause	receptive: non-agentive clause
Category J (Learned and scientific writings)	8	2	1			
Category K (General Fiction)	0	0	0			
Category L (Mystery and detective fiction)	0	0	0			
Category M (Science fiction)	0	0	0			
Category N (Adventure and western fiction)	0	0	0			
Category P (Romance and love story)	0	0	0			
Category R (Humour)	0	0	0			
TOTAL	64	19	9	5	2	21

The analysis of PROCESS TYPE poses more problems than the analysis of voice. The basic challenge is to determine the range of clause types that the verb *translate* can serve in as Process. My investigation of LOB suggests that the lexicogrammar of English seems to offer two basic models — one 'material' and one 'relational'.

In the *'material' model*, translation is construed as a kind of process of transformation. In response to *What is Pound doing these days?*, it is possible to say *Oh, he's translating poetry*, using the unmarked present tense of 'material' clauses — the present-in-present. The outcome of the material change — the target of translation — may be construed as a circumstance — a resultative Role, as in *Oh, he's translating poetry into English.* Examples from LOB include: *but it does mean that it is almost impossible to translate him in a way that is positively misleading; translating letters from Eskimos; after it had been edited, translated and introduced by Dr.*

Gweneth Whitteridge; almost all the nominalizations with *translation* seem to be metaphorized 'material' clauses of this kind, as in *Any new translation of Cavafy is to be welcomed.* Figure 1 provides a transitivity analysis of one of the 'material' clauses in LOB. According to this analysis, *Frederik translated it into English and French* is like *Frederik chopped the onion into cubes.* Here *into* is interpreted as a preposition marking circumstance of Role rather than one of Location in abstract space. The "source" may also be represented circumstantially, as *Another cycle was also translated from the Persian*; and such examples could be expanded to include the "target": *Another cycle was translated from the Persian into Malay.* The prepositional phrase complex *from ... into ...* looks like a path expression in clauses of motion (cf. the second part of the analysis in Figure 1); but processes of transformation or conversion are often construed on this model — *change/ convert/ transform from x to y* (also in their 'relational' guise, as with *turn: he turned it from a disadvantage into an advantage*).

Frederik	translated	it ['the song']	into English and French
Frederik	chopped	the onion	into cubes
Actor	Process	Goal	Role
Actor	Process	Goal	Location
Frederik	translated	it	from Spanish into English and German
	(2) was also translated	(1) another cycle of tales	from the Persian
Frederik	transferred	the table	from the living room into the kitchen

Figure 1. Transitivity analysis of 'material' example with "translate"

In the *'relational' model*, translation is construed as causing to mean. In response to *What does "de" mean?*, it is possible to say *Oh, I translate it as 'of'*, using the unmarked present tense of 'relational' clauses — the simple present. Here *as 'of'* is an inherent third participant rather than an optional circumstantial elaboration of the clause; it cannot be left out: we cannot say *Oh, I translate it* (in the sense intended). This third participant represents the meaning in the target of translation. Examples from LOB include: *This verse contains the same Hebrew word four times and is translated 'blows, goes round, goes round and round, returns on its circuits'; The word translated 'madness' means 'mad revelry and wickedness'; He was usually known as Iain Ciar, which may be translated in English as Dark-complexioned John.* Figure 2 shows an example of a 'relational' analysis of a clause with *translate* as Process. According to this analysis, *The verse has also been translated 'to know that wisdom and knowledge are madness and folly'* is like *The verse has also been glossed as 'to know ...'* and even *The verse has also been declared the most beautiful in the poem*. The analysis relates *translate* to *mean;* thus the example in Figure 2 is agnate with *the verse also means 'to know that wisdom and knowledge are madness and folly'*.

The verse	has also been translated	'to know that wisdom and knowledge are madness and folly'
Token	Process	Value

Figure 2. Transitivity analysis of 'relational' example with "translate"

The 'material' and 'relational' clauses in LOB differ with respect to what they construe as the Medium translated (the Goal of 'material' clauses; the Token of 'relational' clauses). In the 'material' clauses, the Medium is realized by a nominal group that denotes a fairly extensive semiotic entity — a book, a collection, (the work of) a writer, a lyric, a synopsis, letters, romances, (a cycle of) tales, Arabian Nights, songs and so on. These are entities that can also be edited, revised and published. In contrast, in 'relational' clauses, the Medium is realized by a nominal group that denotes a fairly small semiotic abstraction — a movie title, a verse, a word, a name. These are abstractions that can also be glossed and said to mean something.

The lexicogrammar of English thus offers two complementary models of translation — one 'material' model of translation as doing, as transformation or conversion; and one 'relational' model of translation as being, as assignment of meaning. The existence of such complementary models in the grammar always suggests that the phenomenon being construed is of considerable experiential complexity (as was shown with respect to the lexicogrammar of teaching by Halliday 1976) — which is certainly true of translation! The models point to two ways of thinking about translation. We can think of it as transforming a semiotic entity from one language into another (or more generally, from one semiotic system into another — see further below); this relates to the "transfer" metaphor that has been used for translation, particularly in machine translation. (In this connection, it is important to keep in mind the dangers of metaphors based on the conduit metaphor — the dangers of thinking that there is something to be transferred from one language to another.) Alternatively, we can think of translation as an assignment of meaning — as mapping from one language to another; this relates translation to the basic semiotic relationship of signification or meaning.

It is interesting to note that the two models — the 'material' model and the 'relational' one — do not seem to be evenly distributed across the "genres" of LOB. The absolute numbers are too low to be reliable — the investigation needs to be extended to cover a modern corpus of 200 to 400 million words; but it is striking that in LOB_D (Religion), the 'relational' model dominates whereas in LOB_G (Belles lettres, biography, essays), the 'material' model dominates.

1.3. Organization of discussion

Having briefly considered the context of *translation* in the system of English lexicogrammar, I will now turn to the main task of this chapter: I will explore the contextualization of translation starting with the widest environment in which it can be contextualized (in Section 2). The widest environment is that defined by a typology of systems of all kinds — a typology that orders systems in complexity from physical systems to semiotic systems. Here I shall discuss the location of the process of translation in relation to this typology and I shall explore translation among different kinds of semiotic system. In the next section, Section 3, I shall focus on semiotic systems and I shall suggest how translation can be located within a series of related contextualizations defined by the dimensions of systemic functional theory. This series of related contextualizations will help us explore both the notions of "translation equivalence" and "translation shift" and the traditional distinction between "free" and "literal" translation. The series of related contextualization extends from the most global environments of language (in context) to the most local ones. In Section 4, I shall show how this series of contextualizations can be used to map out the resources of the source language and of the target language and in the following section, Section 5, these maps will be used to locate translation equivalences and translation shifts. Finally, in Section 6, I shall move up in abstraction from the languages involved in translation to the context — or meta-context — of the process of translation itself.

2. Translation and kinds of system

2.1. An ordered typology of systems; language as higher-order semiotic

The first step is, then, to locate translation in the most inclusive environment of all — the environment defined by a comprehensive typology of all phenomenal realms known to us from a scientific point of view: see Figure 3. Phenomenal realms are organized into a hierarchy of systems[3] of increasing complexity (Halliday & Matthiessen 1999: 507–511; Matthiessen & Halliday in prep.). There are four orders of systems in this hierarchy.

(i) Systems of the first order are *physical systems*, ranging in size from subatomic particles or strings to the entire universe, but subject throughout to the laws of physics. (ii) Systems of the second order are *biological systems*. They are physical systems with the added property of "life": they are self-replicating. (iii) Systems of the third order are *social systems*. They are biological systems (and hence also physical systems) with the added property of value: this means, among other things, that they are organized as social groups according to some form of division of labour. (iv) Systems of the fourth order are *semiotic systems*. They are social systems (and hence also biological and physical) with the added property of *meaning*. Semiotic systems are systems for making meaning and to be able to make meaning they have to be stratified into at least two levels or strata — content and expression. Stratification is a kind of organization that distinguishes semiotic systems from systems of all other kinds.

A language is a semiotic system, but also a social system [studied in sociolinguistics], a biological system [studied in neurolinguistics and articulatory/ auditory phonetics], and a physical system [studied in acoustic phonetics]. But there are many other forms of semiotic systems — including facial expression, gesture, posture and other systems that accompany spoken language or may be used on their own; drawing, painting, charting and other systems that accompany written language or may be used on their own; systems of performing arts. A number of these have been investigated and described from a systemic functional point of view, giving us a sense of how they share modes of meaning with language but also how they differ in their organization from language (see e.g. Kress & van Leeuwen 1996; O'Toole 1994; C. Martin 1997; McInnes 1998; Matthiessen et al 1997; Martin & Iedema, forthc.; Steiner 1988); and Steiner (1991) shows how language and social action share a number of organizational properties such as a distribution of subsystem by rank.

There are different ways of sorting semiotic systems into different types in a comprehensive typology of such systems; but one distinction that is critical to the interpretation of language as a kind of semiotic system is Halliday's (1995) distinction between primary semiotic systems and higher-order ones. *Primary semiotic* systems are bi-stratal and are, in principle, confined to one mode of meaning at a time (they are micro-functional). In contrast, *higher-order semiotic* systems are tri-stratal (see Figure 3) and they are able to create more than one mode of meaning at a time (they are meta-functional). Their content level is further stratified into semantics and lexicogrammar. The prototypical higher-order semiotic is language (prototypical both in evolutionary terms — it evolved first in the species — and in developmental terms — children learn it first); and language is very likely to be the only truly higher-order human semiotic.

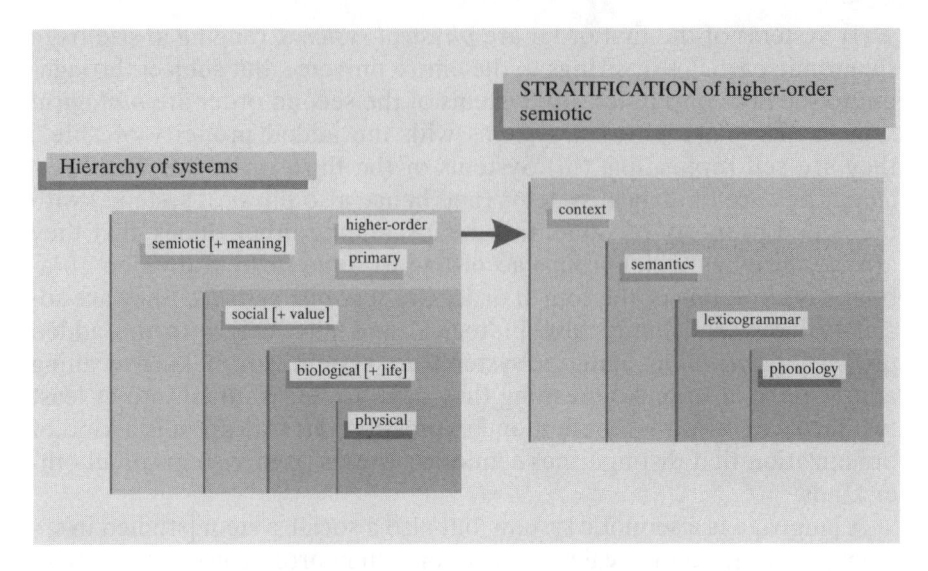

Figure 3. Theoretical modelling of language as social-semiotic system

2.2. Translation as a semiotic process

We can now relate translation to the ordered typology of systems. Translation might be a process occurring within systems of all kinds or between systems of all kinds. As we have seen, it can be modelled in the lexicogrammar of English as a process of transformation; and this aligns it in the grammar's modelling of experience with processes that can occur within, and between, systems of all kinds. Thus the following examples of 'material' clauses (cf. the analysis in Figure 1 above) suggest translation between different orders of system:

> *By nature afar off, alienated and separated from God, spiritually destitute and dead in trespasses and sins, the redeemed soul is "a debtor to mercy alone", born of the Spirit, called from nature's darkness into God's marvellous light, **translated into the Kingdom of His dear Son**, and in everything enriched by Him. [LOB_D]*
> *Schemes such as this, like individual and group piece-work or bonus schemes, raise practical problems of setting rates or measuring standards of performance, i.e the **translation** of ideas of a proper day's work **into terms of physical output or effort.** [LOB_H]*
> *The Urban Stress Test **translates** complex, technical data **into an easy-to-use action tool for concerned citizens, elected officials and opinion leaders.** [From fund-rasing letter analysed in Mann, Matthiessen & Thompson 1992.]*

Interestingly the same is true of the relationship of identity in the following 'relational' clause:

> *To say there is no remembrance **would mean** spiritual annihilation. [LOB_D]*

However, while the "outcome" of the process is represented as a resultative Role (*into*...) in the 'material' clauses above, it does not seem possible to represent the meaning of the translation within them. Thus using a 'relational' clause, we can say *he translated kita:bun into English as 'book'* just as we can *he glossed kita:bun in English as 'book'*, but using a 'material' clause we can hardly say *The Urban Stress Test translates data into a tool as 'xxx'* just as we can hardly say *The Urban Stress Test transforms/ converts data into a tool as 'xxx'* and this points to a critical difference: translation in our sense involves assignment of meaning — as it is construed in a 'relational' clause — and is thus restricted to fourth-order systems.

Translation is unique to semiotic systems; it is a semiotic process. This still leaves open the possibility that translation occurs both *between* semiotic systems and systems of other orders and *within* semiotic systems. We could say that when human beings construe experience of systems of any kind into meaning, they are "translating" non-semiotic patterns into semiotic ones (cf. Bell's 1991: 14, point that in a sense "all communicators are translators"). The limiting case is perhaps the situation where people construe perceptual representations linguistically. If we interpret perception as a set of *bio-semiotic systems* (as suggested in Halliday & Matthiessen 1999: 606–10), we can say — stretching the term "translation" — that bio-semiotic representations, e.g. representations construed by the human visual system, are translated into linguistic representations. The degree of congruence between visual representations and linguistic ones has received considerable attention in the last ten to fifteen years, in particular in the work by Ray Jackendoff and a number of other cognitive linguists.

However, it seems more helpful to model this as a process of *construing* experience as meaning (transforming it into meaning; see Halliday & Matthiessen 1999) and to recognize translation as a special form of construal — one that takes place *within* systems of the fourth order: (experience construed as) meaning in one system is (re)construed as meaning in another.

If we confine translation to semiotic systems in this way, this still leaves open the possibility that translation may occur between semiotic systems of different kinds (what Roman Jakobson called *intersemiotic* translation) as well as between systems of the same kind, e.g. between languages (Jakobson's *interlingual* translation). The terms *translation* and *translate* are certainly not restricted to language in LOB; for example:

> *It represents in impressions of excellent quality such famous prints as Debucourt's "La Promenade Publique" of 1792, the view of Westminster Hall and Abbey engraved by D. Havell after Glendall, and the now rare coaching subjects of James Pollard of which "The Royal Mails preparing to start for the West of England, 1831" (from the "Swan with Two Necks", Cheapside) is a notable example. Joseph Farington gains from* **translation into aquatint** *in the plates from Boydell's "History of the River Thames" and ...* [LOB_H]

But the vast majority of examples in LOB concern interlingual translation. I shall concentrate on interlingual translation; but many of the points I will make could apply equally to translation involving other kinds of semiotic system and it will be helpful to consider some examples of "translation" between language and semiotic systems other than language.

2.3. Construing non-linguistic semiotic presentations linguistically

Let's first consider some examples of "translating" some form of non-linguistic semiotic representation into language as text. Within an educational context, Mohan (1986) provides many examples of "translations" between non-linguistic semiotic representations and linguistic ones (e.g. the tasks of "converting completed tables into speech or writing", p. 87). Often such an "intersemiotic translation" moves from one semiotic system to more than one, as when we "translate" a short story or novel to the stage or the screen — or indeed when we "translate" a play or a screenplay into a performance.

The potential for intersemiotic translation involving language will depend on the "typological distance" between language and the other semiotic. A semiotic semiotic such as painting will be at a greater "typological" distance from language than some form of semiotic that is ultimately derived directly from language such as mathematics or (symbolic) logic. Thus it is comparatively easy to translate mathematical or logical expressions into language: the simple set-theoretic theorem $B \supset A => A \cap B = A$ can be translated into English as an 'enhancing' complex of two 'intensive relational' clauses — *If A is a subset of B, then the intersection of A and B is A*. Of course, the further mathematics or logic moves from its linguistic origins, the harder such expressions will be to translate. I will give an example involving greater typological distance — a "translation" of a visual semiotic representation — William Turner's (1840) *The Slave Ship* — into an English text by John Ruskin.

The painting is from Turner's later period when he was foregrounding the use of colour as a representational resource: see Figure 4. Translating this into a linguistic description is a challenge — especially at a time when photographic reproductions were not available; but Ruskin accepted the challenge with considerable semiotic energy: see Example 1.[4] The entire painting (at the highest rank — that of the "work", see O'Toole 1994: e.g. p. 24) is "translated" by one long paragraph. Ruskin begins by locating the painting ideationally (it is a "sea" and it was the Academy Picture of 1840) and interpersonally (assessed as the noblest ever painted). This is the nuclear information, but it is "external" to the painting itself. The remainder of the paragraph elaborates on this nuclear information. The organization of this elaborating part of the paragraph is revealed very clearly by a thematic analysis of the text — see Table 2.

After dealing with the painting as a whole, the paragraph scans it in two phases — first the sky (the upper half of the painting: *storm — clouds*) and then the sea (the lower part of the painting: *surface of the sea — two ridges — between the two ridges: fire of sunset — waves — spaces of water*), following these two phases with a third that moves from a combination of the two phases (the upper part reflected in the lower part (*images of clouds*) to the 'guilty ship' and its parts (*thin masts*)). The paragraph is thus developed spatially — larger to smaller and top to bottom, moving forward in such a way that the ship is presented as the New information of the whole paragraph. The clausal build-up of New information is also carefully managed: the successive new elements contain a series of interpersonally charged items — culminating with the final elements of the last clause (*with condemnation in that fearful hue* [*which signs the sky with horror, and mixes its flaming flood with the sunlight, and, cast far along the desolate heave* [*of the sepulchral waves*], [7.7A.4] *incarnadines the multitudinous sea*][5]).

It is very clear that the painting could have been scanned or traversed in different ways. Precisely because the "translation" represents a move from one *kind* of semiotic to another, there is a great deal of indeterminacy and play — "freedom" — in the translation potential: the situation would be different if we were to translate Ruskin's paragraph into another language. One aspect of this indeterminacy is that the units of correspondence are not so easy to establish beyond the high-ranking correspondence between painting (at the rank of work) and paragraph. At the same time, this does not mean that the "translation" is random. Ruskin has scanned or "read" the painting in a principled way — whole to part, top part (predominantly light, source of light) to bottom part (predominantly dark, reflection of light) and then followed the vertical path of the light. He has also ensured that "the slave ship", which is wedged between the two halves of the painting, is maximally contextualized by his account while at the same time giving it the kind of prominence suggested by the reflected, cold bluish light at the far left of the painting. (Note that according to Kress & van Leeuwen's 1996: 186–92, account of information structure in images, the horizontal axis is often used to realize the distinction between given and new, with given on the left and new towards the right. We might say that the slave ship is given — deriving from the context at the time of Turner's painting. If so, Ruskin has transformed the information flow in his "translation" into English.)

This then is the textual movement within Ruskin's paragraph. But the paragraph also evokes the movement in Turner's dynamic depiction of the ship struggling in the storm through the use of the ideational resources of English. There are interesting details — such as the motif of v-ing forms of verbs of motion as Epithets in nominal groups (as in *streaming clouds, tossing waves, whirling water, declining sun;* cf. also *burning clouds, flaming flood*), which Coleridge also used in the first part of Kubla Khan (cf. Matthiessen 1995: 705–9), and verbal nouns of motion as Thing in nominal groups (as in *(enormous) swell, (broad) heaving (of the whole ocean), lifting (of its bosom ...), swell (of the sea), (added) motion (of their own fiery) flying, (desolate) heave (of the sepulchral waves)*). But the dominant ideational motifs seem to be those created by COMPLEXING and PROCESS TYPE. As the text unfolds, the clause complexes vary with respect to how many clauses they contain; but clause complex [6] achieves a peak of complexity with 9 ranking clauses (analysed in Table 2), followed closely by the final complex with 7 ranking clauses. The peak comes at the point where the text construes the stormy motion of the waves. This is also where every clause of the complex is 'material' in process type. Ruskin has thus used the grammar both to represent the movement in the painting directly and to symbolize it indirectly. We can see this when we visualize the patterns construed by the grammar of COMPLEXING and PROCESS TYPE: see Figure 6. This "backtranslation" of the linguistic *analysis* into the visual semiotic of a line chart shows Ruskin's paragraph construes "waves" of meaning — waves that evoke the movement in the painting. When complexing peaks, material clauses (as Figure 5) peak; and such peaks of material clauses are followed by a rise in relational clauses.

Example 1:   John Ruskin's account of William Turner's *The Slave Ship*, 1840 (quoted in Schneider Adams 1996: xii-xiii.)

*[1] The noblest sea [that Turner has ever painted], and, if so, the noblest [certainly ever painted by man], is that [of the **Slave Ship**], the chief Academy picture [of the Exhibition [of 1840]]. [2.1] It is a sunset [on the Atlantic, after prolonged storm]; [2.2] but the storm is partially lulled, [2.3] and the torn and streaming clouds are moving in scarlet lines [2.4] to lose themselves in the hollow [of the night]. [3.1] The whole surface [of the sea [included in the picture]] is divided into two ridges [of enormous swell], [3.2] not high, nor local, [3.3] but a broad heaving [of the whole ocean], like the lifting [of its bosom by deep-drawn breath after the torture [of the storm]]. [4.1] Between these two ridges the fire [of the sunset] falls along the trough [of the sea], [4.2] dyeing it with an awful but glorious light, the intense and lurid splendour [which burns like gold, and bathes like blood]. [5.1] <u>**Along this fiery path and valley, the tossing waves** [by which the swell [of the sea] is restlessly divided], **lift themselves in dark, indefinite, fantastic forms**</u>, [5.2] <u>each casting a faint and ghastly shadow behind it along the illumined foam.</u> [6.1] <u>They do not rise everywhere,</u> [6.2] <u>but three or four together in wild groups, fitfully and furiously,</u> [6.3] <u>as the under strength [of the swell] compels or permits them;</u> [6.4] <u>leaving between them treacherous spaces [of*</u>

Figure 4. William Turner's *The Slave Ship* (1840)

level and whirling water], [6.5] <u>now lighted with green and lamp-like fire</u>, [6.6] <u>now flashing back the gold</u> [of the declining sun], [6.7] <u>now fearfully dyed from above with the undistinguishable images</u> [of the burning clouds], [6.8] <u>which fall upon them in flakes</u> [of crimson and scarlet], [6.9] <u>and give to the reckless waves the added motion</u> [of their own fiery flying]. [7.1] Purple and blue, [7.2] the lurid shadows [of the hollow breakers] are cast upon the mist [of night], [7.3] which gathers cold and low, [7.4] advancing like the shadow [of death] upon the guilty ship [7.5] as it labours amidst the lightning [of the sea], [7.6] its thin masts written upon the sky in lines [of blood], [7.7] girded with condemnation in that fearful hue [[7.7A.1] which signs the sky with horror, [7.7A.2] and mixes its flaming flood with the sunlight, [7.7A.3] and, cast far along the desolate heave [of the sepulchral waves], [7.7A.4] incarnadines the multitudinous sea].

Ruskin's paragraph is an example of a "translation" in the sense that it serves as an *alternative* to the painting itself: it represents the replacement of the "source" text by a "target" presentation in another semiotic system. However, many presentations are inherently multimodal, being made up of *complementary* contributions from different semiotic systems, as illustrated by Steiner (1988) in his analysis of the division of labour between language and music in a folk ballad. Examples include printed documents with written texts, photographs, graphs, maps and other visual contributions, online documents or web pages with written texts, visual contributions of the kind found with printed documents but with the po-

56 Christian M.I.M. Matthiessen

Table 2. Thematic analysis of Ruskin's paragraph (different lexico-referential chains as topical Themes represented by columns)

	whole	sky	sea							night	ship
			whole	ridges	fiery path	waves	strength of swell	spaces			
[1]	The noblest sea …										
[2.1]	It										
[2.2]		the storm									
[2.3]		the torn and streaming clouds									
[2.4]		<-"->									
[3.1]			The whole surface [of the sea […]]								
[3.2]				<two ridges>							
[3.3]				<two ridges>							
[4.1]				Between these two ridges	*the fire [of the sunset]*						

The environments of translation 57

Table 2. Thematic analysis of Ruskin's paragraph (different lexico-referential chains as topical Themes represented by columns) (Continued)

	whole	sky	sea whole	ridges	fiery path	waves	strength of swell	spaces	night	ship
[4.2]					<the fire of the sunset>					
[5.1]					Along this fiery path and valley,	*the tossing waves [...]*				
[5.2]						each				
[6.1]						They				
[6.2]						[they]				
[6.3]							the under strength [of the swell]			
[6.4]							<-"->			
[6.5]								<treacherous spaces [...]>		
[6.6]								<-"->		
[6.7]								<-"->		

58 Christian M.I.M. Matthiessen

Table 2. Thematic analysis of Ruskin's paragraph (different lexico-referential chains as topical Themes represented by columns) (Continued)

	whole	sky	sea						night	ship
			whole	ridges	fiery path	waves	strength of swell	spaces		
[6.8]		<the … images […]>								
[6.9]		<-"->								
[7.1]										
[7.2]										
[7.3]									which <night>	
[7.4]									<-"->	
[7.5]										it <the guilty ship>
[7.6]										its thin masts
[7.7]										<-"->

The environments of translation 59

Table 3. "The Slave Ship", clause complex analysis

[5]					α		Along this fiery path and valley, the tossing waves [by which the swell [of the sea] is restlessly divided], lift themselves in dark, indefinite, fantastic forms
					ˣβ		each casting a faint and ghastly shadow behind it along the illumined foam.
[6]	1						They do not rise everywhere,
	+2	α	α				but [they rise] three or four together in wild groups, fitfully and furiously,
			ˣβ				as the under strength [of the swell] compels or permits them;
		ˣβ	α				leaving between them treacherous spaces [of level and whirling water],
			ᵌβ	1			now lighted with green and lamp-like fire,
				+2			now flashing back the gold [of the declining sun],
				+3	α		now fearfully dyed from above with the undistinguishable images [of the burning clouds],
					ᵌβ	1	which fall upon them in flakes [of crimson and scarlet],
						+2	and give to the reckless waves the added motion [of their own fiery flying].

	Along this fiery path and valley,	the tossing waves [by which the swell [of the sea] is restlessly divided],	lift	themselves	in dark, indefinite, fantastic forms
clause: exper.	Location	Actor	Process	Goal	Role or Manner
group/ phrase	prep. phrase: place	nom. gp.	verbal gp.	nom. gp.	prep. phrase

Figure 5. Transitivity configuration in clause

tential for animation and video and sound as well, and spoken presentations (whether performed or spontaneous) with facial expressions, gestures, body postures, paralinguistic features and so on. Such multimodal presentations vary considerably with respect to the division of labour among the contributing semiotic systems. For example, there are many contexts where language is the central constitutive semiotic, but there are other contexts where it is essentially ancillary. Whatever the nature of the division of labour is, it makes sense to ask whether the complementary semiotic contributions are in some way "translations" of one another.

This question can clearly only be answered after a good deal of analysis of samples from a wide range of registers. But there are certainly registers where contributions from different semiotic systems are coordinated by a kind of translation relationship. For example, in an investigation of WHO reports in English and French, I found that charts, tables and maps all stand in elaborating relations to English and French passages. These passages often take the form of an identifying relational clause that construes the name of the chart, table or figure as Token and the parameter(s) being quantified as Value, as illustrated in Figure 7. Thanks to this clause type, it is thus possible in language to gloss displays from other semiotic systems, just as it is possible to gloss linguistic items.

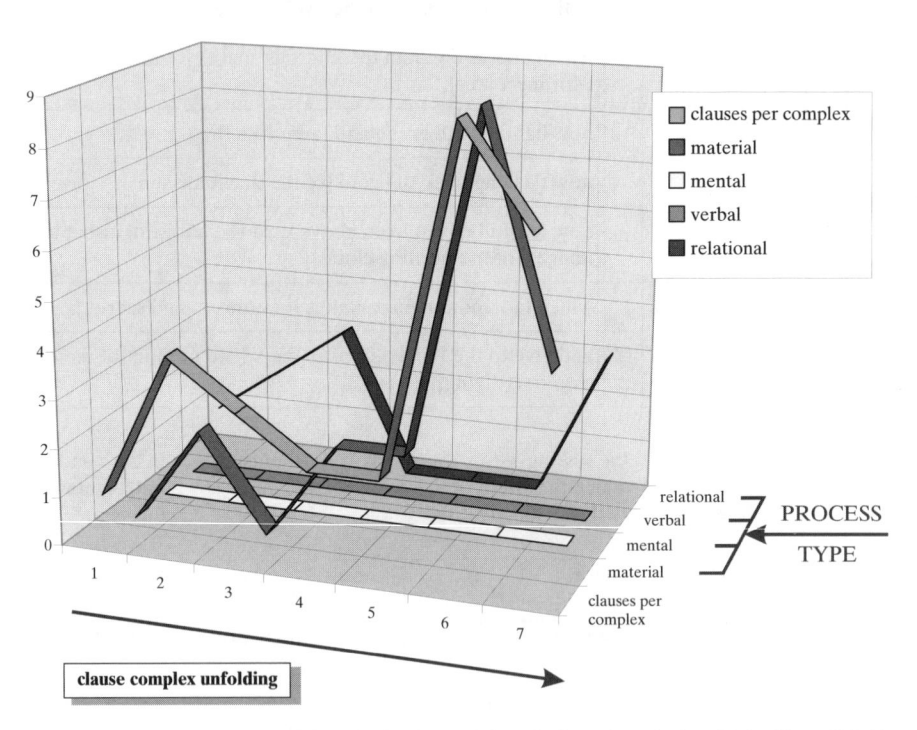

Figure 6. Visualization of partial analysis of verbal description of a painting ("The Slave Ship")

Map 2	**shows**	the estimated regional distribution of HIV-infected adults (including AIDS cases) alive as of mid-1995.
Token	Process	Value
nom. gp.	verbal gp.	nominal group

Figure 7. Identifying relational clause construing "translation" relation between name of quantifying map and parameter being quantified

2.4. Construing texts pictorially

The examples given in the previous subsection illustrate how paintings or other images may be "translated" into language. The reverse is of course also possible; texts may be "translated" into some form of pictorial representation. Thus paintings often have a linguistic "source text" or set of "source texts", as in the case of Turner's *The Slave Ship*. Turner must have heard about, or read, the report describing what happened on the ship. Schneider Adams (1996: 58) describes the context as follows:

> ...Turner's *The Slave Ship* ..., which Ruskin described so vividly in *Modern Painters,* was inspired by revulsion against the slave trade. A Marxist reading of Turner's painting could not ignore the political or economic impetus behind slavery, and its effect on the artist. In 1839, Thomas Folwell Buxton, a member of Parliament and a Quaker who led a crusade against slavery, published *The African Slave Trade and Its Remedy*. His argument detailed the abuse of human beings for economic gain. It included the report of an English captain who had 132 slaves thrown overboard in 1783 in order to claim insurance on the loss: "The master of the ship," Buxton wrote, "called together a few of the officers, and stated to them that, if the sick slaves died a natural death, the loss would fall on the owners of the ship; but, if they were thrown alive into the sea, on any sufficient pretext of necessity for the safety of the ship, it would be the loss of the underwriters ...

The relationship between Buxton's report and Turner's painting is fairly indirect and if Turner's painting can be called a pictorial translation of the report at all, it is certainly a very "free" one. It clearly has many features in common with other paintings by Turner of ships under stormy conditions — the kind of scenes he had experienced himself (cf. Lloyd 1996: 187). In this sense, translations into painting are target-semiotic oriented.

Clearer examples of pictorial "translations" of texts are provided by paintings depicting scenes from novels, shorts stories and plays. As an example, consider Martin Emond's pictorial "translation" shown in Figure 8 of the following passages from Macbeth:

IV.1

Third Apparition: Be lion-mettled, proud, and take no care
Who chafes, who frets, or where conspirers are;
Macbeth shall never vanquished be, <u>until</u>
Great Birnan Wood to high Dunsinane Hill
<u>Shall come against him</u>.

Macbeth: That will never be.
Who can impress the forest, bid the tree
Unfix his earth-bound root? Sweet bodements! Good!

V.5

Messenger: Gracious my lord,
I should report that which I say I saw,
But know not how to do't

Macbeth: Well, say, sir.

Messenger: As I did stand my watch upon the hill
I looked toward Birnan and anon methought
The wood began to move.

Macbeth: Liar and slave!

Messenger: Let me endure your wrath if't be not so.
Within this three mile may you see it coming.
I say, a moving grove.

Macbeth: If thou speak'st false,
Upon the next tree shall thou hang alive
Till famine cling thee. If thy speech be sooth,
I care not if thou dost for me as much.
I pull in resolution, and begin
To doubt the equivocation of the fiend
That lies like truth. "Fear not till Birnan Wood
Comes to Dunsinane" — and now a wood
Comes toward Dunsinane. Arm, arm, and out!

Emond's painting construes what is referred to in the dialogue — in particular the clauses *till Birnan Wood comes to Dunsinane, now a wood comes toward Dunsinane, until Great Birnan Wood shall come against him,* which are all 'locative' 'material' clauses of motion with the structure Actor (wood) + Process (come) + Location (to[ward] Dunsinane, against him), unfolding iconically from the source of motion to the destination; but this may of course also be enacted in a staged performance or a film version of the play. (Emond would most likely have read Macbeth in a Swedish translation; but the difference between English and Swedish is neutralized in the pictorial translation: what is significant is the translation from a linguistic kind of semiotic to a pictorial kind, with a change in context from Elizabethan times to mid-20th century.) The painting construes these material clauses of directed motion as a swell of camouflaged soldiers (Actor) heading (Process) towards the entrance of a castle (Location). According to Kress & van Leeuwen's (1996: 61–2, 73) account, I think this this would be a "narrative" (as opposed to "conceptual") representation, of a "non-transactional action" type. The painting adds considerable detail in comparison with the clause and the groups/ phrases serving in the clause, making the representation more specific e.g. with respect to the weather conditions and time of day (though Emond has also chosen to leave out details such as the soldiers' facial features at the rank of "figure" in O'Toole's rank-based account, thus collectivizing rather than individuating the soldiers).

In the case of this example, the correspondence is thus roughly between one clause in English (or Swedish) and one painting. In the case of

Ruskin's "translation" of the Slave Ship, the linguistic unit was a paragraph. Because we are dealing with two different kinds of semiotic system, we can expect that there will be considerable variation in the size of the unit of correspondence. But size does matter. Shakespeare's work was one of Emond's sources of inspiration and in addition to various paintings such as the one discussed here, he also produced a gigantic mural that covers the left wall of the foyer of Malmö Stadsteater in Malmö, Sweden. This mural draws on all of Shakespeare's work, with certain key scenes selected and brought together in a seamless sequence to represent the whole Shakespearean experience (on a visit to this theatre, consider for example the scenes from *The Tempest* where a tree emerges from a representation of "goodly creatures" dancing in the "brave new world" (Act 5, Scene 1) to link this scene to a representation of Miranda and Ferdinand through its stem but also to frame the second representation through its foliage, thus separating the two scenes). Such experiential complexity would obviously be hard to construe in a single painting and there is a long tradition of epics being represented by murals, as with murals depicting Biblical stories or the Mexican revolution.

Figure 8. "Translation" of scene from Macbeth into oil painting (Martin Emond, between 1950 and 1959)

Emond's painting does not only *construe* the scene from Macbeth. It also *enacts* his assessment or appraisal of the scene through the tone and the colour scheme, indicating threat and foreboding by means of a pervasively dark tone (dominated by the dark clouds running as a prosody through the painting) and skew towards blood red. The linguistic sources of appraisal are not to be found in the individual 'material' clauses of motion quoted above but rather over longer passages of text where there is an accumulation of a negative appraisal of Macbeth in terms of social sanction of the moral subtype (see Martin, in press, for the description of the resources of appraisal): the painting represents the beginning of Macbeth's just punishment within the play — the threatening swell of the soldiers is in harmony with the threatening aspect of nature. And it is organized "textually" in the same way as the 'material' clauses quoted above: it *presents* the source of the swell as "given" whereas the destination of the swell — the black door of the castle — is presented as prominent by means of the surrounding bright yellow of the wall of the castle and (according to Kress & van Leeuwen's 1996, interpretation of information structure in images) by means of the vertical placement to the right of the painting. In other words, Emond's painting — like paintings in general (see Kress & van Leeuwen 1996; O'Toole 1994) — embodies the three metafunctional modes of meaning.

2.5. Language as primary semiotic of translation

Both the examples of "translation" from pictorial representation into text and the examples of "translation" of text into pictorial representation show three points very clearly. First, "translation" is not a passive reflection of the original; it is a creative act of reconstruing the meanings of the original as meanings in the "target".

Second, whether these semiotic transformations are thought of as translations or not, they are located at level of abstraction that is high enough above the modality-specific level of expression to make the transformation possible: to put this in linguistic terms, they are located at the level of semantics rather than at the level of lexicogrammar (or the level of expression); and they are located within the roughly same context (of culture) as the original. This is also very clear when we consider "translations" of protolanguage into language, as illustrated in Example 2. Young children's protolanguages are semiotic systems of the primary kind: they are systems with two levels only — content and expression (Halliday 1975) — and lack a level of lexicogrammar. Protolinguistic content can thus be "translated" into linguistic content only at the level of semantics within language; but since language is a higher-order semiotic with a level of lexicogrammar, the translations will inevitably impose lexicogrammatical patterns on the translations.

Third, the lower-level realization within each semiotic system plays an important part in determining how the meanings are "translated". In partic-

Example 2. Translation from protolanguage (about 9 months) to adult language (English), from Halliday (1975: 61)

[ø] mid-low falling to low	'let's be together'
[ø] mid falling to low	'look (it's moving)'
grasping object firmly	'I want that'
touching object lightly	'I don't want that'
touching person or relevant object firmly	'do that (with it) again (e.g. make it jump up in the air)'

ular, the level of lexicogrammar within language is a resource for construing highly *schematic* representations. These representations are (i) variable in delicacy from very general to very specific, (ii) variable in abstractness from concrete to abstract and (iii) variable in "expansion" from nuclear configurations to highly expanded configurations. For example, when Ruskin writes

> *Along this fiery path and valley, the tossing waves [by which the swell [of the sea] is restlessly divided], lift themselves in dark, indefinite, fantastic forms*

using the lexicogrammatical potential for specifying the clausal schema to evoke as much as possible of the painting, he could also have opted for more highly schematic alternatives still describing the same scene:

> *Along this path and valley, the waves lift themselves in forms*
>
> *The waves lift themselves*
>
> *The waves move up*
>
> *The ridges move up*
>
> *The things move up*
>
> *Something happens*

This is an important aspect of the power of a higher-order semiotic system with a lexicogrammatical level. Other aspects of the power of such a system include the metafunctional organization (simultaneous but independently variable modes of meaning) and the potential for metaphor (the reconstrual of experience within the same system).

The only clearly higher-order (human) semiotic system is language and this gives language a unique position in "inter-semiotic translation". In discussing the role of language in the organization and evolution of the brain, Bickerton (1995: 24) notes: "The linguistic cat is also a holistic cat. ... The word ties together aspects of catness that may well be stored separately in other areas of the brain, suggesting that its neural representation may serve as what has been called a *convergence zone* (Damasio and Damasio 1992)." The notion of *convergence zone* is important because it helps explain why language has the power to integrate meanings from a range of different semiotic systems. It is related to Michio Sugeno's hypothesis that language is the primary resource for *fusing* information from different semiotic sources — a hypothesis that has been tested and is being tested at his laboratory at Tokyo Institute of Technology (see in particular the work by Ichiro Kobayashi, e.g. Kobayashi 1995, and by Kobayashi and Sugeno, e.g. Kobayashi & Sugeno 1994). In this sense, language is the "interlingua" of semiotic systems. In our own work, this hypothesis is represented by the model of a multi-modal semantic system (Matthiessen et al 1997) that is based on language (Halliday & Matthiessen 1999).

As a working hypothesis, we might thus adopt the suggestion that language is the only semiotic system into which all other kinds of (human) semiotic systems can be translated. As we have seen, this does not mean that the translations will be "literal"; they are bound to be very "free" because they have to be done at the level of semantics and thus be abstracted away from lower-level "renderings" of meaning.

2.6. Translating across languages [typological distance]

If we allow for "intersemiotic" translation as one kind of translation, we see clearly that translation has to be modelled as a mapping (or transformation) of meanings (at the level of semantics) in the first instance. We can also begin to get a sense of how indeterminate such a mapping (transformation) can be, suggesting that it needs to be represented as a fuzzy match. When we move from translation between semiotic systems of different kinds to translation between semiotic systems of the same kind, it is reasonable to expect that the potential for translation will increase dramatically. Thus when we translate between two languages, there will be many more points of contact than when we translated between a language and some other kind of semiotic. In particular, we will be able to map between two lexicogrammatical systems as well as between two semantic systems. (In fact we might define "interlingual translation" as translation where it is possible to translate between wordings at the level of lexicogrammar.) This is a difference not just in degree but also in kind; and this is true regardless of what languages are involved in the translation: even if the lexicogrammatical systems of two languages differ significantly with respect to a large number of parameters, this difference is dwarfed by the fact they both languages have lexicogrammatical systems. (We have to keep context in mind: the intersemiotic translations illustrated above were all located within roughly the same context of culture; but both intersemiotic translation and interlingual translation may involve considerable contextual distance.)

At the same time, it is important to get a sense of the outer limits of distance when we translate between languages. It is reasonable to expect that these outer limits can be defined by reference to languages that are maximally typologically distant — or rather, that these outer limits can be defined for certain grammatical systems by reference to languages that are maximally typologically distant as far as these systems are concerned, bearing in mind that linguistic typology is typology of systems rather than of whole languages (Halliday 1966a). Pawley (1987) reports on George Grace's discussion of this issue:

> If languages have markedly different resources for the characterization of situations, i.e. if their grammars require them to report the same bits of observed reality in very different ways, it may be that translation between such reports is impossible — at least, accurate translation. Grace concludes that what he calls 'isomorphic' or 'quasi-isomorphic' translation is rarely possible between languages that are genetically unrelated or associated with radically different cultures. In an isomorphic translation the source text and its translation specify the same conceptual situation ... Usually, the best one can hope to achieve is that kind of matching which Grace refers to as 'paraphrastic' translation — in which the speaker's communicative intent is more or less accurately captured. What is being translated in such cases is not the linguistic meaning or the conceptual situation specified by the source text; rather, it is the translator's reconstruction of the speaker's pragmatic meaning or communicative purpose. (p. 331)

Pawley goes on to compare English and Kalam (a language spoken in the Highlands of Papua New Guinea) — a comparison that he believes "may indicate the outer limits of variation among languages in resources and conventions encoding event-like phenomena". He notes: "In these respects Kalam may be as different from English as any language on earth." From a systemic functional point of view, "these respects" refer to systems within the ideational metafunction (rather than the interpersonal and textual metafunctions). In fact, the most fundamental difference between the two languages seems to be in the division of labour between the two ideational modes of construal — the logical and the experiential (for this interpretation, see Halliday & Matthiessen 1999: 317–8). Thus in construing the flow of goings-on, Kalam relies more on the logical mode, combining clauses into clause complexes, whereas English relies more on the experiential mode, using a single clause for the "same" goings-on.

For example, the Kalam clause complex shown in Figure 9 is a series of four clauses representing a sequence of events, which Pawley glosses as "(1) the man takes hold of the stick, (2) the stick is thrown, (3) it flies over the fence, (4) it falls into the garden"; but the English translation proposed by Pawley is a single clause — *The man threw a stick over the fence into the garden*. The analysis of the English clause is presented in Figure 10. It shows that while Kalam draws on the logical metafunction to create a complex of four clauses, English only uses the logical mode to construe a prepositional phrase complex as a circumstance of Location. The translation shift between the two languages is thus quite considerable.

B	monday	d	yokek	waty	at	amb	wogmgan	yowp
man	stick	hold	he-displaced-different subject	fence	above	it-went	garden-inside	it-fell
Actor	Goal	Process	Process	Location		Process	Location	Process

Figure 9. Kalam clause complex (Pawley 1987: 354; analysis from Halliday & Matthiessen 1999: 317)

The man	threw	a stick	over the fence	into the garden
Actor	Process	Goal	Location	
nom. gp.	verbal gp.	nom. gp.	prepositional phrase (complex)	
			α	ˣβ

Figure 10. English translation equivalent — single clause

The typological distance between Kalam and English with respect to how they construe the flow of events would seem to be quite high; and the two languages may, as Pawley suggests, indicate the outer limits of variation among languages around the world in this respect. For languages that are typologically closer (in this respect) such as English and Chinese, Japanese, Vietnamese, French, or German, we can expect much higher correspondence in translation between clauses and clause complexes. The same principle of "typological distance" is relevant throughout all the systems of language-in-context: see Colin Yallop's contribution on translation between English and Pitjantjatjara in this volume.

2.7. Translating within languages between varieties

If translation between typologically distant languages represents one pole on a scale of translation difference, then it would be reasonable to expect that translation between varieties within one language (what might be called, using Jakobson's term, *intralingual translation*) represents the other pole on this scale. In particular, it seems reasonable to expect that *dialectal varieties* should represent minimal translation differences: since dialect variation is characterized by phonological variation and to some extent by lexicogrammatical variation but the semantics remains constant (as noted in e.g. Halliday 1978, dialects represent different ways of saying the same thing), translation should constitute a minimal transformation of meaning and also a minimal transformation of many lexicogrammatical patterns. This is confirmed by the success of the work on automatic *dialect adaptation* by computer undertaken by David Webber and Bill Mann first on dialects of Quechua and later on dialects of other languages as well. Dialects shade into different languages along dialect chains, with no clear boundary between dialects and languages; so it also makes sense that closely related languages such as Danish and Swedish should be characterized by a fairly low translation difference. The task of relating what Gregory (1967) calls temporal dialects also gives us a useful insight into the way "translation" shades into other kinds of mappings. While Chaucer is often translated into Modern English, Shakespeare is not (one reason being the Great Vowel Shift that separates the two writers); but Shakespeare is often published with glosses and commentary.

We can make sense of the great potential for translating one dialect of a language into another because dialects are characterized not only by fairly low-level variation but also by higher-level constancy — they are essentially constant at the level of semantics. And, as already suggested for intersemiotic translation, it is at the level of semantics that translation has to take place in the first instance (see further below). But by the same token, *registerial varieties* should constitute a considerable challenge to translation. This is so because there is no higher-level constant in register variation (see Matthiessen 1993, and references therein): registers differ semantically — they constitute one kind of semantic variation, being "ways of saying different things" (Halliday 1978: 35). Indeed, it should be impossible to translate one register into another. Thus it is impossible to translate a meteorological forecast into a gossip text. And people are of course aware of this: one source of linguistic humour is the partial adaptation of one register to make it look like another. (This is also a source of pedagogic confusion for children, as when a generalized explanation is dressed up as a particularized narrative.) While a text from one register cannot be translated into a text from another register within a language, register is one of the keys to translation across languages, as researchers working with MT have found (where registers are called "sublanguages" — cf. Catford's 1965: 83 "'sub-languages' or varieties within a total language"): see further below.

Although a text from one register cannot be translated into a text from another register, *partial* translation involving a shift in register is possible and is often practiced (even if it may not be recognized as translation):

this is the shift between written and spoken registers. From the point of view of context, this means that there is a shift within mode but not (in the first instance) within field and tenor. Let me give a brief example of a translation, taken from Halliday (1985: 79):

Example 3. Translation from written to spoken mode

> [*written original:*] ||| *The use of this method of control unquestionably leads to safer and faster train running [in the most adverse weather conditions].* |||

> [*spoken translation, 1:*] ||| *If this method of control is used,* || *trains will unquestionably (be able to) run more safely and faster* || *(even) when the weather conditions are most adverse.* |||

> [*spoken translation, 2:*] ||| *You can control the trains in this way* || *and if you do that* || *you can be quite sure* || *that they'll be able to run more safely and more quickly [than they would otherwise]* || *no matter how bad the weather gets.*

One of the striking differences between the written original and the spoken translations is that the written original deploys only one ranking clause whereas the first spoken translation deploys a complex of 3 clauses and the second a complex of 5 clauses. This is in fact characteristic of the difference between prototypical speech and writing (Halliday 1985). In this respect, the shift that occurs in the translation from written to spoken mode is similar to the shift that occurs if we translate from English to Kalam, which is perhaps not surprising since unlike English Kalam does not have a history of centuries of written varieties. Another difference that is perhaps less immediately obvious but which is just as significant lies in the degree of congruence (metaphoricity). The written original is highly metaphorical (in the sense of ideational grammatical metaphor; Halliday 1994: Ch. 10, Halliday & Matthiessen 1999: Ch. 6, Matthiessen 1995: Section 2.3.2; Halliday & Martin 1993) for example in the use of nominalization such as *use* and of "conjunctive verbs" such as *lead to*. In contrast the spoken translations are progressively more congruent.

The translation from written to spoken thus clearly leads to a change in meaning and it is important to be aware of this when we translate between varieties of a language. I will just add one example — Labov's translation from BEV (Black English Vernacular) in Example 4 to SAM (Standard American English), shown as Example 5. Labov used this translation to demonstrate the logic of BEV; but Atkinson (1985: 106–7) reveals serious problems with the "translation":

> In his demonstration of the logical adequacy of this series of responses by Larry, Labov translates them into a series of propositions. Labov himself is somewhat misleading about the nature of this translation exercise, giving the impression that the differences

between the two formats is a matter of style, claiming that he is involved in 'setting out the Standard English equivalents in linear order'. ... Now it is surely obvious that Labov's act of translation is far more than a transposition from the style of BEV to Standard (American) English. He re-orders and re-creates the 'thesis' that Larry is interpreted as proposing.

In fact, the complexity of the natural logic of casual speech, which is shown in Table 4, has been destroyed in the course of the translation.

Example 4. Black English Vernacular (BEV); J.L. = interviewer; L. = interviewee, Larry

J.L.: What happens to you after you die? Do you know?

L.: Yeah, I know. After they put you in the ground your body turns into — ah — bones 'n shit.

J.L.: What happens to your spirit?

L.: Your spirit — soon as you die, your spirit leaves you.

J.L.: And where does the spirit go?

L.: Well it all depends ...

J.L.: On what?

L.: You know, like some people say if you're good an' shit, your spirit, your spirit goin' t'heaven ... 'n' if you're bad your spirit goin' to hell. Well bullshit! Your spirit goin' to hell anyway, good or bad.

J.L.: Why?

L.: Why? I'll tell you why. 'Cause, you see, doesn't nobody really know that it's a God, y'know 'cause I mean I have seen black gods, pink gods, white gods, all colour gods, and don't nobody know it's really a God. An' when they be sayin' if you good you goin' t'heaven tha's bullshit, cause you ain't goin' to no heaven, 'cause it ain't no heaven for you to go to.

Example 5. Labov's Standard (American) English translation

1 Everyone has a different idea of what God is like.

2 Therefore nobody really knows that God exists.

3 If there is a heaven, it was made by God.

4 If God doesn't exist, he couldn't have made heaven.

5 Therefore he does not exist.

6 You can't go somewhere that doesn't exist.

7 Therefore you can't go to heaven.

8 Therefore you are going to hell.

Table 4. The natural logic of casual speech (from Larry's last turn)

1	1	α	α	'Cause, you see, doesn't nobody really know
			'β	that it's a God, y'know
		ˣβ		'cause I mean I have seen black gods, pink gods, white gods, all colour gods,
	+2	α		and don't nobody know
			'β	it's really a God;
+2	ˣβ	a		an' when they be sayin'
		"β	ˣβ	if you good
			α	you goin' t'heaven
	α	α		tha's bullshit,
		ˣβ		cause you ain't goin' to no heaven,
		ˣγ		'cause it ain't no heaven for you to go to.

2.8. Representation of a multilingual system for translation

In this section I have focussed on the question of what the domain of applicability of translation is within the system of systems that make up our phenomenal world (as we know it from a scientific point of view). I suggested that the domain of translation is that of fourth-order systems — semiotic systems — and I illustrated translation between different kinds of semiotic system before focussing on translation between (and within) languages. The process of translation works in terms of the resources of the systems involved in the translation; but although I have discussed the domain of translation, I have not said anything about how those resources are organized.

We might assume that the resources of each language, or of each semiotic system, are represented independently of one another as a collection of monolingual (or monomodal) systems and that they are only related by statements specifying translation correspondences. Alternatively we might assume that the resources of each language, or of each semiotic system, are fully integrated in a single multilingual (or multimodal) system and that this integration supports translation but exists regardless of whether translation takes place or not. The debate in machine translation revolved around these two positions. The first is represented by the transfer approach in MT; the second is represented by the interlingua approach. However, we might also explore some form of synthesis of the two positions — an approach where each language (semiotic system) is represented as part of an integrated multilingual (multimodal) system but in such a way that it retains its own integrity. This was the approach we developed first in the context of multilingual text generation in the early 1990s (Bateman et al 1991; Matthiessen et al 1991; Bateman, Matthiessen & Zeng 1999; Zeng 1996), then also in the context of register variation (Matthiessen 1993) and multimodality. Since the approach is discussed in some detail in Elke Teich's chapter in this book, there is no need to summarize it here: Teich also shows how the approach is relevant to translation. One important aspect of the approach is that it will allow us to interpret translation in terms of fuzzy theory as a matter of degree: compare the discussion in Section 3.2 below. For example, while both the mood grammars of both English and German include 'imperative' mood types that have the same basic value in the mood systems of the languages, they do not overlap entirely in the grammar and as Teich has found in a study of instructional texts, they differ semantically, at least in the register of procedural instruction.

3. Environments of translation

In the preceding section, I tried to suggest something of the domain of possible applications of the concept of translation by locating it first in relation to a general ordered typology of systems (physical — biological — social — semiotic) and then in relation to different kinds of semiotic system. I tried to show that by considering what Jakobson called intersemiotic translation, we are invited to consider the outer limits of what we would want to model as translation and to focus on what is constant across different environments in which translation may take place. What is constant is the defining property of semiotic systems — the property of meaning. That is, translation is, in the first instance, a semantic mapping (transformation).

3.1. Orders of environments

In the remainder of the chapter, I will continue along the same lines of investigation: I will try to make the environments of translation as explicit as possible, but now focussing specifically on "interlingual" translation. I will try to identify all the *environments* that are relevant to the task of locating translation (and, as part of translation, translation equivalence and translation shift). My basic assumption is that any act of translation is *multiply contextualized* and that we have to identify these contexts or environments.[6] And my working principle is that (in the default case[7]) to make translation maximally effective, we should make it *maximally contextualized*. There is nothing surprising about this principle of contextualization: the wider the context, the more information is available to guide the translation. There is also a typological principle at work here: the wider the environment, the more congruent languages are likely to be; the narrower the environment, the more incongruent languages are likely to be.[8] (When we move towards a wider environment, we are thus moving closer to something like a higher-level constant or relation of equivalence between languages.) Consequently, translation "difference" will be lower the wider the environment in which the translation takes place (for a more detailed discussion, see Section 3.2. below).

Language is organized along a number of dimensions. We can interpret all these dimensions as defining particular manifestations of the very general contrast between 'wider environment' and 'narrower environment'; that is, we can interpret them as different dimensions of contextualization. These different dimensions all define environments of translation and are related to one another in a successive series of contextualizations, as shown in Figure 11.

The diagram says that the most global manifestation of cline between 'wider environment' and 'narrower environment' is the *hierarchy of stratification*: the widest stratal environment is that of context and within that there is a hierarchy of linguistic strata or levels of decreasing stratal scope — semantics, lexicogrammar and phonology (graphology or sign). So the widest stratal environment of translation is that of context.

The whole semiotic complex of language in context is extended along the *cline of instantiation* from particular texts (instances) to the general system (the potential). While translation is always a mapping (transformation) between particular instances (from the "source text" to the "target text"), it takes place in the environment of more general patterns located closer to the potential pole of the cline of instantiation.

Each stratum is organized internally through a series of contextualizations; the diagram in Figure 11 only shows this for the level (stratum) of lexicogrammar, but the general principle is the same for all levels (strata). Locally, each level is organized into a hierarchy of units; this is the *hierarchy of rank* or the rank scale. The number of orders within the hierarchy of rank varies according to level of stratification and according to language; that is, while the number of strata is fixed for all languages, the number of ranks (within a given stratum) is not. Within the lexicogrammar of English, the rank scale is: clause — group/ phrase — word — morpheme. The widest rank environment is that of the clause, the most extensive unit of grammar; the narrowest rank environment is that of the morpheme. So the widest rank environment of translation is that of the clause rather than say that of the word.

What I am calling the principle of contextualization in translation was in fact first stated by Halliday (1966b: 29–30) by reference to rank (The Figure inside the citation is a reproduction of his illustration):

> What is the nature of the equivalence between two languages? We take it for granted that there can be such equivalence; that in some sense at least, and despite the Italian proverb 'traduttore — traditore', an utterance in language 1 may be translated into language 2. If we take two texts in different languages, one being a translation of the other, at what rank (among the grammatical units) would we be prepared to recognize 'equivalence'? In general, this would be at the rank of the sentence,[9] this being the contextual unit of language; it is the sentence which operates in situations. In other words, as could be expected from what is said about the way language works, it is generally the case that (1) a single sentence in language 1 may be represented by a single sentence in language 2: if we have an English text consisting of forty-seven sentences, the French translation could also consist of forty-seven sentences, divided at the same points; and (2) a particular sentence in language 1 can always be represented by one and the same sentence in language 2.
>
> But this equivalence of units and of items is lost as soon as we go below the sentence; and the further down the rank scale we go, the less is left of the equivalence. Once we reach the smallest unit, the morpheme, most vestige of equivalence disappears. The morpheme is untranslatable; the word a little less so, but it is nevertheless very rarely that we can say that a particular word in language 1 may always be translated by one and the same word in language 2 — this being condition (2) above; even condition (1) is not always fulfilled for the word, since one word in language 1 is often the equivalent of part of a word, or of several words, in language 2. The nearer we come to the sentence, the greater becomes the probability of equivalence; yet it remains true to say that the basic unit is the sentence.

	‖	la	jeune	fille	avait +	+ ‖	raison ‖	je	vais +		lui	demand	+ er	pardon ‖
M	X		young	daughter	have	X	X	reason	X	go	X	X	ask for	X	pardon
W		the	young	daughter	had			reason	I	am going		him	to ask for		pardon
G		the girl			had			reason	I am going to ask him for						pardon
C		the girl was right						I am going to apologize to him							
S		The girl was right; I am going to apologize to her.													

       X = grammatical morpheme
       + = fused morpheme (e.g. *avait* consists of three fused morphemes)
       M = morpheme equivalents
       W = word equivalents
       G = group equivalents
       C = clause equivalents
       S = sentence equivalent

Figure. Multilingual correspondence and rank (from Halliday 1966: 31)

As an illustration, here is an example of a sentence in French translated 'rank by rank' into English. First, each of the French morphemes is translated into English, by what as far as one can say would be the most probable equivalent (if one can be found) for that item irrespective of its environment. The translation is incomprehensible and meaningless. Next the same process is repeated at word rank: this shows more meaning but is still not English. Then in turn at group, clause and sentence rank. What is for some reason called 'literal translation' is translation at, roughly, the rank of the group.

Within each rank, each unit is organized into a *hierarchy of axis*. This is a hierarchy of two orders: the wider environment is that of the paradigmatic or systemic axis and the narrower environment is that of the syntagmatic or structural axis. So the widest environment of translation is that of system rather than that of structure; for example, there is likely to be less translation difference between the clause systems of two languages than between their clause structures. So for example, it is usually possible to translate an 'interrogative' clause in one language into an 'interrogative' clause in another, regardless of how 'interrogative' is realized; what matters is that the systemic contrast between 'interrogative' and 'declarative' is maintained in the structural realization.

The paradigmatic axis is organized systemically along the *cline of delicacy*. This cline extends from the most general systemic contrasts to the most delicate. The most general constitute the widest environment whereas the most delicate constitute the narrowest environment. So the widest delicacy environment of translation is that of the most general systems of the language — such as the general mood systems of 'indicative/ imperative', 'declarative/ interrogative'. It is to be expected that as the delicacy increases, we will find greater translation differences. Teruya's (1998) detailed description of the lexicogrammar of Japanese transitivity shows that while English and Japanese are fairly similar in the more indelicate part of the grammar, differences tend to emerge as the description moves towards more delicately specified domains.

The value of mapping out the environments of translation is illustrated convincingly by a study Catford (1965: 30) reports on:

> in a French short story of about 12,000 words the preposition *dans* occurs 134 times. ... In terms of probabilities we can state the [English] translation equivalences as follows: *dans* = *in* .73, *dans* = *into* .19, *dans* = *from* .015, *dans* = *about/ inside* .0075.

These translation equivalences are stated at word-rank, so there is no higher-ranking environment to condition them.

> But the equivalence-probabilities are, in fact, constantly affected by contextual and **co-textual** factors. We must, then, take these factors into account, and consider not merely the unconditioned probabilities, but also the **conditioned probabilities** of the various equivalences. Thus, though the unconditioned probability of the equivalence *dans* = *into*

The environments of translation 77

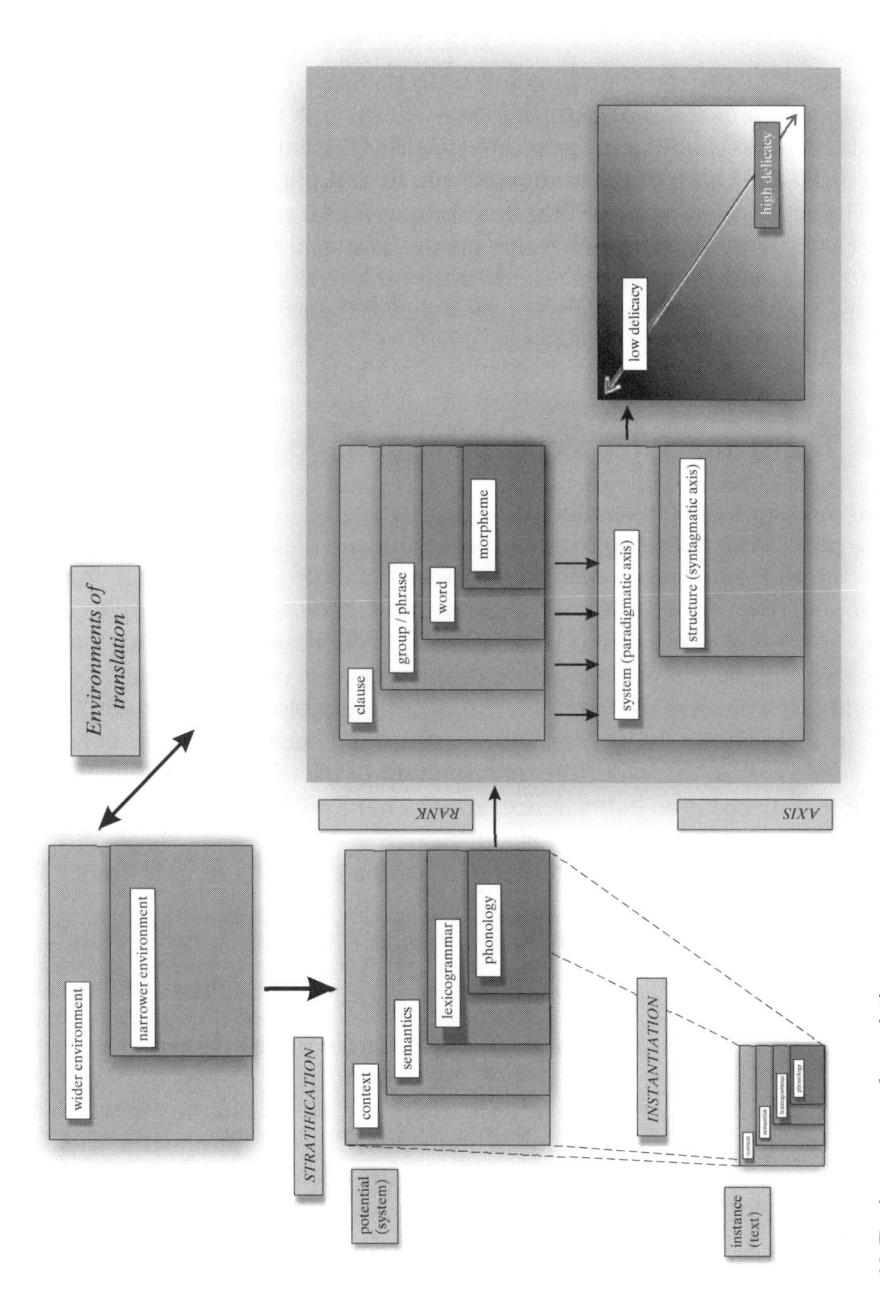

Figure 11. Environments of translation

is only .19, the conditioned probability of this equivalence is very much higher when *dans* is preceded by certain verbs, e.g. *aller*, and must be 1 (certainty), or very nearly so, when such a 'verb of motion' precedes, and a 'noun referring to a place' follows.

This constitutes a move up the rank scale: in effect, the translation of *dans* is now stated in terms of parts of its environment in the clause (the nature of the Process) and the prepositional phrase (the nature of the noun serving as Head/ Thing of the nominal group in that phrase).

The value of mapping out the environments of translation is also shown very clearly by the difference this makes in lexical translation. If we extend the environment from that of word rank to those of group rank and clause rank, we can translate lexical items in their collocational environments (cf. Baker 1992: 47–63).

3.2. Translation equivalence and translation shift

The model of the environments of translation diagrammed in Figure 11 also makes it possible to locate *translation equivalence* (cf. Catford 1965: 49–56) and *translation shift* (cf. Catford 1965: 73–83) that occur in the mapping (transformation) between one language-in-context complex and another. I will assume that translation equivalence and translation shift are two opposite poles on a cline of difference between languages. (We might also conceive of them in terms of congruence: the cline would then be from maximal congruence to maximal incongruence.) The general principle is this: the wider the environment of translation, the higher the degree of translation equivalence; and the narrower the environment, the higher the degree of translation shift.

Catford (1965: 49) characterizes translation equivalence as follows:

> The SL and TL items rarely have 'the same meaning' in the linguistic sense; but they can function in the same situation. In total translation, SL and TL texts or items are translation equivalents when they are interchangeable in a given situation. This is why translation equivalence can nearly always be established at sentence-rank — the sentence is the grammatical unit most directly related to speech-function within a situation.

What Catford refers to as "situation" is the context of situation in which a text occurs. So we can characterize equivalence by reference to the widest environment defined by the hierarchies of stratification, rank and axis; but according to the general principle I suggested above, equivalence is a matter of degree, so we can adjust the characterization of equivalence to say that the highest degree of equivalence is to be found in the widest environment — that of context. If translation is a matter of degree, then we can in principle represent it by means of fuzzy theory (as it has been developed by Zadeh 1987): the degree to which two expressions in two different languages are equivalent will depend on how many features they share. Catford suggests that translation equivalence "can nearly always be established at sentence-rank". In the light of current systemic functional theory, this must be revised: the focus has to be on the semantic unit of text rather than on any grammatical unit.[10] That is, we move up the hierarchy of stratification from lexicogrammar to semantics. This makes good sense since text is "language functioning in context" (cf. Halliday & Hasan 1976: 1-2).

As for translation shifts, it is important to note that there cannot be any shifts along the global dimensions of stratification and instantiation; that is, the process of translation cannot move from a given stratum in the "source" language to another stratum in the "target" language; and it cannot move from a given degree of instantiation in the "source" language to another in the "target" language. These globally defined domains have to be kept constant. However, within the overall grid defined by stratification and instantiation (to be outlined in more detail below; see e.g. Table 5) there can be more local translation shifts: in particular, translation may involve a shift in rank and it may involve a shift in delicacy (though not in axis). In other words, the two main sources of variation in translation environments are rank and delicacy. (Within rank, we can also add grammatical class; and we have to allow for shift in metafunction, to be discussed in the next section.)

3.3. "Free" and "literal" translation

The hierarchies of stratification, rank and axis define the traditional difference between "free" and "literal" translation, as shown in Figure 12. The narrower the environment, the more "literal" the translation — e.g. word for word translation (rather than clause-based translation) or translation of wording [lexicogrammar] rather than translation of meaning [semantics].[11] In the default case, "free" translation is probably preferred as the most effective form of translation. However, freedom is a matter of degree. Perhaps one of the freest types of translation is the translation of comic strips. Ingrid Emond used to translate Donald Duck from Italian[12] into Swedish and she told me she enjoyed this task because the translation could be quite free as long as it made contextual sense — and as long as it was in harmony with the pictorial representation of the narrative. And there are of course contexts of translation (see further below) where "literal" translation has value — e.g. contexts in linguistics or translation studies where we try to indicate how the wording of a particular language works.

If the translation is "free", the environment of translation is the widest possible — that of semantics (language) within context (higher-level semiotic) or even just of context, as when the text to be translated instantiates a register not found in the target language and it becomes necessary to try to find the nearest culturally equivalent context. This does not of course mean that there is no translation within narrower domains. Rather it means that translation within narrower environments is *automatized*. In reference to his analysis of dramatic dialogue, Halliday (1982: 135) characterizes automatization as follows: "language is likely to be fully automatized, with the words and structures and sounds being there in their automatic function of realizing the semantic selections in an unmarked way — getting on with expressing meanings, without parading themselves in patterns of their own". Thus wordings are translated as realizations of meanings, soundings as translations of wordings. However, there are contexts of translation where the translation has to be *de-automatized*. The term is taken over by Halliday from Mukařovský; and he provides the following comments:

> The term "de-automatization", though cumbersome, is more apt than "foregrounding", since what is in question is not simply prominence but rather the partial freeing of the lower level systems from the control of the semantics so that they become domains of choice in their own right. In terms of systemic theory the de-automatization of the grammar means that grammatical choices are not simply determined from above: there is selection as well as pre-selection. Hence the wording becomes a quasi-independent semiotic mode through which the meanings of the work can be projected.

Translation has to try to bring out the meanings created by de-automatization — even if the translation is "free": precisely because the lower levels have been partially freed, they need special attention to bring out the meaning-making power of lower-level resources. This is most likely to happen in literary translation; in the translation of poetry, even the level of phonology may be de-automatized.

3.4. Agnation and translation

The ordered series of related environments diagrammed in Figure 11 represents the series of domains in which translation between two or more languages may take place. But it also represents the domains of agnation within a given language. Agnation plays an important role in translation; I will discuss agnation first and then relate it to translation.

Agnation is always defined systemically by reference to organization along the systemic or paradigmatic axis within the unit at some rank (along the hierarchy of rank) within some stratum (along the hierarchy of stratification) at some degree of instantiation (along the cline of instantiation). But any given expression always enters into an infinite set of relationships of agnation — relationships that are defined throughout the or-

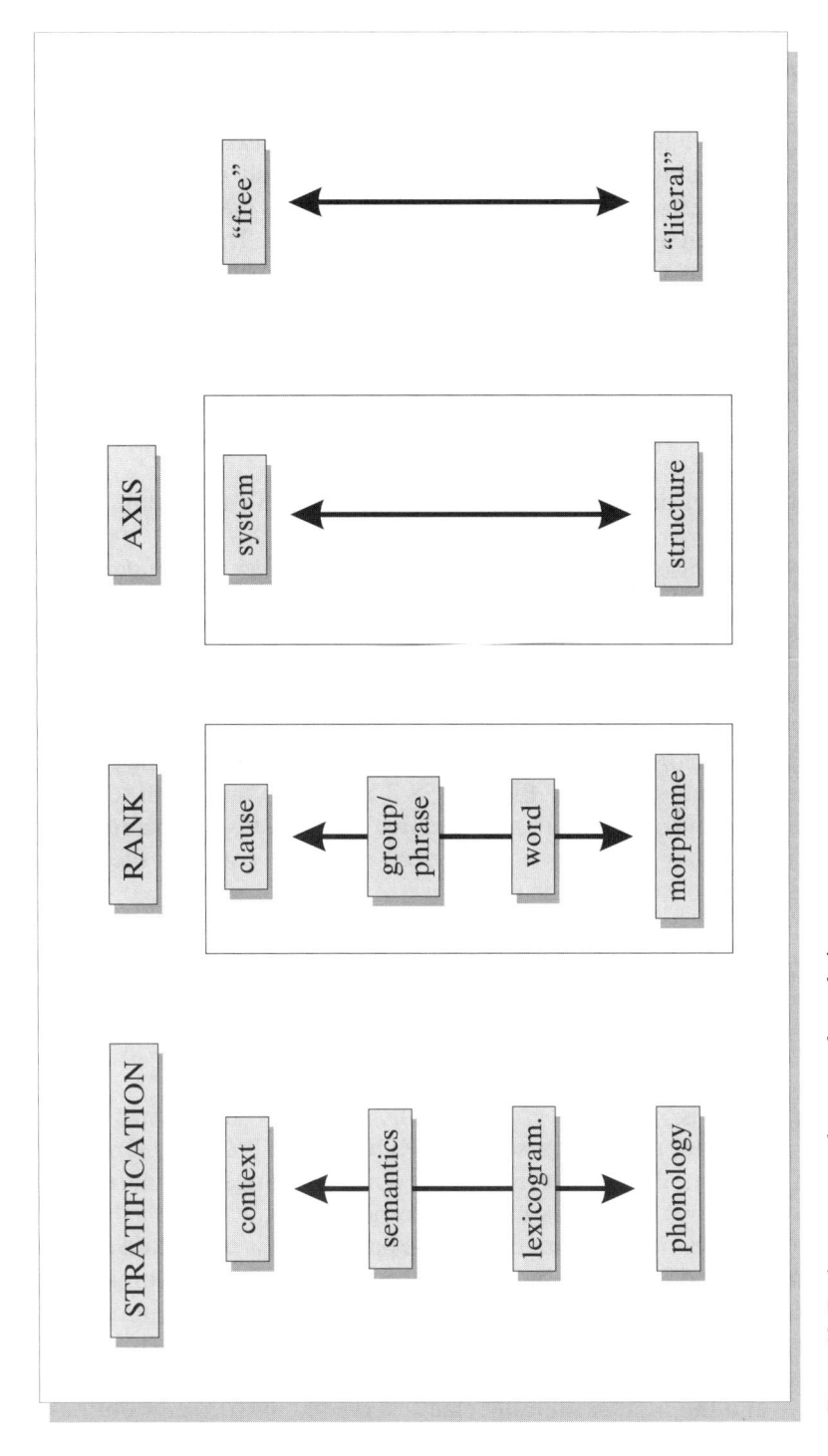

Figure 12. Environments and nature of translation

dered series of environments in Figure 11. In this sense, agnation is always multidimensional.

Agnation is represented by means of the system network (for examples, see Elke Teich's chapter) and this system network defines different degrees of agnation. Two expressions may be closely related within a very delicate system of options in the network or they may be more distantly related within a very indelicate system of options. They may even be unrelated within a particular environment and only be related within a wider environment. For example, two expressions may not be lexicogrammatically agnate, only semantically agnate (see Hasan 1996: Ch. 3, for this point in relation to the realization of elements of generic structure); or they may not be semantically agnate, only contextually agnate. Consider the following two examples from a guide book:

Example 6. Locative existential clause in English guide book

> <u>At the top of Blues Point Road</u> **there is** *a neat little sandstone church and vicarage, St. Peters.*

Example 7. Non-locative existential clause in English guide book

> *Entry to the park is free during the week, but* **there is** *a small fee per car at weekends.*

They are lexicogrammatically agnate within the domain of the clause with respect to the system of PROCESS TYPE: they are both 'existential' clauses, but whereas the first is 'locative' and locates a concrete entity in space the other second is not and does not. Now consider the following example, also from a guide book:

Example 8. Locative perceptive mental clause in English guide book

> <u>Farther north on the right</u> **can be seen** *some of the buildings of the University of California, Los Angeles campus.*

This clause is not lexicogrammatically agnate with the two examples above with respect to the system of PROCESS TYPE: it is 'mental' rather than 'existential'.[13] However, it is lexicogrammatically agnate with the first of the two examples in other respects: it is 'locative', the circumstance of Location is thematic and the participant is presented as New information and is realized by a 'non-specific' ("indefinite") nominal group. And when we move from lexicogrammar as the environment of agnation to semantics, we can describe the examples as agnate also with respect to the semantic correlate of the system of process type: both the 'mental' clause and the first 'existential' clause serve to construe new entities that travellers will encounter on their tour. Semantically, there are two strategies for achieving this; one is to construe a subjective potential (realized by a locative visual perceptive mental clause with a modulation of potentiality) and the other is to construe an objective actual (realized by a locative existential clause in the simple present).

The relevance of agnation to translation is this: any expression in the source text will be agnate to innumerable alternative expressions defined by the systemic potential of the source language and all these agnates are candidates in the source for translation into the target and, by the same token, there will also be a set of agnate candidates in the target language. (If we conceive of translation as problem-solving, then the system network defining relations of agnation can be seen as organization the "search space" of possible solutions. This view has been quite productive in text-generation: see Patten 1988.) At any point in translation it may be one of these agnates rather than the actual expression that serves as the best candidate for translation (cf. Halliday's 1956 suggestion that grammatical and lexical systems, the latter in the form of the thesaurus, should form the basis of translation). The agnates make up the source text's *shadow texts* — texts that might have been because they fall within the potential of the language — and these shadow texts are thus also relevant to translation. By the same token, an actual translation exists against the background of shadow translations — possible alternative translations defined by the systemic potential of the target language. In this way agnation along the paradigmatic axis is a critical part of the environment of translation.

This can be illustrated by reference to the existential and mental clauses discussed above. The English translation of a Spanish guidebook presenting Gaudi's *La Sagrada Família* in Barcelona contains quite a few existential clauses such as the one shown in Example 9. This would seem to be an existential clause that is semantically agnate with a perceptive mental one: the text might have read *in the Cathedral itself, you can see the Chapel of Santa Llúcia* ... The German translation contains many fewer existential clauses — assuming that clauses with *es gibt* + nominal group in the accusative and possibly clauses with *sich befinden* are interpreted as existential. Where an existential clause occurs in the English translation, one of a small number of different process types is used in the German translation and only very rarely do we find an existential clause of the *es gibt* kind. One of the types that occurs fairly frequently is precisely a perceptive mental clause, as in the German version of the English clause in Example 9: see Example 10. This is thus a case where it would be appropriate to translate one of the *agnates* of the English existential clause into German rather than the existential type actually instantiated in the English text.

Example 9. Existential clause from the English text of "El Temple de la Sagrada Família"

In the Cathedral itself, **there is** *the Chapel of Santa Llúcia, opposite the Archdeacon's Palace, which itself contains a Romanesque gallery with arches supported by 12th- and 13th-century columns. [p. 7]*

Example 10. Mental clause from the German text of "El Temple de la Sagrada Família" corresponding to an English existential clause

In der Kathedrale selbst **kann man** *die Kapelle Santa Llúcia (Heilige Luzie)* **bewundern**, *gegenüber dem Palast von l'Ardiaca (Erzdiakon). Heute noch kann man im Palast des Erzbischofs eine romanische Galerie mit Bogen sehen, die auf Säulen des XII. und XIII. Jh. ruhen. [p. 7]*

It is clear then that while both English and German have an existential clause type, this type has fairly different systemic values in the two languages, as can be seen from the fact that they have different agnation sets and from the fact that they have different discourse function in the registers of guidebooks. One further example demonstrates this very nicely. The English clause in Example 11 is an existential clause with an Existent that is realized by a nominal group complex — 1: *many Christian astrologers* ^ 2: *and innumerable references to astrology in churches and cathedrals.* Because of the value of the existential type in the English transitivity system, the complex can be treated as a group complex serving as Existent in a simple existential clause. However, the situation is different in the German text: see Example 12. In German, the complexing has to take place at clause rank rather than at group rank because the value of the existential clause type *es gibt* in German does not include the locative sense of the English counterpart. Only the first part of the complex is truly existential in the grammar of German.

Example 11. Existential clause from the English text of "El Temple de la Sagrada Família" with a complex Existent

and **there have been** *many Christian astrologers and innumerable references to astrology in churches and cathedrals. [S.F. p. 42]*

Example 12. German clause complex from the German text of "El Temple de la Sagrada Família"

Es gab *viele christliche Astrologen, und es* **sind** *unzählige Bilder aus dem Tierkreis in Kirchen und Kathedralen* **zu finden**. *[S.F. p. 42]*

Existence, location and possession are known to form a region in semantic space where there is considerable indeterminacy across languages — or even within a single language — in how they are construed lexicogrammatically. More generally, it seems that there is a significant number of semantic motifs that are typologically indeterminate in this way. This is either because they lie at the borderline between two or more somewhat more stable regions, as I think is the case with existence and also e.g. with quality (located between 'entity' and 'process' in semantic space), or because they are experientially quite complex and the lexicogrammars of languages handle this complexity by providing two or more complementary models for construing these motifs. This second type includes time, emotion and pain — and many other motifs as well. Thus time may be construed grammatically either as tense (as in English) or as aspect (as in Chinese) or as some mixture of the two (as in Russian). Emotion may be construed grammatically either as a process in a mental clause or as a quality in a relational clause or as both, as in many languages including English (see e.g. Matthiessen 1995: 276–9) and Japanese (see Teruya 1998). And pain appears to be handled by a rich repertoire of complementary models, as shown by Halliday (1998). At a higher degree of abstraction, we can also identify motifs of a fractal character that are systematically manifested in different environments throughout the semantic and lexicogrammatical systems. They define major points of variation across languages — see further Section 5.1. below.

3.5. Human translation and machine translation

The model of the environments of translation diagrammed in Figure 11 makes it possible to explain *machine translation* (MT) in relation to human translation. While human translation can be performed throughout the full range of different environments — at least when the translator is skilled, MT is more restricted, still being confined to narrower environments. In a sense, we can understand the history of MT as a gradual move from narrower to wider environments. When it started in the 1950s, MT was largely word-based and many of the humorous examples of the output of MT systems derive from this kind of approach. In the 1960s, MT moved up the rank-scale to the grammar of the clause (thanks to advances in parsing); but the grammar was represented in terms of formal rather than functional categories, so the interpretation of the clause is still "from below" as a bracketed sequence of classes of units serving in the clause. This still seems to be roughly the state of commercially available MT software that can be bought off the shelf for a few hundred dollars. An illustration is provided in Example 13. I used a French to English translation system that comes with both a French manual and an English one to translate part of the French manual into English. The result is tabulated together with the version in the English manual.

Example 13. Getting Power Translator to translate its own manual

	French manual:	English translation of French manual (by Power Translator):	English manual:
[0]	Bienvenue au Power Translator	Welcome to the ++Power ++Translator	Welcome to Power Translator
[1.1]	Vous pouvez utiliser le Power Translator	You can use the ++Power ++Translator	You can use Power Translator
[1.2]	pour traduire pratiquement n'importe quel texte de l'anglais vers le français ou du français vers l'anglais.	to translate practically does not import what text English to French or French to English.	to translate almost any text — from English to French or from French to English.
[2]	Le Power Translator produit un premier jet [2A]	The ++Power ++Translator produces a first throw [2A]	Power Translator produces draft translations [2A]
[2A]	que vous pouvez éditer.	that you can @@éditer.	that you edit into final form.
[3.1]	Vous pouvez également utiliser la fonction Voice	You can equally use the function ++Voice	In addition, you can use the Voice feature
[3.2]	qui permet au Power Translator de vous lire n'importe quel texte en anglais.	that allows the ++Power ++Translator to read you does not import what text in English.	to have Power Translator speak any English text.
[4]	La partie I vous guide pas à pas dans les travaux pratiques [4A]	The part I guides you in works practice	In part I, you'll find a step-by-step tutorial.
[4A]	qui vous sont proposés.	that are proposed you.	

The move upwards in the development of MT has continued into semantics (largely restricted to lexicogrammatical semantics — not extended into discourse semantics) though arguably not into context. The quality of the output of MT systems often suffers from the fact that these systems are not able to translate within a wide enough environment. However, research into MT has produced a rich picture of translation "shifts" within narrower environments (lexicogrammatical shifts, interpreted in formal terms) and translation studies could be enriched by incorporating these results (cf. Bateman, Matthiessen & Zeng, 1999). Further, the debate within MT between those who favour translation based on "transfer" and those who favour translation based on "interlingua" raises interesting issues relating precisely to the question of the environment of translation.

4. Translation in relation to the global dimensions: stratification & instantiation

In the preceding section, I sketched the relevant environments in which translation — including translation equivalence and translation shift — can be located. In this section, I will deal with the most global dimensions that define environments of translation in some more detail.

4.1. The instantiation-stratification matrix

The most global dimensions identified in Figure 11 above are the hierarchy of stratification and the cline of instantiation. Together they can be used to locate translation within the total system (or really system-&-process) complex of language in context — see Figure 13. The figure represents multilinguality as a series of staggered systems, identifying the location of different fields of multilingual studies: translation (studies) at the instance pole of the cline of instantiation and comparison & typology at the potential pole, the two being distinguished merely by the number of languages they take into consideration. Let me comment briefly on instantiation and stratification individually first and then explore how they organize the overall semiotic space of language-in-context as a total system-&-process.

Instantiation: Translation is located at the instance pole of the cline of instantiation: we translate *texts* in one language into texts into another; but we do not translate one *language* into another language. But while translation takes place at the instance pole of the cline of translation, texts are of course translated as instances of the overall linguistic system they instantiate — translation of the instance always takes place in the wider environment of potential that lies behind the instance.[14] And there are other relevant environments intermediate between the two poles of the cline of instantiation. One such environment is that of registers — a region on the cline of instantiation halfway between instance and potential: we will discuss this environment in the next subsection. Another such environment is much closer to the instance pole: this is the environment of previous instance that can serve as (representative) examples of how to translate new instances, as in example-based machine translation. The more experienced a translator is, the more s/he will have accumulated such examples and distilled significant patterns from them.

The potential of one language is, as just noted, not translated into the potential of another language; rather the potential of one language is mapped onto that of another. For a person (such as a translator), a community (such as a multilingual community) or a computational system that engages with the potentials of two or more languages, the potential of one language has to be mapped onto the potential of another language in such a way that they can produce texts instantiating one potential or another and can translate from a text in one language to a text in another. For example such a mapping may be achieved by means of the "transfer rules" of transfer-based machine translation systems. But there are other approaches. As I noted in Section 2.8. above, our approach has been to represent the mapping by defining multilingual system networks. These are system networks where certain parts are common across languages whereas other parts are assigned to partitions that belong to a particular language or set of languages (see Bateman et al. 1991); where partitions specific to one language or another exist, commonality has to be located within a wider environment (higher up the rank scale or the hierarchy of stratification): such networks are described and exemplified in Elke Teich's contribution to this volume.

The potential pole of the cline of instantiation is not the focus of translation studies; but it has been the focus in comparative linguistics (originally associated with historical investigations) and contrastive linguistics (associated with applied linguistics). Here the language systems of a reasonably small number of languages are compared and contrasted. And if such comparative descriptions are generalized to cover many languages or even samples of languages intended to be representative of language in general, we move into the discipline of linguistic typology.

In principle, translation could be informed by findings within comparative and typological linguistics precisely because they are concerned with the potential pole of the cline of instantiation; and by the same token, these endeavors could draw on experience from translation because the potential is nothing more than an accumulation and distillation of innumerable instances. The break-through will come from corpus-based cross-linguistic research of the kind outlined in Johansson (1998a): such corpus-based research involves both corpora of "comparable original texts" and corpora of "original texts and their translations". In her contribution to this volume, Elke Teich explores the relationship between comparison of the English and German systems and translation between English and German texts.

Translators do of course use a certain type of comparative description. They use bilingual or multilingual reference resources that are concerned with the linguistic systems of the languages involved. Such reference resources typically focus on the lexical part of lexicogrammar — bilingual (or multilingual) dictionaries; but in theory they could be part of a more extensive set of bilingual (or multilingual) resources developed by means of linguistic comparison. It seems to me that it would be quite useful in translation not only to have bilingual or multilingual dictionaries of lexical items, but also to have access to such "dictionaries" of other resources such as dictionaries of grammatical items and (fragments of) grammatical structures. For instance, it would be useful to be able to look up *there is* (etc.) [existential] in an English-German grammatical dictionary and find entries such as 1. *es gibt* (etc.) [existential], 2. *sich befinden* [existential], 3. *man kan ... sehen/ bewundern/ finden; ist* (etc.) *... zu sehen/ erkennen* [mental] etc. together with commentary and examples. I should note that in using the term "dictionary" in this way, I take it to be a way of compiling information about the linguistic system according to categories that realize options in the system: the dictionary is not a "component" or "module" of the linguistic system, it is a way of looking at it. By the same token, it would be useful to explore thesaurus-based views not only of the lexical part of lexicogrammar but also of the grammatical part, as well as of other linguistic resources. The value of the thesaurus is that it reveals systemic patterns of agnation that can form the "search space" in translation, as suggested by Halliday (1956) — cf. Section 3.4. above.

Stratification: While translation can be located at one end of the cline of instantiation, it cannot be located only at one stratum along the hierarchy of stratification. Translation takes place throughout the hierarchy of stratification. Or rather, we might say that translation takes place within the content system of language, above the expression system of phonology (graphology, sign); that is, translation takes place within lexicogrammar, within semantics and within context.

This does not mean that we cannot recognize translation at the level of expression: Catford (1965) discusses both "phonological translation" (Chapter 8) and "graphological translation" (Chapter 9); and to this we need to add translation of sign (cf. Johnston 1989). But while allowing for translation at the level of expression, we can still recognize that translation is prototypically a mapping (transformation) of meaning and thus that it takes place at the level of lexicogrammar and above.

As already noted in the previous section, the nature of translation changes depending on where we locate translation along the hierarchy of stratification (cf. Figure 12): in the default case, we aim to translate text as meaning in context and lexicogrammatical translation is "automatized". This is what has been called "free" translation". But we may also focus on text as wording and specifically try to translate patterns of wording at the level of lexicogrammar. The lower the rank of the lexicogrammatical translation, the more "literal" it will be. Translation in relation to the hierarchy of stratification is thus largely a question of what we try to keep as constant as possible and what we allow to vary.

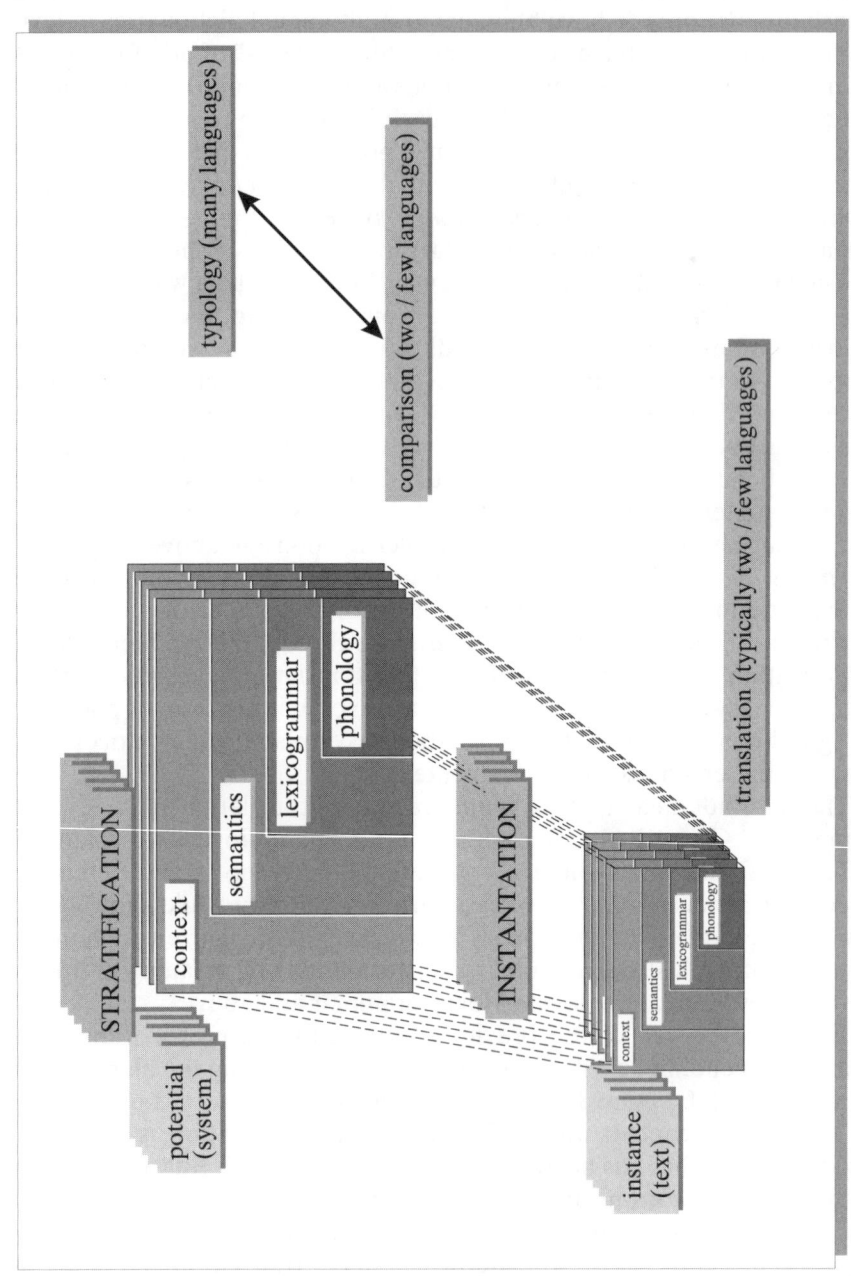

Figure 13. The cline of instantiation and sites of multilingual work

Together stratification and instantiation define the overall space of semiotic systems-&-processes. They can be intersected to map out the total resources of the semiotic complex of language in context. Such a map is called an *instantiation-stratification matrix*. A schematic version of the matrix is set out in Figure 14. Using such a matrix, we can make quite explicit observations about the feasibility and complexity of translation and we can manage that complexity in a theoretically motivated way. For example, we can use the matrix to select certain aspects of the total set of resources to serve in partial translation. Thus we can select items from the lexical part of the lexicogrammatical stratum to perform partial, keyword translation. (Note that the map is a two-dimensional extract from the multi-dimensional overall model diagrammed in Figure 11 above. Various other approaches seem to rely on a more one-dimensional hierarhcy; compare, for example, Hatim & Mason's 1990: 74 "hierarchical relationship between text, discourse, and genre", which they model as social occasions —> genre —> discourse —> text.)

The diagram represents the cline between "free" translation and "literal" translation, it shows the location of translation at the instance pole of the cline of instantiation and it indicates the *systemic frame of reference for translation*. (See Elke Teich's contribution in this volume for a discussion of these aspects that relates them to concerns in translation studies.) To deal with this last part, we need to look at the cline of instantiation in some more detail; in particular, we need to discuss the region on the cline that lies between its two poles.

4.2. The cline of instantiation

The cline of instantiation is, as the name indicates, a non-discrete cline rather than a discrete hierarchy (see Halliday 1992, 1995; Halliday & Matthiessen 1999: 323–7, 382–7; Matthiessen 1993; Matthiessen & Halliday, in prep: Ch. 2). Intermediate between the two poles — the poles defined by reference to the systemic potential of language and textual instances, we also find significant linguistic patterning. This patterning is more general than the patterns we find in particular texts; but it is more particularized than the patterning we find in the overall system. This patterning is contextually significant: its significance can be characterized in terms of the major contextual variables of field, tenor and mode (see e.g. Halliday 1978). But the patterning itself is linguistic patterning, representing variation in language. From the point of view of the instance, we can interpret it as recurrent types of instance — *text types*. From the point of view of the potential, we can interpret it as selective instantiation of the potential — as subpotentials or *registers*.

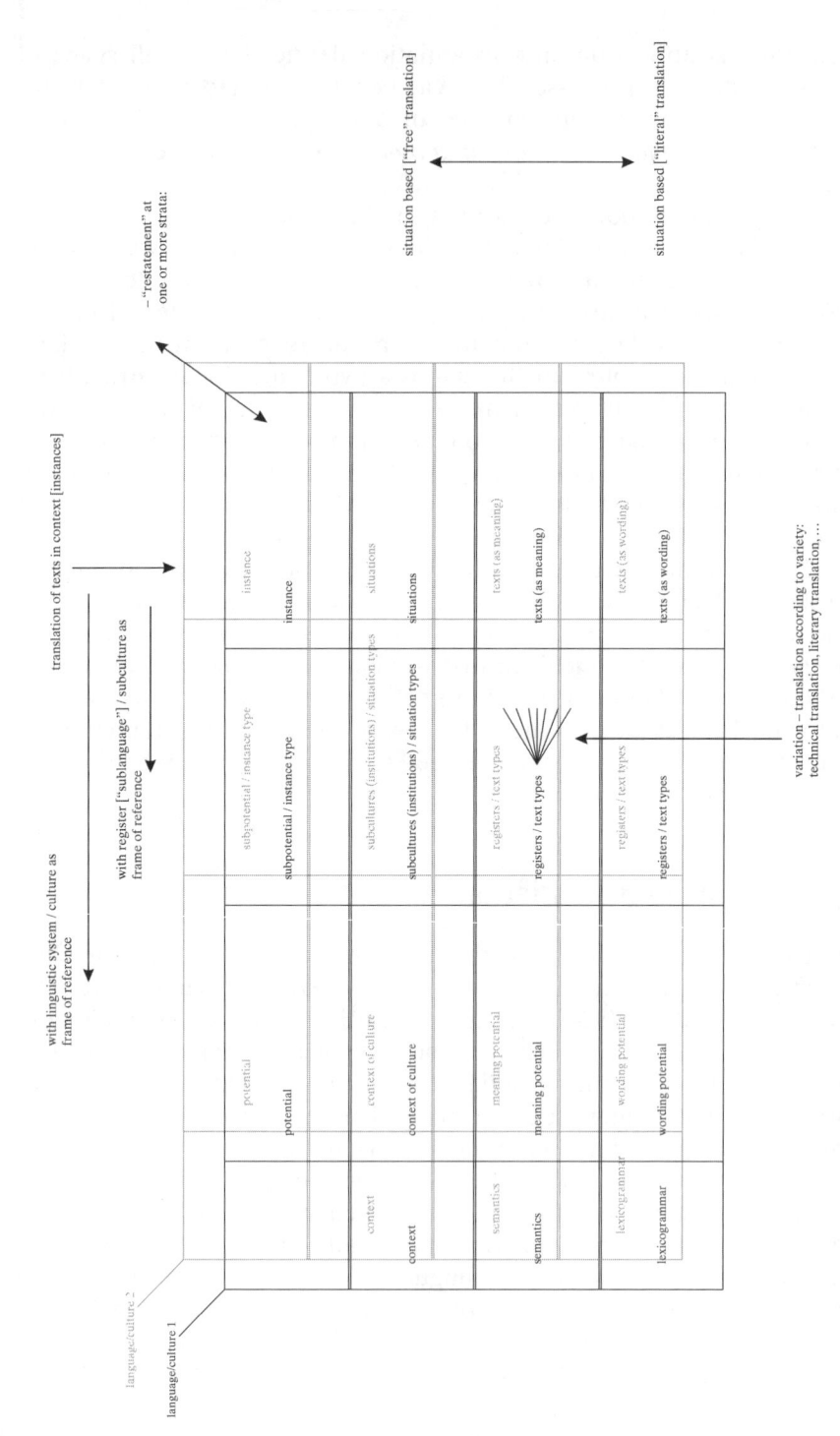

Figure 14. The instantiation-stratification matrix — types of translation

Returning to the question of the systemic frame of reference for translation, mentioned at the end of the previous subsection, we can now note that while this frame of reference may be the overall systems of the languages involved, it may also be the relevant registerial subsystems of those languages. For example, if we are given the task of translating a weather report from French into English, we may use the full resources of those languages as our frame of reference; but we may also narrow the domain to the relevant registerial subsystems — the subsystems of weather reporting in French and English.

Interestingly, one of the keys to successful translation seems to be the choice of register as the frame of reference (for discussion, see Erich Steiner's contribution and Hartley & Paris's contribution to this volume). This has long been recognized in work on translation — at least implicitly — in the very general distinctions among different types of translation such as literary translation, technical translation, business translation, legal translation, bible translation. But these are still very general and registerially heterogeneous categories and it is helpful to sharpen the focus considerably; the more information is available about the specific registers relevant to the translation, the richer the frame of reference. In MT, register has long been recognized under the heading of "sublanguage" as a key to translation (see e.g. Kittredge 1987; Kittredge & Lehrberger 1982). If we regard translation as problem solving, it is easy to see why register is a useful frame of reference: it makes available valuable information to the translation process by significantly reducing the space that has to be searched for appropriate translations and by offering a "compilation" of those semantic strategies appropriate to the contextual task at hand (see Patten 1988 for this perspective with respect to text generation). Thus one translation project we have undertaken was to translate M.A.K. Halliday's paper *Computing meanings* into Chinese and Japanese to be published as a trilingual document with parallel texts in English, Chinese and Japanese. The Chinese translation was undertaken by Wu Canzhong in consultation with Halliday; this posed no registerial problems since Wu is a linguist. Originally the Japanese translation was undertaken by a professional translator with experience in various kinds of translation but not in linguistic translation and this translation was to be checked and revised by another member of the translation project, Kazuhiro Teruya. However, when he received the professional translation into Japanese, it very soon became clear that it was actually unusable since it was too far away from the appropriate register of Japanese linguistics, so Teruya had to set it aside and do the translation himself from scratch. As the person who initiated the project, I should have anticipated this from the start!

One study that demonstrates the importance of register in translation very clearly is Wu (1992). He identifies registerial differences between "university introductions" written in Chinese in the P.R.C. and similar introductions written in North America. For example, the Chinese introductions pay attention to the national status of the university, whereas the North American ones foreground recreational facilities. This of course highlights the importance of describing the contextual value (in terms of field, tenor and mode) of different registers: even apparently similar registers may have different contextual values in different languages and thus deploy different semantic strategies. Another relevant study will be referred to below — Abelen, Redeker & Thompson's (1993) investigation of the difference between Dutch and (American) English in the register of fund-raising letters.

In general, patterns that unfold within the span of a single text derive from — and help define — more general patterns that lie "higher up" the cline of instantiation. Consequently, it is reasonable to expect that translated texts follow this principle; in other words, it is reasonable to expect that the patterns that unfold in translated texts can be related to more general patterns that lie higher up the cline of instantiation. And I think that this is generally the case; I will illustrate the principle by reference to the system of THEME PREDICATION in Section 5.4. below. However, I have the impression that translators may depart from this guiding principle particularly within the textual metafunction because they may not be aware of the significance of textual meaning, since they tend to focus predominantly on ideational meaning (for this point, see M.A.K. Halliday's contribution to this volume). Thus I have found a number of examples of translations from German and Swedish to English where there is a shift from the original in the selection of Theme in the translated text even though this shift is not motivated by the English system of THEME: see Example 14. (This is not to say that there are no systemic differences between English and German — there clearly are (cf. Steiner & Ramm 1995); but the English system is not such that it prevents a more congruent translation from the German original in this example.) In the first two clauses, the English translation has Subject as 'unmarked' Theme even though the circumstantial Locations in space (*in the village*) and in time (*in the spring*) are motivated as Theme. The third clause illustrates the reverse shift: the English translation has a marked circumstantial Theme (a temporal Location) even though the German original does not. Variation is of course an inherent aspect of instantiation: as soon as the systemic potential is being instantiated, there is opportunity for variation; but the critical question is always whether the variation is meaningful.

Cases such as these are in contrast with examples where the translator has attempted to translate the thematic selections from German into English but where systemic differences (i.e., differences at the system pole of the cline of instantiation) still lead to an instantial difference between the two texts. This situation is illustrated by Example 15, from the same source as the earlier examples. In the German version, the interpersonal comment

Example 14. Translation of Theme from German into English — examples of differences[15]

English	German
They used to say **in the village** that he had sec ond sight *[At the Trocadero, p. 105]*	**Im Dorf** sagten sie immer, er hätte das Zweite Gesicht *[Im Trocadero]*
The sheep were always shorn **in the spring** *[At the Trocadero, p. 109]*	**Jedes Frühjahr** wurden die Schafe immer geschoren *[Im Trocadero]*
During this time **the sheep** were enclosed in two pens. *[At the Trocadero, p. 109]*	**Die Schafe** waren während dieser Zeit in zwei Buchten gesperrt. *[Im Trocadero]*

Adjunct *zum Glück* (literally: 'to:the luck') serves as Theme; the English translation of the Theme consists of both the interpersonal comment Adjunct *luckily* and the Subject *my parents*. The systemic difference between the two languages is that while English allows for multiple elements within the Theme, German marks off a single element as Theme quite clearly since this Theme is always followed by the Finite (in a free clause, but not in a bound one): for further discussion, see Elke Teich's chapter in this volume.

Example 15. Translation of Theme from German (simple) into English (multiple)

English	German
Luckily my parents had left me some money. *[Pale Anna, p. 13]*	Zum Glück hatten meine Eltern mir Geld hinter lassen. *[Die Blasse Anna, p. 12]*

The examples in Example 14 illustrate a purely instantial difference; I believe they do not reflect a systemic difference between English and German (though it is of course always very hard to know — only extensive corpus studies will give us some measure of certainty). However, there are certainly cases where two or more linguistic systems look congruent with one another but instantial differences turn up in texts. I referred to one such example at the end of Section 2.8. above — the 'imperative' mood in English in German. When this happens, we have to revise our comparative description of the systems involved. Since the systemic potential is nothing more than a "distillation" of innumerable textual instances, regular instantial differences can only be explained by reference to systemic differences.

Such systemic differences can be quite subtle and may only be observable in a corpus-based investigation. For example, Johansson (1998b), shows how the verbs *hate / love* serving as Process in English 'mental: emotive' clauses differ from their Norwegian translation equivalents *hate / elske* with respect to the nature of the nominal group realizing the Phenomenon. In English original texts, 27% of the nominal groups realizing

Phenomenon in clauses with *hate* denote persons and 73% denote non-persons; the numbers for *love* are somewhat more even — 46% persons, 54% non-persons. But both verbs differ significantly from their Norwegian equivalents. Norwegian strongly favours personal nominal groups as Phenomenon: 65% for *hate* 'hate' (vs. 35% for non-persons) and 61% for *elske* 'love' (vs. 39% for non-persons). Johansson emphasizes that this correlates with different (systemic) senses: "Whereas Norwegian *hate* and *elske* express a strong feeling and typically combine with a personal object, English *hate* and *love* are also used in a weakened sense". Interestingly, the relative frequencies for *hate* and *elske* in Norwegian translations of English texts show a skew in relative frequency towards "non-personal" Phenomena, just as English does. This is thus a powerful example of the connection between variation in instantiation and translation.

The principle that cross-linguistic differences in the relative frequency of instantiation in text represent systemic differences is also in operation at the level of semantics, as demonstrated by Abelen, Redeker & Thompson (1993) in a study of the register of fund-raising letters in Dutch and (American) English. Using Rhetorical Structure Theory (Mann, Matthiessen & Thompson 1992), they are able to identify quantitative differences in the instantiation of different rhetorical relations in the discourse-semantic organization of fund-raising letters in The Netherlands and the U.S. The American letters were found to have "a more overtly persuasive character than Dutch letters' and to be "dominated by interpersonal relations, which played a much less prominent role in the Dutch letters" (p. 343).

4.3. Mapping out the resources for translation

The instantiation-stratification matrix can thus be used to identify and locate translation types and translation issues. But it is also of value in translation as a map of the resources that have to be considered in the course of translation. A more detailed version of the matrix is set out in Table 5.

At the content levels of language (lexicogrammar and semantics) the resources are organized *metafunctionally* into three simultaneous strands of meaning — ideational (with two subtypes: logical and experiential), interpersonal and textual. This metafunctional organization is neither a hierarchy nor a cline since the metafunctions form a *spectrum* of simultaneous modes of meaning, so this organization was not shown in Figure 11 above; but it is still a dimension of organization within lexicogrammar and semantics that is critical to translation. As M.A.K. Halliday notes in his contribution to this volume, while translation should give equal weight to all three metafunctional contributions, there has been a strong tendency to give more weight to the ideational metafunction (cf. my remarks above in connection with the variation in theme selection illustrated in Example 14 above); and this has also been true traditionally of work within MT.

Each one of the cells in Table 5 can be "blown up" in detail and surveyed systematically in terms of a map of the features of the semiotic domain represented by the cell. For example, the resources of the lexicogrammatical system (cell: potential x lexicogrammar) — the wording potential of a language — can be mapped out according to the two dimensions of rank and metafunctional diversification (to be discussed further below). Such a map is called a *function-rank matrix*; Table 6 shows the function-rank matrix for the lexicogrammar of English (see Matthiessen 1995, for a survey of the lexicogrammatical resources of English based on the map). Such maps have also been developed for other languages, as e.g. Rose's (1998: 55) matrix for Pitjantjatjara; Teruya (1998: 35–40) presents a very detailed one for Japanese and the descriptions in Caffarel, Martin & Matthiessen (forthc.) will give a good sense of the distribution of lexicogrammatical resources in a range of languages. (It is also possible to construct such a map of the semantic system of a language — based on an account such as Martin 1992, although this is harder since much less systematic work has been done on mapping out the semantic system of a language: see Matthiessen & Halliday, in prep: Ch. 3, for discussion.)

To support work on translation, we need to develop comparative maps that identify translation equivalences and shifts between languages. Text books in translation do this to some extent; but I believe it is possible to provide more motivated and systematic overviews than what has traditionally been offered. A recent valuable contribution is Baker's (1992) "coursebook on translation" and it is instructive to read her book in relation to a comprehensive function-rank matrix.

Table 5. Stratification-instantiation matrix (adapted from Halliday 1995)

STRATI-FICA-TION:	INSTANTIATION:			
	potential	> subpotential	type of instance <	instance
context	context of culture: the culture as social-semiotic system: networks of social semiotic features constituting the systems-&-processes of the culture; defined as potential clusters of values of field, tenor and mode	"subculture"/ institution: networks of regions of social-semiotic space	situation type: a set of like situations forming a situation type	situation: instantial values of field, tenor & mode; particular social semiotic situation events, with their organization

98 Christian M.I.M. Matthiessen

Table 5. Stratification-instantiation matrix (adapted from Halliday 1995) (Continued)

STRATI-FICA-TION:	INSTANTIATION:			
	potential	> subpotential	type of instance <	instance
semantics	semantic system [meaning potential]: networks of ideational, interpersonal and textul meanings; their construction as texts, subtexts, parasemes, sequences, figures & elements	register: networks of topological regions of semantic space	text type: a set of texts (meanings) forming a text type	text: semantic selection expressions (features from passes through the semantic networks), and their representation as meanings particular texts, with their organization
lexico-grammar	lexicogrammatical system [wording potential]: networks of ideational, interpersonal and textual wordings; their construction as clauses, groups/ phrases, words and morphemes Function-rank matrix: | | ideat. | interp. | textual | | clause | | | | | group | | | | | word | | | | | morph. | | | |	[register:] networks of typological regions of lexicogrammatical space	[text type:] a set of like texts (wordings) forming a text type	lexicogrammatical selection expressions (features from passes through lexicogrammatical networks), and their manifestation as wordings particular texts, spoken or written, with their organization
phonology/ graphology/ sign				

The book starts at word rank — quite a narrow environment along the rank scale within lexicogrammar, the narrower of the two stratal environments within the content plane (Chapter 2: "Equivalence at word level"), moves up (Chapter 3: "Equivalence above word level") until it reaches systems of group/ phrase and clause rank (Chapter 4: "Grammatical equivalence"). This move is essentially based on rank rather than metafunction, which is noteworthy since metafunction is far more likely to remain constant in translation than rank is. Then one of the metafunctions is taken up — the textual one (Chapter 5: "Textual equivalence: thematic and information structures" and Chapter 6: "Textual equivalence: cohesion"). The final chapter is devoted to "pragmatic equivalence" — primarily contextual issues (cf. Table 5).

With the help of the function-rank matrix we can get a good sense of what Baker covers (the textual metafunction and certain other systems, which are not metafunctionally located in her presentation) and what she leaves out (a systematic overview of ideational (logical and experiential) and interpersonal issues). But we can also use the matrix to explore alternative ways of navigating through the resources. We could opt for a tour based on metafunction (rather than one based on rank) that would foreground what languages achieve metafunctionally and how they differ with respect where they locate the systems and realizations along the rank scale. Such a metafunctional tour would start with the clause rather than with the word because among the units of the grammar it is the clause that is the gateway to the text as a unit (process) of meaning and because the principle of contextualization tells us to work with wider rather than narrower environments in translation (see Section 3).

With the help of the matrices in Tables 5 and 6, we can also locate various strands of analysis that have been undertaken in translation studies. For example, "speech act" analysis has been used in the investigation of parallel texts (see Snell-Hornby 1995: Section 3.4 and cf. Hatim & Mason 1990: 60–62). In the systemic functional model presented here, this corresponds to one system within interpersonal semantics — the system of NEGOTIATION (see Martin 1992).

It is impossible within the scope of a chapter to develop a comparative function-rank matrix for translation (even assuming that all the information needed was already available, which it is not!). So I will only illustrate certain equivalences and shifts that can be located within the function-rank matrix shown for English in Table 6.

5. Translation equivalences and shifts: some illustrations

As a working hypothesis, I will assume that there is a high degree of "equivalence" or congruence between languages as far as metafunctions are concerned and that this applies along the full extent of the cline of instantiation, from translation of text instances and to mappings between systems. Thus in translation metafunction tends to be preserved. But within a metafunction, there may be considerable variation — both shifts

Table 6. Function-rank matrix for English

rank	[class]		ideational			interpersonal		textual	
			logical		experiential				(cohesive)
clause		complexes (clause —			TRANSITIVITY (process type)	MOOD MODALITY POLARITY	THEME CULMINATION VOICE	COHESIVE RELATIONS:
phrase	[prepositional]	phrase —			MINOR TRANSITIVITY (circumstance type)	MINOR MOOD (adjunct type)	CONJUNCTION	
group	[verbal]	group —	INTERDEPENDENCY (parataxis/ hypotaxis) & LOGICAL- SEMANTIC RELATION (expansion/ projection)	TENSE	EVENT TYPE ASPECT [if non-finite]	FINITENESS DEICTICITY	VOICE	REFERENCE, ELLIPSIS & SUBSTITUTION,
	[nominal]			MODIFICATION	THING TYPE CLASSIFICATION EPITHESIS QUALIFICATION	PERSON ATTITUDE	DETERMINATION	CONJUNCTION
	[adverbial]			MODIFICATION	QUALITY (circumstance type)	COMMENT (adjunct type)	CONJUNCTION	
word		word)		DERIVATION	(DENOTATION)	(CONNOTATION)		
information unit		info. unit complex	INFO. TAXIS	ACCENTUATION		KEY	INFORMATION FOCUS	
			complexes	simplexes				

across ranks and shifts within ranks (structural in the first instance, but also systemic). I will give some representative illustrations, starting with the marked situation where there is a metafunctional shift.

5.1. Metafunctional shifts

There is one systematic exception to the working hypothesis that languages are metafunctionally congruent: within the ideational metafunction, it seems clear that languages vary considerably in how they divide up the labour of "construing experience" between the logical mode and the experiential mode — the two ideational columns in Table 6. This has in fact already been illustrated with reference to English and Kalam: where Kalam favours the logical mode, English favours the experiential one (see Section 2.6.). And I also pointed out that this kind of shift occurs in "translation" between spoken and written texts within one language (at least, within English). Let me give one more example of a divergence between two languages that involves the logical and experiential modes of construing experience. Example 16 presents an English clause and its French counterpart taken from a 1996 WHO weekly report. These reports appear in both languages, which are set out in parallel columns.

Example 16. English and French versions from a parallel text (the WHO weekly report)

Shigellosis or typhoid fever were suspected

On a pensé qu'il pouvait s'agir de shigellose ou de fièvre typhoïde.

In the English wording, there is a simple clause — a cognitive mental clause in the passive voice with the Senser left implicit: see Figure 15.

English	Shigellosis or typhoid fever	were suspected
TRANSITIVITY	Phenomenon	Process: cognitive

Figure 15. Analysis of English clause

This mental clause is metaphorical; a more congruent version would be *(Health workers) suspected that (the disease) was shigellosis or typhoid fever* — or *(the disease) was probably shigellosis or typhoid fever*. The French version suggests something along these lines; it deploys a clause complex of projection, with a mental clause where the Senser is the generalized person *on* (which may be translated as 'one' — but which is much more common than this English translation equivalent) and a projected

102 Christian M.I.M. Matthiessen

idea clause of a relational type (*s'agir de* might be translated as 'be about, concern'; *être* would be an alternative): see Figure 16.

French	On	a pensé		qu'il pouvait s'agir de shigellose ou de fièvre typhoïde.
COMPLEXING	α		—>	'β
TRANSITIVITY	Senser	Process: cognitive	—>	(projected idea clause)

Figure 16. Analysis of French clause complex

In addition to shifts within the ideational metafunction between the experiential and logical modes of construing experience, it also seems that there are true metafunctional shifts.

One such shift occurs between the interpersonal metafunction and the logical mode of the ideational metafunction in the context of projection. In a study of German and English translations of a guide book in Spanish (or probably Catalan, since the book is concerned with Barcelona), I found a number of places where the German translation had an interpersonal selection of modality (the modal *sollen*) within a simple clause but English had a clause complex of (impersonal) projection, as in Example 17. This difference is not just instantial but rather it is systemic: it reflects a difference in the semantic domains of the English and German systems of modality; in this particular area, the German system extends into "evidentiality" whereas the English does not (cf. Palmer 1986: 52–3; 72).

Example 17. English clause complex of projection (logical) as translation of German modal clause (interpersonal)

English [Barcelona]	German
where **tradition holds** —> *that the patriots who died defending the city in September 1714 are buried.* [p. 28]	wo die Patrioten begraben sein **sollen**, die bei der Verteidigung der Stadt im September 1714 starben. [p. 28]
where the waters of a bronze fountain, **it is said**, speed the return of all visitors who drink them. [p. 36]	dessen Wasser die Trinker zur Rückkehr ermutigen **soll**. [p. 36]
It is said —> *that the fitters, glaziers, thatchers, bricklayers, and so on now have no paint-splashes on their smocks,* [p. 129]	Die Schlosser, Glaser, Dachdecker, Kaminbauer usw. **sollen** auch keine Farbflecken mehr an ihren Kitteln haben
projection: complex	"interpersonal projection": modal simplex

Other translation shifts between the ideational and interpersonal metafunctions appear to be similar: the ones I have been able to identify all involve clause complexes of projection construed by the logical mode of the ideational metafunction. For example, English clausal modulation within the interpersonal metafunction would be translated into Tagalog by a projecting clause complex (Martin 1990). Similarly, English clauses of negative polarity have to be translated as projecting clause complexes in Tongan, as illustrated in Figure 17 (example from Churchward 1956: 56, quoted in Payne 1985: 208; my analysis).

Na'e	'ikai		ke	'alu	'a	Siale
aspect	negative verb		aspect	go	absolute	Charlie
projecting clause		—>	projected clause			

'Charlie didn't go'

Figure 17. Tongan translation equivalent of English negative clause

Another related kind of shift occurs between languages that construe direct and indirect speech logically as projection within clause complexes and languages that enact this as an assessement of evidentiality or the like within the interpersonal metafunction using so-called quotative particles or affixes.

These strategies are not unlike English interpersonal metaphors of modality where the resources of projection within a clause complex are marshalled by the interpersonal metafunction, as in *I don't think —> Charlie went* where the modality and the polarity are part of the projecting clause. And it is of course quite possible — or even likely — that this is precisely what we find in languages such as Tagalog and Tongan.

If there is a translation shift between the logical mode of the experiential metafunction and the interpersonal metafunction, what remains "equivalent" in the translation? We might argue that while there is metafunctional shift at the level of lexicogrammar, the higher-level meaning of modality or negative polarity is approximately equivalent at the level of semantics. But this does not help us explain why it is these meanings that may shift metafunctionally in their lexicogrammatical realization. We might be able to explain why by reference to *fractal types* in the semantic system (Halliday & Matthiessen 1999: 223–6). Fractal types are very general patterns of meaning that are manifested in different environments throughout the content system of a language — that is, throughout its semantic and lexicogrammatical systems. Expansion is one of the major fractal types (see Halliday 1994: 328–9) and projection is another.

In the translation shifts referred to above, one of the languages uses the logical manifestation of projection — projection within the logical domain of the clause complex. The other language uses an interpersonal system within the simple clause — modality or polarity. But these systems might in fact be interpreted as manifestations of projection within the interpersonal metafunction. Such interpersonal projections can be glossed as 'I think', 'I deny' and the like (although it is important that, being interpersonal, they are enactments rather than ideational construals): they represent the speaker's evaluative projection of a proposition or a proposal. If this line of interpretation works, we can then explain the translation shifts as "cross-overs" in the manifestation of projection within one metafunction or another.

And the earlier set of examples of translation shifts between the logical and experiential modes of the ideational metafunction can in fact be explained along the same line: these are shifts in the domain of manifestation of the fractal type of expansion. Here expansion is manifested either logically as a clause complex or experientially as transitivity patterns within the clause (as in Kalam vs. English or as in spoken English vs. written English).

5.2. Metafunctional equivalence: shift within metafunction

As I suggested above, the default case is that metafunctions remain constant as we translate text from one language into another. Within one metafunction, there may still of course be translation shifts. These shifts may be local to a given rank on the rank scale (see Sections 5.4. and 5.5. below) or they may be less local, involving a shunt along the rank scale (see Section 5.3. below). Wherever the shifts occur, as much as possible of the metafunctional effect has to be preserved even if there are fairly significant systemic differences between the languages involved. Let me just give one example, taken from the textual metafunction (see also Steiner 1989, on diathesis across languages).

One well-known challenge in translation is the task of translating between languages such as English where every nominal group has to select in the system of DETERMINATION and languages such as Chinese where it is possible to "opt out" of the choice and most nominal groups do not in fact select in the system of DETERMINATION. This problem would seem to be insurmountable until we look at it more holistically, in a wider environment than that of the nominal group. If we see it in terms of strategies within the textual metafunction for introducing and tracking discourse referents (see Martin 1983, for a typological study demonstrating this principle), we can begin to relate it to patterns within the textual metafunction as a whole. When we do so, we find that the introduction and tracking of discourse referents is part of the textual metafunction's concern with managing the assignment of textual statuses in discourse (cf. Matthiessen 1992).

The system of DETERMINATION is thus related to the systems of THEME and INFORMATION and while they are independently variable in English, there are certain preferred combinations such as 'specific & given & thematic'. Such skews in the system can help the task of translation: even if a nominal group is not overtly marked as specific ("definite") or non-specific ("indefinite"), it is more likely to present a discourse referent as identifiable if it is given and thematic, but more likely to present it as non-identifiable if it is new and rhematic. In fact, languages may grammaticalize as categorical what are merely favoured combinations in English. Thus Li & Thompson (1980: 85) note that the topical Theme in Mandarin "always refers to something that the hearer already knows about — that is, it is definite — or to a class of entities — that is, it is generic". For example, they translate the Chinese clause *gou wo yijing kan-guo le* (tones left out in my representation of it) as either *The dog I have already seen* or *Dogs* (generic) *I have already seen* and note that it cannot be translated as *A dog I have already seen* (Li & Thompson 1980: 86). This last version would of course be highly marked in English.

5.3. Metafunctional equivalence: shift in rank

When metafunctional equivalence is maintained in translation but there is a shift up or down the rank scale, the metafunctional meaning is maintained but the work of construing that meaning is done in different ranking environments in the grammars of the languages involved. In terms of the function-rank matrix (see Table 6), this means that the metafunctional column remains constant but the rank row is varied. We have to distinguish two degrees of variation here. The move along the rank scale may be systemic or merely realizational.

> (i) When the move is systemic, the points of origin of the metafunctional systems in question are different in the languages involved; for example, the point of origin may be group rank in one language but word rank in the other.

> (ii) When the move is merely realizational, the points of origin of the systems are the same but the languages differ in where along the rank scale terms in the system are realized structurally.

Examples that at first sight seem to be of the first kind may turn out to be of the second kind on closer inspection: it is often hard to know when descriptions of languages are not comprehensive and are stated in an informal framework. For example, it would seem that at least certain parts of the nuclear transitivity system in a number of so-called "polysynthetic" languages operate at word rank (within the class of verb) rather than at clause rank as in English and many other languages: the verb is the domain not only of the Process but also of pronominal affixes[16] that represent participants involved in it. While participants may be represented nominally in the clause, this appears to happen essentially for textual reasons rather than for experiential ones. However, it is fairly likely that a comprehensive systemic functional interpretation of such a language would indicate that the transitivity *system* (paradigmatic axis) has the clause as its point of origin even though the domain of the *realization* of nuclear transitivity is the verb at word rank (syntagmatic axis). In either case, a translation from English into a language with this kind of transitivity system would entail a move down the rank scale from clause rank to word rank.

By the same token, translating from a language such as Japanese, Finnish or Turkish that does a fair amount of work at word rank into a language such as English, Chinese or Vietnamese that depends more on group (and clause) rank means moving up the rank scale. For example, temporal or modal affixes at word rank are likely to have to be translated as auxiliaries at group rank. Thus the verb *hanasitagaranaku* in the Japanese clause *Ami-ga soitu-tono geemu-no naiyoo-o hanasitagaranaku natte* ('Ami began not to want to talk about the content of the game with the person') has to be translated into English as a verbal group complex — *not to want to talk about* (example taken from Teruya 1998: 135).

5.4. Equivalence in metafunction and rank: shift in system

When metafunctional and rank equivalence is maintained in translation but there is a systemic shift, the extent of the shift depends on where along the cline of delicacy it takes place. It may be a fairly small shift occurring at a high point in delicacy; this will be a lexical shift (cf. Hasan 1996: Ch. 4, on lexis as the most delicate part of lexicogrammar). It may also be a major shift occurring at the indelicate pole of the cline of delicacy; this will be a grammatical shift involving fairly primary grammatical systems. I will give an example of the latter, from the textual metafunction at clause rank. (The shift may also be a shift in delicacy itself, either between different degrees of delicacy within lexis [cf. Baker 1992: 22–3; Halliday & Matthiessen 1999: 310–1 on Chinese and English] or between grammar and lexis.)

As I was analysing a German short story, Heinrich Böll's *Die Blasse Anna*, and a translation of it into English, *Pale Anna*, by Christopher Middleton, I was struck by the fact that the first clause of the English translation had a marked thematic selection of the 'predicated theme' type (see Halliday 1994: 58–61; Matthiessen 1995: 556–60) even though the German original did not: see Example 18. Here the (marked) circumstantial theme selection has been translated from German into English; but the

English translation adds the selection of 'predicated theme'. The aspect of the German clause that would seem to "trigger" this selection in the translation is *erst*, 'first', which has not been translated as an item; and clauses with 'predicated theme' do occur text-initially in English as one strategy of opening a narrative. To explore this translation shift further, I identified all the 'predicated theme' clauses in the collection of short stories that *Die Blasse Anna* appears in, Penguin's parallel text anthology of German short stories with English translations. I found only five examples in the whole anthology, which is not surprising since 'predicated theme' is quite a marked option in the English system of THEME. Three out of the five examples have *erst* in the German original. In the other two examples, the elements predicated in English appear as the newsworthy culmination of the clause in German (cf. Matthiessen 1995: 600–3) — a feature which the English translation picks up since what is predicated is also marked as the focus of New information.

Example 18. German circumstantial Theme translated into English as predicated circumstantial Theme

English	German
It wasn't until spring 1950 that I came back from the war and I found there was nobody I knew left in the town. [Pale Anna, p. 13]	Erst **im Frühjahr 1950** kehrte ich aus dem Krieg heim und ich fand niemanden mehr in der Stadt, den ich kannte. [Die Blasse Anna, p. 12]

To extend the exploration a little further, I repeated the exercise for two Spanish guidebooks translated into English and German, thus changing the sample to parallel translated texts. In this sample there are ten 'predicated theme' clauses in the English text but only one in the German.

Out of the ten English 'predicated theme' clauses, seven correspond to German clauses where the equivalent element is thematic (one with *erst*) — but not predicated: see Table 7. Three correspond to German clauses where the equivalent is element is rhematic, one of which is culminative within the clause. This suggests strongly that English and German are *textually congruent* in the sense that the texts show similar tendencies to assign thematic status — but only up to a point since English clauses are 'predicated theme' where German clauses are not. This is illustrated by the parallel clauses in Example 19. If we translate the German clause into English, we get the clause *In Plaça d'Espanya the Exhibition of 1929 was born*, with a marked circumstantial Theme but without theme predication (so-called "it-cleft").

The single 'predicated theme' clause in the German guidebooks is shown in Example 20. The corresponding English clause also thematizes

Example 19. German circumstantial Theme corresponding to English predicated circumstantial Theme

English [Barcelona]	German [Barcelona]
and ***it was in Plaça d'Espanya*** *that the Exhibition of 1929 was born, [p. 82]*	***An der Plaça Espanya*** *enstand die Expo 1929. [p. 82]*

Table 7. German textual selections corresponding to translated English 'predicated theme' in two guidebooks

English predicated Theme thematic in German	without *erst*	5
	with *erst*	1
English predicated Theme included within Theme in German		1
English predicated Theme rhematic in German		2
	English predicated Theme culminative in German	1

the universal exhibition, but not as a predicated Theme: instead it deploys a particular kind of ideational metaphor where a congruent circumstantial element of Location in time is represented metaphorically as the Senser of a perceptive mental clause and which serves as unmarked (participant) Theme. (There are three such examples, including this one, in the English guidebooks, none of which corresponds to metaphorical German clauses of perception: in her contribution to this volume, Elke Teich points out that German does not use this particular metaphorical strategy.)

Example 20. German predicated Theme corresponding to English circumstantial Theme reconstrued as thematic Senser of perceptive mental clause

English [Barcelona]	German [Barcelona]
Firstly, the Universal Exhibition of 1888 *saw the urbanisation of the slopes of Montjuic look ing over the city. [p. 81]*	***Zuerst war es die Weltausstellung 1888****, die den Berghang zum Parallel erschloss. [p. 81]*

These instantial differences between English and German with respect to the selection of 'predicated theme' in text should not come as a surprise. The instantial differences derive from systemic differences between the two languages. The system of THEME PREDICATION is quite restricted in German. It is much more restricted in German than in English (cf.

Baker 1992: 137–8) or in Swedish (see Brandt et al 1977: 209–10). Thus while the theme systems of German and Swedish are closer in certain respects than either is to that of English, in the area of theme predication, English and Swedish are much closer and we could predict from their systems that 'predicated theme' clauses in English will be translated as 'predicated theme' clauses in Swedish (and vice versa). To check this prediction in an exploratory way, I investigated how 'predicated theme' clauses in Joseph Conrad's *The End of the Tether* were translated into Swedish by Tryggve Emond in *Den yttersta gränsen*. As predicted, 'predicated theme' clauses in the English original were translated into Swedish as 'predicated theme' clauses; two examples from the beginning of the short story are given in Example 21. This picture can now be sketched more systematically: Stig Johansson (p.c.) has informed me about important doctoral research by Mats Johansson using a parallel corpus of English and Swedish. The systemic potentials for theme predication appear to be very similar in English and Swedish, but in terms of the systemic probabilities of instantation they are actually significantly different. For example, 'theme predication' is selected twice as often in Swedish (original) texts as in English (original) texts; and while English theme-predicated clauses are generally translated by Swedish ones, only about a third of Swedish theme-predicated clauses are translated by English ones. Johansson has found a similar situation with English and Norwegian.

Example 21. English 'predicated theme' clauses translated into Swedish as 'predicated theme' clauses

English [The End of the Tether]	Swedish [Den yttersta gränsen]
It was the serang, an elderly, alert little Malay, with very dark skin, who murmured the order to the helmsman [p. 157]	*Det var serangen, en äldre, vaksam liten malaj med mycket mörk hy*, som hade mumlat ordern till rorsmannen [p. 5]
It was she who volunteered to look after the little one, [p. 158]	*Det var hon* som erbjöd sig att ta hand of den lilla, [p. 11]

5.5. Equivalence in metafunction, rank and system: shift in structure

While translation shifts affecting systems along the paradigmatic axis can, as we have seen, be fairly extensive, shifts in structure under the condition of systemic equivalence are much less dramatic: they are fully "automatized" (in the sense discussed in Section 3.3. above). An example from the experiential metafunction is the realization of (intensive) 'relational' clauses within the system of PROCESS TYPE. The unmarked variant of this clause type in English and many other languages has a Process which is realized by (a verbal group containing) an unstressed, often monosyllabic verb meaning 'be' (often phonologically reduced) — the "copula" of traditional grammar. However, in many other languages the unmarked variant of this clause type is realized by the absence of the structural element Process: the clause consists of two participants only, either Carrier + Attribute or Token + Value. One such language is (Modern Standard) Arabic, as illustrated in Example 22. (In clauses that are marked with respect to polarity and/or tense/aspect, a Process is present to realize the marked features.) We can analyse this example as a configuration of Token + Value (my transliteration and analysis): see Figure 18. The English translation is also an identifying relational clause — *Omar's brother is the most ignorant boy in the school;* but this clause is a configuration of Token + Process: 'be' + Value. Systemically the Arabic original and the English are the same — they stand in the same relation to other process types in the transitivity system, so there is no difficulty in matching them up as translation equivalents; but structurally they are different. (In marked cases, Arabic clauses of this type would have a Process realized by a verb such as *ka:na* or *laysa*.)

This short example illustrates the general principle of structural shift located within metafunctional and systemic equivalence. Comparable examples within the other metafunctions are not hard to find; for example, in Bateman et al (1991), we illustrate how equivalent options within the mood systems of different languages are realized by different strategies such as relative sequence of Subject and Finite, interpersonal mood particles and tone.

Example 22. Example of identifying relational clause in Modern Standard Arabic (from Cowan 1958: 45)

أَخُو عُمَرَ أَجْهَلُ وَلَدٍ فِي ٱلْمَدْرَسَةِ

'*akhū ͑umara 'ajhalu waladin fi ∩l-madrasati,*
Omar's brother is the most ignorant boy in the school.

ˀaxu:	͑umara	ˀajhalu	waladin	fi	l-madrasati
brother: nom	Omar: gen (/acc)	ignorant:most	boy: gen: indef	in	def-school: gen
Token		Value			
nom. gp.		nom. gp.			

Figure 18. Structure of (unmarked) identifying relational clause in Modern Standard Arabic

6. Translation: (meta-)contexts

I have suggested that we can locate translation within a series of environments extending from the most global to the most local. These environments are part of the object of translation — the language-in-context that serves as the "source" and the language-in-context that serves as the "target". But the most all-encompassing environment must of course be the context of the process of translating itself and as a final step in my exploration of the contextualization of translation, I will discuss this environment briefly. We might call this the *meta-context* of translation to highlight the fact that this context is more abstract than what is being translated (Hatim & Mason 1990: 12 speak of the "socio-cultural context in which the act of translation takes place; my "meta-context" also includes the context in which the translation is read or listened to). It is in fact part of the meta-language — or meta-language in context — of translation. Since a meta-language is a semiotic system just as a language is, we can use our theory of language to conceptualize meta-language (see Matthiessen 1988; Matthiessen & Nesbitt 1996). In particular, it will be helpful to explore the field, tenor and mode of the meta-context of translation.

field: The field is the social process of translation in which the translator plays a part — interpretable as one kind of multilingual text production (along with of kinds such as glossing and multilingual text generation). Translation is part of a sequence of processes concerned with the creation of text, including the production of the original before the translation (possibly according to guidelines for how to write translatable text), the preparation of it for translation and also the processes of editing and evaluating the output of the translation process. An important aspect of this sequence is the division of labour between human and computer.

tenor: The tenor is the role-relationship associated with translation involving the original writer, the translator, the editor, the reader and other roles entering into the total process of translation. (These are roles not persons; one and the same person may take on more than one of these roles as when writers translate their own work or when translators also edit the text.) Also relevant within tenor are the translator's degree of expertise and authority (in relation to both the text and the reader) and the status of the translation. The status of the translation includes both the translator's (or translation agency's) angle on it (e.g. is it a draft or an authorized translation?) and the reader's angle on it (e.g. is it a natural translation or a wooden one?). The reader may be a critic evaluating the translation, drawing on the particular strategies of appraisal applied to translations (cf. Venuti 1995: 2ff).

mode: The mode includes the channel of translation (written, spoken; electronic [fax, e-mail, WWW], non-electronic), the medium of translation (human translation only, machine translation only, machine-assisted human translation, human-assisted machine translation), the role of the translation in relation to the original (translation as constitutive, replacing source/ translation as ancillary, aiding understanding of source; focus on source ["source-language oriented"]/ focus on target ["target-language oriented"] — see Anwyl et al 1991) and the rhetorical mode of the translation (for cataloguing, for information retrieval, for reference etc.).

All three aspects of the meta-context of translation need to be developed further; but I will only take up one or two issues very briefly here. The first issue concerns the nature of the translation — where is it located on the cline from "free" to "literal" translation; is it "total" translation or only "partial"? Such distinctions depend on the meta-context of the translation. For example, if the rhetorical mode of the translation is "for information retrieval" or "for cataloguing" and if the readers are experts in the field of the source text, it may be appropriate to undertake a partial translation based on key words — a kind of translation that can be automated. If the intended readers of the target text are language learners, it may be appropriate to undertake both a "free" translation and a fairly "literal" translation. And so on.

The second issue concerns the field of translation — more specifically the roles that may be taken on by human translators and computational translation systems and the division of labour between the two. It is important to recognize that they are complementary participants in the translation process; they are not competing alternatives. The challenge is to model the complementarity between the two so that they can work together in a unified hybrid system that benefits human translators and consumers. A very simple model based on field considerations is presented in Figure 19. This model is based on a cline of participation from one pole where the computer does the translation (computer as "agent", human as "beneficiary") to the other pole where the computer helps do the translation (human as "agent", computer essentially as "means"). Along this cline there are various kinds of computer system involved in the translation process — from full-fledged MT systems at one end (where the computer does the translation) to translation aids such as online bilingual dictionaries, grammars and spell-checkers at the other (where the computer helps do the trans lation). Already over a decade ago, Carbonell & Tomita (1987) identified the following kinds of computer system:

1. Translation aids
2. Post-editing systems
3. Pre-editing systems
4. Knowledge-based systems
5. Interactive systems
6. Multilingual composition aids
7. Knowledge-based interactive systems

And since then increasing attention has been paid to computational environments for developing and maintaining linguistic resources (see e.g. Estival et al 1997), to systems for translating WWW pages, and to systems for operating and developing translation systems over the WWW, via e-mail and the like (e.g. Blanc & Guillaume 1997). Looking into the 21st century, Minako O'Hagan (1997) has outlined a vision of a global network of translation expertise where human translators and computational systems are seamlessly integrated. For a general, recent survey of computational approaches to multilinguality, see Chapter 8, Multilinguality, of the online book *Survey of the State of the Art in Human Language Technology*.[17]

But there is another aspect of this kind of development that will blur the boundaries between translation and other kinds of multilingual text production. If we start with the traditional concept of translation, we can note that it is essentially source-language oriented: the emphasis is on the mapping from the source text. However, we also need to recognize translation of a kind where the emphasis is on the creation of target-language texts and source language texts may not be the only source that the writer draws on (see e.g. Anwyl et al 1991). Here translation from the source-language text may thus only be one part of the production of texts in various languages.

This type of activity may shade into what is known as multilingual text generation (for example our own Multex system — Matthiessen et al 1998 — and the KPML system — Bateman 1997) — see further Hartley & Paris's contribution to this volume. Here a computational system generates texts in various languages drawing on higher-level specifications of meaning that are in some sense shared across languages without treating one particular language as the source. These higher-level specifications may come from various sources — data base systems, expert systems, summarization systems or translation systems. A multilingual text generation system working together with a summarization system may be able to produce texts that can serve as a kind of translation, as in the TREE project (Somers et al 1997). Further, such systems are very likely to be both multilingual and multimodal (as Multex already is).

114 Christian M.I.M. Matthiessen

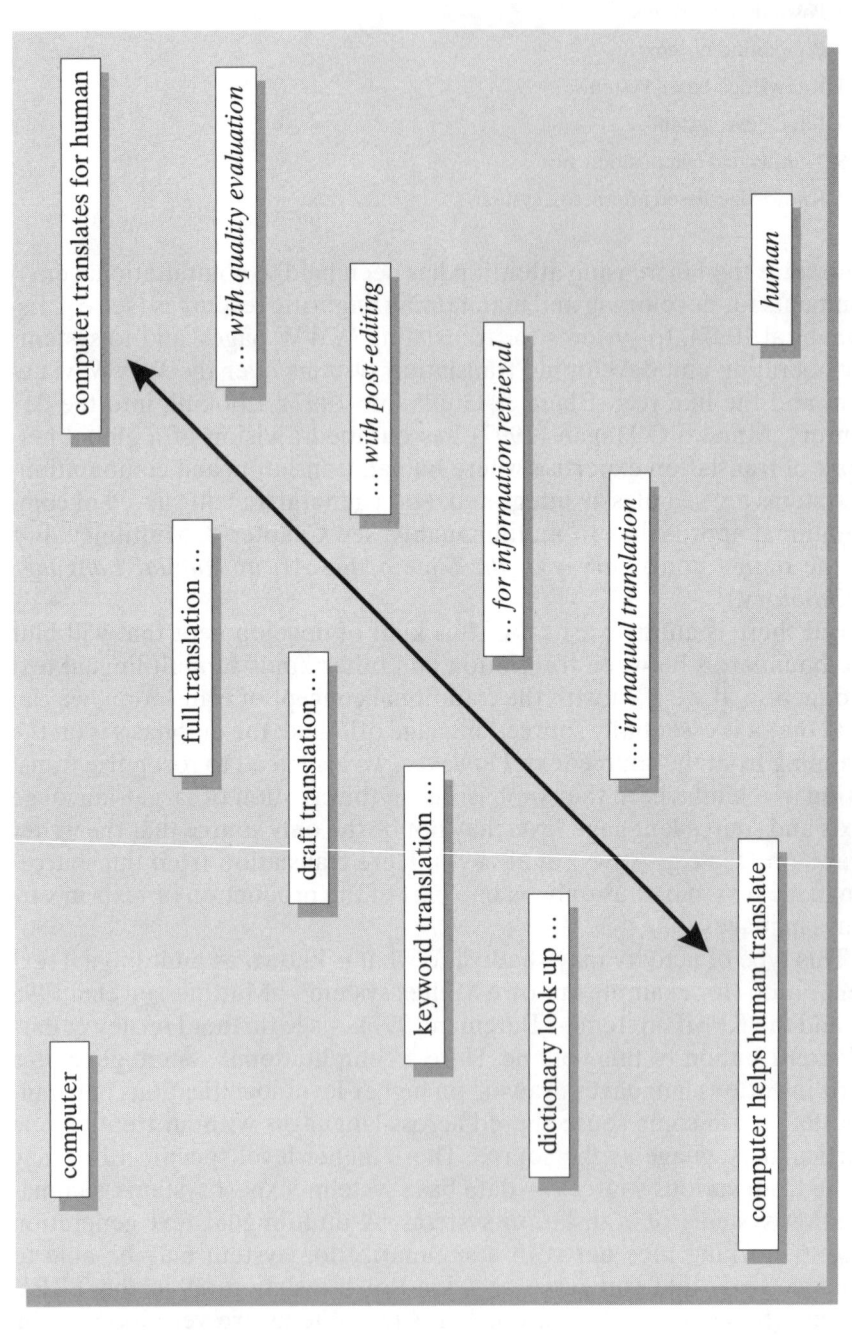

Figure 19. The division of labour between computer and human in the process of translation

7. Conclusion

In this chapter, I have sketched the "environments of translation". I started with the most global environment and moved progressively to more local ones. I adopted this strategy because I believe it reflects the successive contextualization of the act of translation itself: the act is contextualized "top-down" rather than "bottom-up"; or rather, it has to be contextualized in this way since the literature is full of observations about problems that "bottom-up" approaches run into.

I began by placing translation in the widest environment of all — that of a comprehensive typology of systems. This made it possible to explore the fuzzy boundaries of translation as a semiotic (4th-order) process (of transformation or mapping). I explored some examples of "intersemiotic translation". This exploration underlined the point that translation has to take place in wider rather than narrower environments in the first instance and it illustrated a point that was developed later that "translation equivalence" is a matter of degree where the degree depends on the nature of the systems involved in the translation.

Having established translation as a semiotic process (mapping) I then focussed on the semiotic environments of translation: I discussed its location in relation to an ordered series of contextualizations from the most global (widest) environments to the most local (narrowest). I suggested that two translation clines move from the most global environment to the most local ones: both "free" translation and "translation equivalence" are located as poles on these clines within the most global environment and both "literal" translation and "translation shift" are located as the opposite poles on these clines within the most local environments.

Finally I moved up in abstraction from the object of translation — languages in context — to meta-context of the process of translation itself. This is the widest environment of all in the sense that it allows us to locate translation in relation to other multilingual processes and to identify the range of values within field, tenor and mode that are characteristic of translation.

Let me conclude this chapter with a few comments on the act of translation. I have treated the act of translation as an act of meaning (cf. Halliday 1993): I have suggested that it is in the first instance a process at the semantic stratum and that it is located at the instantial pole of the cline of instantiation. This also means that it is a *logogenetic act* — it is an act in the creation of meaning that takes place as a text unfolds. Or, in this case: as two texts unfold — the "source text" and the "target text": both are sequences of logogenetic acts. We see this most clearly in the case of simultaneous interpretation of spoken text since this task hardly leaves any time for viewing the source text as product: is has to be translated as process. But it is important to keep in mind that written texts are also sequences of logogenetic acts.

One of the most pressing tasks for the study of translation within functional linguistics seems to me to be to develop detailed descriptions of the patterns that such logogenetic acts create. And since the clause (complex) is a likely candidate as the "unit of translation" — a critical logogenetic act — detailed lexicogrammatical analysis of source texts and corresponding target texts will be an important source of insight. A number of our research students at Macquarie University are engaged in research of this kind. At the same time, we must keep in mind that we need to operate at a high degree of semiotic abstraction to handle translation differences: this means operating at the stratum of (discourse) semantics and identifying semantic motifs that can be treated as fairly constant across languages — such as the task of introducing and tracking discourse referents discussed by Martin (1983). Many such motifs are likely to emerge most clearly midway along the cline of instantiation as register-specific strategies.

Notes

1. In preparing this chapter, I have benefited from the insights of a number of people and I am very grateful to them. In the context of research into multilingual text generation, I have learned from John Bateman, Elke Teich, Kazuhiro Teruya, Wu Canzhong and Zeng Licheng; and in the context of a project involving the translation of M.A.K. Halliday's *Computing meanings: some reflections on past experience and present prospects,* I gained a great deal from a series of discussion with M.A.K. Halliday, Kazuhiro Teruya (who undertook the translation into Japanese) and Wu Canzhong (who undertook the translation into Chinese). I am also grateful to participants in the translation workshop organized by Colin Yallop and Erich Steiner at the 25th ISFC, in Cardiff, 1998, for their contributions and comments, to Stig Johansson for comments on a draft version of the chapter and to Kazuhiro Teruya for help with the preparation of the chapter for publication.
2. Catford (1965: 20) characterizes translation theory as a "branch of Comparative Linguistics" — which it is, in theory, although in practice it does not seem to be treated as such. Compare also Halliday's remarks in this volume.
3. The term *system* stands for *system-&-process:* the organization has to be interpreted both synoptically as system and dynamically as process.
4. Another source for Ruskin must have been the report written about the ship — see the next subsection.
5. This is an echo from Macbeth, thus adding the intertextual allusion to bloody deed and retribution to the final new: *No, this hand will rather / The multitudinous seas incarnadine, making the green one red.* (II.2)
6. I am using the term *environment* rather than the term *context* simply because *context* has come to refer to one particular kind of environment — the stratal environment of language (and other denotative semiotic systems; cf. Martin, 1992).
7. "In the default case" because there are marked types of translation — such as the interlinear glossing linguist use together with more idiomatic translations of examples from languages they are working with.

The environments of translation   117

8. This has to be qualified: we have to allow for significant differences in the wider environment — in particular, we have to allow for those contextual differences that derive from differences in the contexts of culture in which the languages being translated are embedded: cf. Colin Yallop's contribution to this volume.
9. At that time, the sentence was treated as a separate rank, above the rank of clause. In more recent work, this has been replaced by the clause complex; that is, the "sentence" is interpreted not as a rank in its own right but as a complex at clause rank.
10. Bell (1991: 29) writes that "there is good psychological and linguistic evidence to suggest that the unit [of translation, CM] tends to be the clause". It seems very plausible that it is the clause or the clause complex since it is the clause (complex) that is the focus of text processing; but this is not in conflict with the observation that it is the text that is the unit of the highest degree of translation equivalence.
11. Catford (1965: 25) recognizes three popular terms — "free", "literal" and "word-for-word". He characterizes free translation as "unbounded", word-for-word translation as "rank-bounded at word-rank, and literal translation as lying "between these extremes". I have generalized the notions of free and literal translation so as to be able to apply them to all three hierarchies in Figure 12, and I treat word-for-word translation just as a special case of literal translation with reference to one of the three hierarchies — the hierarchy of rank.
12. These Donald Duck stories were Italian originals, not translations from stories produced in the U.S. Ingrid Emond observed that they were culturally different from the American ones, e.g. in the degree of violence.
13. The use of a modulation of potentiality is characteristic of perceptive mental clauses. It is of course possible to explore an existential interpretation of the clause. One interesting issue is what the agnate tagged version of the clause is: is it ... *can't they?* as it should be if the clause is mental; or is it *can't there?* (i.e. *farther north on the right there can be seen some of the buildings ... can't there?*) as it should be if the clause is existential? But even if the answer is the second alternative, we can certainly find more unambiguously perceptive mental clauses with an explicit Senser serving a very similar discourse function; for example: *At the centre is Alice Springs where you can see Ayers Rock, the most spectacular sight in this area; There you can see the first settlers' houses, church, and cemetary; after a short distance you can see on your right the Chinese Gardens.*
14. There is a real difficulty here, however. The consumers of a translation will very likely not have access to the system that lies behind the original text they are accessing through the translation. For example, Vibeke Emond translated Banana Yoshimoto's wonderful short novel *Kitchen* into Swedish. The novel was reviewed in a local Swedish paper, *Helsingborgs Dagblad,* and the reviewer's evaluation was fairly negative. This was not because of the quality of the translation — it was very high. Rather the reason was that he did not understand the Japanese system that lies behind the original Japanese text and he was too parochial to take this into account or too lazy to make an effort to do some homework before passing judgment; so he read it as if it had been a text instantiating a system he was familiar with — which of course it was not. (There are after all no meta-critics: critics are not held directly accountable for their evaluations.) The translator of fiction has of course no way of making the system behind the original text accessible to the reader; as Venuti (1995) notes, translators are supposed to be "invisible". In other kinds of translation it is of course possible to include footnotes or extended comments that describe aspects of the system that lies behind the original text (and this may be used with translations of literary classics).
15. The examples have been taken from *Penguin Parallel Texts — German Short Stories 1,* edited by R. Newnham.
16. That is, pronominal affixes rather than concord affixes.
17. URL: http://www.cse.ogi.edu/CSLU/HLTsurvey/HLTsurvey.html; Chapter 8, URL: http://www.cse.ogi.edu/CSLU/HLTsurvey/ch8node2.html.

References

Abelen, E., Gisele Redeker and Sandra A. Thompson
1993   The rhetorical structure of US-American and Dutch fund-raising letters. *Text* 13.1: 323–350.

Anwyl, Phyllis, Toru Matsuda, Katsuhiko Fujita and Masayuki Kameda
1991   Target-language driven transfer and generation. In *Proceedings of The 2nd Japan-Australia Joint Symposium on Natural Language Processing* (JAJSNLP '91), October 2–5 1991, Kyushu Institute of Technology, Iizuka City, Japan. pp. 234–243.

Atkinson, Paul
1985   *Language, structure and reproduction: an introduction to the sociology of Basil Bernstein.* London: Methuen.

Bateman, John A.
1997   *KPML Development Environment: multilingual linguistic resource development and sentence generation.* IPSI/ GMD, 15 Dolivostrasse, Darmstadt, Germany.

Bateman, John A., Christian M.I.M. Matthiessen, Keizo Nanri and Licheng Zeng
1991   The rapid prototyping of natural language generation components: an application of functional typology. In *Proceedings of IJCAI 91,* Sydney. New York: Morgan Kaufman. pp. 966–971.

Bateman, John A., Christian M.I.M. Matthiessen and Licheng Zeng
1999   "Multilingual language generation for multilingual software: a functional linguistic approach." *Applied Artificial Intelligence: An International Journal.* 13.6: 607–639.

Bell, Roger T.
1991   *Translation and translating: theory and practice.* London & New York: Longman.

Bickerton, Derek
1995   *Language & human behaviour.* London: UCL Press.

Blanc, E. and P. Guillaume
1997   Developing MT lingware through INTERNET: ARIANE and the CASH interface. In *Proceedings of PACLING '97,* September 2–5 1997, Meisei University.

Brandt, Margareta, Ingemar Persson, Inger Rosengren and Lars Åhlander
1977   *Tysk grammatik för universitets bruk.* Lund: Liber Läromedel.

Caffarel, Alice, James R. Martin and Christian M.I.M. Matthiessen (eds.)
forthc.   *Language typology: a functional perspective.* Amsterdam: Benjamins.

Carbonell, Jaime G. and M. Tomita
1987   Knowledge-based machine translation. In: Sergei Nirenburg (ed.). *Machine translation: theoretical and methodological issues.* Cambridge: Cambridge University Press.

Catford, J. C.
1965   *A linguistic theory of translation.* London: Oxford University Press.

Churchward, Maxwell C.
   1956   *Tongan grammar.* London: Oxford University Press.

Cowan, David
   1958   *An introduction to Modern Literary Arabic.* Cambridge: Cambridge University Press.

Damasio A.R. and H. Damasio
   1992   Brain and language. *Scientific American* 267: 88–95.

Estival, D., A. Lavelli, K. Netter and F. Pianesi (eds.)
   1997   *Computational environments for grammar development and linguistic engineering.* Proceedings of a Workshop Sponsored by the Association for Computational Linguistics, 12 July 1997, Universidad Nacional Educación a Distancia, Madrid, Spain.

Gentzler, Edwin
   1993   *Contemporary translation theories.* London & New York: Routledge.

Gregory, Michael J.
   1967   Aspects of varieties differentiation. *Journal of Linguistics* 3.

Halliday, M.A.K.
   1956   The linguistic basis of a mechanical thesaurus. *Mechanical Translation* 3.3: 81–89.

Halliday, M.A.K.
   1966a   Typology and the exotic. In: Halliday and McIntosh. pp. 165–83.

Halliday, M.A.K.
   1966b   General linguistics and its application to language teaching. In: Halliday and McIntosh. pp. 1–41.

Halliday, M.A.K.
   1975   *Learning how to mean: explorations in the development of language.* London: Edward Arnold.

Halliday, M.A.K.
   1976   "The teacher taught the student English": an essay in applied linguistics. *LACUS.* Hornbeam Press: Columbia.

Halliday, M.A.K.
   1978   *Language as social semiotic: the social interpretation of language and meaning.* London & Baltimore: Edward Arnold & University Park Press.

Halliday, M.A.K.
   1982   The de-automatization of grammar: from Priestley's "An Inspector Calls". In: J. Anderson (ed.), *Language form and linguistic variation: papers dedicated to Angus McIntosh.* Amsterdam: Benjamins. pp. 129–159.

Halliday, M.A.K.
   1985   *Spoken and written language.* Geelong, Vic.: Deakin University Press.

Halliday, M.A.K.
   1992   The notion of 'context' in language education. In: Thao Le and Mike McCausland (eds.), *Interaction and development: proceedings of the international con-*

ference, Vietnam, 30 March — 1 April 1992. University of Tasmania: Language Education.

Halliday, M.A.K.
1993 The act of meaning. In *Georgetown University Round Table on Languages and Linguistics 1992: language, communication and social meaning*. Washington, D.C.: Georgetown University Press.

Halliday, M.A.K.
1994 *An introduction to functional grammar*. London: Edward Arnold.

Halliday, M.A.K.
1995 *Computing meanings: some reflections on past experience and present prospects*. Paper delivered at PACLING '95. To appear. (In English, with parallel translations in Chinese and Japanese).

Halliday, M.A.K.
1998 The grammar of daily life: construing pain. *Functions of Language* 5.2.

Halliday, M.A.K. and Angus McIntosh
1966 *Patterns of language: papers in general, descriptive and applied linguistics*. London: Longman.

Halliday, M.A.K. and Ruqaiya Hasan
1976 *Cohesion in English*. London: Longman.

Halliday, M.A.K. and James R. Martin
1993 *Writing science: literacy and discursive power*. London: Falmer.

Halliday, M.A.K. and Christian M.I.M. Matthiessen
1999 *Construing experience as meaning: a language based approach to cognition*. London: Cassell.

Hasan, Ruqaiya
1996 *Ways of saying: ways of meaning*. London: Cassell.

Hatim, Basil and Ian Mason
1990 *Discourse and the translator*. London: Longman.

Johansson, Stig
1998a On the role of corpora in cross-linguistic research. In: Stig Johansson and S. Oknefjell, *Corpora and cross-linguistic research: theory, method, and case studies*. Amsterdam: Rodopi. pp. 1–24.

Johansson, Stig
1998b Loving and hating in English and Norwegian: a corpus-based study. In: D. Albrechtsen, B. Henriksen, I.M, Mees and E. Poulsen (eds.), *Perspectives on foreign and second language pedagogy*. Odense: Odense University Press. pp. 93–103.

Johnston, Trevor
1989 *AUSLAN dictionary: a dictionary of the Sign Language of the Australian Deaf Community*. Petersham, NSW: Deafness Resources Australia Limited.

Kittredge, Richard and L. Lehrberger (eds.)
1982 *Sublanguage: studies of language in restricted semantic domains*. Berlin: de Gruyter.

Kittredge, Richard
    1987   The significance of sublanguage for automatic translation. In: Sergei Nirenburg (ed.), *Machine translation: theoretical and methodological issues.* Cambridge: Cambridge University Press. pp. 59–67.

Kobayashi, Iichiro
    1995   *A social system simulation based on human information processing.* Ph.D. thesis, Tokyo Institute of Technology.

Kobayashi, Ichiro and Michio Sugeno
    1994   "An Approach to Social System Simulation based on Linguistic Information — An Application to the Forecast of Foreign Exchange Rate Changes." *Journal of Japan Society for Fuzzy Theory and Systems,* Vol. 6, No. 4, August 1994. (In Japanese.)

Kress, Gunther and Theo van Leeuwen
    1996   *Reading images: the grammar of visual design.* London: Routledge.

Li, Charles N. and Sandra A. Thompson
    1980   *Mandarin Chinese: a functional reference grammar.* Berkeley: University of California Press.

Lloyd, Michael
    1996   Being there. In Michael Lloyd (ed.), *Turner.* Port Melbourne, Vic., London & New York: Thames and Hudson. pp. 186–202.

Mann, William C., Christian M.I.M. Matthiessen and Sandra A. Thompson
    1992   Rhetorical Structure Theory and text analysis. In W.C. Mann and S.A. Thompson (eds.), *Discourse description: diverse linguistic analyses of a fund-raising text.* Amsterdam: Benjamins. pp. 39–79.

Martin, Catherine A.
    1997   *Staging the reality principle: systemic-functional linguistics and the context of theatre.* Ph.D. thesis, Macquarie University.

Martin, James R.
    1983   "Participant identification in English, Tagalog and Kate." *Australian Journal of Linguistics* 3.1: 45–74.

Martin, James R.
    1990   "Interpersonal grammaticalisation: mood and modality in Tagalog." *Philippine Journal of Linguistics* (Special Monograph Issue celebrating the 25th Anniversary of the Language Study centre, Philippine Normal College).

Martin, James R.
    1992   *English text: system and structure.* Amsterdam: Benjamins.

Martin, James R.
    in press   Beyond exchange: appraisal systems in English. In: S. Hunston and G. Thompson (eds.), *Evaluation in text.* Oxford: Oxford University Press.

Martin, James R. and Rick Iedema (eds.)
    forthc.   *Multimodality: the Inter-Semiotics of Communication* London: Routledge.

Matthiessen, Christian M.I.M.
    1988   Representational Issues in Systemic Functional Grammar. In: James D. Benson and William S. Greaves (eds.), *Systemic functional approaches to dis-*

course: selected papers from the Twelfth International Systemic Workshop. Norwood, NJ.: Ablex. Also as ISI/ RS-87–179.

Matthiessen, Christian M.I.M.
1992   Interpreting the textual metafunction. In: Martin Davies and Louise Ravelli (eds.), *Advances in systemic linguistics.* London: Pinter. pp. 37–82.

Matthiessen, Christian M.I.M.
1993   Register in the round: diversity in a unified theory of register analysis. In: Mohsen Ghadessy (ed.), *Register analysis: practice and theory.* London: Pinter.

Matthiessen, Christian M.I.M.
1995   *Lexicogrammatical cartography: English systems.* Tokyo: International Language Sciences Publishers.

Matthiessen, Christian M.I.M., Keizo Nanri and Licheng Zeng
1991   Multilingual resources in text generation: ideational focus. In: *Proceedings of the 2nd Japan-Australia Symposium on Natural Language Processing,* Japan, October 1991.

Matthiessen, Christian M.I.M. and Christopher Nesbitt
1996   On the idea of theory-neutral descriptions. Ruqaiya Hasan, Carmel Cloran and David G. Butt (eds.), *Functional descriptions: theory in practice.* Amsterdam: Benjamins. pp. 39–85.

Matthiessen, Christian M.I.M., Marilyn Cross, Ichiro Kobayashi and Licheng Zeng
1997   Generating Multimodal Presentations: Resources and Processes. In: *Proceedings of the Artificial Intelligence in Defence Workshop AI '95,* ed. by S. Goss, Eighth Australian Joint Conference on Artificial Intelligence, Canberra 14 November 1995. pp. 91–109.

Matthiessen, Christian M.I.M., Licheng Zeng, Marilyn Cross, Ichiro Kobayashi, Kazuhiro Teruya and Canzhong Wu
1998   The Multex generator and its environment: application and development. In: *Proceedings of the International Generation Workshop '98,* August '98, Niagara-on-the-Lake.

Matthiessen, Christian M.I.M. and M.A.K. Halliday
in prep.   *An outline of systemic functional linguistics.*

McInnes, David
1998   *Attending to the instance: towards a systemic based dynamic and responsive analysis of composite performance text.* Ph.D. thesis, Sydney University.

Mohan, Bernard A.
1986   *Language and content.* Reading, Mass.: Addison-Wesley.

O'Hagan, Minako
1997   A teletranslation scenario in distributed VR environments: role of language agent. In *Proceedings of PACLING '97,* September 2–5 1997, Meisei University.

O'Toole, Michael
1994   *The language of displayed art.* London: Leicester University Press (Pinter).

Palmer, F. R.
  1986   *Mood and modality.* Cambridge: Cambridge University Press.

Patten, Terry
  1988   *Systemic text generation as problem solving.* Cambridge: Cambridge University Press.

Pawley, Andrew
  1987   Encoding events in Kalam and English: different logics for reporting experience. R.S. Tomlin (ed.). *Coherence and grounding in discourse.* Amsterdam: Benjamins. pp. 329–61.

Payne, John R.
  1985   Negation. In Timothy Shopen (ed), *Language typology and syntactic description. Clause structure.* Cambridge: Cambridge University Press. pp. 197–243.

Rose, David
  1998   *The Western Desert Code: an Australian cryptogrammar.* Ph.D. thesis, University of Sydney.

Schneider Adams, Laurie
  1996   *The methodologies of art: an introduction.* New York: HarperCollins.

Snell-Hornby, Mary
  1995   *Translation studies: an integrated approach.* Amsterdam: Benjamins.

Somers, H., B. Black, J. Nivre, T. Lager, A. Multari, L. Gilardoni, J. Ellmann and A. Rogers
  1997   Multilingual generation and summarization of job adverts: the TREE project. In *Proceedings of the Fifth Conference on Applied Natural Language Processing,* 31 March — 3 April 1997, Washington Marriot Hotel, Washington DC, USA. pp. 269–76.

Steiner, Erich
  1988   The interaction of language and music as semiotic systems: the example of a folk ballad. In: J.D. Benson, M.J. Cummings and W.S. Greaves (eds.), *Linguistics in a systemic perspective.* Amsterdam: Benjamins. pp. 393–443.

Steiner, Erich
  1991   *A functional perspective on language, action and interpretation.* Berlin and New York: Mouton de Gruyter.

Steiner, Erich
  1989   Predicate-argument structures for transfer. In: Erich Steiner (ed.), *Argument structure: grammatical issues.* IAI Working Papers 11.

Steiner, Erich and W. Ramm
  1995   On theme as a grammatical notion in German. *Functions of Language* 1.2: 57–93.

Teruya, Kazuhiro
  1998   *An exploration into the world of experience: a systemic-functional interpretation of the grammar of Japanese.* Ph.D. thesis, Macquarie University.

Venuti, Lawrence
  1995   *The translator's invisibility: a history of translation.* London & New York: Routledge.

Wu, Canzhong
   1992   *A functional approach to the problem of translating university introductions.* MA thesis, Xi'an Jiaotong University.

Zadeh, Lotfi A.
   1987   *Fuzzy sets and applications: selected papers by L.A. Zadeh.* Eds. R.R. Yager, S. Ovchinnikov, R.M. Tong, H.T. Nguyen. New York: Wiley.

Zeng, Licheng
   1996   *Planning text in an integrated multilingual meaning space.* Ph.D. thesis, Sydney University.

Part II
Modeling translation

How do we know when a translation is good?

Juliane House

1. Introduction

How do we know when a translation is good? This question is one of the most important questions to be asked in connection with translation, and it is crucial to attempt to answer this question on the basis of a theory of translation and translation criticism. In this chapter I will try just this: present a theory-guided approach to the linguistic analysis and evaluation of a translation. The structure of the chapter is as follows:

First I will give a brief review of how translations have been evaluated inside different traditions and schools of thought. Second, I will present a functional-pragmatic model for evaluating translations first proposed some twenty years ago, and revised in the late nineties. In the third part of the chapter the theoretical assumptions and distinctions made in the model are put to the test in a detailed analysis of a German translation of an English children's book. In the fourth and last part of the chapter I will briefly discuss the scope of translation criticism.

In trying to answer the title question 'How do we know when a translation is good', we must first address the crucial question any theory of translation faces, namely what translation actually is. This question can be split up and made more concrete by asking the following three sub-questions:

(1) How does a source text relate to its translation?

(2) How are features of the source text and features of the translation related to one another, and how are they perceived by human agents (author, translator, translation recipients)?

(3) In the light of (1) and (2) above, how can we tell when a translation is a translation, and when it is a text resulting from a different textual operation?

These three basic questions can be taken as yardsticks against which different approaches to evaluating a translation can be measured and compared. In the following section some of the most influential views on how to assess the quality of a translation will be described and critically discussed.

2. Translation evaluation in different schools of thought

2.1. Anecdotal, biographical and neo-hermeneutic views

Subjective and intuitive assessments of the quality of a translation have been undertaken since time immemorial by generations of translators, writers, philosophers, philologists and many others. Such informal assessments of translations tend to also appear in reviews of literary works in newspapers and magazines, more often than not consisting of global judgements such as "the translation does justice to the original" or "the humorous tone of the original is unfortunately not kept up in the translation" and so forth.

While such incidental and anecdotal evaluations of translations may have their legitimate place in journalism and other non-scientific genres, they should be viewed with reservation in the academic field of translation studies, if this field is to gain respectability as a scientific undertaking. Anecdotal evaluations of the quality of a translation, based largely or exclusively on the translator's or translation critic's own knowledge, intuition and experience are even today frequently offered in many philological traditions of writing about translation, especially literary translation. One such approach is the neo-hermeneutic approach. Its propagators look at translation as an individual creative act depending exclusively on subjective interpretation and transfer decisions (cf. e.g., Stolze 1992).

Instead of striving to set up criteria for evaluating translations that are empirically based, transparent and intersubjectively reliable, propagators of this approach think that the quality of a translation must most importantly be linked to "the human factor", i.e., the translator himself whose interpretation of the original and his moves towards an "optimal translation" are seen as rooted in his artistic-literary intuitions and interpretative skills and knowledge. Translation is understood to be an individual's creative act. Texts have no fixed meanings at all, rather their meanings change in any historic moment, depending on individual speakers' positions.

It is inappropriate in the context of this paper to expand on a critique of the hermeneutic position (the reader is however referred to the recent lucid discussion in Bühler 1998), suffice it to say that such an extremely relativising stance as propounded in much hermeneutic work, and especially the relativisation of "content" and "meaning" is particularly inappropriate for the evaluative business of deciding when, how and why a translation is good.

With respect to the three above questions, we can state that the hermeneutic approach only sheds light on what happens between the translator and features of the original text. The superordinate question of how one can tell when a translation is good cannot be answered in any satisfactory manner.

2.2. Response-based behavioural approaches

As opposed to the subjective-intuitive approach to evaluating a translation, supporters of the response-based view expressly aim at a more reliable, more "scientific" way of evaluating translations. They dismiss the translator's mental actions as belonging to some in principle unknowable "black box". This tradition, which is influenced by American structuralism and behaviourism, is most famously associated with Nida's (1964) and Nida and Taber's (1969) pioneering work in the sixties, as well as with the few attempts to put translation criticism on a more respectable empirical footing undertaken by psychologists and psycholinguists such as Carroll (1966).

Basically, adherents of this approach tried to look at translation recipients' reactions to a translation as their main yardstick for assessing a translation's quality, positing global behavioural criteria, such as e.g., intelligibility and informativeness and Nida's "equivalence of response" based on his principle of "dynamic equivalence of translation", i.e., that the manner in which receptors of a translation respond to the translation be "equivalent" to the manner in which the source text's receptors respond to the source text. Assuming that it is true that a "good" translation should elicit an equivalent response to its original, we must immediately ask whether it is at all possible to measure an "equivalent response", let alone "informativeness" or "intelligibility". If these phenomena cannot be measured, it is useless to postulate them as criteria for translation evaluation.

Despite the fact that a number of impressively imaginative tests were designed to test the responses a translation presumably evokes — using for instance reading aloud techniques, various cloze and rating procedures — all these methods, in which observable, verifiable responses to a translation were sought and taken as ultimate criteria of its quality, nevertheless failed because they were unable to capture the complex phenomenon of an "overall quality of a translation". Further, the source text is largely ignored in all these methods, which means that nothing can be said about the relationship between original and translation, nor about whether a translation is in fact a translation and not another secondary text derived via different textual operations.

2.3. Literature-oriented approaches: descriptive translation studies

This descriptive-historical approach is oriented squarely towards the translation text, the consequence being that a translation is evaluated predominantly in terms of its forms and functions inside the system of the target culture and literature (cf. Toury 1995). The source text is of subordinate importance, the main focus — retrospective from translation to original — being "actual translations", and the textual phenomena that have come to be known in the target culture as translations. As a first step, for instance, a translation is on principle taken to be a translation if, in the context of the culture enveloping it, it is "assumed" to be a translation. Interestingly, Toury's empirical-descriptive appproach implies a "clear wish to retain the notion of equivalence, which various contemporary approaches ... have tried to do without" (1995: 61). His notion of equivalence, which might serve as a yardstick for measuring the quality of a translation, does not refer, however, to a single relationship (between translation and original) but to "any relation which is found to have characterized translation under a specified set of circumstances" (1995: 61) and its norms responsible for the way this equivalence is realised. According to Toury, translation equivalence in the descriptive translation studies' paradigm is thus never a relationship between original and translation, but a "functional-relational concept", i.e., that set of relationships which has been found to distinguish appropriate from non-appropriate modes of translation performance for the particular culture in which the translation operates.

The aim of scholars working in this paradigm is to not prescriptively prejudge features of a translation text in their relation to some other text, (e.g., the original), but rather to first of all "neutrally" describe the characteristics of that text as they are perceived on the basis of native culture members' knowledge of comparable texts in the same genre. This aim is certainly legitimate and commendable. However, if one aims at judging a particular text which is plainly not an "independent", "new" product of one culture only, then such a retrospective focus seems peculiarly inappropriate for making reasonable statements about why a translation qua translation is "good".

While the strength of this approach is its solid empirical-descriptive work and its emphasis on contextualization at the micro-level of the reception situation and the macro-level of the receiving culture at large, as well as the inclusion of both a "longitudinal" (temporal, diachronic) and a (synchronic) systemic perspective (considering the polysystemic relations into which the translation enters with other texts in the receiving cultural system), it nevertheless clearly fails to provide criteria for judging the merits and weaknesses of a particular "case". In other words, how are we to legitimately say that one text is a translation, and another one not? And what are the criteria for judging merits and weaknesses of a given "translation text"?

2.4. Functionalistic, "skopos"-related approaches

Adherents of this approach (cf., above all, Reiss and Vermeer 1984) claim that it is the "skopos" or purpose of a translation that is of overriding importance in judging a translation's quality. The way target culture norms are heeded or flouted in the process of translation is thus regarded as the crucial yardstick in evaluating a translation. According to Reiss and Vermeer, it is the translator or more frequently the translation brief he is given by the person(s) commissioning the translation, who decides on the function the translation is to fulfil in its target environment. The notion of function, critical in this theory, is, however, never made explicit let alone operationalized. The reader can only hypothesise that "function" in this paradigm is conceived as something very similar to the real-world effect of a text.

A distinction is made by Reiss and Vermeer (1984) between equivalence and adequacy in translation. Equivalence in Reiss and Vermeer's view refers to the relationship between an original and its translation whenever both fulfil the same communicative function, and adequacy is the relationship between an original and a translation where no functional match is obtained, and where the "skopos" of the translation has been consistently attended to.

Whether such a terminological distinction is necessary and useful for clarifying the complicated matter of determining the quality of a translation, is open to debate. Further, the authors do not specify how exactly one is to go about determining the (relative) equivalence and adequacy of a translation, let alone how exactly one is to go about determining the linguistic realization of the "skopos" of a translation. Most importantly, however, it naturally follows from the crucial role assigned to the "purpose" of a translation that the original is reduced to a simple "offer of information" ("Informationsangebot"), with the word "offer" making it immediately clear that this "information" can freely be accepted or rejected, changed or "improved upon" as the translator sees fit.

In sum, how the global "skopos" of a text is realized linguistically, and, even more critical, how the adequacy of a translation vis-à-vis this skopos is to be determined, is not clear. Functionalistic approaches are solely concerned with the relationships between features of texts and the human agents concerned with them. But translation is by its very nature characterised by a double-bind relationship, i.e., any translation is simultaneously bound to its source text and to the presuppositions and the conditions governing its reception in the new target linguistic and cultural environment. Skopos theory is not an adequate theory to handle the question of evaluating a translation in this fundamental sense.

2.5. Post-modernist and deconstructionist approaches

Scholars belonging to this approach (cf. e.g., Venuti 1995) try to critically examine translation practices from a socio-philosophical and political stance in an attempt to unmask unequal power relations, which may, for instance, be reflected in a certain skewing in the translation. In a plea for making translations (and translators) "visible" revealing ideological and institutional manipulations, proponents of this approach believe they can make politically pertinent (and "correct") statements about the relationship between features of the original and the translation. They focus on the hidden forces shaping both the process of selecting what gets translated in the first place and how an original text is bent and twisted in the interests of powerful individuals and groups "pulling strings" when selecting texts to be translated and adopting particular strategies of re-textualisation. This is certainly a worthwhile undertaking, especially when it comes to explaining the influence translators can exert through their translation on the recipient national literatures and their canons. Further, the application of currently influential lines of thinking such as e.g., post-colonialism (Robinson 1997) to translation studies may certainly yield interesting results. However, one wonders if it is wise to busy oneself with matters that are extraneous to the translation process itself. In other words, criticising the lowly, clearly invisible status of the translator, and giving priority to the socio-cultural and ideological constraints and influences on the "cultural practice" of translation may be fascinating in itself but it also detracts from the many still unsolved problems in the centre of translation and translation evaluation. Surely, translation is first and foremost a linguistic procedure — however conditioned this process may be by "external forces". In other words, before adopting a critical stance of the translation process from a macro-perspective, one needs to consider the micro-perspective, the linguistic "nitty-gritty" of the text, or, and this seems to me the optimal strategy with regard to tackling the problem of evaluating a translation, one might fruitfully consider the interaction of context and text in a systematic way, as has been attempted in some linguistic approaches to translation (see below 3).

If comparative analyses of original and translation focus primarily on the shifts and skews through ideological constraints and unconscious manipulations, and if an agenda is given priority which "stresses" the theoretical, critical and textual means by which a translation can be studied as a "locus of difference" (Gentzler 1993: 93), one wonders how one can ever differentiate between a translation and a version, i.e., a text that results from a textual operation which can no longer claim to be in a translation relationship with an original text.

With respect to the three questions (relationship between source and target texts; between texts and persons involved in a translation; delimitation of a translation from other textual operations), we can state that critical post-modern approaches can give no answer to the crucial question of when a text is a translation and when a text belongs to a different textual procedure.

2.6. Linguistically-oriented approaches

Approaches in which the source text — its linguistic and textual structure as well as its meaning potential at various levels — is seen as an important factor in translation, can be found in many different linguistic schools. Linguistic-textual approaches take the relationships between source text and translation text seriously, but they differ in their capacity to provide detailed procedures and techniques for analysis and evaluation. Most promising for translation evaluation seem to be approaches which explicitly take account of the interconnectedness of context and text.

A pioneering linguistically-oriented approach to evaluating a translation is Reiss' (1971) attempt to develop a translation-relevant text typology. Reiss believed that the text type to which the original belongs is the most important invariant for a translation, determining all important subsequent translational decisions. Text types are to be derived from Bühler's three functions of language, yielding the three global textual categories of content-oriented, form-oriented and appellative (conative) texts. Reiss suggested that these textual types were to be upheld in translation, without however — and here the same criticism made above with respect to her later work also holds — giving specific indications as to how precisely one should go about establishing whether and how original and translation are in fact equivalent in terms of textual types (and otherwise).

Other pioneering linguistic work in translation evaluation includes the programmatic suggestions by Catford (1965) and Koller (1979), as well as by scholars in the so-called Leipzig school of translation. In this early work, however, no specific procedures for assessing the quality of a translation were offered.

In more recent times, several linguistically oriented works on translation such as e.g., by Hatim and Mason (1990), Bell (1991), Baker (1992), Doherty (1993), Fawcett (1997) and Gerzymisch-Arbogast and Mudersbach (1998) have made valuable contributions to evaluating a translation by the very fact that all these authors — although not directly concerned with translation quality assessment — widened the scope of translation studies to include recent linguistic concerns with speech act theory, pragmatics, sociolinguistics, stylistics and discourse analysis.

Linguistic approaches take the relationship between source and translation text seriously, but they differ in their capacity to provide detailed procedures for analysis and evaluation. Features of the texts and how they are perceived by language users are mostly well documented, but the consequences of these relationships determining whether a text is a translation or not, have not been a major concern in most of the above studies.

Whenever the "context of situation" is explicitly taken into consideration, features of the texts and how they are perceived by language users are also necessarily accounted for. Attempts to explicitly link text and context, and at the same time take account of the human agents involved in text reception and production operating from a functional-systemic approach provide one of the most fruitful basis for analysing and evaluating source and target texts (see e.g., Steiner 1998 and this volume). Such an approach has been adopted by the present author, who designed a model for translation quality assessment in the mid-seventies (House 1977, 2d. ed. 1981). This model was recently revised (House 1997). It will be described in the next section.

3. A functional-pragmatic model of translation evaluation

3.1. Basic concepts

While the functional model for translation provided by House (1977, 1997) is mainly based on Hallidayan systemic-functional theory, it also draws eclectically on Prague school ideas (functional style and functional sentence perspective, foregrounding etc.), speech act theory, pragmatics, discourse analysis and corpus-based distinctions between spoken and written language. The original model also adapted Crystal and Davy's (1969) register based schema for contrastive stylistic analysis.

The revised model provides for the analysis and comparison of an original and its translation on three different levels: the levels of Language/Text, Register (Field, Mode and Tenor) and Genre. In what follows I give a brief sketch of the model's operation.

One of the basic concepts underpinning the model is "translation equivalence". This concept also underpins our everyday understanding of translation, i.e., "normal", non-linguistically trained persons think of translation as a text which is some sort of "reproduction" of a text originally produced in another language, with the "reproduction" being of comparable value. (This is the result of an infomal interview study conducted by the present author with 20 non-linguistically trained native speakers of German). Over and above its role as a concept constitutive of translation, "equivalence" is also a fundamental notion for translation criticism. Translations must be conceived as texts which are doubly bound: on the one hand to its source text and on the other hand to the (potential) recipient's communicative conditions. This double-linkage nature is the basis of the so-called "equivalence relation". One of the aims of a theory of translation criticism is then to specify and operationalize the equivalence relation by differentiating between a number of frameworks of equivalence, e.g., extra-linguistic circumstances, connotative and aesthetic values, audience design and last but not least textual and language norms of usage that have emerged from empirical investigations of parallel texts, contrastive rhetoric and contrastive pragmatic and discourse analyses.

In a recent attempt to make "a case for linguistics in translation theory", Ivir (1996) expresses the inherent relativity of the equivalence relation very well: "equivalence is ... relative and not absolute, ... it emerges from the context of situation as defined by the interplay of (many different factors) and has no existence outside that context, and in particular ... it is not stipulated in advance by an algorithm for the conversion of linguistic units of L1 into linguistic units of L2" (1996: 155).

The notion of equivalence is the conceptual basis of translation and, to quote Catford, "the central problem of translation-practice is that of finding TL (target language) equivalents. A central task of translation theory is therefore that of defining the nature and conditions of translation equivalence" (1965: 21). But the concept of equivalence is also the basis of translation criticism, it is the fundamental criterion of translation quality.

Equivalence is a relative concept, and has nothing to do with identity. "Absolute equivalence" would be a contradictio in adiecto. Equivalence is a relative concept in several aspects: it is determined by the socio-historical conditions in which the translation act is embedded, and by the range of often irreconcilable linguistic and contextual factors, among them at least the following: source and target languages with their specific structural constraints; the extra-linguistic world and the way it is "cut up" by the two languages resulting in different representation of reality; the original reflecting particular linguistic and stylistic source language norms; the linguistic norms of the translator and the target language and culture; structural features of the original; target language receptors' expectation norms; the translator's comprehension and interpretation of the original and his "creativity"; the translator's explicit and/or implicit theory of translation; translation traditions in the target culture; interpretation of the original by its author.

Given these different types of equivalence in translation, it is clear that — true to the nature of translation as a decision process (Levy 1967) — it is necessary for the translator to make choices, i.e., the translator must set up a hierarchy of demands on equivalence which he wants to follow. It is also clear that the many recent polemical attacks against using the concept of "equivalence" in translation theory, because of its imputed vicinity to "identity" and formal linguistic equivalence, are quite unfounded. Views of equivalence as simply based on formal, syntactic and lexical similarities alone have been criticised for a long time — not least because it has long been recognised that any two linguistic items in two different languages are multiply ambiguous. Further, purely formal definitions of equivalence have long been revealed as deficient in that they cannot explain appropriate use in communicative performance. This is why functional, pragmatic equivalence has been a concept accepted in contrastive linguistics for a long time, and it is this type of equivalence which is most relevant for translation. It is consequently used in the functional-pragmatic model where it is related to the preservation of "meaning" across two different languages and cultures. Three aspects of that "meaning" are particularly important for translation: a semantic, a pragmatic and a textual aspect, and translation is viewed as the replacement of a text in the source language by a semantically and pragmatically equivalent text in the target language. An adequate translation is thus a pragmatically and semantically equivalent one. As a first requirement for this equivalence, it is posited that a translation text have a function equivalent to that of its original. This requirement will later be differentiated given the empirically derived distinction between overt and covert translation, concepts to be discussed below (3.2) in greater detail.

The use of the concept of "function" presupposes that there are elements in a text which, given appropriate tools, can reveal that text's function. The use of the concept of function is here not to be equated with "functions of language" — different language functions clearly always co-exist inside any text, and a simple equation of language function with textual function/textual type (a procedure adopted e.g., by Reiss 1971 and also many others) is overly simplistic. Rather, a text's function — consisting of an ideational and an interpersonal functional component — is defined pragmatically as the application or use of the text in a particular context of situation, the basic idea being that "text" and "context of situation" are not viewed as separate entities, rather the context of situation in which the text unfolds "is encapsulated in the text ... through a systematic relationship between the social environment on the one hand and the functional organisation of language on the other" (Halliday 1989: 11). This means that the text must be referred to the particular situation enveloping it, and for this a way must be found for breaking down the broad notion of "context of situation" into manageable parts, i.e., particular features of the context of situation or "situational dimensions". Inside systemic-functionalist linguistics, many different systems have been suggested featuring situational dimensions as abstract components of the context of situation, as e.g., Crystal and Davy's (1969) scheme which was, in fact, the system adopted and adapted as the basis for the original eclectic model of translation quality assessment by House (1977, 1981).

3.2. The original functional-pragmatic model of translation evaluation

The original assessment model used three dimensions characterising the text's author according to her/his temporal, geographical and social provenance and five dimensions of language use elaborating, for instance, on the text's topic and social activity and on the interaction of, and relationship between, author and recipients in terms of social role relationship, social attitude, degree of participant involvement and orality. The operation of the model involved initially an analysis of the original according to this set of situational dimensions, for which linguistic correlates are established. The linguistic correlates of the situational dimensions are the means with which the textual function is realized, i.e., the textual function is the result of a linguistic-pragmatic analysis along the dimensions with each dimension contributing to the two functional components, the ideational and the interpersonal, in characteristic fashion. Opening up the text with these dimensions yields a specific textual profile which characterises its function, which is then taken as the individual textual norm against which the translation is measured. The degree to which the textual profile and function of the translation (as derived from an analogous analysis) match the profile and function of the original is the degree to which the translation is adequate in quality. The set of situational dimensions is thus a kind of "tertium comparationis", with the model enabling a detailed linguistic-textual analysis by distinguishing for each individual dimension lexical, syntactic and textual means of realizing certain features of the context of situation. In evaluating the relative match between original and translation, a distinction is made between "dimensional mismatches" and "non-dimensional mismatches". Dimensional mismatches are pragmatic errors that have to do with language users and language use, non-dimensional mismatches are mismatches in the denotative meanings of original and translation elements and breaches of the target language system at various levels. The final qualitative judgement of the translation consists then of a listing of both types of errors and of a statement of the relative match of the two functional components.

3.3. The revised model of translation evaluation

In the revised model, the classic Hallidayan concepts of "Field", "Mode" and "Tenor" are used. The dimension of Field captures social activity and topic, with differentiations of degrees of generality, specificity or "granularity" in lexical items according to rubrics of specialised, general and popular. Tenor refers to the nature of the participants, the addresser and the addressees, and the relationship between them in terms of social power and social distance, as well as degree of emotional charge. Included here are the text producer's temporal, geographical and social provenance as well as his intellectual, emotional or affective stance (his "personal viewpoint") vis-à-vis the content he is portraying and the communicative task he is engaged in. Further, Tenor captures "social attitude", i.e., different styles (formal, consultative and informal). Mode refers to both the channel — spoken or written (which can be "simple", i.e., "written to be read" or "complex", e.g., "written to be spoken as if not written"), and the degree to which potential or real participation is allowed for between writer and reader. Participation can be "simple", i.e., a monologue with no addressee participation built into the text, or "complex" with various addressee-involving linguistic mechanisms characterizing the text. In taking account of (linguistically documentable) differences in texts between the spoken and written medium, reference is also made to the empirically established corpus-based oral-literate dimensions hypothesised by Biber (1988). Biber suggests dimensions along which linguistic choices may reflect medium, i.e., involved vs. informational text production; explicit vs. situation-dependent reference; abstract vs. non-abstract presentation of information.

The type of linguistic-textual analysis in which linguistic features discovered in the original and the translation are correlated with the categories Field, Tenor, Mode does not, however directly lead to a statement of the individual textual function. Rather, the concept of "Genre" is newly incorporated into the analytic scheme, "in between", as it were, the register categories Field, Tenor, Mode, and the textual function. The category of Genre is an important addition to the analytic scheme for evaluating a translation in that it enables one to refer any single textual exemplar to the class of texts with which it shares a common purpose. Although the category "register" (Field, Tenor, Mode) captures the relationship between text and context, register descriptions are basically limited to capturing individual features on the linguistic surface. In order to characterise "deeper" textual structures and patterns, a different conceptualisation is needed. This is attempted via the use of "Genre". Genre is thus conceived of as a category superordinate to register. While register captures the connection between texts and their "microcontext", Genre connects texts with the "macrocontext" of the linguistic and cultural community in which texts are embedded. Register and Genre are both semiotic systems realized by language such that the relationship between genre, register and language/text is one between semiotic planes which relate to one another in a Hjelmslevian "content-expression" type, i.e., the genre is the content plane of register, and the register is the expression plane of genre. Register in turn is the content plane of language, with language being the expression plane of register (Martin 1993).

The resultant scheme for textual analysis, comparison and assessment is shown inTable 1 (see next page).

Taken together, the analysis provided in this model yields a textual profile characterising the individual textual function. But as mentioned above, whether and how this textual function can be kept depends on the type of

Table 1. A Scheme for Analysing and Comparing Original and Translation Texts

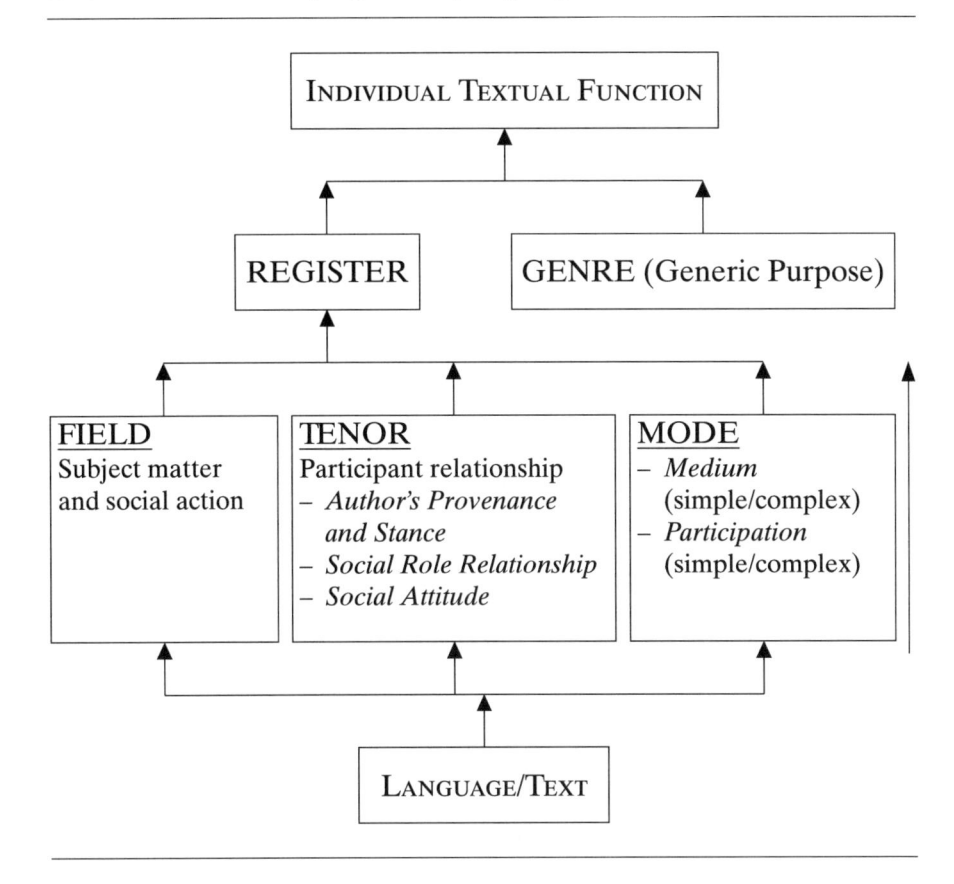

```
                    ┌──────────────────────────────┐
                    │  INDIVIDUAL TEXTUAL FUNCTION │
                    └──────────────────────────────┘
                              ▲         ▲
                    ┌──────────────┐   ┌──────────────────────┐
                    │   REGISTER   │   │ GENRE (Generic Purpose)│
                    └──────────────┘   └──────────────────────┘
                       ▲    ▲    ▲              ▲
```

FIELD	TENOR	MODE
Subject matter and social action	Participant relationship – *Author's Provenance and Stance* – *Social Role Relationship* – *Social Attitude*	– *Medium* (simple/complex) – *Participation* (simple/complex)

```
                    ┌──────────────────────┐
                    │    LANGUAGE/TEXT     │
                    └──────────────────────┘
```

translation sought for the original. In the following section two fundamentally different types of translation and versions will be discussed.

3.4. Two types of translation

The distinction between two different types of translation: overt and covert translation goes back at least to Friedrich Schleiermacher's famous distinction between "verfremdende" and "einbürgernde Übersetzungen", which has had many imitators using different terms. What sets the overt-covert distinction apart from other similar distinctions and concepts is the fact that it is integrated into a coherent theory of translation criticism, inside which the origin and function of the two types of translation are consistently described and explained. The basic distinction is as follows: In an overt translation the receptors of the translation are quite "overtly" not being addressed, an overt translation is thus one which must overtly be a translation, not a "second original". The source text is tied in a specific manner to the source language community and its culture. The original is specifically directed at source culture addressees, but at the same time points beyond the source culture community because it is also of general human interest. Source texts that call for an overt translation have an established worth in the source language community, they are either tied to a specific occasion in which a precisely specified source language audience is/was being addressed or they may be timeless source texts, i.e., those transcending as works of art and aesthetic creations a distinct historical meaning.

A covert translation is a translation which enjoys the status of an original source text in the target culture. The translation is covert because it is not marked pragmatically as a translation text of a source text but may, conceivably, have been created in its own right. A covert translation is thus a translation whose source is not specifically addressed to a particular source culture audience, i.e., it is not firmly tied to the source language and culture. A source text and its covert translation are pragmatically of equal concern for source and target language addressees, both are, as it were, equally directly addressed. A source text and its covert translation have equivalent purposes, they are based on contemporary equivalent needs of a comparable audience in the source and target language communities. In the case of covert translation texts, it is thus both possible and desirable to keep the function of the source text equivalent in the translation text. This can be done by inserting a "cultural filter" (see below for details) between original and translation with which to account for cultural differences between the two linguistic communities.

Translation involves text transfer across time and space, and whenever texts move, they also shift frames and discourse worlds. "Frame" is a psychological concept and it is thus, in a sense, the psychological pendant to the more "socially" conceived concept of context, delimiting, like context, a class of messages or meaningful actions. A frame often operates unconsciously as an explanatory principle, i.e., any message that defines a frame gives the receiver instructions in his interpretation of the message included in the frame. Similarly, the notion of a "discourse world" refers to a superordinate structure for interpreting meaning in a certain way, e.g., as in Edmondson's (1981) discourse model, a locutionary act acquires an illocutionary value by reference to an operant discourse world.

Applying the concepts of frame and discourse world to overt and covert translation, we can state the following: In overt translation, the translation text is embedded in a new speech event, which gives it also a new frame. An overt translation is a case of "language mention" (as opposed to "language use" in the case of covert translation), it is similar to a quotation. Relating the concept of "overt translation" to the four-tiered analytical model (Function — Genre — Register — Language/Text), we can state that an original and its overt translation are to be equivalent at the level of Language/Text and Register as well as Genre. At the level of the individual textual function, functional equivalence, while still possible, is of a different nature: it can be described as enabling access to the function the original has in its discourse world or frame. As this access is to be realized in a different language and takes place in the target linguistic and cultural community, a switch in discourse world and frame becomes necessary, i.e., the translation is differently framed, it operates in its own frame and its own discourse world, and can thus reach at best second-level functional equivalence. As this type of equivalence is, however, achieved through equivalence at the levels of Language/Text, Register and Genre, the original's frame and discourse world are co-activated, such that members of the target culture may "eavesdrop", as it were, i.e., be enabled to appreciate the original textual function, albeit at a distance.

In overt translation, the work of the translator is important and visible. Since it is the translator's task to give target culture members access to the original text and its cultural impact on source culture members, the translator puts target culture members in a position to observe and/or judge this text "from outside".

In covert translation, on the other hand, the translator must attempt to re-create an equivalent speech event. Consequently, the function of a covert translation is to reproduce in the target text the function the original has in its frame and discourse world. A covert translation operates therefore quite "overtly" in the frame and discourse world provided by the target culture, with no attempt being made to co-activate the discourse world in which the original unfolded. Covert translation is thus at the same time psycholinguistically less complex and more deceptive than overt translation. It is the translator's express task to betray the original and to hide behind the transformation of the original, he is clearly less visible, if not totally absent. Since true functional equivalence is aimed at, the original may be legitimately manipulated at the levels of Language/Text and Register via the use of a cultural filter. The result may be a very real distance from the original. While the original and its covert translation need thus not be equivalent at the levels of Language/Text and Register, they have to be equivalent at the levels of Genre and the Individual Textual Function.

In evaluating a translation, it is thus essential that the fundamental differences between overt and covert translation be taken into account. These two types of translation clearly make different demands on translation criticism. The difficulty of evaluating an overt translation is generally reduced in that considerations of cultural filtering can be omitted. Overt translations are "more straightforward", as the originals can be taken over "unfiltered". The major difficulty in translating overtly is, of course, finding linguistic-cultural "equivalents" particularly along the dimension of Tenor and its characterisations of the author's temporal, social and geographical provenance. However, here we deal with overt manifestations of cultural phenomena, which are to be transferred only because they happen to be manifest linguistically in the original. Judging whether a "translation" of e.g., a dialect is adequate in overt translation can ultimately not objectively be given, i.e., the degree of correspondence in terms of social prestige and status cannot be measured in the absence of complete contrastive ethnographic studies — if, indeed, there will ever be such studies. In other words, such an evaluation must necessarily remain subjective to a certain degree. However, as opposed to the difficulty of evaluating differences in cultural presuppositions, and communicative preferences between text production in the source and target cultures, which characterises the evaluation of covert translation, explicit overt transference in overt translation is still easier to judge.

In connection with evaluating covert translations, the translation assessor has to consider the application of a "cultural filter" in order to be able to differentiate between a covert translation and a covert version. In the following section, the concept and function of the cultural filter will be discussed in more detail.

3.5. The concept and function of a "cultural filter"

The concept of a "cultural filter" is a means of capturing socio-cultural differences in expectation norms and stylistic conventions between source and target linguistic-cultural communities. These differences should be based on empirical cross-cultural research. Whether or not there is an empirical basis for changes made along any of the pragmatic parameters is reflected in the assessment of the translation. Given the goal of achieving functional equivalence in a covert translation, assumptions of cultural difference should be carefully examined before any change in the source text is undertaken. The unmarked assumption is one of cultural compatibility, unless there is evidence to the contrary. In the case of the German and Anglophone linguistic and cultural communities evidence of differences in communicative norms seems now available, i.e., the concept of cultural filter has been given some substance and validity through a number of empirical contrastive-pragmatic analyses, in which Anglophone and German communicative differences and priorities along a set of hypothesized dimensions were hypothesized. Converging evidence from a number of cross-cultural German-English studies conducted with different data, subjects and methodologies suggests that there are German communicative preferences which differ from Anglophone ones along a set of dimensions, among them directness, content-focus, explicitness and routine-reliance. (For a summary of this research see House 1996.)

For the comparative analysis of source and target texts and the evaluation of covert translations, it is essential to take into account whatever knowledge there is about cultural differences between target and source communities. It must be stressed at this point that there exists far too little empirical research in the area of language-pair specific contrastive pragmatic analysis — in fact, empirical research in this area seems to be one of the major research desiderata in translation studies for the coming millennium.

3.6. Distinguishing between different types of translations and versions

Over and above distinguishing between covert and overt translation in translation criticism, it is necessary to make another important distinction: between translations and versions.

Overt versions are produced whenever a special function is overtly added to a translation text. There are two different cases of overt version production: 1. when a "translation" is produced which is to reach a particular audience. Examples are special editions for a youthful audience with the resultant omissions, additions, simplifications or different accentuations of certain features of the source text etc., or popularisations of specialist works (newly) designed for the lay public, and 2. when the "translation" is given an added special purpose. Examples are interlingual versions or "linguistic translations", resumés and abstracts, where it is the express purpose of the version producer to pass on only the most essential fact of the original.

A covert version, on the other hand, results whenever the translator — in order to preserve the function of the source text — has applied a cultural filter non-objectively and consequently undertook changes on the situational dimensions, i.e., the original has been manipulated with this manipulation not being substantiated by research.

In discussing different types of translations the distinction between a translation and a version, we implicitly assume that a particular text may be adequately translated in only one particular way. The assumption that a particular text necessitates either a covert or an overt translation does, however, not hold in any simple way. Thus any text may, for a specific purpose, require an overt translation, i.e., it may be viewed as a document which "has an independent value" existing in its own right, e.g., when its author has become, in the course of time, a distinguished figure, and then the translation should be evaluated as an overt translation.

There may also well be source texts for which the choice overt-covert translation is a subjective one, e.g., fairy tales may be viewed as products of a particular culture which would predispose the translator to opt for an overt translation, or as non-culture specific texts, anonymously produced, with the general function of entertaining and educating the young, which would suggest a covert translation. Or consider the case of the Bible, which may be treated as either a collection of historical literary documents, in which case an overt translation would seem to be called for, or as a collection of human truths directly relevant to all human beings, in which case a covert translation might seem appropriate.

Further, the specific purpose for which a "translation" is produced, i.e., the particular brief given to the translator, will, of course, determine whether a translation or an overt version should be aimed at. In other words, just as the decision as to whether an overt or a covert translation is appropriate for a particular source text may depend on factors such as the changeable status of the text author, so clearly the initial choice between translating or version-producing, cannot be made on the basis of features of the text, but may depend on the arbitrarily determined purpose for which the translation or version is required.

Returning to the three basic issues with reference to translation criticism — relationship between original and translation, between texts and human agents, distinction between translation and other secondary textual operations — addressed initially in order to assess the differences in theoretical and empirical potential between different approaches to translation criticism, the assessment model presented above is firmly based on a view of translation as a double-linkage operation. As opposed to views that show a one-sided concern with the translation, its receptors and the translation's reception in the target culture, the model attempts to take account of both source and target texts by positing a cline along which it can be shown which tie of the double-linkage has priority in any particular translation case — the two endpoints of the cline being marked by the concepts overt translation (source text focussed) and covert translation (target text focussed). The relationship between features of the text(s) and the human agents involved (as author, translator, reader) is explicitly accounted for through the provision of an elaborate system of pragmatic-functional analysis of original and translation, with the overt-covert cline on which a translation is to be placed determining the type of reception sought and likely to be achieved. Finally, explicit means are provided for distinguishing a translation from other types of textual operation by specifying the conditions holding for a translation to turn into a version.

Integrating cultural filters that are empirically verified into the evaluation process might be taken to mean that there is greater certainty as to when a translation is no longer judged to be a translation but rather a covert version. True, in the past twenty years the field of contrastive pragmatics has begun to make an important contribution to assessing covert translations in a non-arbitrary way. However, given the dynamic nature of socio-cultural and communicative norms and the way research necessarily lags behind, translation critics will have to struggle to remain abreast of new developments if they want to be able to fairly judge the appropriateness of changes through the application of a cultural filter in a translation between any given language pair.

4. Testing the model: Analysing the translation of a children's book

The analysis of the original text and its translation is based eclectically on Neo-Firthian grammar, rhetorical-stylistic concepts, and concepts and notions adapted from the Prague school of linguistics, as well as from speech act theory, pragmatic and discourse analysis. On each of the dimensions FIELD, TENOR, MODE, I differentiate lexical (choice and patterns of lexical items, collocations, co-occurrence etc.), syntactic (parataxis, hypotaxis, nature of the verb phrase, mood, tenses, etc.), and textual means (cohesion and coherence, theme dynamics, clausal and iconic linkage) although it might not always be the case that all categories are found to be operative on a particular dimension. The terminology will be as in Table 1 above, with sub-categories of FIELD, TENOR and MODE printed in italics.

In order to be able to make grounded statements about why and how a translation is "good", both source and translation text will be analysed at the same level of delicacy, and the translation text will then be compared with the source text's textual profile.

In the following I will try out the above model with an analysis and comparison of an English children's book: *Peace at Last* by Jill Murphy and its German translation *Keine Ruh für Vater Bär* (see appendix for the two texts; numbers refer to lines in the texts).

4.1. Analysis of original

FIELD
The original is a short picture book for 2 to 6 year olds. It presents a harmless, peaceful family idyll in the form of a story about a bear family: *Mr.*

Bear, *Mrs. Bear* and *Baby Bear*. The plot is simple, an everyday experience is described: Mr. Bear can't sleep, wanders about the house, and finally drops off to sleep back in his own bed only to be woken up by the alarm clock. He is comforted, however, by Mrs. Bear and a nice cup of tea — a simple story full of warmth and gentle humour, just right for a bedtime story for young children. The title of the book "Peace at last" is well in line with this characterisation.

Lexical Means:
Preponderance of lexical items that are likely to be part of the nascent verbal competence of young children developed in interactions in the immediate hic-et-nunc environment, i.e., their home and neighbourhood surroundings*: tired, go to bed, fall asleep, sleep, snore, Baby Bear's room, living-room* etc.

Syntactic Means:
Short clauses with simple structures throughout the text.

Textual Means:
Strong textual cohesion which makes the text easily comprehensible and digestible for young children. Textual cohesion is achieved through a number of different procedures, most prominently through iconic linkage and theme dynamics.

Iconic Linkage:
There is iconic linkage between many clauses in the text highlighting (for the children's benefit) a reassuring similarity, and thus recognizability of states and actions, and also heightening the dramatic effects, as for instance in:
2, 3: *Mr. Bear was tired. Mrs. Bear was tired; Baby Bear was tired.*
6, 10, 13, 16, 21, 27: *Oh NO! I can't stand THIS.*
6, 11, 14, 17, 22, 28: *So he got up and went to sleep in Baby Bear's room (the living room, the kitchen, in the garden, in the car). So he got up and went back into the house.*

Theme Dynamics:
Thematic movement frequently arranged in sequences of theme-rheme movements to ensure given-new ordering, e.g., 28–29; foregrounded rhematic fronting in all clauses with onomatopoetic items: 9, 12, 15, etc. for dramatic effect.

TENOR

Author's Temporal, Geographical and Social Provenance
Unmarked, contemporary, standard middle-class British English.

Author's Personal (Emotional and Intellectual) Stance
The author views the characters she creates with a warm sense of humour, empathy and involvement, without becoming sentimental. The characters keep their dignity and are not infantilized.

Lexical Means:
Characters keep their names including titles: *Mr.* and *Mrs. Bear*, which results in a neutral, detached manner of description that also adds a humorous note, considering that the characters are "teddy bears".

Syntactic Means:
Monotonous repetition of phrases for humorous effect, e.g.: 34, 35: *Did you sleep well — Not VERY well.*

Social Role Relationship
Author-reader: symmetric, intimate relationship between both types of addressees, i.e., adults (parents and other caretakers) and children, no "talking down", no evidence of educational, pedagogic motivation, no hidden, ideologically induced lecturing.

Author-characters in the story: respect for individuality of characters through leaving titles and generic terms (*Mrs. Bear*), sympathy, empathy.

Characters amongst themselves: tolerance, sympathy, irony and good humour.

Lexical Means:
Title and names (*Mr., Mrs. Bear*) throughout the text for humorous effect.
34, 35: Use of address form "dear" to create intimacy.

Syntactic Means:
18: Direct address of readers creates involvement and intimacy.

Textual Means:
34–35: Presence of ritualized move "How-are-you" and ritualized second-pair part (*Not very well*) as well as ensuing uptake (*never mind*) to provide stark contrast to the preceding story of Mr. Bear's misery and thus has humorous effect.

37: Short-clipped final phrase to seal the preceding promising move: also closing and "sealing" the relationships in comfort, intimacy and reassurance.

Social Attitude
Informal style level: conversational, intimate style characterising the type of talk occurring in a family.

Syntactic Means:
Simplicity of clauses, co-ordination rather than subordination, simplicity of noun phrases, lack of pre- and post-modification.

Lexical Means:
Use of lexical items marked as informal through their use in familiarity inducing settings; onomatopoetic elements e.g., DRIP, MIAAOW, followed by informal "*go*" in the past tense ("*went*"); informal conjunction "*So*".

MODE
Medium: Complex
"Written to be read aloud as if not written", creating for the young listener the illusion that the person doing the reading aloud is inventing it simultaneously with the reading, i.e., real-life spontaneous oral language is being simulated. Along Biber's three (oral-written) dimensions: involved vs. informational, explicit vs. situation dependent, abstract vs. non-abstract, this picture book can be located at the involved, situation-dependent, and non-abstract end of the cline.

Syntactic Means:
Frequency of short co-ordinated clauses linked with *and*; use of conjunction *so* characterising spoken language.

Phonological Means:
Presence of emphatic stress frequent in oral encounters, and marked in writing through capitalisation (e.g., *BRRRRR went the alarm clock*).

Textual Means:
Ample use of repetition for redundancy throughout the text in order to make comprehension easier for young readers/listeners.

Participation
Complex: monologue with built-in (fictional) dialogic parts.

Lexical Means:
Use of *well*, a token typically used at the beginning of a response in a dialogue (18).

Syntactic Means:
Presence of rhetorical, addressee-directed utterance (18).

Textual Means:
Heavy use of direct speech designed to increase listeners'/readers' involvement in the story. This direct speech includes a deliberate "animation" of the animals and the objects such as the tap and the living-room clock that are depicted as emitting (intentionally?) noises in a way suggesting interaction with Mr. Bear.

GENRE
Picture book for young children designed to be read aloud by adults, often as a bed time story. The "communicative purpose" of such a book is to entertain children, comfort and reassure them, and (maybe) also "elevate" i.e., educate them. In the English tradition, children's books often use humour to gently socialise the young into family life and the world beyond. The text is supported by pictures. I have omitted them here as they do not add anything that the words themselves do not make explicit. In fact the pictures are the same in the original and the German translation.

STATEMENT OF FUNCTION
The function of the original text consisting of an ideational and an interpersonal functional component may be summed up as follows: Although the ideational functional component is not marked on any of the dimensions, it is nevertheless implicitly present, in that the text informs the readers about certain social activities and events involving the protagonists depicted in the text, in other words, it tells a story! However, the ideational component is clearly less important than the interpersonal one, which is marked on all the dimensions used for the analysis of the text.

The particular GENRE, picture books written for young children, determines that the interpersonal function is primary, its purpose being to provide reassurance and comfort, a sense of belonging, and increased understanding of how the world around the child functions.

On FIELD, too, the interpersonal component is strongly marked: The description of a typical piece of family life, where a member of the family experiences a sleepless night, is presented in a light-hearted, good-natured, long-suffering and humorous way, making the story amusing, entertaining and easily comprehensible. On TENOR, the author's personal stance as well as the particular social role relationship and social attitude evident in the text strongly mark the interpersonal functional component: The relationship between both author and reader, and between the (fictional) characters are characterised by good humour. The informal style level also clearly feeds into the interpersonal functional component by enhancing the text's intimate humorously human quality. On MODE, the medium characterised as "written to be read as if not written" marked as involved, situation-dependent and non-abstract, as well as the many stretches of simulated speech (monologue and dialogue) clearly also strengthen the interpersonal function because of the emotive effect of spontaneous immediacy and directness.

4.2. Comparison of original and translation and statement of quality

As opposed to the original, the translation is far from presenting a peaceful family idyll, already the translation's title: *Keine Ruh für Vater Bär* points to a rather different story, i.e., the translation transforms the original's positive soothing atmosphere into a "negative" one, falsely ironic and "funny" in the sense of the German *Schadenfreude*, i.e., enjoying another person's misery. In the translation one recognises a motive found in many post-68 German children's books (see House forthcoming): a deliberate attempt to reach what is (presumably) perceived as a pedagogically desirable goal, namely to encourage children to "emancipate themselves", i.e., to stand up to their parents. This ideological stance is expressed in a forcedly ironic and "funny" storyline which (barely) cloaks a clear didactic mandate. The original's harmless, peaceful story is changed into a series of minor disasters. This impression is substantiated by the following individual mismatches along Field, Tenor, Mode, and Genre.

FIELD
Textual Mismatches:
Loss of Cohesion: the onomatopoetic lexical items are not consistently rendered: (28/29): *Und die Sonne schien immer heller* vs. (26) *SHINE, SHINE went the sun*, presumably in an attempt to "correct" the original in that the sun does not make noises and should therefore (presumably) not be presented in the same vein as the other noise making objects in the story. This mismatch results in a loss of humour, precisely because the imaginative agency of the sun is omitted.

The consistent use of an equivalent of the conjunction *so* throughout the text is not kept up in the translation: apart from some repetitions of the phrase *dort wollte er schlafen* at the beginning of the text (7, 11, 15, 18) different structures are used. Thus, for example (22): *So he went off to sleep* is rendered as (23): *Er stand auf und ging in den Garten* or (28): *So he got up and went back into the house* is turned into (30): *Er stieg aus und ging ins Haus*.

Syntactic Mismatches:
The use of onomatopoeia in English is based on "normal", i.e., lexicalized verbs (e.g., *snore, drip, snuffle*), the German "equivalents" often resemble infantilized comic-strip-like interjections (*sch-sch-sch, schnüff-schnüff*).

TENOR
Author's Personal (Emotional and Intellectual) Stance
Loss of humour, sentimentalization and infantilization of characters in the story.

Lexical Mismatches:
The characters *Mr. Bear, Mrs. Bear*, and *Baby Bear* are changed into the sentimentalized and infantilized German collocation*s Vater Bär, Mutter Bär, Baby Bär*. This change also means a loss of humour, created in English precisely through the clash between the titles *Mr., Mrs.* and the fact that we are here dealing with teddy bears functioning also as children's toys.

Syntactic Mismatches:
Clause structures are even simpler than in the English original, i.e., two simple short clauses are made out of one longer co-ordinated one: (6/7*):
So he got up and went to sleep in Baby Bear's room* vs. *Er stand auf und ging ins Kinderzimmer. Dort wollte er schlafen.*

Social Role Relationship
Between author and readers, between author and the protagonists, and between the protagonists: These three role-relationships are clearly interdependent such that the relationship between the protagonists is a reflection of the author's assessment of her readers and her view of her characters. The relationships are changed quite radically in the German translation, witness the following mismatches.

Textual Mismatches:
The German translation transforms the book's positive atmosphere into a negative one. To start with, the original's title *Peace at last* is turned into *Keine Ruh für Vater Bär*, a total contradiction of the original's title. And in keeping with the German title's ominous prediction (which flies in the face of the original's hopeful promise) a consistently negative storyline is continued until the end of the story, which is also the very opposite of "peaceful". Compare here lines 34 to 37 in the original with the German text's lines 28–34. The entire sequence starting with *Und die Post* is invented, and added by the translator (presumably on the basis of the final picture in the book, in which an official-looking envelope can be detected).

At the end of the original story, the mother is nice, warm, friendly (*never mind, ... a nice cup of tea*), and her final words *and she did* indicate that she brings the tea as a "sealing" comfort. In the German translation, however, the clause *Warte, ich bring dir das Frühstück ans Bett* merely hints that this act is part of her sober daily routine.

Lexical Mismatches:
Framed by the major manipulations of title and ending, the body of the German text contains a pattern of negativisation and problematisation, and it is not only the relationship between father and son that is presented in a negative and problematic way but also the relationship between mother and father. Implicitly authoritarian role-relationships are therefore built into the translator's version of the story. The very first sentence: *The hour was late* is translated in such a way as to evoke a different role-relationship between parents and child: *Es war Schlafenszeit*, this clause implies a parental regime (when it's late and dark, children must be in bed asleep), where the English original remains a neutral statement. As noted above, the "neutral" Mrs. and Mr. Bear become Mutter and Vater Bär, which typecasts them exclusively as parents. Similarly, Baby Bear's room becomes *das Kinderzimmer,* a generic term, i.e., the room is then not an individual's room but belongs to someone in the role of a child, the role relationship between child and parent then being marked as fixed and normative.

Further, the use of the German expressions *mein Lieber* und *meine Liebe* (29/30) helps to disrupt the harmony of the happy family idyll portrayed in the English original. Despite the deceptive formal equivalence between *my dear* and *mein(e) Liebe(r)*, these phrases are certainly not pragmatically equivalent. *Mein Lieber* has a distinctively ironic (not humorous!) overtone.

30: The uncaring and dismissive phrase *Macht nichts* is also clearly not equivalent with *never mind*. In fact, *macht nichts* is much more direct, and less concerned and polite. The use of *macht nichts* and *warte* by the German Mutter Bär in particular give her a superficial and indifferent air: whereas in English *never mind* relates to alter (*never you mind*) and is thus comforting, the German *macht nicht*s refers to self, (*das macht mir nichts aus*) a crucial difference not only in terms of perspective but also in terms of illocutionary force.

8: *(Baby Bär) lag im Bett und spielte Flugzeug* is different from *Baby Bear was lying in bed pretending to be an aeroplane* in that the German expression implies a division between the world of adults and the world of children, the latter "playing at things". In the English original, Baby Bear is taken more seriously, treated more as an equal. The German translation infantilizes and sentimentalizes the character. Similarly, (24)

He was just falling asleep is rendered with a metaphorical expression typically used in German child-talk (25) *die Augen fielen ihm zu.*

The "bourgeois" family is presented in the German translation as a unit which allows for no peace, and Mr Bear, who in English (30) *got into bed and closed his eyes, schlüpfte unter die Decke und seufzte tief* in German (32/33), and he is not content to *yawn* as he is allowed to do in the English original, rather he must grumble: (36) *brummte Vater Bär.*

At the very end of the story (40) the compound noun *Parksünder* (followed and intensified by the collocation *Parksünder Daddy* (40) epitomizes the "Schadenfreude" and the forcedly funny one-up-manship of the child over his father.

MODE
Participation
In one instance ((18) in the original, (19) in the translation), the attempt, via a rhetorical question, to directly involve participants is not kept up in the translation. Instead, the German translation presents an impersonal, rather laid back statement with an initial informal, regional starter *tja.*

GENRE
In as much as the translation is still a children's picture book to be read to young children, there has been no change in the GENRE of the translation. However, the "framing" is very different in the text: both title and ending set a very different tone: a humorous, innocent book to be read with pleasure, amusement and joy is turned into an ideologically laden, pedagogically motivated book embued with a certain forced wit, and a trend to infantilize the protagonists in the story through lexical and textual means.

As the analysis of a larger corpus (n= 62) of German-English and English-German translations of children's books has revealed (House forthcoming), there seem to be patterned differences between texts in this Genre in the two linguistic and cultural communities. In German children's books there seems to be a tendency to depict a type of role relationship between children and adults in much the same way as was outlined above, i.e., there is more sentimentalization, more infantilization as well as less (and different) humour, greater explicitness and a greater need to impose edifying pedagogic ideas and ideologies on the stories told in German children's books.

STATEMENT OF QUALITY
The analysis of original and translation has revealed mismatches along the dimensions of FIELD, MODE and in particular TENOR, with a consequent substantial change of the interpersonal functional component of the text's function. On FIELD, loss of cohesion was established in several

cases detracting from the aesthetic and emotive pleasure a well-knit text will elicit.

On TENOR, the author's stance is changed such that the translation loses the original's subtle and warm humour superimposing instead a new note of infantilization and sentimentalization onto the text through syntactic simplification and changes of protagonists' names and titles. Most incisive however are the changes in the social role relationship portrayed in the original and the translation: the original's positive reassuring atmosphere is transformed into a negative one. "Schadenfreude" is substituted for comfort and friendliness. Children are depicted as generically different from adults and a more authoritarian relationship and, consequently, a general "negativisation" and "problematisation" of the role relationship between all the story's characters is implied, such that "no peace" can be found — a situation which may have been designed as "funny", but is, if pitted against the original, clearly the very opposite.

If we interpret the above results in the light of the analyses of a larger corpus of German and English children's books (House forthcoming), they reflect a culturally conditioned, ideologically tinted difference in the realization of GENRE between English and German children books. This difference is most clearly visible in the different framing in the German translation: the title and the end of the German story guide the reader/listeners along a different path than is suggested in the original.

These differences may be interpreted as reflecting differences in German and English communicative preferences and norms established in cross-cultural research (see e.g., House (1996)). For a full understanding of these culture-conditioned differences, however, one would need much more data, and a comprehensive comparative analysis of the various strands of intellectual, artistic, economic, legal and socio-political forces in the two cultures in question and their influence on text production and reception. Such a broad ethnographic approach coupled with a detailed linguistic analysis may be less utopian than it may seem. It certainly is the most promising and fruitful way of relating context to text, and text to context.

The German translation analysed above can be described as a covert translation, in which a cultural filter has been applied. One wonders, however, why the translator or the publisher had not opted for an overt translation. It is a sad truth that translators of children's books seem to feel particularly licensed to produce covert translations making changes whenever they think these are appropriate thus barring children from access to the original's voice. Children are often totally underrated in their imaginative and learning capacities. Their natural curiosity and their desire to be exposed to strange, foreign and different worlds and norms is simply overrun.

One reason for this tendency to adapt original texts to the receiving cultures' dominant GENRE may be the current one-sided, often dogmatic reception-oriented, hermeneutic climate, which needs, in the opinion of this author, to be counteracted by solid text- and context-based linguistic analyses.

5. Possibilities and impossibilities of translation criticism

In translation criticism it is important to be maximally aware of the difference between (linguistic) analysis and (social) judgment, i.e., there is a difference between comparing, describing and explaining differences established in linguistic analysis and judging "how good a translation" is.

Instead of taking the complex psychological categories of translation receptors' intuitions, feelings, reactions or beliefs as a cornerstone for translation criticism, the above model's functional-pragmatic approach focusses on texts, i.e., products of human decision processes. Such an approach, however, cannot ultimately enable the evaluator to pass judgments on what is a "good" or a "bad" translation. In the last analysis, any evaluation depends on a large variety of factors that necessarily enter into a social evaluative judgement. An evaluative judgment emanates from the analytic, comparative process of translation criticism, i.e., the linguistic analysis provides grounds for arguing an evaluative judgment. As intimated above, the choice of an overt or a covert translation depends not on the translator alone or on the text to be translated, or on her subjective interpretation of the text, but also on the reasons for the translation, the implied readers, on publishing and marketing policies, i.e., factors which have nothing to do with translation as a *linguistic* procedure. Such factors are social factors, which concern human agents as well as socio-cultural, political or ideological constraints and which are often more influential than linguistic considerations or the translator herself. However, despite all these "external" influences, translation is at its core a linguistic-textual phenomenon, and it can be legitimately described, analysed and evaluated as such. More forcefully argued, the primary concern for translation critics remains linguistic-textual analysis and comparison. A consideration of social factors is, if it is divorced from textual analysis, of secondary relevance. Linguistic description and explanation must not be confused with evaluative assertions made on the basis of social, political, ethical or individual grounds. It seems imperative to emphasize this distinction given the current climate in which the criteria of scientific validity and reliability are often usurped by criteria such as social acceptability, political correctness, vague emotional commitment or fleeting zeitgeist tastes. Translation as a phenomenon in its own right, as a linguistic-textual operation should not be confused with issues such as what the translation is for, what it should, might, or must be for. One of the drawbacks of an overriding concern with covert translation is that the borders between a translation and other multilingual textual operations become blurred. In view of this confusion some conceptual clarity can be reached by theoretically distinguishing between translations and versions and by positing functional equivalence as a sine qua non in translation.

The core concept of translation criticism is translation quality. This is a problematical concept if it is taken to involve — as it mostly, and informally, is — individual value judgments alone. It is of course extremely difficult to pass any "final judgment" of the quality of a translation that fulfils the demands of scientific objectivity. This should not, however, be taken to mean that translation criticism as a field of inquiry is worthless. But one should be aware that in translation criticism one will always be forced to move from a macro-analytical focus to a micro-analytical one, from considerations of ideology, function, genre, register to the communicative value of individual linguistic items. In taking this dual, complementary perspective, the translation critic will be enabled to approximate the reconstruction of the translator's choices and to throw some light on his decision processes in as objective a manner as possible. That this is a complex undertaking which, in the end, yields but probabilistic outcomes, should not detract from its usefulness. In translation criticism, one should try to reveal, in any individual case, exactly where and with which consequences and (possibly) for which reasons (parts of) translated texts are what they are in relation to their "primary texts". Such a modest goal might guard the translation evaluator against making prescriptive, apodictic and global judgments (of the "good" vs. "bad" type), which are not intersubjectively verifiable.

The difference between linguistic analysis and value judgement is often ignored when one talks about the quality of a translation. Both components, the linguistic and the judgemental are, of course, implicit in translation evaluation, but they should not be mixed up, nor should the evaluative component be used in isolation from the linguistic component.

In summary and to conclude, translation criticism, like language itself, has two basic functional components, an ideational and an interpersonal one, which lead to two separable steps: the first and primary one referring to linguistic analysis, description and explanation based on knowledge and research, the second and secondary one referring to value judgments, social, interpersonal and ethical questions of relevance and personal taste. Without the first, the second is useless, in other words, to judge is easy, to explain and understand less so. In other words, we know when a translation is good, when we are able to make explicit the grounds for our judgement on the basis of a theoretically sound and argued set of procedures.

Appendix:

Source Text:
Jill Murphy 1980 *Peace at Last*. London: Macmillan.

1 The hour was late.
2 Mr. Bear was tired, Mrs. Bear was tired and
3 Baby Bear was tired, so they all went to bed.
4 Mrs. Bear fell asleep. Mr. Bear didn't. Mrs. Bear began to snore. "SNORE,"
5 went Mrs. Bear, "SNORE, SNORE, SNORE."
6 "Oh NO!" said Mr. Bear, "I can't stand THIS." So he got up and went to sleep
7 in Baby Bear's room.
8 Baby Bear was not asleep either. He was lying in bed pretending
9 to be an aeroplane. "NYAAOW!" went Baby Bear, "NYAAOW! NYAAOW!"
10 "Oh NO!" said Mr. Bear, "I can't stand THIS."
11 So he got up and went to sleep in the living-room.
12 TICK-TOCK …went the living-room clock …TICK-TOCK, TICK-TOCK.
13 CUCKOO! CUCKOO! "Oh NO!" said Mr. Bear,
14 "I can't stand THIS." So he went off to sleep in the kitchen.
15 DRIP, DRIP …went the leaky kitchen tap.
16 HMMMMMMMMMMM …went the refrigerator. "Oh NO," said Mr. Bear,
17 "I can't stand THIS." So he got up and went to sleep in the garden.
18 Well you would not believe what noises there are in the garden at night.
19 "TOO-WHIT-TOO-WHOO!" went the owl.
20 "SNUFFLE, SNUFFLE," went the hedgehog.
21 "MIAAOW!" sang the cats on the wall. "Oh, NO!" said Mr. Bear, "I can't stand
22 THIS." So he went off to sleep in the car.
23 It was cold in the car and uncomfortable, but Mr. Bear was so tired that
24 he didn't notice. He was just falling asleep when all the birds started
25 to sing and the sun peeped in at the window. "TWEET TWEET!" went the birds.
26 SHINE, SHINE …went the sun.
27 "Oh NO!" said Mr. Bear, "I can't stand THIS."
28 So he got up and went back into the house.
29 In the house, Baby Bear was fast asleep, and Mrs. Bear had
30 turned over and wasn't snoring anymore. Mr. Bear got into bed and closed
31 his eyes. "Peace at last," he said to himself.
32 BRRRRRRRRRRRRRR! went the alarm-clock, BRRRRRR!
33 Mrs. Bear sat up and rubbed her eyes.
34 "Good morning, dear," she said. "Did you sleep well?"
35 "Not VERY well, dear," yawned Mr. Bear.
36 "Never mind," said Mrs. Bear. "I'll bring you a nice cup of tea."
37 And she did.

Translation Text:
Jill Murphy 1981 *Keine Ruh für Vater Bär*. Translation by Ingrid Weixelbaumer. Wien/ München: Annette Betz Verlag.

1 Es war Schlafenszeit.
2 Vater Bär war müde. Mutter Bär war müde und Baby Bär war müde ... also gingen
3 sie alle ins Bett. Mutter Bär schlief sofort ein. Vater Bär nicht.
4 Mutter Bär begann zu schnarchen. "SCH-CH-HHH", machte Mutter Bär.
5 "SCH-CHCH-HHH, SCH-CHCHCH-HHH" "Oh, NEIN!" sagte Vater Bär.
6 "DAS halte ich nicht aus." Er stand auf und ging ins Kinderzimmer.
7 Dort wollte er schlafen.
8 Baby Bär schlief auch noch nicht. Er lag im Bett und spielte Flugzeug.
9 "WIEEE-AUUU, WIEEE-AUUU-UMM!" "Oh, NEIN" sagte Vater Bär.
10 "DAS halte ich nicht aus." Er stand auf und ging ins Wohnzimmer.
11 Dort wollte er schlafen.
12 TICK-TACK ... machte die Kuckucksuhr im Wohnzimmer...TICK-TACK,
13 TICK-TACK, KUCKUCK! KUCKUCK! "Oh, NEIN!" sagte Vater Bär.
14 "Das halte ich nicht aus." Er stand auf und ging in die Küche.
15 Dort wollte er schlafen.
16 TROPF, TROPF ... machte der undichte Wasserhahn. HMMMMMMMMMMMM... machte der Kühlschrank.
17 "Oh, NEIN!" sagte Vater Bär. "DAS halte ich nicht aus."
18 Er stand auf und ging in den Garten. Dort wollte er schlafen.
19 Tja, nicht zu glauben, was es da an Geräuschen gibt, nachts im Garten.
20 HUH-WITT-HUHUHUHHH!" machte die Eule. "SCHNÜFF, SCHNÜFF" machte der Igel.
21 "MIAAU!" sangen die Katzen auf der Mauer. "Oh, NEIN!" sagte Vater Bär.
23 "DAS halte ich nicht aus." Er stand auf und ging zu seinem Auto.
24 Es war kalt und ungemütlich im Auto. Aber Vater Bär war so müde,
25 daß er es gar nicht merkte. Die Augen fielen ihm zu. Er war schon fast
26 eingeschlafen, da finden die Vögel zu singen an, und die Sonne blinzelte
27 zum Fenster herein.
28 "ZIWITT ZIWITT!" zwitscherten die Vögel, und die Sonne schien
29 immer heller. "Oh, NEIN!" sagte Vater Bär. "DAS halte ich nicht aus."
30 Er stieg aus und ging ins Haus zurück.
31 Alles war still und friedlich. Baby Bär schlief fest, und Mutter Bär
32 hatte sich umgedreht und schnarchte nicht mehr. Vater Bär schlüpfte unter
33 die Decke und seufzte tief. "Endlich Ruh' im Haus!" sagte er zu sich.
34 BRRRRRRRRRRR! machte der Wecker. BRRRRR! Mutter Bär rieb sich die Augen
35 und gähnte. "Guten Morgen, mein Lieber" sagte sie. "Hast du gut geschlafen?"
36 "Nicht SEHR, meine Liebe", brummte Vater Bär. "Macht nichts", sagte Mutter Bär.
37 "Warte, ich bring dir das Frühstück ans Bett."
38 "Und die Post!" rief Baby Bär.
39 "Oh, NEIN!" sagte Vater Bär, als er den Polizeistempel sah.
40 "PARKSÜNDER!" rief Baby Bär. "Parksünder-Daddy!".

References

Baker, Mona
    1992   *In Other Words. A coursebook on translation.* London: Routledge.

Biber, Douglas
    1988   *Variation Across Speech and Writing.* Cambridge: Cambridge University Press.

Bell, Roger
    1991   *Translation and Translating.* London: Longman.

Bühler, Axel
    1998   Vier Vorurteile über Hermeneutik — Eine Polemik. In: Bernulf Kanitschneider and Franz Josef Wetz (eds.), *Hermeneutik und Naturalismus*, 83–97. Tübingen: Mohr Siebeck.

Carroll, John
    1966   An Experiment in Evaluating the Quality of Translations. *Mechanical Translation* 9: 55–66.

Catford, John
    1965   *A Linguistic Theory of Translation.* Oxford: Oxford University Press.

Crystal, David and Derek Davy
    1969   *Investigating English Style.* London: Longman.

Doherty, Monika
    1993   Parametrisierte Perspektive. *Zeitschrift für Sprachwissenschaft* 12: 3–38.

Edmondson, Willis
    1981   *Spoken Discourse. A Model for Analysis.* London: Longman.

Fawcett, Peter
    1997   *Translation and Language. Linguistic Theories Explained.* Manchester: St. Jerome Press.

Gentzler, Edwin
    1993   *Contemporary Translation Theories.* London: Routledge.

Gerzymisch-Arbogast, Heidrun and Klaus Mudersbach
    1998   *Methoden des wissenschaftlichen Übersetzens.* Tübingen: Francke.

Halliday, Michael A.K.
    1989   *Spoken and Written Language.* Oxford: Oxford University Press.

Hatim, Basil and Ian Mason
    1990   *Discourse and the Translator.* London: Longman.

House, Juliane
    1977   *A Model for Translation Quality Assessment.* 2d. ed. 1981. Tübingen: Narr.

House, Juliane
    1996   Contrastive Discourse Analysis and Misunderstanding. The Case of German and English. In: Marlis Hellinger and Ulrich Ammon (eds.), *Contrastive Sociolinguistics*, 345–361. Berlin: de Gruyter.

House, Juliane
1997   Translation Quality Assessment: A Model Revisited. Tübingen: Narr.

House, Juliane
forthcoming   Cross-Cultural Pragmatics and Translation. Oxford: Oxford University Press.

Ivir, Vladimir
1996   A Case for Linguistics in Translation Theory. Target 8: 149–157.

Levy, Jiri
1967   Translation as a Decision Process. In: To Honor Roman Jakobson on the Occasion of his Seventieth Birthday. vol. 2, 1171–1182. The Hague: Mouton.

Koller, Werner
1992   Einführung in die Übersetzungswissenschaft. 4th ed. (1st ed. 1979). Heidelberg: Quelle und Meyer.

Koller, Werner
1995   The Concept of Equivalence and the Object of Translation Studies. Target 7: 191–222.

Martin, James R.
1993   A Contextual Theory of Language. In: Bill Cope and Mary Kalantzis (eds.), The Powers of Literacy: A Genre Approach to Teaching Writing, 116–136. London: Falmer.

Nida, Eugene
1964   Toward a Science of Translation. Leiden: Brill.

Nida, Eugene and Charles Taber
1969   The Theory and Practice of Translation. Leiden: Brill.

Reiss, Katharina
1971   Möglichkeiten und Grenzen der Übersetzungskritik. München: Hueber.

Reiss, Katharina and Hans Vermeer
1984   Grundlegung einer allgemeinen Übersetzungstheorie. Tübingen: Niemeyer.

Robinson, Douglas
1997   Translation and Empire. Postcolonial Theories Ex-plained. Manchester: St. Jerome Press.

Steiner, Erich
1998   A Register-Based Translation Evaluation: An Advertisement as a Case in Point. Target 10: 291–318.

Stolze, Radegundis
1992   Hermeneutisches Übersetzen. Tübingen: Narr.

Toury, Gideon
1995   Descriptive Translation Studies and Beyond. Amsterdam: Benjamins.

Venuti, Lawrence
1995   The Translator's Invisibility. A History of Translation. London: Routledge.

Intralingual and interlingual versions of a text — how specific is the notion of *translation*?

Erich Steiner

> We started the last division on a paradoxical quest: how to translate untranslatable phrases and words. Our argument, which incidentally enabled us to solve the riddle of the paradox landed us in another apparent antinomy: words are the elements of speech, but words do not exist. Having once recognised that words have no independent existence in the actual reality of speech, and having thus been drawn towards the concept of context, our next step is clear: we must devote our attention to the intermediate link between word and context, I mean to the linguistic text. (Malinowski 1935: 23)

1. Introduction[1]

In this paper, an attempt will be made to relate the notion of "versions" of a text to the notions of *textual variation* and *translation* as relationships between texts. Section 1, after introducing the notion of *register*, illustrates intralingual versions of a text, discussing a small set of English texts and a small set of German texts in turn. Within each set, the texts can informally be said to be versions of each other. We shall then argue that this informal notion of version can be more technically analysed as a relationship of register variation within these intralingual sets. Section 2, by contrast, will focus on interlingual versions, especially translations, arguing that here, again, we find register-variation, this time across texts realized in different lexicogrammatical systems (languages). In particular, it will be seen that translated texts are registerial variants of each other, but so are other, e.g. co-generated, texts in different languages. We thus want to draw attention to the relationship between translation and multilingual generation. Chapter 3 will then pose the central question of this paper: Can translation be comprehensively modelled by conceptualising it as (restricted) register variation plus realization in different language systems of some invariant *ideational*, i.e. propositional, content, or is translation as a relationship between texts characterised by specific and different properties? We shall start with an inspection of passages from an original English advertising text and from its original German translation. This will be followed by some observations on these two texts which will show that the translated text has properties beyond those of a registerial variant in a different language system. We shall then suggest three alternative translations of our English original, two of them as translations on the *semantic level* and a third one as a translation on the *lexicogrammatical level*, in order to show that the notion of translation needs to be defined with reference to some (stratified) model of language and texts, rather than simply in the pre-theoretical sense of "being produced in a process called translation". In chapter 4, we shall produce further monolingual registerial variants of our translated passages, thereby illustrating the fact that whereas register variation is an overriding phenomenon within sets of intertextually related texts, those texts that are in a specific relationship of translation with each other have additional characteristic properties which are not found in the same distribution in co-generated registerial variants. Section 6 will relate the notions of *translation, paraphrase*, and *variation* to each other, before finally raising the question of what the specific challenges are of the phenomenon of translation for a linguistic theory, such as *Systemic Functional Linguistics*.

The question of what the specific properties of translated texts are has long been at the centre of attempts at modelling translation (cf. Baker 1995, Koller 1995, 1992: 80–89, House 1997: 24–28, George Steiner [1975] 1992: 28–40, Wilss 1977: 279–80, Neubert 1986). We shall attempt to address this question in an example-based way, using notions from Systemic Functional Linguistics (cf. Halliday 1994, Halliday and Hasan 1989, Martin 1992, Halliday and Matthiessen 1999), register theory in general (Biber 1993), but also language typology (Hawkins 1986) and its implications for translation studies (Doherty 1991, 1993, Matthiessen's and Teich's contributions to the current volume) as our theoretical background. We are also much indebted to efforts in translation studies using concepts from Systemic Functional Linguistics (cf. Catford 1965, Hatim and Mason 1990, Bell 1991, House 1997, Taylor 1998, Taylor-Torsello 1993, Munday 1997, Spence 1998). Some of our own earlier attempts can be seen as directly related to the present paper (cf. Steiner 1991, 1997, 1998a, 1998b, 2000).

2. Intralingual versions of texts and the notion of register

This section will begin with a brief explanation of the notion of *register* (cf. also Steiner 1998a: 292–295). Illustrations of register variants will then be given in the form of excerpts from three English and three German advertising texts, taken from one series of *Rolex* advertisements. Some passages of the German texts are translations from English texts, others are written as German original passages, but all of them are intertextually related, being parts of one series. Our focus in this section will be on the intralingual relationships, i.e. on the texts within each of the two language sets as registerial variants of each other. For reasons of practicality, and because we shall be concentrating on the linguistic texts in this paper, rather than on their interaction with visual codes, we shall not reproduce the original formatting of the texts (for which the reader is referred to my own papers referred to above and Plenker 1994 for examples D2,3 and E2,3 below).

Before proceeding with an illustration of our small intralingual sets of versions of a text, let us give a short introduction to the notion of *register*

Register theory, as formulated in Halliday, McIntosh and Strevens (1964), and Halliday and Hasan (1989), should not be seen as yet another view of textual and linguistic variation competing with others for the same conceptual space. It is, rather, a theoretically motivated view of contexts of situation, how texts are embedded therein, and what systematic relationships there are to the lexicogrammar of natural languages. The work of House (1997 and this volume) provides an insightful and creative exploration of the concept in translation quality assessment. The contributions of Matthiessen and of Teich in this volume situate the notion of register within overall models of language, and of translation.

For present purposes, let us regard the register of a text as constrained by the variety of a given language which this text instantiates. We shall furthermore assume that this variety is best conceptualised as a registerial sub-grammar of the overall language. The text itself can be seen as classified in terms of a number of interrelated properties, or feature combinations, which are derivable from this sub-grammar. We shall furthermore assume that these properties are indicative of, or make reference to, some context of situation in which the text may be said to function. The text is thus of a certain type, or register.

The register itself will be discussed in terms of the three major dimensions of variation, *field*, *tenor* and *mode* of discourse, which are common to all versions of the theory. We shall, on the next level of delicacy, assume a few sub-dimensions for each of these three variables, which vary somewhat across versions of register theory, but not too widely.

Finally, it may be said that an almost unique characteristic of the concept of register is to be found in the theoretically motivated realization relationships between register and the lexicogrammar of languages, most clearly as relationships between field, tenor, mode of discourse on the one hand, and the general language functions *ideational, interpersonal, textual* in the grammar.

The first variable under field of discourse is *experiential domain*. This is what is frequently referred to as "subject field" or "subject matter" elsewhere. Its most direct realizations in lexicogrammar are the structure of lexical fields set up in texts, terminologies, if they have already been established for a domain, lexical and other referential chains in texts, as well as headings of various types, paragraphing, transitivity of clauses, expressions of time, sometimes perspective and Aktionsart.

Also under field of discourse, as a second variable, we find *goal orientation*, sometimes subdivided into short term goal and long term goal. We assume that the notion of goal is one that can be applied in various degrees of granularity (cf. Steiner 1991: 84–101). Granularity here translates into different ranks on which a text structure can be discussed, i.e. the text as a whole, paragraphs and clause complexes. Some of the more prominent lexicogrammatical realizations of goal structure include clause mood, presence or absence of ellipsis of some types, tense selection, transitivity, in particular agency patterns, patterns of identifiability, types and realization of conjunctive relations, patterns of thematic progression, typical patterns of topic construction, and certainly paragraphing in written texts. We would like to draw attention to the fact that these patterns run across entire texts and paragraphs, defining properties of entire discourses rather than being segmental parts which can easily be localised in only one unit or constituent of a text or sentence.

The third variable under field of discourse is *social activity*, i.e. general types of activity which are recognized across a society as meaningful and which can be related directly to needs in a society. Examples are activities such as production, exchange, communication, reproduction, consumption, etc., or their subtypes. Any text and its lexicogrammatical properties are partly constrained by which of these activities it is part of or a realization of. For example, a text about a given domain will have very different properties, depending on whether it is an advertising text, i.e. part of an exchange of commodities, or whether it is an instruction for production of those commodities.

Let us next turn to a discussion of tenor of discourse. The first variable, *agentive roles*, refers to semiotic roles assigned through the text to author and reader/ hearer, such as vendor vs. customer; giver vs. receiver; sayer vs. listener; teacher vs. learner etc. Important lexicogrammatical realizations are mood selections, ellipsis, modality, the use of specialist language, options in key, etc.

The second variable under tenor, *social role*, categorises various dimensions along which a text or discourse encodes social power relationships between participants. Most human societies are stratified into types of social hierarchies according to various dimensions. Some of the more important hierarchies have to do with social class, gender, level of expertise, age, ethnicity, religious affiliation etc. The basic options here seem to be equal vs. unequal, and then subtypes of these. Major lexicogrammatical realizations of such choices are located in the interpersonal systems of the grammar, but also in systems structuring texts and dialogues in response to hierarchies between participants.

The third variable under tenor is *social distance*. It stands for the amount of shared contextual space which the participants assign to themselves and to each other. It is determined, in the first instance, by the frequency and range of previous interaction. Realizations include tagging, modality, use of forms of address, use of accents and dialects, use of sociolects etc.

Sometimes (e.g. in the work of Martin 1992: 533–535) a fourth variable is introduced under tenor, which is the variable *affect*. This variable is used to control variation as to negative/positive affect, towards self/other, and permanent/transient (more delicate distinctions have been elaborated since).

The final register variable to be discussed here will be the mode of discourse, i.e. the encoding and maintaining of texts and discourses in terms of the role language is playing, the channel used for communication, and the medium of discourse.

In terms of *language roles*, the endpoints on a cline of orientations would be something like constitutive vs. ancillary. Texts differ depending on whether they are part of a linguistic activity (constitutive), or a non-linguistic activity (ancillary). In terms of lexicogrammatical realization, some of the systems involved would be ellipsis, mood, theme, and reference.

In terms of *channel* of discourse, what is at issue is the physical channel employed for the particular stretch of discourse under investigation. Major possible options are sound waves, electronic channels, paper, telephone lines etc. The various types of channel are of interest here to the extent that they offer and constrain choices in meanings and their realizations. A channel which does not allow face-to-face interaction, for example, limits the use of gesture and body-language in communication, but may allow other things instead, such as parallel display of texts, etc.

Finally, in terms of *medium* of discourse, the major variables are spoken vs. written. Patterns of realization involved are use of pronouns vs. full words, exophoric vs. endophoric reference, types of cohesion in general, certain types of clause complexity, etc. Figure 1 below is a graphic representation of the distinctions just made in our explanation of the notion of register

In our present attempt to clarify the notions of *register* and *translation*, one of the interesting questions is that of whether a register analysis overconstrains a translation. In other words, do the values that our register variables have taken in the source language text have to remain unchanged in translation? For instance, if a given source language text in its tenor encodes social distance as minimal, does that imply, for any translation of that text, that this variable has to remain constant? Quite obviously, if there were a built-in assumption of that nature, it would be a source of over-constraining, because due to changes in other register variables, e.g. the goal under the field of discourse, any of the variables, and therefore any property of the text, may have to change. The concept of register has no such built-in assumption, however. It simply provides a meta-language to raise the question. Having said this about register analysis in its application to translation, it can be seen as a prototypical case of translation, rather than multilingual text production, that the register remains relatively constant (cf. also Halliday's contribution, this volume). To the extent that we require a notion of translation which is separate from other forms of multilingual text production, a relative stability of register across source texts and target texts may be assumed to be a criterion. The more register variables change, the more the resulting text will not be a translation in the narrower sense.

Let us now move on to a brief consideration of a small set of English texts, explaining in what sense they are registerial variants of each other:

(1Ea): *A Rolex does more than just tell you the time* (Newsweek, 24.2.1992)

> *Even as you read these words someone, somewhere on this planet will be venturing into the unknown.*
> *They might be at sea — a tiny speck in the ocean aboard a frail craft inching its way across the Pacific*
> *Or deep below the surface of the water, probing Earth's inner space.*
> *Or weathering a dust storm in the pitiless heat of an unmapped desert.*
> *Or braving temperatures 60 degrees below freezing as they urge their dog-sled across the Polar ice-cap.*
> *Only a fool would enter the inhospitable environments that these people seek out without weeks, months, or even years of preparation.*
> ...
> *The sheer ability of a Rolex Oyster to keep going under the most severe conditions is legendary. Only the strong survive. And, to ensure this, the case of every Oyster is hewn from a solid block of stainless steel, 18ct gold, or platinum. This operation involves pressures of up to sixty tons.*
> *Such force is necessary because what is being created is, itself, massively strong.*

Example (1Ea) above contains two short excerpts from a Rolex advertisement, the first excerpt from the beginning, the second one roughly from the middle of the text (for a comprehensive analysis of the whole text cf. Steiner 1997). We shall be using most of the second passage from this excerpt later on in our detailed investigations of whether translation is only restricted register variation plus realization in different lexicogrammatical systems (cf. texts (1Eb-d) and their translational counterparts in German below).

(2E): *Why explorers are willing to stake their lives on a Rolex* (Time International, No. 41/93)

> *Part of what makes a Rolex so dependable is the design of its rugged case, which is sculptured from a solid block of metal, using as much as sixty tons of pressure.*
> *Such force is necessary because what is being produced is, itself, massively strong. It has to be; inside every Oyster case beats a movement that has taken a year to make, from the first operation on the first tiny part through to final assembly by our craftsmen in Geneva.*

This excerpt comes from a second English advertisement in the same series. The full advertisement structures its relationship between written and visual messages quite differently from the full text (1E) in terms of overall lay-out (i.e. the language role under mode of discourse is quite different), but it preserves its experiential domains to a very considerable extent, as well as much of the tenor, down to extended verbatim citations of parts of (1Ea).

(3E): *Aquanaut Sylvia Earle probes earth's other space* (The Economist, 3.10.1992)

> *In Maui a woman hangs suspended in the depths of the Pacific, eye to eye with the great humpback whales of Hawaii.*
> ...
> *For her deepest dive — 1,250 feet down to the floor of the Pacific — Dr. Earle relied on a massive diving suit to protect her in such an alien environment. In just such a way, the Rolex that Dr. Earle wears relies on its massively strong case to protect the delicate movement within. Indeed, so rugged is the Oyster case that sculpting it from a solid block of metal requires pressures of up to sixty tons.*

Example (3E) above varies more than (2E) in terms of register, relative to (1Ea). Whereas the general experiential domains are preserved (Rolex watches and Challenging Adventures), there are few verbatim quotations, and subdomains differ substantially, e.g. the adventurers themselves, especially in terms of gender. There are also interesting changes in terms of tenor, in so far as this advertisement partly addresses the female gender rather than the male. On the other hand, there are still enough commonalities between the texts to justify regarding them as strongly related intertextually, possibly even as different variants of one text. Do they share a super- and/ or sub–text? This is not the topic of the present paper, but is highly relevant in studies of translation and ideology.

Let us now move on to an inspection of a small set of German texts, asking the question again of whether and in what sense they may be considered to be registerial variants. Translations of the German examples will not be given locally, because the issue is exactly to what extent they

168   Erich Steiner

are translations of our English examples (1Ea)-(3E) (cf. also our discussion of interlingual versions below):

(1Da): *Die Zuverlässigkeit, der man sogar sein Leben anvertraut.* (Der Spiegel 21/93)

> *Seit Menschengedenken wird die Welt erforscht und neu entdeckt. Suchen Menschen die Herausforderung ihrer selbst. Überwinden alte Grenzen, um neue zu stecken.*
> *Nur die Kühnsten unter ihnen erreichen ihr Ziel. Ein Ziel, dessen Weg von Dramatik und extremen Strapazen geprägt ist.*
> *Die Ausrüstung für diese abenteuerlichen Expeditionen wird mit größter Sorgfalt zusammengestellt. Denn nicht selten entscheidet sie über Leben und Tod. Kein Wunder, daß sich viele Abenteurer und Entdecker für eine Rolex Oyster entschieden haben.*
> ...
> *Die Stärke einer Rolex Oyster, egal welchen Bedingungen und Situationen sie auch ausgesetzt wird, ist legendär.*
> *Das Gehäuse jeder Oyster ist aus einem massiven Metallblock herausgearbeitet oder aus 18karätigem Gold oder Platin geformt. Ein Vorgang, bei dem ein Druck von bis zu 60 Tonnen ausgeübt wird.*
> ...
> *Uhren, die als präzise Zeitmesser arbeiten, gibt es viele. Aber nur wenigen vertraut man sein Leben an.*

Example (1Da) above is an excerpt from a text which, as a whole text, was produced as a translation from a text from which (1Ea) is an excerpt (for a comprehensive analysis of the entire text cf. Steiner 1998a). As we shall see below, the claim that this is a translation has to be relativised: on the one hand, there are passages in the full German text which are newly produced rather than translated (such as the beginning of (1Da)), and on the other, as we shall argue below, even in the passages that were "translated", there are types of changes which are not necessary in a translation. At the moment, though, our focus is on the relationships between the German texts (1Da — 3D) intralingually.

(2D): *Warum Entdecker ihr Leben einer Rolex anvertrauen* (Der Spiegel 24/93)

> ...
> *Doch Leistungsstärke und Perfektion kommen nicht von ungefähr. Die Zuverlässigkeit einer Oyster fängt schon bei der Herstellung des Gehäuses an: Es wird mit einem Druck von sage und schreibe 60 Tonnen aus einem massiven Metallbock gestanzt. So entsteht ein perfekter Schutzmantel, in dem das hochentwickelte Uhrwerk seine Arbeit aufnehmen kann. Ein Mechanismus, der so akribisch gefertigt wird, daß unsere Uhrmacher in Genf bis zu einem Jahr für dessen Herstellung benötigen.*
> ...
> *Uhren, die als präzise Zeitmesser arbeiten, gibt es einige. Aber nur wenigen vertraut man sein Leben an.*

Text (2D) is closely related to (1Da) in terms of register variables, except for the language role under mode of discourse, and except for the fact that the experiential domains, for the whole text rather than for this excerpt, represent a sub-set of those of (1Da). Parts of (2D) are verbatim citations from (1Da), but most passages are not. So, informally speaking, it is not simply the case that (2D) is a collection of excerpts from (1Da). Rather, (2D) is a registerial variant of (1Da), with the occasional verbatim citation as the limiting case.

(3D): *Aquanautin Sylvia Earle — Raumforscherin der Tiefe* (Reiter Revue No. 10/90)

> Vor der Insel Maui hängt in der Tiefe des Pazifiks eine Frau an einem Seil — Auge in Auge mit einem riesigen Buckelwal.
> ...
> Mit ihrer fast unerschöpflichen Energie engagiert sich Dr. Sylvia Earle vehement für die Erhaltung des ökologischen Gleichgewichts der Meere. Für den Schutz deren Flora und Fauna. Für die Rettung der bedrohten Wale. Dazu katalogisiert sie Meereslebewesen und hilft bei der Entwicklung von neuen Geräten zur Erkundung der noch unberührten Welten unter Wasser. Daß Dr. Sylvia Earle auf eine Rolex vertraut, ist keine Überraschung. Wer in seiner Tätigkeit auf Perfektion und Zuverlässigkeit setzt, macht auch bei seiner Uhr keine Kompromisse.

(3D) stands in much the same relationship to (1Da) and (2D) as (3E) stands to those of the English set. However, (3D) is in no way a translation of (3E). Substantial passages differ completely between the two texts, both in the full versions and in the excerpts given here.

In what sense, then, are the 3 texts within each of the language specific sets registerial variants of each other?

Assume we are using a notion of register as a 10-dimensional space within which to model textual variation in contexts of situation (cf. also House 1997, as well as her contribution to this volume). Figure 1 below gives a schematic overview of this notion, as we have introduced it above.

Within each of the two language-specific sets of texts given above, all the texts are closely related registerial variants of each other. They share parts of their experiential domains, goals and activities (field), they also share characteristics of their agentive roles, social roles, social distance, and encoded affect (tenor), and they are of similar registers in terms of their language role, medium and channel (mode). In other words, sets of intralingually related texts such as the ones illustrated here are not simply either the same or different — rather, they share parts of their textual properties, which is why they may be called informally "versions" of each other. There is an associated question of what the difference may be between different texts, and different versions of "a text", a question which

```
                              ┌─ experiential
                              │   domain           ┌─ instruction
                              │                    ├─ persuasion
                              │                    ├─ argumentation
                              │   ┌ goal           ├─ description
                              │   │ orientation    ├─ exposition
                      field   │◄──┤                ├─ narration
                        ──────┤   │                └─ ...
                              │   │
                              │   │
                              │   └ social
                              └─ activity


                                                      ┌─ information giver vs. seeker
                              ┌─ agentive roles ─────►│
                              │                       └─ ...                    ┌─ higher or same
                              │                              ┌─ authority ─────►│
                      tenor   │                              │                  └─ ...         ┌─ ...
                        ─────►│─ social roles ──────────────►│─ expertise ───────────────────►│
                              │                              │                                └─ higher
                              │                              │   level of             ┌─ ...       or same
                              │─ social distance ─► ┌─ low   └─ education ───────────►│
                              │                     └─ high                           └─ higher or same
                              └─ affect


                                                    ┌─ constitutive
                              ┌─ language role ────►│
                              │                     └─ ancillary
                              │                                      ┌─ graphic
                      mode    │─ channel ──────────────────────────►│
                        ─────►│                                      └─ phonic
                              │
                              │                     ┌─ written
                              └─ medium ───────────►│
                                                    └─ spoken
```

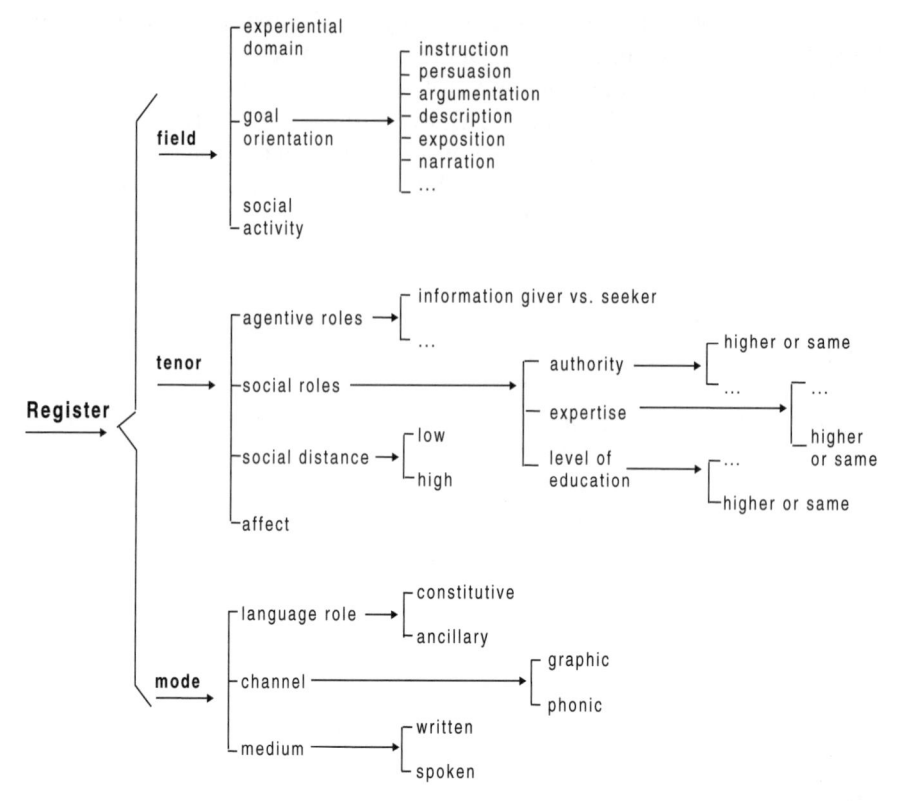

Figure 1. Register

we cannot go into here, but which we have addressed, using a related set of texts, in a different investigation (cf. Steiner 1998b).

3. Interlingual versions

Moving on to a consideration of the full set of 6 texts presented above, we note that corresponding pairs of English-German texts are partly translations, in an informal sense. Where this is the case, the direction was from English to German. Still, the linguistic texts overall vary to different degrees: in the first pair ((1Ea), (1Da)), the linguistic text of the full advertisement is largely a translation, in the second pair ((2E), (2D)) less so, and least of all in the third ((3E), (3D)). The overall visual and graphic design of matching texts (not displayed in this paper), an important aspect of their respective modes of discourse, are almost identical. Example (2D) above is particularly noteworthy, in that it is taken from an advertisement which preserves the layout of that of (2E) almost completely. On a superficial view, the texts from which (2E) and (2D) are taken look very much like translations — except that upon closer examination, e.g. in our passages quoted here, we can see that the linguistic texts are reminiscent more of loose "versions" than of translations in any stricter sense. Examples (3D) and (3E) are relevant to our present discussion in yet a different way: as far as the full texts are concerned, these look again very similar, almost identical, in terms of general layout, so that mode variables are held constant to a considerable degree. The same applies to the tenor variables. However, the experiential domains are only the same on a very general level, and hardly a single clause of (3D) is actually translated, or encodes the same message as any of the clauses in its parallel (3E).

Let us, for a moment, concentrate on those passages which are translations in the narrower sense. Are they passages which preserve the register and only have an encoding in the different language systems of English and German respectively? This does not seem to be the case, in the sense that a full preservation of register is not given even in translated passages. On the other hand, the variation that we observe seems to be less than the variation within the intralingual sets. And, very importantly, the members of each pair in our interlingual set have registers related to different contexts of culture.

All register variables are systematically linked to their lexicogrammatical realization, which is strongly language-specific. From this it follows that lexicogrammatical patterns, even where they realize very similar registers of two texts in a translation relationship, are necessarily different. Minimally, i.e. even in cases in which literal translation is applied as a global strategy for a text (cf. Vinay and Darbelnet 1958: ch. 1.4.1.), the two texts are differentiated by the application of obligatory translation procedures.

What we have illustrated so far, then, is that the translated passages in our little set above are similar in register, though not identical. We have also pointed out that lexicogrammatical structures are, of course, widely different between translated pairs, and we have at least hinted at the possibility that the apparent similarity in register of translated passages may be interestingly problematic, because the registers are linked to respectively different contexts of culture. The following section will attempt to substantiate our claims about register and translation in some detail.

4. Is translation (only) restricted register variation plus realization in different lexicogrammatical systems?

In this section, we shall try to identify a specific relationship of *translation* between texts by investigating in some detail properties of translated passages, attempting to contrast these passages with other passages which are registerial variants, sometimes in different languages, yet not translations.

We shall argue that translation can be conceptualised at different linguistic levels: lexicogrammar, semantics, or register, with resulting differences in translation strategies and evaluation criteria (cf. also Halliday this volume; for the model architecture, and particularly for the linguistic levels assumed cf. the overviews of Systemic Functional Linguistics in Teich's and in Matthiessen's contributions to this volume).

We shall start with a short passage from the original English advertising text (1Ea). This excerpt will be referred to as (1Eb) in subsequent parts:

(1Eb) *The sheer ability of a Rolex Oyster to keep going under the most severe conditions is legendary. Only the strong survive. And, to ensure this, the case of every Oyster is hewn from a solid block of stainless steel, 18ct gold, or platinum. This operation involves pressures of up to sixty tons.*

The German original translation of this passage, i.e. a version which was produced in a process called "translation", is given below:

(1Db) *Die Stärke einer Rolex Oyster, egal welchen Bedingungen und Situationen sie auch ausgesetzt wird, ist legendär. Das Gehäuse jeder Oyster ist aus einem massiven Metallblock herausgearbeitet oder aus 18karätigem Gold oder Platin geformt. Ein Vorgang, bei dem ein Druck von bis zu 60 Tonnen ausgeübt wird.*

We give a literal back-translation into English of the German passage in (1Ec) below. By "literal back-translation" we mean a translation which makes all and only those adjustments which are obligatory because of lexicogrammatical constraints of the target-language system. In terms of modelling in Systemic Functional Linguistics, we are producing a translation with our focus on the lexicogrammatical level.

(1Ec) *The strength of a ROLEX Oyster, no matter what conditions and situations it is subjected to, is legendary. The case of every Oyster is produced from a massive metal block or formed from 18ct gold or platinum. A process, in the course of which a pressure of up to 60 tons is exercised.*

What we can see immediately in (1Ec) is that this back-translation is a registerial variant of the English original (1Eb), and in particular a variant with a few idiosyncratic properties, yet it is not the original English text of (1Eb). What does this tell us about the nature of translation? Obviously, there is no bi-uniqueness between passages of texts standing in the relationship of translation. But we shall attempt to go a bit further than this obvious statement. Our assumption is that a) the relationship between corresponding lexicogrammatical constructions between the two languages is not one-to-one, but many-to-many, and b) the translation between two texts has properties additional to the closest possible lexicogrammatical correspondences. What are these properties? Our two assumptions a) and b) together should account for the differences between (1Eb) and (1Ec).

The following are some relevant observations on the translation (1Db) quoted above, observations of a kind which have been made about translations in general before, and which we exemplify here to take stock of possible properties of translated texts before proceeding further to modelling these (cf. Baker 1995, Toury 1995: 259–280 and Fawcett 1997: 100 for an overview).

– The German translation is almost as long in terms of number of words (46 words) as the English original (52 words), although the following passages (12 words) are left out: *sheer, to keep going, only the strong survive, and, to ensure this*. We shall add some remarks about the final unsuitability of using "number of words" as a measure of "length" of translations in section 5 of this chapter, but let us stay with it for the moment, and postpone discussions of more theoretically motivated criteria until later.

– Several lexicogrammatical realizations encoding high affect (tenor of discourse) have disappeared from the German (cf. some of those just listed, as well as *is hewn from*) .

– The German passage is shifted in terms of the goal (field of discourse) from the persuasive and argumentative region of the cline of text-types to the more descriptive region by the dropping of the conjunctive/ extensional (*and*) and purpose *(to ensure this)* conjuncts, or adjuncts, depending on one's analysis of purpose adjuncts in the grammar.

– The German translation disambiguates, and specifies some elements of its portrayed states of affairs, or *figures* in the sense of semantics, more clearly cf. *"Das Gehäuse jeder Oyster ist aus einem massiven Metallblock herausgearbeitet oder aus 18karätigem Gold oder Platin geformt." ("is produced from a massive metal block or formed from 18ct gold or platinum"),* cf. also *"egal welchen Bedingungen und Situationen sie auch ausgesetzt wird (no matter what conditions ...in" (1Ec)).*

– We notice a slight shift away from unmarked written language through the use of an ellipsis at the end of the German text, which is actually an observation counteracting the effects of the other observations made here, because at this point the German translation has features of markedness not present in the English.

– In the English original, the referent of the Subject in *Only the strong survive* is ambiguous between some 'adventurers' and the 'Rolex Oysters', an ambiguity which does not cause any disturbance in the interpretation, because in English, for typological reasons, either is acceptable. The literal translation in (1De) below as *nur die Starken überleben* is problematic in that it either enforces some human beings as agents, or else the Rolex Oysters, which latter, however, feels strongly and inelegantly metaphoric (both in terms of *lexical metaphor* and of *grammatical metaphor* as used by Halliday (1994: 340–368), cf. Hawkins 1986: 53–74, Doherty 1993: 9–11 for a discussion of the typological basis of the phenomenon between English and German). The actual translation reviewed here (1Da) avoids the problem by leaving out this passage altogether.

Observations such as those above have been made about translated texts before. What we would like to emphasise at this point is that these observations are not random and coincidental. Textual properties of translations — other than arbitrary changes or lexicogrammatical mistakes — are not due to some individual "fault" of the translator, but point to inherent properties of translations, as we hope to demonstrate further below. It is those translation-specific properties which are responsible for many of the differences that the back-translation (1Ec) shows respective to (1Eb). We shall now present three alternative translations of the same passage which are the results of attempting to base the translation strategy on the level of semantics in the first and second case ((1Dc)) and its variant (1Dd)), and on the level of lexicogrammar in the third (1De)). This should serve as an illustration of our claim that, given a target-culture oriented translation strategy, a semantically-based translation will on the one hand avoid arbitrary changes in a translated text, and it will avoid typologically-caused weaknesses of the target text on the other. However, it will still show traces of the translation-specific processes of understanding and of a tendency towards unmarked texts.

The first of these translations is an attempt to create a German translation, holding values constant on the level of semantics (cf. Halliday and Matthiessen 1999 for ideational semantics, Martin 1992 for interpersonal and textual, Ramm, Rothkegel, Steiner and Villiger 1995: 34–43 for specifically thematic meaning; the contribution by Teich in this volume gives an overview of the architecture of the Systemic Functional model, and the place of semantics within it). Note that there would be a small set of alternatives within the set of semantically-based translations of such a passage, and we shall point to one or two of them in our subsequent discussion.

(1Dc) Schon die Eigenschaft einer Rolex Oyster, auch unter den härtesten Bedingungen funktionsfähig zu bleiben, ist legendär. Qualität ist die beste Garantie! Und, um dies sicherzustellen, fertigen wir das Gehäuse jeder Oyster aus einem massiven Block von rostfreiem Stahl, 18karätigem Gold, oder Platin. Bei diesem Prozeß entsteht ein Druck von bis zu 60 Tonnen.

A literal, i.e. lexicogrammatical back-translation into English, given below as (E1d), is meant to illustrate the results of our semantically-based strategy for readers without a knowledge of German:

(E1d) Even the property of a Rolex Oyster to remain able to function even under the most severe conditions is legendary. Quality is the best guarantee! And, to ensure this, we produce the case of every Oyster from a massive block of stainless steel, 18ct gold, or platinum. In this process (there) develops a pressure of up to sixty tons.

Let us add a short commentary to the semantically-based translation suggested here, repeating the original English passage (1Eb) for ease of reference:

(1Eb) The sheer ability of a Rolex Oyster to keep going under the most severe conditions is legendary. Only the strong survive. And, to ensure this, the case of every Oyster is hewn from a solid block of stainless steel, 18ct gold, or platinum. This operation involves pressures of up to sixty tons.

We have translated *The sheer ability of a Rolex Oyster* as *Schon die Eigenschaft einer Rolex Oyster, auch* ... The grammatical epithet *sheer* in this case has the semantic function of focusing on its phrase. In our translation, we have preserved this semantic function, choosing the focusing-adverb combination *schon...auch,* which seems better in German than the collocationally awkward formulation chosen in our literal translation in (1De) below.

To keep going has been translated as *funktionsfähig zu bleiben.* The reason is that *to keep going* in English is a *material doing process* grammatically, one which takes an *actor* as its first role. German does not easily allow this process type with inanimate referents as actors, or if such a construction is chosen, it reads more metaphorical than in English (cf. Doherty's (1993: 8) "inadvertent personification"). We have therefore decided to change the experiential grammar of the English clause from an *action* process with only an *Actor* into a *relational* process type with a predicative adjective as *Value/Subject Complement* in addition to the Subject, a structure which collocates well grammatically with the semantically inanimate referent *Rolex Oyster.*

Only the strong survive has been translated as *Qualität ist die beste Garantie.* The (inter-)textual motivation here is that the English phrase seems to be something of a cliché, which is why we have chosen one for German as well, assuming that we want to preserve the affectual meaning of using a cliché. We have already given the typologically motivated reason why it is better to avoid the *material process "survive"* of the English version in (1Eb) above. Thereby, of course, we are sacrificing the thematic progression of the original at this point, a question of the trade-off between locally maintaining thematic progression on the one hand and maintaining affect and degree of markedness on the other.

The grammatically passive *the case of every Oyster is hewn...* receives a translation as *fertigen wir das Gehäuse jeder Oyster...*, with the verbal group in active voice grammatically. The reason here is that both the English and the German sentences take a hypotactically dependent enhancing clause of purpose *(to ensure this/ um dies sicherzustellen)*. Semantically, purpose clauses, and to a somewhat lesser extent grammatical purpose adjuncts expressed as phrases, presuppose a conscious *Actor,* which is encoded through arbitrary reference in English. This kind of arbitrary reference in passives is sometimes felt to be stylistically awkward in German, which is why we have chosen an active and specific, even if pronominal, reference. We are paying the price, though, of not being able to preserve the somewhat literary affectual heightening of the English *is hewn from* here. An alternative, preserving the affectual semantics of *hewn* better, as well as local thematic progression, would be something like *und deswegen ist das Gehäuse jeder Oyster aus ... geschaffen.* The resulting translation may actually be preferable, as a semantically-based translation:

(1Dd) Schon die Eigenschaft einer Rolex Oyster, auch unter den härtesten Bedingungen funktionsfähig zu bleiben, ist legendär. Qualität ist die beste Garantie! Und deswegen ist das Gehäuse jeder Oyster aus einem massiven Block von rostfreiem Stahl, 18karätigem Gold, oder Platin geschaffen. Bei diesem Prozeß entsteht ein Druck von bis zu 60 Tonnen.

Aus einem massiven Block von rostfreiem Stahl, 18karätigem Gold, oder Platin in our semantically-based German versions preserves the semantic ambiguity of the English, rather than attempting to resolve it.

This operation involves pressures of up to sixty tons is translated as *Bei diesem Prozeß entsteht ein Druck von bis zu 60 Tonnen.* The motivation comes again largely from a typological comparison of English and German: the relational process of the English version cannot easily be used in German, because German does not as easily allow the conflation of a semantic process, or event, with the grammatical participant role of *Carrier,* as in English. We have therefore chosen to de-metaphorize the construction into the *material event* Process of the German version, which involves a complete re-conflation of participant roles and syntactic functions. Observe that the thematic structure in terms of Theme and Rheme now remains as in English.

What we hope to have demonstrated in (1Dc) and (1Dd) above is that a preservation of the semantics of a text is possible under translation, and that a translation strategy based on the semantic level of a model of language, Systemic Functional Linguistics in this case, yields a specific kind of translation, in fact, probably a kind of translation which is the preferred one in target-culture-oriented translation contexts.

Another type of translation, often called *literal translation* (where that term is used to refer to both a local translation procedure and a global translation method, cf. Newmark 1988: 45–53), is one which operates with only the obligatory changes necessary in the target language text to conform to the lexicogrammatical constraints of the target language. In other words, the literal translation is one, in terms of Systemic Functional Linguistics, which holds lexicogrammatical features and structure constant to the largest extent possible under the constraints of the target language system. Our translation (1De) illustrates this method for our short sample text:

(1De) Die bloße Fähigkeit einer Rolex Oyster, unter den härtesten Bedingungen weiterzulaufen, ist legendär. Nur die Starken überleben! Und, um dies sicherzustellen, ist das Gehäuse jeder Oyster aus einem massiven Block von Edelstahl, 18karätigem Gold, oder Platin gearbeitet (geschnitten, gehauen). Diese Operation beinhaltet Druckverhältnisse von bis zu 60 Tonnen.

We are not giving another literal back-translation of (1De) here, because this is, by definition and as a matter of fact, our text (1Eb) above. As we can see, what we obtain in (1De) is a lexicogrammatically correct text, but one which violates certain register- and genre constraints of its target language. The text is typically marked in its lexicogrammatical choices and to that extent reads "foreign" in the target culture. Depending on the languages involved, on the registers and on questions of context of culture, literal translations may be more or less advisable. They may even, precisely because of their "foreignizing potential", be a consciously chosen strategy depending on ideological context (cf. Venuti 1995: 148–186 for more general thoughts along these lines). In typologically very closely related languages, literal translations may be perfectly acceptable, and each literal translation would also be a semantically-based translation, though not the only one. In typologically more different languages — and the pair of English and German is a case in question — literal translations are often not semantically-based translations, and, in addition, are usually marked in terms of grammatical and lexical metaphorization, as well as information flow.

We have tried to illustrate in this section that texts which stand in a relationship of translation are usually registerial variants of each other, although the variation should be restricted in the case of semantically-based translations. But we have also tried to illustrate that source texts impose a particular set of constraints on target texts, which give target texts many of their specific properties as translations. We have also tried to illustrate that some properties of target texts may be due to the specific process of understanding and translation, rather than to constraints within the source text alone. Furthermore, a target text may be a valid translation in one sense, e.g. a literal translation, without being a very felicitous text in the context of culture of the target language. Finally, the relationship *translation-of* is not necessarily a transitive relationship, as we have tried to illustrate in back-translations in this section. We shall come back to these observations below, where we shall also suggest explanations for some of them.

5. Target-language variations

This section is meant to illustrate that the four texts (1Db), (1Dc), (1Dd) and (1De), which are all of them translations (in a theoretically weak sense in the case of (1Db)), and which among themselves are registerial variants (with very little registerial variation between the two semantically-based translations (1Dc) and (1Dd)), now have other possible registerial variants in their target language, but variants which are not translations of any other text accessible to us.

Let us first create a variation shifting from persuasive/ argumentative in terms of goal orientation towards descriptive/expository (cf. Halliday and Martin 1993 for more and original theoretical background, as well as Steiner 1998b for an extensive experiment along these lines with the English text). In examples (4D) — (6D), we shall give a word-for-word gloss in English, rather than a semantic (or "idiomatic") translation, because the point of our illustration here is exactly that of what lexicogrammatical means are available in German for realizing the register variations discussed:

(4D)   *Die Rolex Oyster hat die bekannte und positiv bewertete Eigenschaft, unter äußerst schwierigen Bedingungen funktionsfähig zu bleiben. Nur hohe Qualität garantiert diese Sicherheit. Sie ist für Anforderungen konzipiert, die ein Höchstmaß an Stärke und Stabilität erfordern. Das Gehäuse ist aus rostfreiem Stahl, 18karätigem Gold oder Platinum hergestellt. Bei diesem Vorgang wird ein Druck von bis zu 60 Tonnen erzeugt.*
The Rolex Oyster has the known and positively valued property under utterly difficult conditions functionable to remain. Only high quality guarantees this security. It is for challenges conceived which a highest-measure of strength and stability demand. The case is from stainless steel, 18ct gold or platinum produced. In this process is a pressure of up to 60 tons produced.

(5D) below instantiates a variation increasing formality and distance:

(5D)   *Bereits die Qualität einer Rolex Oyster, auch gegen diffizilste Konditionen resistent zu sein, findet in weiten Kreisen ihre Würdigung. Qualität ist eine Stilfrage. Zur Ab-*

sicherung dessen dient die exklusive Verwendung von Edelstahl, 18karätigem Gold oder Platin bei der Fertigung des Gehäuses, einem Prozeß mit Pressionsamplituden zwischen 0 und 60 Tonnen.
Indeed the quality of a Rolex Oyster also against most difficult conditions resistant to be finds in wide circles its appreciation. Quality is a style-question. To the ascertainment of this serves the exclusive use of quality-steel, 18ct gold or platinum in the creation of the case, a process with pressure-amplitudes between 0 and 60 tons.

(6D) below instantiates variation decreasing formality and distance:

(6D) *Alle finden es unglaublich, wie stark sie ist! Egal, wie schwer die Lage ist. Da kommen nur die Härtesten durch. Das ist bei denen von Rolex das absolute Muß, und deshalb verwenden die für ihre Oyster nur den härtesten Stahl, Gold von 18Karat, oder Platin. Dabei gibt es dann einen Druck von beinahe 60 Tonnen.*
Everyone is finding it unbelievable how strong it is! No matter how bad the situation is. There are coming only the toughest through. This is with those of Rolex an absolute must, and therefore use those for their Oyster only the hardest steel, Gold of 18 carat, or Platinum. There is then a pressure of almost 60 tons.

Let us at this point look back at the complete set of texts that we have used so far. Figure 2 gives an overview of the relationships that obtain between them.

As has been explained in our attempts so far, there obtains a translation relationship in a weak "procedural" sense between two of the texts in the first group. Next, as was shown in our experiment here, semantic and/or lexicogrammatical translation relationships obtain between selected texts of the middle group. The semantically-based translations are furthermore close registerial variants of their sources. Finally, among the third set of texts, the only (monolingual) relationship which obtains is that of register-variation. It is specifically semantics which is made to change in going from (4D) to (6D), and this would definitely not be a translation, according to our assumptions in the previous section. Quite in accordance with this view, texts (1Dc) and (1Dd) come very close to being (monolingual) translations, but this is precisely because they are both semantically-based translations of the same source text. And, of course, being close to monolingual translations, they are partly lexicogrammatically identical.

6. Discussion: translation vs. paraphrase vs. variation

It has been argued so far that

– there are intralingual versions of "a text" which are related to each other as (registerial) variants (section 1);

180   Erich Steiner

```
1E a) ─────────── procedural Tr ──────────▶ 1D a)
       ─ ─ ─ ─ ─ ─ ─ ─ ─ ─ ─ ─ ─ ─ ─ ─ ─

2E              procedural
       ─ ─ ─ ─ ─ ─ ─ ─ ─ ─ ─ ─ ─ ─ ─ ─ ▶    2D

3E              co – generation
       ─ ─ ─ ─ ─ ─ ─ ─ ─ ─ ─ ─ ─ ─ ─ ─ ▶    3D
```

─ ─

1E b)   "procedural Tr"   1D b)
            semantic Tr   literal

1E c)   semantic Tr   1D c)

            literal   literal Tr
1E d)   1D d)

                                               1D e)

─ ─

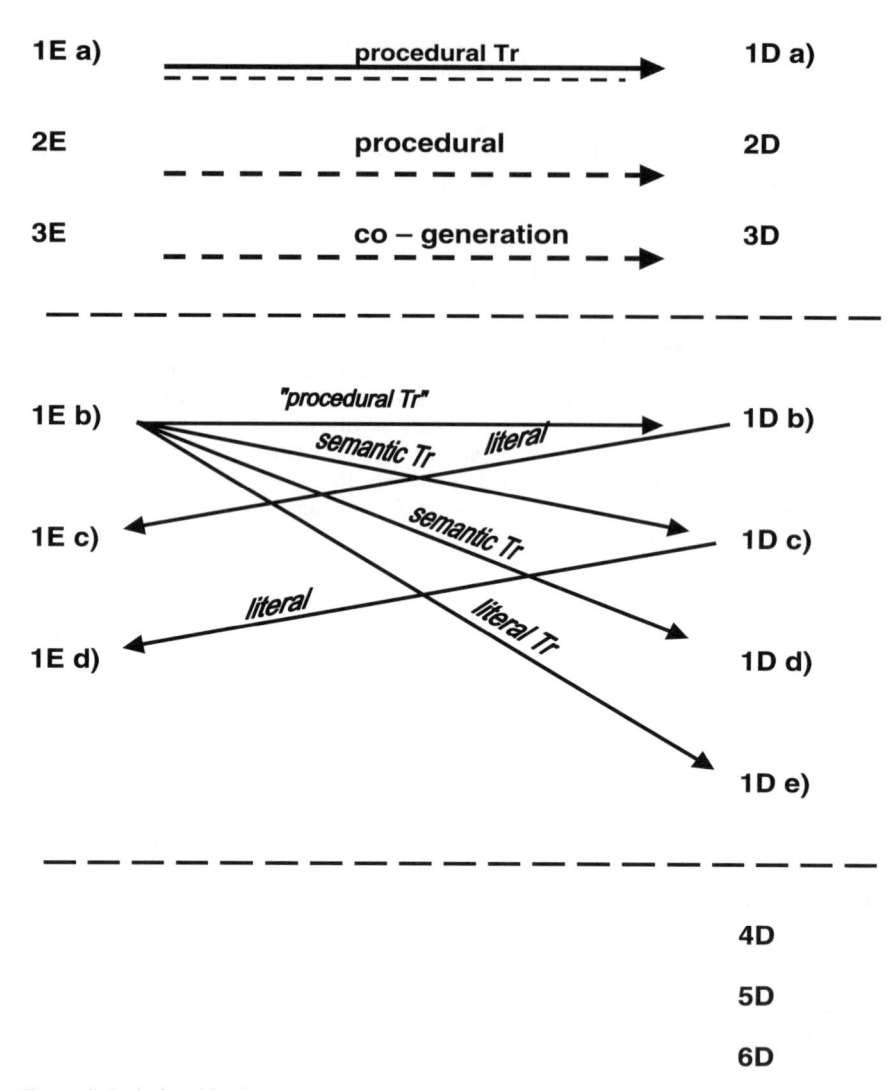

                                               4D

                                               5D

                                               6D

Figure 2. Relationships between texts

– there are also interlingual versions of "a text", some of which are translations (in the superficial sense of "being produced within an activity called translating"), and some of which are not (section 2). They are also related to each other as registerial variations and even the translated texts show (limited) registerial variation;

– in section 3 it was argued that the translation in a merely "procedural" sense (1Da,b) shows specific properties beyond those of other texts in the multilingual sample. We then offered translations of the same passage, two of them semantically-based translations, and the other a literal translation, discussing to what extent they are "translations" in a theoretically-motivated sense, and also what some of their properties are;

– in section 4 we offered three further monolingual variants of our translations, arguing that these now also belong in our set of sample texts, yet not as translations of any text, but as monolingual registerial variants within the German set of texts.

We shall now attempt to theorise our notion of *translation*, starting with a discussion of a few central properties and then by relating it to the terms *paraphrase* and *variation*.

We assume that our three terms would all refer to subtypes of *intertextual relationships*. The three terms *paraphrase, registerial variant,* and *translation* constitute a non-exhaustive set of hyponyms, i.e. there are additional types of intertextual relationships. Furthermore, translated texts may be registerial variants (within limits) and very locally even paraphrases. What are the properties that characterise the notion of *translation* vis-a-vis that of *registerial variant, encoded in a different language system*? We want to argue here that translated texts are a register in themselves, a register, whose properties are due to its nature as translation.

Starting again with our observations on text (1Db) above, it appears that translated texts are often longer and affectually less powerful than originals. As we have argued, there would seem to be several mutually related reasons for this: in order to ascertain the meaning of a text, i.e. in order to understand it, a reader frequently has to relate clauses and other units to their less metaphorical variants even in the source text and source language — where 'less metaphorical' is to be interpreted in the sense of both grammatical metaphor and lexical metaphor. Take the passage *this operation involves pressures of up to 60 tons* from(1Ea): understanding it may involve relating it to a version such as *while the cases of Oysters are being produced, those working on them will create pressures of as much as 60 tons (per square centimetre?)*. Due to this phenomenon of de-metaphorization within the source text before translating, we are faced by the constant need to disambiguate in the process of understanding, e.g. in the passage *is hewn from a solid block of stainless steel, 18ct. Gold, or platinum*. How far does the scope of *block of* extent? The translator of our original German translation (plausibly) decided that it has narrow scope, which is shown in his/her translation, yet which also necessitates the use of an additional verb and makes the translation longer than its source. Less metaphorical variants of a text are usually longer than more metaphorical ones (cf. Halliday and Martin (1993: 77–78) for theoretically motivated reasons), and this is borne out by what we have seen here. Still staying with length as a phenomenon, let us turn to the observation of the frequent loss of affect in translated texts. An example in our passage is the translation of ... *the case of every Oyster is hewn from a solid block of stainless steel, 18ct gold, or platinum* into either of the translated variants (1Dc) or (1Dd) offered here. As we do not have an easy equivalent in German, we may again unwrap the meaning, at first in English: *to be hewn from* means something like *to be cut with a cutting tool, signifying literary usage* (paraphrasing the relevant entry in the Longman Dictionary Of Contemporary English). As German does not seem to offer that combination of meanings in one verb, we either have to resort to verbs of non-literary usage, sacrificing a specific marking of tenor of discourse, or we try to preserve part of the tenor, but have to choose a verb with a somewhat more general meaning, not implying any specific instruments, such as *schaffen*, as suggested above as an alternative translation in (1Dd). This provides another example of the general fact that in order to understand and translate a passage, we create reformulations which are longer and/or involve fewer register- and semantic features in terms of affect. So far, then, it seems that translated texts are longer and less marked in terms of affect than original texts, and we have attempted to explain why this might be so: the process of understanding, an essential part of source-text analysis, frequently involves a specific kind of "unpacking", known as *grammatical de-metaphorization* in Systemic Functional Linguistics. In producing the target text, not all of this unpacking is undone, and it is this latter phenomenon which causes lengthening, in the first place, and loss of affect in the second.

Yet we have to beware of the simplistic fallacy of counting "length" in terms of number of words: while we know that movement upwards on the rank-scale in the process of grammatical de-metaphorization often involves an increase in the number of words, there are several methodological caveats here. One is that this correlation between moving on the rank scale and number of words will be weaker, the more *synthetic*, in a typological sense, a language is. For incorporating and polysynthetic languages, it may be negligible or even negative. When more than one language is involved, different mechanisms of morphological compounding, as between English and German, interfere heavily (cf. Hansen 1999: 45ff) and provide another factor making the concept of "a word" highly problematic. A further caveat has to do with the typological relationship of the language-pair involved in each particular translation: with respect to English and German, there are comparative phenomena leading to lengthening, and others leading to shortening in terms of number of words — and the complex interplay of these factors additionally interacts with those mentioned before. Thus, theoretically more motivated measures of what is often called "lengthening" are needed, and formulations in terms of "direction of movement on the rank-scale", "de-metaphorization" and other factors have to be developed, in order to allow meaningful hypotheses and quantifications.

A third reason why translations are systematically different from other types of texts is the following: it has been argued before that, depending on the language pair involved in translation, and depending on the direction of translation, entire types of grammatical metaphors, as Halliday would call them, have to be systematically undone. The main reasons would seem to be different, language-specific mappings of semantic functions onto grammatical ones, as well as language specific-differences in information distribution. But this, again, leads to processes of de-metaphorization between source and target language texts, at least in one direction. As we have argued in the discussion of our own semantically-based translation above, we have avoided the conflation of *Rolex Oyster* with the actor or agent roles in several places, even in this short passage, and we have de-metaphorized *this process involves pressures...* into *bei diesem Prozess entsteht ein Druck...* (1De), which is a de-metaphorization by at least one step (an entirely de-metaphorized variant being *während dies geschieht...* 'while this happening') This general process of de-metaphorization which happens between relatively weakly inflecting and fixed word order languages, such as English, and relatively highly inflecting and free word order languages, such as e.g. German or Russian, is another systematic influence making translations longer than originals, yet in contrast to what we have said above about the process of understanding as a motivating force for lengthening, the typologically-induced process depends very much on language pair and direction, rather than being a general property of translations across arbitrary language pairs. That is to say, in translations from German and Russian into English (or, to a lesser extent, French), typological effects may actually, to some extent, counteract the other processes going on during translation, thus reducing the lengthening. We would hypothesize, though, that the target texts would still be longer than parallel non-translated texts. How big the relative weights of the various effects are seems to be an empirical question, which has not been addressed on a larger scale so far (but see Baker's ongoing work cf. Baker 1995, or some of the work in Lavinosa ed. 1998).

In the case of the original translation of our sample passage given in (1Db), we claimed that the translation was somewhat too "free", being less constrained by its source text than would be expected of a translation. At the other end of the spectrum, we illustrated in text (1De) that a translation which preserves functional structure on the lexicogrammatical level is in several senses too much constrained by the source text, or rather, constrained on the wrong level. Alternatively, we suggested two semantically-based translations, bringing in the specific constraints arising out of language comparison and of the process of translation itself. It appears to us that such a semantically-based translation is very promising in many contexts, but may, in fact, still lead to a mismatch in register in a given context of culture (for an attempt to relate the semantic level used here to controlled language and multilingual generation cf. the contribution by Hartley and Paris, this volume). Where registers are realized by very different semantic configurations between languages, or where the same register functions very differently in two cultures, we will have a mismatch — but it would appear that these are precisely the circumstances in which we would advise against a translation and in favour of multilingual text production. The more a particular task requires adaptation to culturally very different contexts (with their concomitant registers), and the more *scopus-adapted* (Reiss and Vermeer 1984, Nord 1991) a translation is, the less will it be a translation in the stricter sense. Hence we stipulate that the meaning of *translation* is not co-extensive with *multilingual register variation*; rather, translation is itself a specific register whose properties are due to the semiotic and psychological processes making up the process of translating, different degrees of intended conformity with the target-culture registers, as well as to the language combination involved and the direction of translation.

To conclude this section, let us return to the differentiation between *variation, paraphrase,* and *translation* (for a related discussion see Yallop's contribution to this volume).

Variation, more specifically register-variation, is possible and necessary within sets of intertextually related texts, both intra-lingually and inter-lingually. Sets of translated texts may or may not differ in register from their sources, with the theoretically motivated stipulation that the register differences should be small in the case of semantically-based translations, but may often be quite strong in the case of literal translations.

Paraphrase is a relationship among sets of propositions, and sentences expressing them, which preserves the truth value. Paraphrases generally do not preserve the textual semantics, and they have no very clear relationship towards the interpersonal semantics at all. Paraphrases are possible within and between languages, but the only relationship they have to a translation is that they preserve important aspects of the experiential and logical semantics of sentences, which both underdetermines and even overdetermines what a translation usually has to be.

Translation, in the sense of literal translation, is only possible between languages, in the sense that a literal translation within one language would have to be a lexicogrammatical copy of itself. A semantically-based translation within one language would be possible because of the non-bi-uniqueness of lexicogrammar and semantics, but would yield a highly constrained set of possibilities. If we added the property of understanding, we would additionally introduce de-metaphorized variants into the set. Yet all the important criteria from language comparison and typology would be missing, and at least in that sense, translation is again only possible between languages.

In the end, we may say that translation is an approximation to a multifunctional paraphrase — rather than the mono-functional paraphrases of logic-oriented semantics — under the constraints of the process of understanding and of the typology of the language systems involved (for the latter see particularly Teich, this volume). Finally, each individual translation, i.e. situated language (instantiation), is text production under the constraints of a source text, in the sense of Neubert (1986).

7. Modelling translation: challenges for a linguistic theory

Based on the arguments presented above, and illustrated by the exercises we went through as one way of illustrating our arguments, it seems reasonable to claim that modelling translation will be a productive challenge to any linguistic theory. We would like to outline the challenge for the theory of Systemic Functional Linguistics here in particular (cf. the contributions by Halliday, but also those by Matthiessen, by Teich, and by Gregory in this volume).

Let us first address the question of the relationship between translation and the levels of linguistic theory: translation methods have been labelled as ranging between the extremes of literal and free for a long time in history, or *transferierend* (transferring) vs. *adaptierend* (adapting) (cf. Koller 1992: 60). For a stratified linguistic theory, such as Systemic Functional Linguistics, it is relatively straightforward to model these translation methods, or strategies, as the preservation of features and structures on different linguistic levels (cf. Catford 1965). Three obvious levels at which features and structures can be preserved would be lexicogrammar vs. semantics vs. register. Preservation on the first of these would specify a relatively literal translation, preservation on the last a relatively free one. However, remembering that each of these levels is internally organised in terms of *delicacy*, we could also investigate the question whether it is not rather the case that on each level, the literal translations are those based on high delicacy (specific classes of units), whereas the free translations are those based on low delicacy. Any in-depth investigation of these questions will increase our understanding of the concepts of *level* and *delicacy*. Finally, in terms of the *rank* scale within lexicogrammar (and semantics), modelling translation as preservation of features and structures on lower ranks, say the morpheme, will yield relatively literal translations, modelling on higher ranks relatively free ones. This stratified model can be interpreted in a "declarative mode", as modelling relationships between texts, and in a "procedural" mode as modelling translators' (and interpreters') cognitive processes.

A closely related question is the clarification of the status of the semantic level of linguistic organisation as worked out in Halliday and Matthiessen 1999. In modelling language, one could either attempt to dissolve the *local* semantics into a functionally very rich lexicogrammar, including a full account of grammatical metaphor, or else one could claim that the local semantics is nothing but register specified to full delicay and being brought down, or related to, the rank of the clause complex (but see Halliday and Matthiessen 1999: 227ff, for quite convincing arguments against such a view). In other words, the notion of a *semantic level*, on a par with phonology, lexicogrammar, and context, somehow hovers between its neighbours. The status of this level can be conceptualised more clearly by testing it in the modelling of certain phenomena, and I would suggest that one of them is translation: within a model of translation, we could conceptualise the local semantics as the most plausible level at which to hold features constant. This conceptualisation would still be language-oriented enough to hold the information about linguistic constraints of the source text, but it would not be so specific to the particular lexicogrammatical realizations as to make the resulting translation too *foreignizing*. At the moment I would prefer to model translation — in most contexts — on this level. We have to emphasise in this connection that semantics in Systemic Functional Linguistics is a multifunctional semantics, i.e. we are not privileging experiential meaning here, but instead translation would be the preservation — or maximally close preservation — of experiential, logical, interpersonal and textual meanings in the relationship of translation between texts, or in the process of translation by the translator.

So far, we have claimed that the phenomenon of translation, both as a relationship between texts and as a process, can shed light on the nature and type(s) of levels in models of language. But translation is also involved, at least in the sense implied below, in processes of "understanding" in general, as we have tried to illustrate in the discussion of some of our examples (cf. our discussion of disambiguation, or of *to be hewn from*, in text (1Eb) and its various translations above). We have also argued that understanding can partly be modelled as the relating to each other by the understander of more and less metaphorized lexicogrammatical expressions of maximally similar meanings. Understanding often requires de-metaphorization, whereas proceeding from an understanding to more generalised and abstract representations often seems to require the opposite (cf. Halliday and Martin 1993). If we could show, in a model of translation, what the specific traces are that the understanding of some source text has left in its target text(s), we could be tapping a very rich source for a better notion of what human text-understanding is.

Finally, the relationship between translation on the one hand, and language comparison and typology on the other: translation is more than comparison and typology of languages, that is to say it is a relationship between instantiations (texts), rather than between language systems. It is a relationship between texts where languages of different types are involved (one set of constraints), where these are compared, i.e. co-classified, under certain parameters (comparison) and where instantiations of these languages, i.e. situated texts, are related to each other against a background of a model of translational equivalences on certain levels. A modelling of translation will force the systemic linguistic community more than hitherto — and give them the tools — to face the interesting challenge of language typology and comparison generally.

Notes

1. I am grateful to a number of people for critical comments: Michael Halliday, Robert Spence, Elke Teich, Colin Yallop. None of these can be held responsible for remaining weaknesses.

References

Baker, Mona
    1995   Corpora in translation studies: an overview and suggestions for future research. *Target*, 7(2): 223–244.

Bell, Roger T.
    1991   *Translation and Translating*. London: Longman.

Biber, Douglas
    1993   *Dimensions of register variation: a cross-linguistic comparison*. Cambridge: Cambridge University Press.

Catford, J.C.
    1965   *A linguistic theory of translation*. Oxford: Oxford University Press.

Doherty, Monika
    1991   Informationelle Holzwege. Ein Problem der Übersetzungswissenschaft. *Zeitschrift für Literaturwissenschaft und Linguistik*, 21(84): 30–49.

Doherty, Monika
    1993   Parametrisierte Perspektive. *Zeitschrift für Sprachwissenschaft*, 12(1): 3–38.

Fawcett, Peter
    1997   *Translation and Language: Linguistic Theories Explained*. Manchester, UK: St. Jerome Publishing.

Halliday, M. A. K.
  1994   *An Introduction to Functional Grammar.* 2nd edition. London: Edward Arnold.

Halliday, M. A. K., Angus McIntosh, and Peter Strevens
  1964   *The linguistic sciences and language teaching.* London: Longman.

Halliday, M. A. K. and Ruqaiya Hasan
  1989   *Language, context, and text: aspects of language in a social-semiotic perspective.* 2nd edition. Oxford: University Press Language Education.

Halliday, M. A. K. and James R. Martin
  1993   *Writing Science: Literacy and Discursive Power.* London and Washington D.C.: Falmer Press.

Halliday, M. A. K. and Christian M.I.M. Matthiessen
  1999   *Construing Experience Through Meaning. A Language-Based Approach to Cognition.* London: Cassell.

Hansen, Silvia
  1999   A Contrastive Analysis of Multilingual Corpora (English-German). Diploma Thesis. Department of Applied Linguistics, Translating and Interpreting. University of Saarland, Saarbrücken.

Hatim, Basil and Ian Mason
  1990   *Discourse and the Translator.* Language in Social Life Series. London: Longman.

Hawkins, John A.
  1986   *A Comparative Typology of English and German.* 1st edition. London: Croom Helm.

House, Juliane
  1997   *A Model for Translation Quality Assessment. A Model Revisited.* Tübingen: Gunter Narr.

Koller, Werner
  1992   *Einführung in die Übersetzungswissenschaft.* 4. Edition. Heidelberg/ Wiesbaden: Ullstein.

Koller, Werner
  1995   The Concept of Equivalence and the Object of Translation Studies. *Target,* 7(2): 191–222.

Lavinosa, Sara (ed.)
  1998   *Meta Translators Journal.* Vol. 43 No. 4. Special Issue on "The Corpus-Based Approach".

Malinowski, Bronislaw
  1935   *Coral Gardens and Their Magic. A Study of the Methods of Tilling the Soil and of Agricultural Rites in the Trobriand Islands. Vol.2. The Language of Magic and Gardening.* New York: American Book Company.

Martin, James Robert
  1992   *English Text. System and Structure.* John Benjamins, Amsterdam, 1st edition.

Munday, Jeremy
1997 Systems in translation: a computer-assisted systemic analysis of the translation of Garcia Marquez. Ph.D dissertation., Bradford: University of Bradford.

Neubert, Albrecht
1986 *Text und Translation, Übersetzungswissenschaftliche Beiträge Bd. 8.* Leipzig: Verlag Enzyklopädie.

Newmark, Peter
1988 *A Textbook of Translation.* New York: Prentice Hall.

Nord, Christiane
1991 *Textanalyse und Übersetzen.* Heidelberg: Julius Groos Verlag.

Plenker, Birgit
1994 Englische Werbetexte und ihre deutschen Entsprechungen. Eine sprachvergleichend-übersetzungskritische Untersuchung. Diploma Thesis. Department of Applied Linguistics, Translating and Interpreting. University of Saarland, Saarbrücken.

Ramm, Wiebke, Annely Rothkegel, Erich Steiner, and Claudia Villiger
1995 Discourse Grammar for German. Deliverable of ESPRIT Basic Research Project DANDELION Deliverable R2.3.2., Commission of the European Union, Brussels.

Reiss, Katharina und H.J. Vermeer
1984 *Grundlagen einer allgemeinen Translationstheorie.* Tübingen: Niemeyer.

Spence, Robert
1998 A functional approach to translation studies. PhD Thesis. Philosophische Fakultät. University of Saarland, Saarbrücken.

Steiner, Erich
1991 *A Functional Perspective on Language, Action, and Interpretation.* Berlin and New York: Mouton de Gruyter.

Steiner, Erich
1997 An Extended Register Analysis as a Form of Text Analysis for Translation. In Gerd Wotjak and Heide Schmidt, editors, *Modelle der Translation. Models of Translation*, pages 235–256. Frankfurt am Main: Vervuert Verlag.

Steiner, Erich
1998a A register-based translation evaluation. *Target. International journal of translation studies.* 10(2): 291–318.

Steiner, Erich
1998b How much variation can a text tolerate before it becomes a different text? An exercise in making meaningful choices. In Rainer Schulze, editor, *Making meaningful choices.* 235–257. Tübingen: Gunter Narr Verlag.

Steiner, Erich
2000 Translation evaluation — some methodological questions arising from the German translation of Goldhagen's "Hitler's Willing Executioners". In Eija Ventola (ed.), *Discourse and the Community.* Tübingen: Gunter Narr Verlag, pp. 291–308.

Steiner, George
    1992   *After Babel: aspects of language and translation.* Oxford: Oxford University Press. First published 1975.

Taylor, Christopher
    1998   *Language to Language.* Cambridge: Cambridge University Press.

Taylor-Torsello, Carol
    1993   *Grammatica e Traduzione.* Torino: Universita degli Studi di Torino.

Toury, Gideon
    1995   *Descriptive Translation Studies.* Amsterdam/ Philadelphia: John Benjamins Publishing Company.

Venuti, Lawrence
    1995   *The translator's invisibility. A history of translation.* London and New York : Routledge.

Vinay, Jean-Paul and Jean Darbelnet
    1958   *Stylistique comparée du francais et de l'anglais.* Paris: Les Éditions Didier.

Wilss, Wolfram
    1977   *Übersetzungswissenschaft — Probleme und Methoden.* Stuttgart: Klett Verlag.

Towards a model for the description of cross-linguistic divergence and commonality in translation

Elke Teich

The goal of this paper is to sketch a model for describing the contrastive-linguistic resources involved in translation. Working on three texts, an English source language text, a translation of that text into German and a back translation of the German text into English produced by machine, some general dimensions of contrastive-linguistic description useful for talking about translation are presented.

The more general argument brought forward is that a model of contrastive-linguistic resources such as the one elaborated in this paper allows us to theoretically contextualize some of the basic notions of translation theory (such as translation strategy, translation procedure, equivalence etc.) and to discuss particular translation problems typically arising when translating between English and German. It will be suggested that a model such as the one presented that is firmly grounded in the notion of *language in use* can contribute to bridging the perceived gap between the theoretical and the applied branches of translation studies.

1. Introduction: Starting assumptions, goals and methodological basis

The goal of this paper is to sketch a model for describing the contrastive-linguistic resources involved in translation.

Two assumptions are entailed here:

- translation involves contrastive-linguistic knowledge;
- describing this contrastive-linguistic knowledge using a suitable model to do so provides some essential insights about the properties of translations.

I make these assumptions based on the following observations about the state-of-the-art in translation studies, on the one hand, and about the nature of translation, on the other hand.

Translation studies is by no means a unified academic discipline with a consensus on goals and methods. Broadly speaking, there is a division into *theoretical* and *applied translation studies* (cf. e.g., Snell-Hornby

(1988), Bell (1991) or Wilss (1977) for a similar distinction).While the former is concerned with analysing translation as process and product in order to gain insights about the nature of translation, the latter is predominantly concerned with the techniques and methods needed to produce translations.

Applied translation studies tends to discuss specific translation problems that arise in translating between two particular languages. Extrapolation from these specific problems results in classifications of such problems and of the methods to solve them, such as *translation procedure* (transposition, modulation, paraphrase etc.; cf. Vinay and Darbelnet 1995), *translation strategy* (literal vs. free translation), and a basic classification of translations into *translation types*, such as literary, technical translation, translation preserving/changing intention (cf. e.g., Sager 1994). While the basic inventory of translation methods constitutes a major part of a translator's tool kit, what remains problematic is the criteria for applying them. Application criteria are often insufficient or rather fuzzy, so that a motivated choice of translation method is impeded. One conceivable reason for this inadequacy lies in the kind of vocabulary used in applied translation studies. For discussing the local translation methods, such as translation procedures, the vocabulary used rarely goes beyond established grammatical terms, such as, for example Quirk et al. (1985) for English. For discussing the more global translation methods, such as translation strategy, which operate on the textual level of linguistic organization and are influenced by contextual factors, the terminology used draws on text linguistic and pragmatic terms that often lack a precise definition. These terminological deficits thus both limit the discussion of translation at the grammatical level and prevent an explicit account of the more abstract linguistic and extra-linguistic parameters that are translationally relevant.

While applied translation studies does not attempt to come up with a general model of translation, developing models of translation, both of process and of product (e.g., Reiß and Vermeer 1984; Hatim and Mason 1990; Bell 1991) is the major goal in theoretical translation studies. Typically, these models are linguistically informed, mainly drawing on text linguistics, stylistics, or psycholinguistics. However, often they remain rather abstract, practical translation problems and the methods to solve them are not the major concern, and they hardly achieve much of a heuristic function.

Based on these observations, it appears that

- from the perspective of applied translation studies, it is desirable to contextualize translation methods, i.e., to ground them in a theory

and corresponding model of translation, to the effect of making their application criteria more explicit;
- from the perspective of theoretical translation studies, it is desirable to give translation models more of a heuristic function so that they gain more applicational relevance.

I maintain that a model of the contrastive-linguistic resources involved in translation can be a step in this direction. This is motivated based on the following view of translation. Translation is *language in use*, and thus comparable to text production or text understanding. It is a particular kind of language in use in that it involves competence in two languages, requiring a specific set of skills and specific kinds of knowledge. The skill set consists of the techniques and methods available to solve translation problems. The kinds of knowledge needed in translation crucially include *linguistic* knowledge, in particular *contrastive-linguistic knowledge* about the languages between which translation is carried out. Therefore, a major component of theorising translation and building models of translation is to uncover this contrastive-linguistic knowledge and provide the means to describe it. Also, the basic unit translators operate on is a *text*. Therefore, in translation, as opposed to other kinds of application of contrastive-linguistic knowledge, such as for instance, contrastive grammar in second language teaching, in addition to contrastive-linguistic knowledge of language *systems*, what comes into play is knowledge about commonalities and divergences in the *instantiation* of language systems in text and according to context.

For building a model of the contrastive knowledge involved in translation, large-scale contrastive-linguistic analyses of translations have to be carried out. This has been argued for recently by a number of researchers in the field, including e.g., Baker (1995). However, apart from collecting suitable multilingual corpora, there is then the question of categories for analysis. For this purpose one needs a model of linguistic description that can be applied contrastive-linguistically, i.e., one that uses categories that are cross-linguistically relevant. Also, translation being an operation that takes texts as primary units, the linguistic model should have something to say about the relation of language systems and their instantiation in actual *texts*. Finally, the model must lend itself as an anchor for translational concepts, such as translation strategy, translation procedure, translation type etc. What is crucial here is the possibility of representing the set of translation options available at particular points in the translation process and the motivations for choosing one of them. There is no such model off-the-shelf; but there are linguistic theories which fulfil some of these desiderata and could serve as a basis. One such theory is Systemic Functional Linguistics (Halliday 1978, 1985). Systemic functional theory is used in a variety of areas, ranging from text analysis in literary studies over language teaching to computational linguistic application. Also, it has been applied to a variety of languages, both in monolingual description and for the modelling of multilinguality, e.g., in functional typology (e.g., Caffarel et al. forthcoming), translation (e.g., Catford 1965; Hatim and Mason 1990; Hatim and Mason, 1997; Bell 1991) and automatic multilingual text generation (e.g., Bateman et al. 1991,Teich et al. 1996, Teich 1995). The research presented in this paper constitutes a first step towards a model of contrastive-linguistic resources in which translational categories can be anchored, taking as a basis the theoretical concepts and representational constructs of Systemic Functional Linguistics.

The paper is organised as follows. First, I introduce some general dimensions of contrastive-linguistic description (Section 2). These dimensions are coextensive with the major representational categories assumed for monolingual description in Systemic Functional Linguistics. This forms the backbone of a model of contrastive-linguistic resources as it has been employed for the purpose of automatic multilingual generation in the Komet-Penman MultiLingual (KPML) system (Bateman et al. 1991) with further extensions by (Bateman and Teich 1995; Teich 1995). On this basis, I present a contrastive-linguistic analysis of an English sample text, a German translation of that sample text and a back translation of the German translation into English produced by machine, focusing on differences and commonalities in the choice of transitivity, the choice of theme and the use of grammatical metaphor (Section 3). Looking at a back translation produced by machine in addition serves the purpose of pointing out some inherent differences between human and machine translation in terms of translation strategy[1]. In Section 4, the relation to translation studies is established explicitly and some of the basic technical terms of application-oriented translation studies, such as translation procedure, translation strategy etc., are placed in the model of contrastive-linguistic description presented. The translation methods that are implied by the differences and commonalities uncovered by the contrastive analysis are motivated against the background of the contrastive-linguistic model. Section 5 briefly summarizes the main points made in the paper and concludes with relating them to some of the issues treated in other papers in this volume.

2. A model of contrastive-linguistic resources

As a basis for subsequent discussion, in the present section the general dimensions of linguistic description used in Systemic Functional Linguistics are introduced (Section 2.1); then it will be shown how these can serve to set up a model of contrastive-linguistic description (Section 2.2).

2.1. General categories of linguistic description in Systemic Functional Linguistics

Systemic Functional Linguistics maintains that language can be described as a *stratified resource*, the strata among which descriptive responsibility is divided being *lexicogrammar, semantics,* and *context*. Between these strata there is the relation of realization: Context is realized by semantics, semantics is realized by grammar. The second central property of systemic functional descriptions is *metafunction*: Language is said to fulfil three major functions, the ideational, the interpersonal and the textual. The ideational is concerned with states-of-affairs and their circumstances (reflected in the grammar of a language in configurations of processes and the participants therein, such as Actor, Goal, Medium, and accompanying Circumstantials of Time, Space etc.),[2] the interpersonal is to do with the role relations of speaker and hearer in a discourse (reflected in the grammar of a language e.g., in the mood of a clause), the textual represents the patterns with which cohesive and coherent texts are created. In addition, each linguistic description, at each stratum, has two aspects, one representing linguistic *systems* (the paradigmatic aspect), the other the *realizations* of these systems (the syntagmatic aspect). This is referred to as *axiality*. The systemic functional means used for the representation of systems are system networks. For an example see Figure 1, which shows a simplified system network of English MOOD. The features of a system are mutually exclusive (e.g., interrogative vs. declarative in the MOOD system in Figure 1), and we speak of them being ordered in *delicacy*, e.g., declarative is more delicate (i.e., more specific) than indicative. System networks are set up for different *ranks*; on the grammatical plane, these are clause, group/phrase, word, and possibly morpheme ranks.

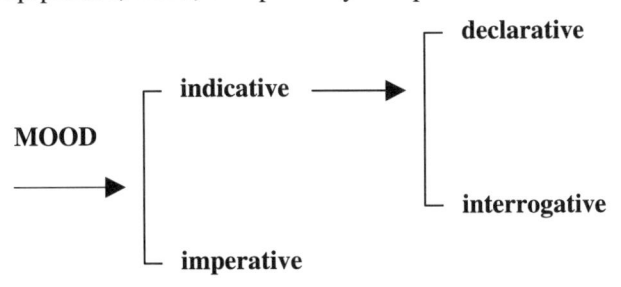

Figure 1. A system network for MOOD

Metafunctional diversification, stratification, axiality, rank and delicacy are the general categories of linguistic description used in the systemic functional model. Figure 2 displays these five dimensions graphically: The arrows indicate the five dimensions, the ellipses folded into each other represent the three strata — lexicogrammar, semantics and context.

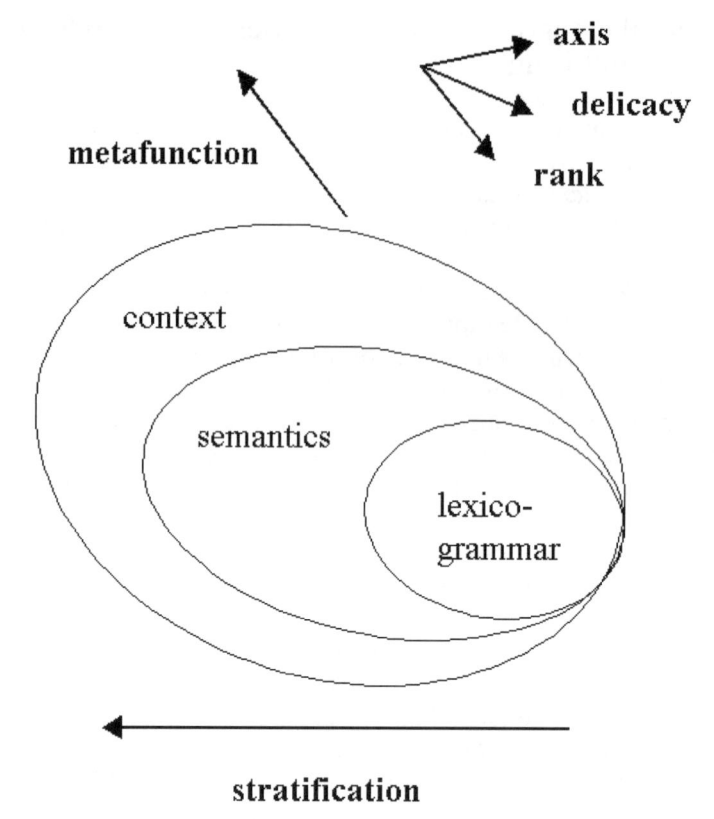

Figure 2. Dimensions of linguistic description in Systemic Functional Linguistics

2.2. Dimensions of contrastive-linguistic description

Comparing any two languages one will always find similarities and differences. A model of language comparison therefore has to accommodate both cross-linguistic commonality and divergence. It is commonly known that depending on the level of linguistic abstraction at which one compares two languages, one will detect more or less commonality: As a tendency, languages show more similarity on the semantic plane and more differences on the grammatical plane. This insight is the basis of interlingua-based machine translation approaches, where semantic or conceptual descriptions are taken to apply multilingually, and grammatical descriptions are taken to be language-specific. For example, languages tend to indicate whether referents are newly introduced or identifiable from context or co-text. Grammatically, this meaning is expressed by word order in some languages, as in most of the languages of the Slavonic family, and by determiners in other languages (as in English or German). However, stratification is only one parameter of cross-linguistic variation. Concentrating on the level of grammar and applying the systemic functional representational categories just introduced, the following further observations can be made (cf. Bateman et al. 1991; Degand 1996; Teich et al. 1996; Teich 1995):

- Languages tend to be similar in terms of paradigms (systems) and different in terms of syntagmatic, surface-syntactic realization (axiality).
- Grammatical systems of low delicacy (less specific grammatical types) tend to be similar across languages, and systems of higher delicacy tend to be dissimilar.
- There may be different preferences in different languages concerning the grammatical rank at which a certain phenomenon is grammatically expressed.
- A particular grammatical means may serve different metafunctions in different languages.

An example of variation according to axiality from English and German is the different realization of imperative mood. Comparing the English and German MOOD systems there is a high degree of similarity: Both English and German distinguish between declarative, interrogative and imperative — so the system of MOOD displayed above (Figure 1) holds for both English and German. However, whereas in English imperative is realized by a nonfinite verb form, in German, imperatives are mostly realized by finite verbs.

Variation according to delicacy can be illustrated using the example of mood again: While English has only one option for imperative, German distinguishes different forms of imperative according to the number of addressees and politeness. See Figure 3 displaying differences and commonalities between English and German mood.

Cross-linguistic variation according to rank can be illustrated using again the example of marking referents in a discourse as identifiable or new. In some languages the status of referents in terms of identifiability is expressed at clause rank by word order; in other languages, including English and German, it is realized at nominal group rank, employing determiners. For an illustration of cross-linguistic variation according to metafunction consider the case where the same kind of grammatical means can serve different functions in different languages, e.g., in Slavonic languages or in German, word order serves a textual function, such as marking Theme-Rheme and Given-New, in other languages, such as English, it mainly marks the Subject (and other syntactic functions thus serving the interpersonal metafunction.

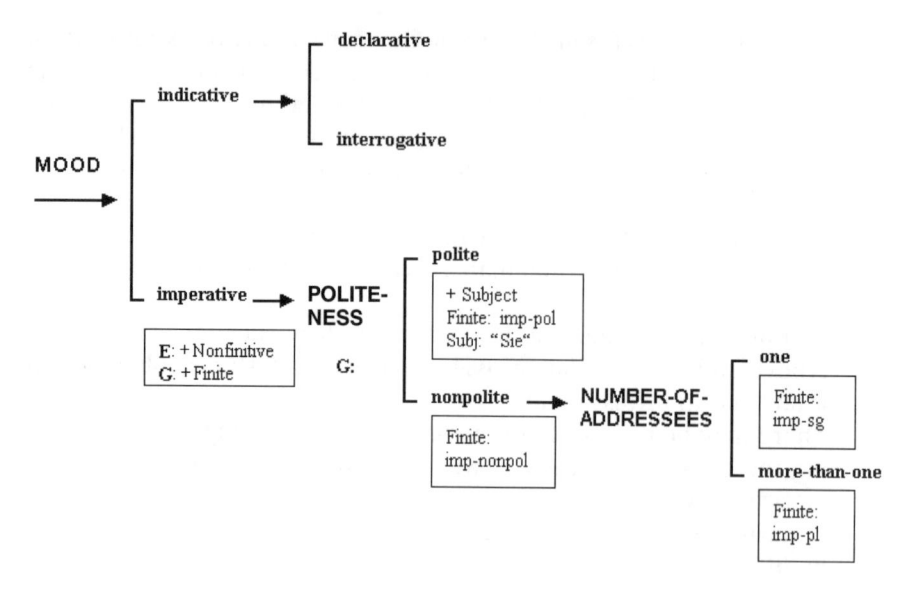

Figure 3. English and German mood options

The representational constructs of stratification, metafunctional diversification, ranking, axiality and delicacy thus set up a space of dimensions of potential variation between languages. Assuming that for translation, knowledge about the potential variation between the languages between which translation is carried out is indispensable, trying to anchor translational concepts and categories in a model of cross-linguistic variation that uses these dimensions appears a promising step.

In the next section, I show by a contrastive analysis of an English sample text, a German translation of that text and a German-English back translation produced by machine that the general dimensions of linguistic description introduced by Systemic Functional Linguistics are not only useful as parameters for describing divergence and similarity between language systems, but that they can also be taken as a basis for the contrastive analysis of texts that are in a translation relation. Even if there is a high degree of commonality between two linguistic systems, such as between English and German, so that in parts systemically equivalent options are available, looking at translations we will find that often the systemically equivalent option is not the translational choice. The motivation for this is said to lie in culture-specific conventions of text types. Since texts are the primary unit on which translation operates, what is involved in translation is not just contrastive knowledge about language systems, but crucially knowledge about the systems in use, i.e., in instantiations of language systems (semantic, lexicogrammatical) according to certain situational and text-type specific conditions.

Therefore, a contrastive analysis of a text and its translation must be able to say something about the contrasts between language systems and about the instantiation of these contrasts in texts. For theorizing translation on a linguistic basis, the notion of instantiation is thus doubly significant and must be added to the model as another dimension of cross-linguistic variation. Figure 4 shows the complete set of dimensions that I maintain are relevant for the contrastive-linguistic description of translations or other parallel text in multiple languages. It is along these dimensions that the contrastive analysis I present in the next section has been carried out.

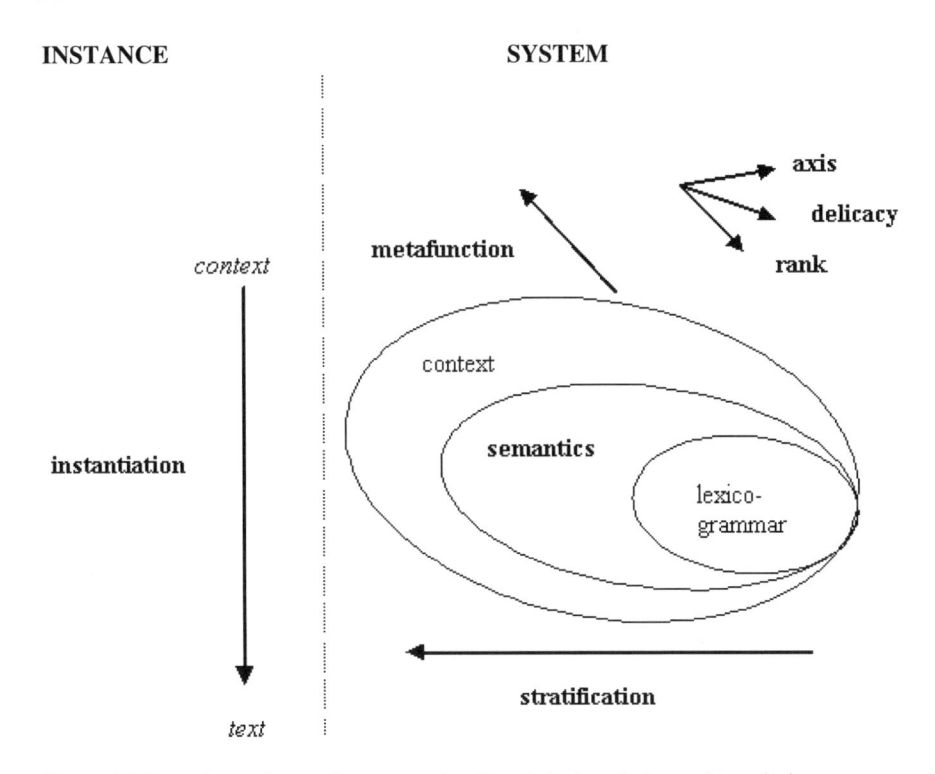

Figure 4. Dimensions relevant for contrastive-linguistic descriptions of translations

3. Contrastive analysis: transitivity, theme, and grammatical metaphor in English and German

The goal of the contrastive analysis of the English original text and its German translation is to show how some typical translational choices in translating from English to German can be described with the contrastive-linguistic model just presented. I focus on three phenomena: the selection of theme (Section 3.1), the choice of process types (Section 3.2) and the usage of grammatical metaphor (Section 3.3). The notions of theme and process type will be made more precise below; the term 'grammatical metaphor' is closely related to 'paraphrase'.

The descriptive basis for this analysis is Halliday (1985) and Matthiessen (1995) for English, and Steiner et al. (1988), Steiner and Ramm (1995) and Teich (1999) for German.

3.1. Theme in English and German

3.1.1. Definition: Theme

Theme is defined in Halliday (1985) as the point of departure of a message, marking what is being talked about in the clause. Theme in English is said to be realized by placement in the initial constituent position(s) of the clause. Typical distinctions drawn in this area are unmarked vs. marked theme, simple vs. multiple theme, predicated vs. nonpredicated theme. What do the English and German theme systems look like then, in comparison to each other?

3.1.2. Theme in English and German: the grammatical systems

Theme being realized predominantly by linear order and German having a rather 'free' word order and English a rather 'fixed' one, we can already predict that there will be differences. While the basic distinctions mentioned above hold for both English and German, there are some major differences in the more delicate options, notably concerning theme markedness. Since English is strictly Subject-Verb-Object (SVO), we can predict that often the Theme will be filled by the Subject. This is how the unmarked theme option is realized in English. The notion of unmarkedness subscribed to here means the placement of elements in Theme position when intonation is "neutral", i.e., when the focus falls on the last lexical element of the clause. German, in contrast, is more flexible in its placement of constituents in front position. First, syntactic functions other than Subject can fill the Theme; second, unmarked theme can also be realized by circumstantial elements, such as locational or temporal Adjuncts. This correlates with another typological difference between English and German: English is much more flexible in the kinds of participant roles that the Subject can take on and in the semantic filling of these roles (cf. Section 3.2 and Hawkins 1986). English Subjects can be Actors in material processes, Sensers in mental processes etc. Examples (1–3) below illustrate this property of English[3].

(1) **Alice**   drives   a Nissan.
     (Actor) (Process) (Goal)

(2) **I**   like   the book.
     (Senser) (Process) (Phenomenon)

(3) **The fifth day** saw   them   at the summit.
     (Senser)   (Process) (Phenomenon) (Location)

German equivalents to (1–3) keeping thematic structure constant are given in (4–6):

(4) **Alice**   fährt   einen   Nissan.
     Alice-NOM   drives   ACC-a   ACC-Nissan
     (Actor)   (Process) (Goal)

(5) **Mir**   gefällt   das   Buch.
     me-DAT   pleases   NOM-the NOM-book
     (Senser) (Process) (Phenomenon)

(6) **Am fünften Tag** erreichten sie
     on-the fifth day   reached   NOM-they
     (Circumstantial)   (Process)   (Actor)

     den   Gipfel.
     ACC-the ACC-summit
     (Goal)

The German equivalents show that unmarked theme can be realized as Subject as in (4), but also it may be realized by an Indirect Object (dative case) as in (5) or as a Circumstantial as in (6). All of (4), (5) and (6) show verb-second ordering — a major basic word order feature of German independent clauses (cf. Hawkins 1986). Thus, the notion of Theme used here is the same as that of 'Vorfeld', i.e., the position(s) before the finite verb, as it is described in work on the grammar of German. In this view, unmarked theme is described as being realized either by conflation with the Most-inherent-participant-role in a process (Actor, Senser, Carrier, Sayer) or by conflation with a Circumstantial or Conjunct/Disjunct (cf. Steiner and Ramm 1995). Figure 5 displays the main systemic commonalities and differences between English and German in THEME-SELECTION and THEME-PREDICATION[4].

Concerning multiple vs. simple theme, the options in English and German are rather similar: combinations of textual, interpersonal and ideational elements in the Theme are possible. However, multiple Themes including a textual element are much rarer in German than in English. Consider examples (7)-(10)[5]:

(7) **But he** couldn't say no.

(8) **Aber er** konnte nicht nein sagen.
    but he could not no say

(9) **Nonetheless he** couldn't say no.

(10) **Trotzdem** konnte er nicht nein sagen.
     nonetheless could he not no say

(7) has a multiple Theme consisting of a Conjunct and the Subject (SVO must be adhered to). The German equivalent (8) has a multiple Theme as well, consisting of the Conjunct and the Subject. However, with textual Adjuncts, German behaves differently from English: in (10) the textual Adjunct alone is in the Theme position, whereas in English again, there is a multiple Theme consisting of the textual Adjunct and the Subject (9).

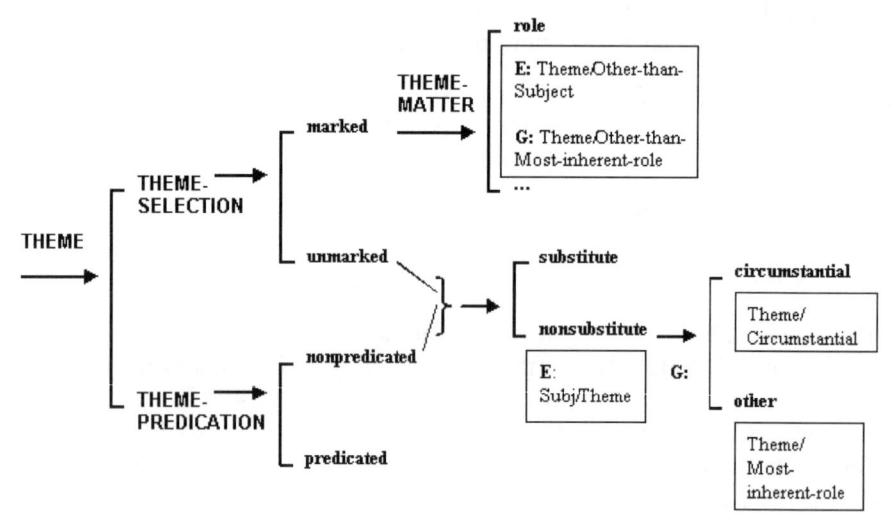

Figure 5. English and German theme options (ideational)

3.1.3. Instantiation: Theme selection in the sample texts

Analysing the English text, its German translation and the English back translation in our Appendix on the basis of this contrastive description of THEME systems, the following observations can be made:

- The German translation often chooses the systemically equivalent option (e.g., unmarked theme in the source language text to unmarked theme in the German target language text), for example (10-E) and (10-G), (11-E) and (11-G), (20-E) and (20-G).

- In cases where systemically equivalent options are not chosen, we find translational correspondence between Theme/Circumstantial and Theme/Subject, e.g., (3-E) and (3-G), (4-E) and (4-G), i.e., in German one of the more delicate options is chosen.
- The English original text has more multiple Themes that include a textual element, e.g., (14-E) and (14-G), (15-E) and (15-G), (19-E) and (19-G). Apart from reflecting the fact that multiple Themes are rarer in German, this shows that the English text chooses to explicitly signal discourse relations, whereas the German translation does not. The differences in Theme choice are thus also a consequence of different selections in marking logico-semantic relations.
- When we compare the E-G translation with the G-E back translation by machine we can see that more systemically equivalent choices have been made in the latter, e.g., consider the translational pairs (2-E)-(2-G) and (2-G)-(2-E') or (3-E)-(3-G) and (3-G)-(3-E').

Theme choice is thus fairly constant across G and E', but much less so across the E original and the G translation: the machine translation G-E' is more literal than the human translation E-G. Where systemic grammatical equivalents cannot be chosen, choice among more delicate options, if available, must be made. Consider for example (3-E) and (3-G): In the German translation, the temporal information is also thematized, however not expressed within a Subject. Hence, there is a Circumstantial-Theme (*vor kurzem* — 'recently') rather than a Subject-Theme and *research* is transposed to a verbal expression with a change to an impersonal construction (*entdeckte man* — 'discovered one').

3.2. Transitivity in English and German

3.2.1. Definition: Transitivity

Transitivity describes the kinds of processes that can be expressed in a clause and the number and kinds of participants therein. The English transitivity system distinguishes between four *process types*: material, mental, verbal and relational, each having associated a set of unique participant roles, such as Actor and Goal for material, Senser and Phenomenon for mental, Sayer and Message for verbal, and Carrier and Attribute for relational. Another feature of the transitivity system is *agency*, which is described as a parallel system to that of process type, accounting for the possibility of a process to extend to another entity or not (effective vs. middle). This encodes notions such as ergative, transitive and intransitive.

3.2.2. Transitivity in English and German: the grammatical systems

The basic process type and agency options also hold for German. Differences between English and German transitivity arise in the following respects.

- Realization of agency. The typical realization of the middle option in the German AGENCY system is reflexivization, e.g.

    (11) *The book sells well.*
    (12) *Das   Buch   verkauft sich gut.*
          the-NOM book-NOM sells   itself well

    See Figure 6 where this difference is given in the realization statement associated with the feature middle. However, compared to English, the ergative pattern (middle) is much less prominent in German.

- Realization of participant roles. German being a rather strongly inflecting language, it has morphological cases (nominative, genitive, dative and accusative). Case government is largely a realization of transitivity type. See again example (5) in Section 3.1, where the first participant is realized by a nominal group in dative case. This is a realization open to Sensers in mental processes and Carriers in relational processes, but not to Actors in material processes or Sayers in verbal processes.

- Mapping of syntactic functions and participant roles. German shows a much tighter correlation of syntactic functions with participant roles than English (cf. Section 3.1). Consider the following examples (partly taken from Hawkins 1986: 59):

    (13) *This hotel forbids dogs.*

    (14) *My guitar broke a string.*

    (15) *This book reads well.*

    (16) a. **Dieses   Hotel   verbietet Hunde.*
              NOM-this NOM-hotel fobids dogs
          b. *In diesem   Hotel   sind Hunde   verboten.*
              in DAT-this DAT-hotel are   NOM-dogs forbidden

(17) a. *Meine   Gitarre   zerriss   eine   Saite.
          NOM-my   NOM-guitar broke   ACC-a   ACC-string
     b. An meiner   Gitarre   riss   eine   Saite.
          at DAT-my DAT-guitar broke   NOM-a NOM-string

(18) a. *Dieses   Buch   liest   gut.
          NOM-this   NOM-book   reads   well
     b. Dieses   Buch   liest   sich   gut.
          NOM-this   NOM-book   reads   itself   well

These examples show the greater flexibility of English to fill Subjects by a variety of participant roles and some typical ways of compensation in translating from English to German: Subjects in English become Circumstantials in German (as in (16b)), the process is passivized as in (16b) or reflexivized as in (18b), or a different lexical verb is chosen as in (17b).

Figure 6 shows some of the main differences in the TRANSITIVITY systems of English and German.

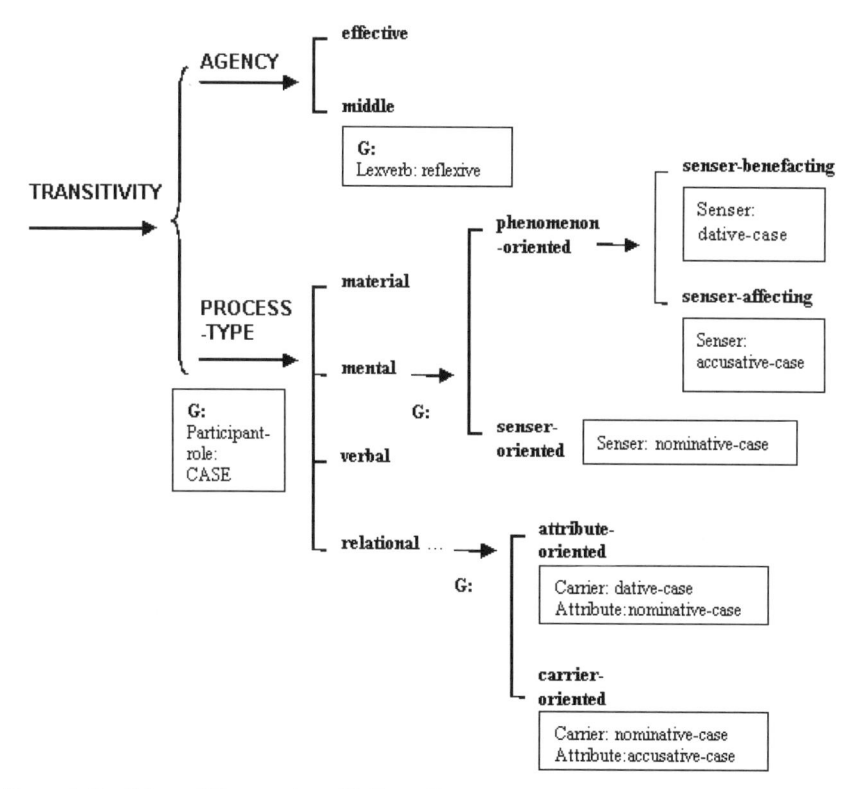

Figure 6. English and German transitivity options

3.2.3. Instantiation: Transitivity choice in the sample texts

In the sample texts, often the systemically equivalent process type is chosen, e.g., (2-E) and (2-G), (4-E) and (4-G) or (5-E) and (5-G), but the above mentioned differences also show, e.g., in (19) below[6].

(19) *Latest research reveals* (3-E)

(20) *Vor kurzem erst entdeckte man...* (3-G)
  recently only discovered one

where putting *Forschung* ('research') as Subject could result in unwanted personification and the translation choice is thus an impersonal construction with *man* ('one'); or

(21) *the hydrogen atoms exchange...billions of times per second.* (15-E)

(22) *werden   die   Wasserstoffatome   Billionen*
  are   NOM-the NOM-hydrogen-atoms billions

  Male pro Sekunde   ausgetauscht. (15-G)
  times per second   exchanged

where the German translation uses a passive construction—the German *austauschen* ('exchange') cannot be used as a middle, so reflexivization is not an option and the translation compensates by a passive; or

(23) *text books write this process as...* (17-E)

(24) *In   Lehrbüchern   wird   dieser   Prozess   als ...*
  in   DAT-text-books is   NOM-this NOM-process as ...

  dargestellt. (17-G)
  represented

where the Subject becomes a Circumstantial in the German translation and the process is passivized. Again, this is because *Lehrbücher* ('text books') is a nonconscious entity and, using *Lehrbücher* as a Subject could result in undesired personification. Compare (25) which gives a literal back translation:

(25) *In text books this process is ... represented as...* (17-E')

In all of these examples, the German translation resorts to grammatical means from a different area of the grammar (notably: diathesis is changed from active to passive) and the process type and/or agency is changed.

Comparing the human translation and the machine translation, again, there are more instances of systemically equivalent options across G and E' than across E and G — the machine translation is more literal than the human translation.

3.3. Grammatical metaphor in English and German

3.3.1. Definition: Grammatical metaphor

The systemic functional term *grammatical metaphor* is related to what is commonly called paraphrase, covering e.g., nominalization of a process. The underlying assumption here is that there is one *congruent* lexico-grammatical realization of a given experiential content (e.g., a semantic process is realized by a clause, a semantic entity is realized by a nominal group, etc.) and a number of *noncongruent* ones which are textually and/or interpersonally not identical with the congruent one[7]. For example, the congruent way of expression of a process or event is as a major clause (26). The same experiential content can be expressed as a verbal group (27), a nominal group (28) or a minor clause (29) — these are the noncongruent ways of expression:

(26) *the student objects to the theory*

(27) *the student's objecting to the theory*

(28) *the student's objection to the theory*

(29) *that the student objects to the theory*

The set of realizational possibilities other than the congruent one is referred to as grammatical metaphor. The crucial parameters here are rank and grammatical class: the same experiential content can be expressed by locating it at different ranks or by assigning it different grammatical classes (cf. Matthiessen 1995: 71–121). Motivations for the choice between congruent and noncongruent realizations are said to lie predominantly in registerial variation, i.e., variation according to situation. So, for example, the register of scientific texts in English uses more nominalizations than, say, the register of instructional texts. Cross-linguistically, grammatical metaphor occurs when, for instance, in a translation the equivalent congruent realization in the target language is not chosen, e.g., a clause is translated as a nominal group (relocation in rank) or a material process is translated by a relational process (relocation in class) (cf. also Bateman 1992). Such cases imply that a translation procedure of transposition or shift has been applied.

3.3.2. Instantiation: grammatical metaphor in the sample texts

There is predominantly equivalent choice of congruent or noncongruent realizations across English and German, e.g.[8],

(30) *When bonded to carbon...* (13-E)

(31) *Verbindet sich das Wasserstoffatom mit*
bonds itself NOM-the NOM-hydrogen-atom with

Kohlenstoff... (13-G)
DAT-carbon

(32) *Hydrogen can form stronger bonds...* (14-E)

(33) *kann Wasserstoff stärkere Bindungen*
can NOM-hydrogen ACC-stronger ACC-bonds

eingehen... (14-G)
form

but there are also some different choices, e.g., congruent choice in English and noncongruent choice in German:

(34) *Hydrogen links up with other atoms...* (2-E)

(35) *Wasserstoff bildet mit anderen Atomen*
NOM-hydrogen forms with DAT-other DAT-atoms

Verbindungen (2-G)
ACC-connections

(36) *this is the gas that is piped...* (7-E)

(37) *könnte dieses Gas... Verwendung finden* (7-G)
could NOM-this NOM-gas ACC-use find

Also, there is translational correspondence between noncongruent and noncongruent, but using different kinds of grammatical metaphor across E and G in that there is a different change in process type from the underlying congruent option:

(38) *Chemists find hydrogen particularly interesting...* (9-E)

(39) *Für   den   Chemiker   ist Wasserstoff   von*
     for   ACC-the ACC-chemist   is   NOM-hydrogen   of

   besonderem   Interesse... (9-G)
   DAT-particular   AT-interest

(40) *Oxygen and nitrogen atoms are particularly attractive to H+* (20-E)

(41) *Sauerstoff-   und Stickstoffatome üben*
     NOM-oxygen and   NOM-nitrogen exercise

   eine   besonders große
   ACC-a   particularly ACC-large

   Anziehungskraft auf H+ aus (20-G)
   ACC-attraction   on   H+ SEPARABLE-VERB-PREFIX

(38) and (39) are noncongruent realizations of the same experiential content ('to be interested in something'). All of the German translational correspondences are so-called *Funktionsverbgefüge* ('support verb constructions'), in which, compared to the congruent base realization with a simple lexical verb, the realization of the semantic process is spread over the verb and a nominal group (as e.g., in (41)). Thus, there is an apparent change in grammatical process type, e.g., between (40) and (41) from relational to material.

It is in the area of grammatical metaphor that the differences in underlying translation models between the human translation and the machine translation become most obvious: In all the sentences with differences in grammatical metaphor between E and G, there are no differences between G and E'. This shows again that the machine translation is more literal than the human translation.

4. Locating translational concepts and categories in the model

In the preceding section I have carried out a contrastive analysis of three texts that are in a translation relation, focusing on three grammatical phenomena. I have employed the general dimensions of potential cross-linguistic variation introduced in Section 2.

On the basis of a sketch of the differences and commonalities in the grammatical systems of theme and transitivity of English and German, I looked at how they are instantiated in the three sample texts. Also, I looked at differences and commonalities in the usage of grammatical metaphor. The next steps are to take some central notions of translation studies and locate them in the model (Section 4.2), thus making its relevance for discussing translation more explicit, and to try to refine their definitions with the help of the terms introduced by the proposed contrastive-linguistic model. Before doing so, it is necessary to say precisely what these notions are and how they are typically defined in translation studies (Section 4.1).

4.1. Translation strategy, equivalence, translation type and translation procedure: common definitions

Translation strategy refers to the classification of translation into *literal* vs. *free*. The extreme case of literal translation is word-for-word or interlinear translation (cf. Wilss 1977), which is defined as operating at the level of words, translating one word in the source language text by one word in the target language without establishing syntactic correctness in the target language expression. This strategy is retrospective, favoring the source language. An example of word-for-word translation is given in (42) below:

(42) a. *Ich bin gestern   abend   spät nachhause gegangen.*
         I am yesterday evening late home   gone

   b. *I am yesterday evening late home gone.*

In word-for-word translation translational correspondence is established at word rank (cf. Catford 1965). In free translation, in contrast, there is no clear limit to what is held constant; translation is prospective, i.e., the target language is favored. Also literal translation (excepting word-for-word translation) is prospective. It typically operates on units larger than the word and leaves rank constant, i.e., prepositional phrases are translated as prepositional phrases, nominal groups as nominal groups etc. In contrast to word-for-word translation, literal translation does establish correctness of the target language expression. See (43) in contrast to (42) above:

(43) a. *Ich bin gestern   abend   spät nachhause gegangen.*
     I am yesterday evening late home   gone

   b. *I went home late last night.*

Literal and free translation are on a cline rather than being absolute categories. Any one translation can be more literal or more free. While the extreme points of this cline can be more or less precisely defined, in between them is a considerable grey area. The same is true of the notion of *equivalence*, which is said to be either *formal* or *dynamic* (cf. e.g., Nida 1964), where formal equivalence implies a source language orientation and dynamic equivalence a target language orientation.

Choice of *translation type* is typically determined by the context in which a translation is carried out, i.e., the client of the translation, the purpose of the translation, its intended readership etc. I adopt here Sager's classification of translation types (cf. Sager 1994: 51–83; the term 'translation type' I employ here is the same as Sager's 'target language documents'), which is shown in Figure 7[9].

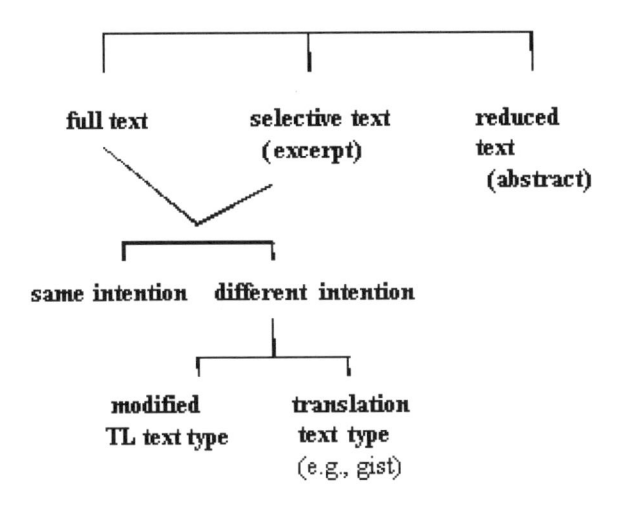

```
              ┌─────────────┼─────────────┐
          full text    selective text    reduced
                         (excerpt)       text
               ╲_____╱         (abstract)
                      │
              ┌───────┴───────┐
        same intention   different intention
                              │
                      ┌───────┴───────┐
                  modified       translation
                  TL text type   text type
                                 (e.g., gist)
```

Figure 7. Translation types

Translation procedures are the basic techniques of translation. I assume the classification of Vinay and Darbelnet (1995) here, which distinguishes between calque, emprunt, literal translation, transposition, modulation, paraphrase etc. The problem with classifications of translation procedures is that the definitions of the single procedures are often rather vague or formulated as operating on rather shallow linguistic levels (e.g., syntactic category). As a consequence, the criteria for their application are not made explicit enough.

The relation between translation type, translation strategy, equivalence and translation procedures is roughly as follows: the choice of translation type will basically determine the global translation strategy and the kind of equivalence sought in the translation, and the translation strategy is an indicator for the kinds of translation procedures that are most likely to be suitable. However, neither translation type or translation strategy, which are global parameters of translation, can determine the translation procedures that are suitable locally, i.e., at the level of grammar, in each instance of translation of a clause or smaller grammatical unit.

Having made explicit the terms of translation type, translation strategy, equivalence and translation procedure, they can now be located in the model of contrastive-linguistic description sketched in Section 2.

4.2. Contextualizing translation strategy, translation type and translation procedure

Figure 8 re-expresses the dimensions of contrastive-linguistic description given in Figure 4 as a table arranged centrally around the dimensions of stratification and instantiation.

Translation type is located in the column between system and instance: The choice of a translation type, i.e., a target language text type, must refer to the type of situation in which a translation is carried out; an appropriate text type or register in the target language has to be determined accordingly.

Translation strategy is located along the dimension of stratification — whether translational correspondence is sought primarily at the stratum of context, semantics or grammar. The terms of translation strategy and equivalence can thus already be made more precise: Translational correspondence at the stratum of context implies free translation and dynamic equivalence. Translational correspondence at the level of grammar can either be sought at the realizational level (syntagmatic axis) or at the systemic, functional level (paradigmatic axis). Formal equivalence can be located more precisely at the syntagmatic axis, and another kind of equivalence at the paradigmatic axis can be defined: functional equivalence. Both formal and functional equivalence can then be subsumed under the more general term of grammatical equivalence. In both cases, the translation strategy is literal translation: When formal equivalence is established, a translation is more literal; when functional equivalence is established, a translation is less literal and moves closer to the free end of the literal-free cline. What is equally important for making more precise what a less literal/more free translation is the third dimension that organises the grammatical stratum: rank. Translational correspondence can be established at the same rank or at a different rank. When a translation is rather constant with respect to rank choices compared to the original, the translation strategy is more literal; when rank is left relatively inconstant throughout a translation, the translation strategy is less literal and translation procedures frequently used are transpositions and modulations (cf. also Section 4.3). In terms of equivalence, with different choices in rank there is a move further away from grammatical (formal, functional) equivalence and closer to contextual or dynamic equivalence.

Translation procedures are located in the model at instance level, where instance is related to the system via register/text type. This is crucial in translation, because in order to decide which translation procedure to apply locally, a translator needs knowledge about differences and commonalities in language systems (both axes) and about the typical choices in the systems according to a situation type (register).

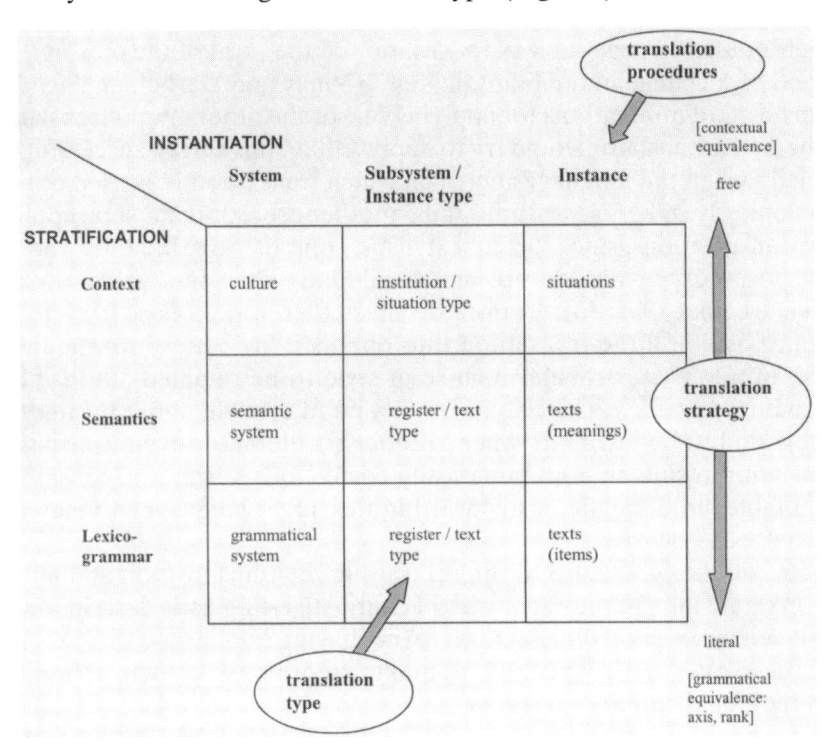

Figure 8. Locating translation methods

Thus, all four notions — translation type, translation strategy, equivalence, translation procedure — can be contextualized in the proposed model of contrastive-linguistic description and each of them can be refined using the dimensions according to which the model is organised (stratification, axiality, delicacy, metafunction and instantiation).

To further illustrate the added value of this contextualization, let us look at the problem of translation procedures being too vaguely defined and the according difficulty of motivating their application.

4.3. Placing translation procedures in the model

In an attempt at making more precise the term of translation procedure, I focus on the three most commonly applied translation procedures: literal translation, transposition and modulation.

Literal translation is defined by Vinay and Darbelnet (1995) as "the direct transfer of a source language text into a grammatically and idiomatically appropriate target language text…" (Vinay and Darbelnet 1995: 33). Transposition "involves replacing one word class with another without changing the meaning of the message"(Vinay and Darbelnet 1995: 36). Modulation is defined as "a variation of the form of the message obtained by a change in the point of view" (Vinay and Darbelnet 1995: 36).

In terms of motivations for applying one or the other, literal translation is the first a translator would try to apply. Often, this can be successful, especially when the languages between which translation is carried out are typologically rather close. If this fails, another procedure must be applied. For transpositions, since "from a stylistic point of view, the base and the transposed expression do not necessarily have the same value" (Vinay and Darbelnet 1995: 36), "translators must, therefore, choose to carry out a transposition if the translation thus obtained fits better into the utterance, or allows a particular nuance of style to be retained" (Vinay and Darbelnet 1995: 36). The change of view point brought about by modulation is said to be justified "when, although a literal, or even transposed, translation results in a grammatically correct utterance, it is considered unsuitable, unidiomatic or awkward in the target language" (Vinay and Darbelnet 1995: 36).

How do the procedures of literal translation, transposition and modulation relate then to the categories of contrastive-linguistic description introduced in the preceding sections? And, having established this relation, can these categories contribute to making more precise their definitions and their application criteria?

Transpositions typically reflect cross-linguistic grammatical metaphor of the first kind, i.e., relocation in rank (see again the translational pairs

(34–35), (38–39) or (40–41) above: In all of these transpositions have been applied). Also modulations often reflect grammatical metaphor[10], namely grammatical metaphor of the second kind, i.e., relocation in grammatical class (see again e.g., (40–41 above). Literal translation establishes translational correspondence at the syntagmatic axis, in the simplest case, e.g., same word order in source and target languages, or at the paradigmatic axis, possibly with differences in syntagmatic realization between source language and target language.

Taking the perspective of the multi-dimensionality of contrastive-linguistic description introduced, two classes of motivation for the application of translation procedures can be distinguished:

1. Procedures related to difference/commonality in grammatical systems:
Literal translation is appropriate when a systemically equivalent grammatical option is available in the target language, whether that option comes with different syntagmatic reflexes or not, e.g., a declarative, independent clause in an English source language text being translated as a declarative, independent clause in a German target language text, possibly accompanied by a basic word order change.
Transpositions may have to be carried out when there is a difference in system delicacy between source language and target language. There are two cases of delicacy difference (cf. also Steiner 1994 for a similar classification):

- more delicate options available in the target language. When there are more delicate options in the target language, a transposition may be required. e.g., English unmarked Subject-Theme to German Circumstantial-Theme as in (3-E)-(3-G).

- only less delicate option available in the target language. An example of this is the inverse of the example just mentioned: Translating from German to English, the systemically closest option to the German unmarked Circumstantial-Theme is the Subject-Theme. Again, a transposition may be required.

Finally there is the case in which there is no systemically equivalent option available in the target language. An option that is in disjunction to the one chosen in the source language text might have to be chosen or other parts of the grammar of the target language may have to be drawn upon to make a translational choice. See for example (15-E) and (15-G), where the middle option is not available in German. Therefore, effective is chosen and the process is passivized. Such cases imply the application of a modulation.

2. Procedures related to differences/commonalities in the mapping of situational attributes and lexico-grammatical expression, i.e., register:
Even if literal translation is often systemically possible (i.e., a systemically equivalent option is available in the target language), transpositions or modulations are often carried out for register reasons. For example, a possible literal translation of (2-E) *Hydrogen links up with other atoms...* is *Wasserstoff verbindet sich mit anderen Atomen...* However, noncongruent versions of *sich verbinden* ('link up'), such as *Bindung eingehen* ('enter into a connection') or *Verbindung bilden* ('build a connection') are expressions that are rather characteristic of the register of scientific chemistry texts and can therefore be a more appropriate translational choice.

Thus, choosing an appropriate translation procedure amounts to balancing the constraints arising from differences and commonalities between language systems and the constraints imposed by registerial differences.

5. Summary and conclusions

This section briefly summarises the main points made in this paper and tries to put it in a wider context by relating some of the issues discussed to what is presented in some other papers in this volume. I conclude with some remarks on the value of translations for multilingual investigation in general.

In this paper I have suggested to root a theory of translation in a model of contrastive-linguistic resources that takes into account multiple dimensions of cross-linguistic differences and commonalities. These dimensions are identical to the representational constructs assumed by Systemic Functional Linguistics, which are stratification, metafunction, axis, rank, delicacy and instantiation. With a sample analysis of selected linguistic phenomena in three texts that are in a translation relation — an English source language text, a German translation of that text and a German-English back translation produced by machine — I have shown the relevance of these parameters for contrastive analysis, on the one hand, and for the linguistic analysis of translation, on the other hand. Finally, I have shown how some of the central concepts of translation theory — translation type, translation strategy, equivalence and translation procedure — can be located in the model of contrastive-linguistic description proposed, indicating how they can be made more precise using the dimensions of cross-linguistic contrast and commonality assumed in the model. For showing the applicational relevance of the proposal, e.g., its use for teaching translation and translation theory, more extensive analyses of translations have to be carried out using the terms suggested.

There is a note in place here about the comparability of the linguistic-descriptive categories I employed in the contrastive analyses. Throughout the paper I have been assuming that there is something like 'equivalent systemic options' across two languages which can be used as a ground of comparison. What we encounter here is a similar problem to that of language typology when it has to make sure that the categories it uses for comparison are actually cross-linguistically applicable. For example, if I want to make a comparative statement about Subjects in English and German, can I simply assume that 'Subject' denotes the same kind of thing in both languages? A common answer to such questions is that if Subjects share a sufficient amount of common properties, then we can apply the term cross-linguistically. This kind of answer is still not entirely satisfactory, but I adapt it for the present context in the following way: Systemically equivalent options across two languages are those options that are located in the same grammatical system (e.g., MOOD, TRANSITIVITY or THEME) and carry roughly the same function in the overall linguistic systems of the languages under investigation. One aspect of future work using the framework presented here will be to make the notion of systemically equivalent option more precise (cf. also work on typology based on Systemic Functional Linguistics, such as Caffarel et al. forthcoming).

On a theoretical level, I would like to place the present paper in the following context. There are a number of notions and terms in translation studies that are very well established and have clearly been useful in theorizing translation. One such notion is that of equivalence. The way equivalence is commonly discussed in translation studies implies that there is something in a translation that is shared with its source language text, something that is held constant across the source language text and a translation of it. One of the central questions in translation studies is then: What is it exactly that is held constant, what is it that can be considered shared? However, establishing equivalence is not only to do with leaving something constant, but it is also to do with accommodating differences. In translation studies it seems, however, that the former mode of thinking about equivalence as looking for a constant is favored. In machine translation research these two views on equivalence are reflected more evenly, namely in the form of interlingua-based vs. transfer-based systems. In the former, equivalence is established by assuming a constant across source language and target language, the interlingua; in the latter, the assumption is that there is no constant, and the mismatch or divergence between the source language and the target language has to be accounted for by transfer rules. Now, one can argue which of the two approaches is more successful, but the point I would like to make is that each of the two views reflects valuable, often complementary, insights into the specific properties of translations. Each adopted on its own, however, remains a simplification.

Consequently, there seem to be two promising methodological paths that have hardly been explored in translation studies:

1. Combining the two views sketched above, i.e., equivalence as the search for a constant and equivalence as the accommodation of differences, may yield a more realistic model of translation.
   The model of contrastive-linguistic resources I have proposed in this paper is a step in exactly this direction because it allows to accommodate both diversity and commonality between language systems and their instantiation in texts, including translation. A similar direction is taken in Matthiessen (this volume).

2. Rather than assuming that there is a constant across a source language and a target language, starting from the assumption that there is no constant may well provide new insights into the properties of translations.
   Using some of the terms discussed in this paper and other papers in this volume, why not instead of seeing equivalence as the search for identity try to approach it as diversity and then constrain this diversity as 'diversity of similarities' (Yallop this volume)? Or why not start with asking whether translation could be considered simply a variant of a text (register) encoded in another language (Steiner this volume)? In both perspectives, there is no a priori assumption about holding anything constant. The challenge then is to be able to say where the limits of this inconstancy or diversity are in translation. Approaching translation from this angle is unusual, but it has the potential of resulting in a more precise definition of equivalence, a clarification of what the range of possibilities between free vs. literal translation is more precisely, and also of what a good translation is.

The final point I would like to make concerns the value of translations for multilingual linguistic investigation in general. One reason why a true interaction, potentially fruitful, between translation studies and linguistics has not really happened is that translations have not been acknowledged as a valuable object of investigation in linguistics. It is true that what translation studies is interested in first of all is the relation between texts and that linguistics, when it is concerned with more than one language, is interested in language systems (cf. Halliday this volume). But texts are instantiations of language systems, their grammars and their semantics, according to particular contextual requirements. So, the two perspectives are actually complementary. In translation studies, this complementarity is more readily acknowledged than in linguistics: It is indispensable when translating to know about differences and commonalities in language systems and how these are realized in different text types and instantiated in the exponents of those types. Multilingual studies in linguistics (language typology, contrastive linguistics) should therefore consider translations as interesting data, use translation as a test bed and consult translation studies for valuable contrastive-linguistic insights. For Systemic Functional Linguistics in particular, investigating translations offers the chance of making some of its notions more precise — in particular that of instantiation.

Acknowledgments

The research reported on here was partly supported by a fellowship from the Australian-European Awards Programme (AEAP). Also, I am grateful to John Bateman, Erich Steiner and Colin Yallop for helpful comments on draft versions of this paper and to Christian Matthiessen, who inspired the basic line of thought of the paper.

APPENDIX: Sample texts

Sample text 1: English original (E)

(1-E) The hidden strength of hydrogen

(2-E) **Hydrogen** links up with other atoms in many ways, forming a wide variety of compounds, from methane to DNA.

(3-E) **Latest research** reveals the strong hydrogen bond — a previously unknown way for hydrogen to form compounds.

(4-E) **Of all the chemical elements**, hydrogen is the simplest in structure, and first in the diversity of its chemical behaviour.

(5-E) **The element itself** exists as the molecule H_2 which is well known as the lightest of all gases.

(6-E) **Although industry** uses this gas on a large scale, it is rarely encountered in everyday life except to fill balloons.

(7-E) **However in 25 years time** this may be the gas which is piped into our homes to fuel boilers and cookers — once we have used up supplies of natural methane gas, CH_4.

(8-E) **Hydrogen** burns to form water, and hence is cleaner than gases containing carbon.

(9-E) **Chemists** find hydrogen particularly interesting because of the versatility of its chemical bonding, as apparent from the many different types of compound that it can form.

(10-E) **The hydrogen atom** consists of a nucleus containing a single proton with an electron in orbit around it.

(11-E) **This orbit** can accommodate at most two electrons, so hydrogen can form only one covalent bond — a bond in which a pair of electrons is shared by two atoms — to another element.

(12-E) **This** it does in most of its compounds.

(13-E) When bonded to carbon as in CH4 and the many other organic compounds with C-H bonds, the hydrogen atom is firmly held by this covalent link to the carbon atom.

(14-E) **On the other hand, hydrogen** can form stronger bonds with oxygen yet still be mobile.

(15-E) **Thus in water, H2O**, the hydrogen atoms exchange between different oxygen atoms billions of times per second.

(16-E) **In some compounds, namely acids**, the molecules are so averse to the hydrogen they contain that they will readily donate the hydrogen to other molecules.

(17-E) **One such** is hydrogen chloride, HCl, and textbooks often write this process as HCl H+ + Cl-.

(18-E) **But H+** is a "bare" proton, and as it has an overwhelming attraction to any electron pair in its vicinity it cannot exist apart from a molecule.

(19-E) **Thus the H+ from an acid** is drawn immediately to another molecule, especially to any atom within that molecule which has a pair of electrons in its outer shell, unattached to any other atom.

(20-E) **Oxygen and nitrogen atoms** are particularly attractive to H+ because of the lone-pair electrons they contain.

(21-E) **Some acids, such as "magic acid"**, are so strong that they can donate their protons to almost any other molecule whether it has a "free" electron-pair or not.

(22-E) **"Magic acid"** is a mixture of fluorosulphuric acid, HSO3F, and antimony pentafluoride, SbF5.

(23-E) **The acid** is so strong that when sulphuric acid is dissolved in it, the sulphuric acid is forced to play the part of accepting a hydrogen and so becomes H3SO4+!

Sample text 2: German translation (G)

(1-G) Die geheime Kraft des Wasserstoffs

(2-G) **Wasserstoff** bildet mit anderen Atomen viele verschiedene Verbindungen, angefangen vom Methan bis zur DNS.

(3-G) **Vor kurzem erst** entdeckte man die starke Wasserstoffbrückenbildung — eine vordem unbekannte Art der Wasserstoffbindung.

(4-G) **Wasserstoff** ist seinem Aufbau nach das einfachste, aber seinem Verhalten nach das vielseitigste von allen chemischen Elementen.

(5-G) **Es** existiert als Molekül H2, das als das leichteste aller Gase allgemein bekannt ist.

(6-G) Obwohl es industriell in grossem Umfang genutzt wird, kommt es im täglichen Leben — ausser beim Füllen von Ballons — kaum vor.

(7-G) **Doch** könnte gerade dieses Gas in einem Vierteljahrhundert, wenn die Vorräte an natürlichem Methangas, CH4, aufgebraucht sind, in den Gasgeräten unserer Haushalte <u>Verwendung finden</u>.

(8-G) **Wasserstoff** verbrennt zu Wasser und ist somit weniger umweltbelastend als Gase, die Kohlenstoff enthalten.

(9-G) **Für den Chemiker** ist das Element Wasserstoff von besonderem Interesse, weil es, wie aus der Vielfalt der Wasserstoffverbindungen ersichtlich, zahlreiche chemische Bindungen eingehen kann.

(10-G) **Das Wasserstoffatom** besteht aus einem Kern mit einem einzelnen Proton und einer Hülle mit einem Elektron.

(11-G) **Die Hülle des Kerns** nimmt höchstens zwei Elektronen auf, so dass der Wasserstoff mit einem anderen Element nur <u>eine kovalente Bindung eingehen</u> kann — eine Bindung, bei der ein Elektronenpaar gleichzeitig von zwei Atomen gebunden wird.

(12-G) **Von dieser Art** sind die meisten Verbindungen des Wasserstoffs.

(13-G) Verbindet sich das Wasserstoffatom mit Kohlenstoff wie in CH4 oder den vielen anderen organischen Verbindungen mit C-H-Bindungen, so ist es durch die kovalente Atombindung fest an das Kohlenstoffatom gebunden.

(14-G) **Mit Sauerstoff** kann Wasserstoff stärkere <u>Bindungen eingehen</u>, ohne seine Bindungsfähigkeit einzubüssen.

(15-G) **Im Wasser etwa** werden die Wasserstoffatome zwischen den Sauerstoffatomen des H2O mehrere Billionen Male pro Sekunde ausgetauscht.

(16-G) **In einigen Verbindungen — besonders in Säuren —** sind die Abstossungskräfte zwischen Molekül und Wasserstoff so gross, dass der Wasserstoff sofort an andere Moleküle abgegeben wird.

(17a-G) **Salzsäure, HCl**, ist eine solche Verbindung.

(17b-G) **In Lehrbüchern** wird dieser Prozess oft durch die Gleichung HCl H+ + Cl- dargestellt.

(18-G) Da aber H+ ein "nacktes" Proton ist und jedes in seiner Nähe befindliche Elektronenpaar anzieht, kann es nicht wirklich ausserhalb eines Moleküls existieren.

(19-G) **Das von einer Säure stammende H+** wird sofort von einem anderen Molekül angezogen, genauer von jedem Atom eines Moleküls, das in seiner Hülle ein Elektronenpaar besitzt, welches noch nicht an ein anderes Atom gebunden ist.

(20-G) **Sauerstoff- und Stickstoffatome** üben eine besonders grosse Anziehungskraft auf H+ aus, weil sie freie Elektronenpaare besitzen.

(21-G) **Einige Säuren, wie z.B. die "magische Säure"**, sind so stark, dass sie ihre Protonen an fast jedes andere Molekül abgeben können, ob es nun ein "freies" Elektronenpaar besitzt oder nicht.

(22/23-G) **"Magische Säure"** ist ein Gemisch aus Fluorschwefelsäure, HSO3F, und Antimonpentafluorid, SbF5, und ist so stark, dass selbst Schwefelsäure, die in ihr gelöst wird, Wasserstoff aufnehmen muss und zu H3SO4+ wird!

Sample text 3: back translation German-English (E')

(1-E') The secret strength of the hydrogen

(2-E') **Hydrogen** forms many different connections with other atoms, begun from methane to the DNS.

(3-E') **Recently only** one discovered the strong hydrogen bond formation — a heretofore unknown kind of the hydrogen connection.

(4-E') **Hydrogen** is its structure the simplest after, but after its behavior the most versatile of all chemical elements.

(5-E') **It** exists as molekule H2, which admits as the easiest all gases generally is.

(6-E') Although it is used industrially to a large extent, it occurs in the daily life — except when filling balloons — hardly.

(7-E') **But straight this gas could find** in a quarter century, if the supplies of natural methane gas, are used up CH4, in the gas units of our households use.

(8-E') **Hydrogen** burns to water and is thus less environmentalloading than gases, which contain carbon.

(9-E') **For the chemist** the element hydrogen is of special interest, because it, as from that variety of the hydrogen connections evidently, can be received numerous chemical connections.

(10-E') **The hydrogen atom** consists of a core with an individual proton and a covering with an electron.

(11-E') **The covering of the core** takes up at the most two electrons, so that the hydrogen with another element only a kovalente connection can be received — a connection, with which a pair of electrons is bound at the same time by two atoms.

(12-E') Are from this kind most connections of the hydrogen.

(13/14-E') If the hydrogen atom connects itself with carbon as in CH4 or the many other organic compounds with CH connections, then it is by the kovalente atomic bond firmly to the carbon atom bind along oxygen can hydrogen stronger connections be received, without losing its connection ability.

(15-E') **In the water** about the hydrogen atoms between the oxygen atoms of the H several trillions time per second are exchanged.

(16-E') **In some connections — particularly in acids —** the repulsive forces between molecule and hydrogen are so large that the hydrogen is transferred immediately to other molecules.

(17a-E') **Hydrochloric acid, HCl**, is such a connection.

(17b-E') **In text books** this process is often represented to Cl by the equation HCl H+ +.

(18-E') Since however H+ is a naked proton and each pair of electrons in its proximity tightens, it cannot really exist outside of a molecule.

(19-E') **The H+ coming from an acid** is tightened immediately by another molecule, more exactly from each atom of a molecule, which possesses a pair of electrons, which is not yet bound to another atom in ist covering.

(20-E') **Oxygen and nitrogen atoms** exercise a particularly large attraction on H+, because they possess free pairs of electrons.

(21-E') **Some acids, e.g. the magic acid**, it is so strong that they can deliver their protons to nearly every other molecule, whether it possesses now a free pair of electrons or not.

(22/23-E') **Magic acid** is a mixture from fluorine sulfuric acid, HSO3F, and Antimonpentafluorid, SbF5, and is so strong that even sulfuric acid, which is loosened in it, hydrogen take up must and H3SO4+ becomes!

Notes

1. The English original text and the German translation are extracts from texts of a small translation corpus compiled from SCIENTIFC AMERICAN and SPEKTRUM DER WISSENSCHAFT by Monika Doherty at Humboldt University, Berlin. The English back translation has been produced by the SYSTRAN system (http://www.systranet.com/; last visited in September 1997). The sample texts are given in the appendix; the English original is referred to as **E**, the German translation as **G** and the back translation into English as **E'**. The individual sentences in the sample texts are labeled by numbers with E, G and E' identifying the text in which they occur.
2. For systemic functional terms, the following notational conventions are used: Functional elements, such as Actor, Goal, Theme, Circumstantial are given with the first letter capitalized; system options, such as declarative, interrogative etc., are given in small letters; system network names, such as e.g., MOOD, are given in small capitals.
3. Themes are given in bold face.
4. A more detailed account of German theme based on Systemic Functional Grammar is Steiner and Ramm (1995); English theme is described in detail in Halliday (1985) and Matthiessen (1995).
5. Theme is annotated in bold face in the sample texts. Clause complexes are not treated and thus left out of the thematic analysis.
6. The number behind the displayed examples is the identifier for the sentence in the sample texts in the appendix.
7. For a definition of grammatical metaphor see Halliday 1985: 319–346.
8. Instances of grammatical metaphor are marked by underlining in the sample text in the appendix; in E', the underlining marks the direct translations of what is grammatical metaphor in G.
9. The translation type in the sample texts is 'full text, same intention'.
10. More prominently, they reflect lexical metaphor; cf. Vinay and Darbelnet 1995: 246–255.

References

Baker, Mona
    1995   Corpora in translation studies: An overview and some suggestions for future research. *Target* 7(2): 223–243.

Bateman, John A.
    1992   Towards Meaning-Based Machine Translation: using abstractions from text generation for preserving meaning. *Machine Translation* 6(1): 1–37. (Special issue on the role of text generation in MT).

Bateman, John A. and Elke Teich
    1995   Selective information presentation in an integrated publication system: an application of genre-driven text generation. *Information Processing and Management* 31(5): 753–768. (Special Issue on Summarizing Text).

Bateman, John A., Christian M.I.M. Matthiessen, Keizo Nanri, and Licheng Zeng
    1991   The re-use of linguistic resources across languages in multilingual generation components. In: *Proceedings of the 1991 International Joint Conference on Artificial Intelligence*, Sydney, Australia, volume 2, 966–971.

Bateman, John A.
   1997   Enabling technology for multilingual natural language generation: the KPML development environment. *Journal of Natural Language Engineering* 3(1): 15–55.

Bell, Roger T.
   1991   *Translation and translating: theory and practise.* London: Longman.

Biber, Douglas and Edward Finegan (eds.)
   1993   *Perspectives on register: situating register variation within sociolinguistics.* Oxford: Oxford University Press.

Biber, Douglas
   1995   *Dimensions of register variation: a cross-linguistic comparison.* Cambridge: Cambridge University Press.

Caffarel, Alice, James R. Martin and Christian M.I.M. Matthiessen
   forthcoming *Systemic Functional Typology*, Amsterdam: Benjamins.

Catford, J.C.
   1965   *A linguistic theory of translation.* Oxford: Oxford University Press.

Degand, Liesbeth
   1996   A Dutch component for a multilingual systemic text generation system. In: Giovanni Adorni and Michael Zock (eds), *Trends in Natural Language Generation: An Artificial Intelligence Perspective*, 350–367. (Number 1036 in Lecture Notes in Artificial Intelligence.) Berlin/New York: Springer.

Ghadessy, Mohsen
   1993   *Register Analysis. Theory and Practice.* London: Pinter.

Halliday, Michael A.K., Angus McIntosh, and Peter Strevens
   1964   *The linguistic sciences and language teaching.* London: Longman.

Halliday, Michael A.K.
   1978   *Language as social semiotic.* London: Edward Arnold.

Halliday, Michael A.K.
   1985   *An Introduction to Functional Grammar.* London: Edward Arnold.

Halliday, Michael A.K.
   this volume Towards a theory of good translation.

Hatim, Basil and Ian Mason
   1990   *Discourse and the translator.* London: Longman.

Hatim, Basil and Ian Mason
   1997   *The translator as communicator.* London and New York: Routledge.

Hawkins, John A.
   1986   *A comparative typology of English and German.* London/Sydney: Croom Helm.

Matthiessen, Christian M.I.M.
   1995   *Lexicogrammatical cartography: English systems.* Tokyo/Taipei/Dallas: International Language Science Publishers.

Matthiessen, Christian M.I.M.
   this volume   The environments of translation.

Nida, Eugene
   1964   *Toward a Science of Translating*. Leiden: E. J. Brill.

Quirk, Randolph, Sidney Greenbaum, Geoffrey Leech, and Jan Svartvik.
   1985   *A comprehensive grammar of the English language*. London: Longman.

Reiss, Katharina and Hans J. Vermeer
   1984   *Grundlegung einer allgemeinen Translationstheorie*. Tübingen: Niemeyer.

Sager, Juan C.
   1994   *Language Engineering and Translation: Consequences of Automation* (Volume 1 of Benjamins Translation Library.) Amsterdam: John Benjamins.

Snell-Hornby, Mary
   1988   *Translation Studies — An Integrated Approach*. Amsterdam: John Benjamins.

Steiner, Erich and Wiebke Ramm
   1995   On theme as a grammatical notion for German. *Functions of Language* 1(2): 57–93.

Steiner, Erich, Paul Schmidt and Cornelia Zelinksy-Wibbelt (eds.)
   1988   *From Syntax to Semantics: insights from Machine Translation*. London: Pinter.

Steiner, Erich
   1994   A Fragment of a Multilingual Transfer Component and its Relation to Discourse Knowledge. In: Wiebke Ramm (ed.) *Text and Context in Machine Translation: Aspects of Discourse Representation in Discourse Processing*, 77–116. (Studies in Machine Translation and Natural Language Processing.) Brussels/Luxembourg: European Commission.

Steiner, Erich
   1996   An extended register analysis as a form of text analysis for translation. In: Gerd Wotjak and Heide Schmidt (eds.), *Modelle der Translation — Models of Translation*, 235–256. (Leipziger Schriften zur Kultur-, Literatur-, Sprach- und Übersetzungswissenschaft).

Steiner, Erich
   this volume   Intralingual and interlingual versions of a text — how specific is the notion of translation?

Teich, Elke, Liesbeth Degand and John A. Bateman
   1996   Multilingual textuality: Experiences from multilingual text generation. In: Giovanni Adorni and Michael Zock (eds.), *Trends in Natural Language Generation: an artificial intelligence perspective*, 31–349. (Number 1036 in Lecture Notes in Artificial Intelligence.) Berlin/New York: Springer.

Teich, Elke
   1995   Towards a methodology for the construction of multilingual resources for multilingual generation. In: *Proceedings of the IJCAI '95 Workshop on Multilingual Generation*, Montreal, Quebec, August 1995, 136–148.

Teich, Elke
   1999   *Systemic Functional Grammar in Natural Language Generation: Linguistic Description and Computational Representation*. London: Cassell.

Vinay, J.P. and J. Darbelnet.
   1995   *Comparative stylistics of French and English. A methodology for translation.*
               Amsterdam: Benjamins (French original appeared in 1958, Paris: Didier).

Wilss, Wolfram
   1977   *Übersetzungswissenschaftliche Probleme und Methoden.* Stuttgart: Klett.

Yallop, Colin
   this volume   The construction of equivalence.

The construction of equivalence

Colin Yallop

1. Uniqueness and similarity

Common sense and scientific analysis tell us that everything is unique and everything keeps changing. We all know that no two people are exactly identical, no two trees are identical, no two rocks are identical; that people change over time, not only physically but in their experience and perceptions and social relationships; that one moment in time can never precisely repeat the conditions and circumstances of a previous moment. Less obviously, but with the help of scientific analysis, we know that even fingerprints, blades of grass and snowflakes are unique.

As humans we are not always content to acknowledge this. Not only do we try to cling to constancy, to recreate circumstances of the past, to recapture lost youth, we also devote extraordinary effort to a technological culture that promotes standardisation of products and procedures and mass production of uniform manufactures and components. Motor vehicles and household appliances are produced in supposedly identical batches, with interchangeable spare parts; banknotes and postage stamps of particular values and series are meant to be identical to each other; and thousands of manufactured items — batteries, bottles, envelopes, light bulbs, paperclips, pencils, screwdrivers and so on — are produced in standard shapes and sizes.

We know that these items are not truly identical. The most advanced manufacturing techniques still produce items that fail to meet the standard, and even when products are up to standard, they are identical within allowable limits, within what engineers call tolerances. When a panel beater replaces a panel on a car and matches the paintwork, it will seem to most people as good as new — but the experienced car mechanic or dealer will probably be able to see that it has been replaced. If I can remove the worn drive belt from my vacuum cleaner and replace it with another that fits and works, I have an identical new belt — except that careful inspection would show that the belt is not exactly identical. I can take any of the two-litre bottles of soft drink from a supermarket shelf knowing that it has been filled to two litres — but a scientific laboratory would be able to show that there are minute variations from one bottle to another. In short, these identical items are identical within limits, identical for relevant purposes, in a particular functional context.

2. The uniqueness of texts

Our texts, spoken and written, are no less unique. Without the technology of writing, printing or sound recording, what we say is fleeting, sometimes perpetuated by memorisation and repetition but impermanent and never repeated identically. Even with technological innovations, our texts are not always as enduring as we want to believe. The work of Shakespeare, printed and bound and available in your bookshop, is rather different in detail from what Shakespeare was writing down 400 years ago — if indeed it was Shakespeare who was writing it down. Highly valued documents, like wills and contracts and constitutions, can now be written down, even preserved in filing cabinets or museum cases, but they too are subject to revision and amendment as well as to physical decay.

We tend to be rather optimistic about the sameness of texts: we refer to "this morning's newspaper", easily disregarding variant editions; we print 100,000 copies of a book and refer to any one of them as "the book"; we photocopy a document and assume that we have exactly replicated it. But sometimes we are forced to curb this optimism and we are reminded of the true uniqueness of everything under the sun, as when we engage in literary studies of how much editing a text has undergone or when we are obliged to show the original birth or marriage certificate, not a copy.

If texts are unique, then we can hardly be confident about the identity of a translation and the original on which it is based. But again, common discourse, at least in English, tries to persuade us otherwise. It seems reasonable to judges in Australian courts of law to ask interpreters to translate exactly what the witness or defendant has said, no more and no less. Interpreters themselves know that while accuracy and faithfulness are of the utmost importance, translating "exactly what someone has said" is often an illusory goal. A multinational company may believe it provides the "same" product information in many languages. And perhaps it is near enough the same for the purpose, but it is not exactly identical in every respect. Someone tells me that they have read a novel by Solzhenitsyn, but I do not assume they have read the Russian original. And as we talk easily of "this morning's paper" or "the dictionary", heedless of variant editions, so also we talk about "the Bible", often overlooking not only the number of languages in which this text exists, but also the variety of English translations now published. (But Muslims are less confident about the Qur'an and deny that it can be preserved in translation.)

3. Translation equivalence

If everything is unique, it is not surprising that judgments about similarity, about identity for relevant purposes, about equivalence across cultural and linguistic boundaries, are problematic.

In the linguistic literature, there is considerable problematisation of sameness and equivalence. I mention three quite different examples. In the course of elaborating his theory of "etics" and "emics", Pike notes that judging whether two linguistic items are the same or different is "an exceedingly complex process — not the simple choice of a 'yes' or 'no'" (1967: 62) and he discusses synonymy in the light of "cultural sameness and difference" (1967: 613); Halverson provides a useful recent review of the concept of equivalence in translation studies, in the context of the human ability to compare ("In studying translation and equivalence, we are studying the means by which all things can be compared", 1997: 227); and Statham, in a spirited defence of Nida's "dynamic equivalence" against deconstructionist criticism, argues that the issue is not whether "purported samenesses" are "identities" but rather in what ways and to what extent we can identify shared semantics (1997: 32).

More specifically, the problems of how to distinguish translation from paraphrase or adaptation and of how to conceptualise "equivalence" in translation are explored in various ways elsewhere in this volume. Matthiessen (chapter 4) speaks of translating "shading into" paraphrasing, and House (chapter 5) addresses the distinction between a translation and a text "resulting from a different textual operation". Shore (chapter 9) also raises questions about how to understand equivalence in the context of training translators, and Teich (chapter 7) does likewise in the course of elaborating a model of contrastive-linguistic resources. Steiner (chapter 6) and Hartley and Paris (chapter 11) particularly examine texts that may be considered variants of each other, and both chapters respond to the need to move beyond simplistic assumptions about equivalence in translation.

It is not the purpose of this chapter to repeat discussion which is carefully pursued elsewhere in the book. The next section will look at a text that may seem to stretch translation to — or beyond — its limits. The main point of this will be to show that even where translators may seem to have moved away from a concern with accuracy and well into free adaptation, it is still possible to find points of correspondence. Such correspondences may be unusual, even unique, but they are, in a sense, only the extreme instances of a process of trying to make sameness out of difference, a process of manoeuvring similarities into relationships that we are willing to accept as equivalent for the occasion and purpose.

4. Alice in Wonderland, Alitji in the Dreamtime

4.1. Background

Lewis Carroll was the pen name of Charles Dodgson, an English mathematician and writer who lived from 1832 to 1898. Carroll — as we will call him from now on — wrote some mathematical works but is more famous for his books for children, among which the most well-known is *Alice's Adventures in Wonderland* (1865). The story tells of a young girl who, dozing off beside her sister on a river bank, catches sight of a large white rabbit which hurries past her taking a watch out of its waistcoat pocket and talking to itself about being late. Alice follows the rabbit down a hole and falls into a fantasy world in which she meets a variety of other strange beings, such as a grinning Cheshire cat, comes upon a March hare and a hatter taking tea with a dormouse, and joins a game of croquet in which the balls are live hedgehogs and the mallets live flamingoes.

The story is at once very English — even in its initial setting in a countryside with daisies, fields and hedges — and highly fantastic. The story has enjoyed great popularity with children but also appeals to adult readers who discern comments on life's absurdities. The book is full of extended puns and plays on words: at one point, for example, Alice is being told about fish and life under the sea, with plays on the names of the fish "whiting", "sole" and "eel" (boots and shoes under the sea are done with whiting rather than blacking, and the boots and shoes have soles and eels) and a further pun on wise fish having a porpoise (purpose). Carroll's playfulness sometimes draws attention to the oddity of customary or proverbial ways of talking, sometimes even touches satirically on serious questions about truth and justice, as in a brief debate about whether "I mean what I say" is the same as "I say what I mean", and in an extraordinary depiction of a court of law in which the judge (the King of Hearts) calls for a verdict before any evidence is heard, the jurors (all animals) write down their names on slates for fear they might forget them before the end of the trial, and cheering in the court is violently suppressed.

Alice in Wonderland was "adapted and translated" by Nancy Sheppard into the Australian language Pitjantjatjara and published as *Alitji in the Dreamtime* in 1975. The very title indicates the extent of adaptation: the name Alice appears in a Pitjantjatjara version as Alitji and the wonderland has become the dreamtime. There are many creative leaps throughout the book. At the very beginning of the story, Alice is sitting beside her sister on a river bank, with nothing to do while her sister reads; whereas Alitji is sitting in a creek bed playing a Pitjantjtatjara story telling game with her sister. Alice sees a white rabbit and follows it, while Alitji sees a white kangaroo.

Alitji in the Dreamtime includes a "back translation" of the Pitjantjatjara into English, and each page of the book is in two columns, with the Pitjantjatjara on the left and the English on the right. In fact this English text sometimes differs substantially from the Pitjantjatjara, notably by including lengthy excursions which are explanations of Pitjantjatjara customs and practices rather than translations of wording in the Pitjantjatjara text. One example near the beginning of the book is a description of the story telling game which Alice and her sister are playing, presumably an explanation which is considered unnecessary for those who can read Pitjantjatjara.

Appendices at the end of this chapter give the opening paragraphs of the text in Carroll's original (Appendix 1), the Pitjantjatjara version (Appendix 2), and the English back translation (Appendix 3). As a further aid to studying these text samples, Appendix 4 provides a rough interlinear gloss of a portion of the Pitjantjatjara, and Appendix 5 shows, if nothing else, the difficulty of aligning the original English with the English of the back translation. Further references to these appendices will be made later.

An "Introduction to Alitji", written by the editor, Barbara Ker Wilson, gives some background to the work and draws attention not only to the cultural equations (such as the white kangaroo for the white rabbit, the witchety grub for the caterpillar and the stockman for the hatter) but also to the inclusion in the Pitjantjatjara of plays on words, not of course as direct translations of the English but as attempts to provide the same kind of enjoyment of the text (Sheppard 1975: ix). Thus Carroll's dormouse begins a story about three sisters called Elsie, Lacie and Tillie, who lived at the bottom of a well. When Alice asks what they lived on, the dormouse replies "treacle" (a play on the old meaning of "treacle" as "remedy" and the phrase "treacle well" for a well believed to provide water with healing powers). The play on "treacle" goes further a little later when the dormouse says that the three sisters were learning to draw. Alice asks what they were drawing and the dormouse replies "treacle", adding that if you can draw water from a water-well, you should be able to draw treacle from a treacle-well.

In *Alitji in the Dreamtime*, the koala (corresponding to the dormouse) begins a story about three sisters called Tili, Iltji and Itjila. All three names are acceptable as names in Pitjantjatjara; but *tili* is a word meaning "flame" or "light", *iltji* is both a word meaning "desert" and the Pitjantjatjara adaptation of Elsie (as Alitji is of Alice), while Itjila is an anagram of Alitji (as Lacie is an anagram of Alice). In the koala's story, the three sisters lived in a *tangka*, which is both a borrowing of the English word "tank" and a Pitjantjatjara word meaning "cooked food". Thus when Alitji asks what the three sisters lived on, the koala replies *mai tangka*, "cooked (vegetable) food". Alitji then asks in surprise how they could cook it, and the koala says on "on a fire", reminding Alitji that they had *tili*.

Enough has been said here to indicate the ingeniousness of both the English original and the Pitjantjatjara translation (or adaptation), and it is beyond the scope of this paper to debate in full the literary merits of the original and the success of the Pitjantjatjara version. The Preface to the Pitjantjatjara version by Jim Warburton, the Director of Adult Education at the University of Adelaide (Sheppard 1975: xiii) suggests that the provision of interesting and enjoyable reading material in Pitjantjatjara both for Pitjantjatjara people and for other Australians who might want to learn the language was an important motive. The inclusion of the English "back translation" alongside the Pitjantjatjara perhaps indicates that the book was also intended to appeal to those who might read the English with little or no reference to the Pitjantjatjara. Certainly the book seems to have been read and enjoyed by readers who had no real intention of learning Pitjantjatjara.

The title, with its equation of "dreamtime" with "wonderland" raises a worry that Aboriginal "dreaming", which in traditional Aboriginal life is most definitely *not* a world of children's fairy tales or fantastic daydreams, but a fundamental concept in understanding and explaining reality, is being romanticised or denigrated. And there are places in the text itself where notions such as "corroboree" and "spirit" may be treated rather more lightheartedly than they would have been customarily in Pitjantjatjara. It seems nevertheless evident that the Pitjantjatjara text, taken as a whole, with its accompanying introduction and preface, is intended as an imaginative exercise, demonstrating the resources and value of the Pitjantjatjara language, and not as any kind of negative comment on customary Aboriginal life and world-views. Any unintended degoratory implications should at least be balanced against the compliment paid to Pitjantjatjara by the effort and skill involved in producing and publishing such a work in the language.

4.2. Discrepancies between Alice in Wonderland and Alitji in the Dreamtime

The reaction of many readers is that *Alitji in the Dreamtime* is simply not a translation but an adaptation, and the book's own declaration that it is "adapted and translated" suggests that the translator and publishers are also cautious about calling it a translation.

We have already noted some striking examples of cultural adaptations or transferences, not only in the substitution of one being for another (a white kangaroo for a white rabbit, a koala for a dormouse, a stockman for a mad hatter, and so on) but also in the reworking of episodes (as in the opening, when Alitji has tired of the story telling game and seems to be collecting gumnuts and decorating her hair with them, whereas the original Alice was getting bored of sitting next to her sister, who was immersed in a book, and was thinking rather lethargically about the possibility of making a daisy-chain).

There are also ingenious attempts to build word play into the Pitjantjatjara, as in the example of the dormouse's (koala's) unfinished story about three sisters described in the preceding section. It is of course (almost always) impossible to "translate" puns and word plays into another language. What translators commonly do is just what is done here: use their imaginative skill to create a new play which is certainly not identical with the the source but shows some kind of general affinity or resemblance to it.

The Appendices also show the complexity of intertextual relations by including the English back translation of the Pitjantjatjara. The opening of the text provides an illustration of the extent to which this "back translation" goes beyond conventional translation by adding an explanation of the *milpatjunangi* story telling game, not in the form of a note explaining the practice in the style of an encyclopedia, but by amplifying the text with a running description of what Alitji and her sister had been doing.

Having noted such striking discrepancies as these, we should not overlook the more mundane details which would have created problems even for a translator who had set out to be as literal or accurate as is humanly possible. An example of the kind familiar to translators is found in the very first line, where English "sister" requires a choice in Pitjantjatjara between the meanings "older sister" and "younger sister" (actually "younger sibling", since Pitjantjatjara distinguishes "older sister" from "older brother" but has a single lexical item for a younger sibling of either sex). In fact, the choice is not particularly difficult here, as Carroll's original text strongly suggests an older sister — a sister who is reading a book which has "no pictures or conversations in it", the kind of book which Alice herself seems to find boring. Nevertheless, we end up with slightly different meanings in the two texts: Carroll's English leaves open the relative age of the sisters, the Pitjantjatjara must specify whether Alitji's sister is older or younger (and if younger, will leave open the sex of the sibling).

A rather more serious challenge to the translator is that Carroll's text is firmly located in the English countryside, with rivers, fields and hedges. The Pitjantjatjara simply do not live in such an environment. While Sheppard has chosen to place Alitji and her sister, more appropriately it may be argued, in a dry creek bed, and to ignore entirely any reference to following the rabbit "across a field" to the rabbit-hole "under the hedge", even a more literal-minded translator would have faced the difficulty of translating the words "field" and "hedge". The use of English loan words or of explanatory footnotes could have evoked the details of an English landscape — and Pitjantjatjara readers are not entirely unaware of English-style pastoral and agricultural practices — but it would have contributed to the "foreignness" of the translation, tending to produce a "foreign" text, read as a story based elsewhere rather than in familiar territory. In cases such as these, there is of course no neutral choice between the intrusion of these "foreign" details, in loanwords or explanations, and the adaptation or suppression of the foreign details to create a "local" or "natural" translation. To make the point bluntly, you cannot create a field surrounded by hedges in an indigenous Pitjantjatjara landscape: either you import the hedge and make the landscape foreign, or you get rid of the hedge and abandon or change details of the source text.

For further indication of differences between the texts, the reader is invited to look at the Pitjantjatjara in Appendix 4, with the benefit of the rough English gloss; and at Appendix 5, which interweaves a portion of the original English text with the English back translation of the Pitjantjatjara.

4.3. Correspondences between Alice in Wonderland and Alitji in the Dreamtime

Despite these substantial differences between Carroll's text and the Pitjantjatjara translation, there are also many correspondences, some of them equivalences as close as one could ask of a translation: Alice was beginning to get very tired, Alitji was getting very tired; Alice was sitting beside her sister, and so was Alitji; Alice falls down a deep hole, and so did Alitji; and so on and so on. Even where the translator has adapted, there are nevertheless correspondences: daisies and the possibility of making a daisy-chain correspond to the gumnuts or tjintjulu berries and decorating one's hair with them; the white rabbit is matched by a white kangaroo; and so on.

Appendix 5 offers an alignment of the original English text (in capitals) and the English back translation of the Pitjantjatjara (in italics) for a small portion of the text. In some instances, correspondences should be obvious and straightforward, for example:

ALICE = *Alitji*

WAS BEGINNING TO GET VERY TIRED OF SITTING
= *was getting very tired of sitting*

Some of the less obvious correspondences are numbered, in square brackets, in Appendix 5. In a few cases, the numbering may help to locate correspondences which are some distance away from each other. The correspondence numbered [7], for example, is uncontroversial (both the rabbit and the kangaroo are white) but Carroll presents this information about colour immediately, as an epithet preceding the word "rabbit" at its first occurrence, whereas the Pitjantjatjara delays it and presents it as explicitly surprising (and of course a white kangaroo is more suprising than a white rabbit). Compare the two below:

When suddenly a [7] white rabbit with pink eyes ran close by her there was nothing so very remarkable in that, nor did Alice think it so very much out of the way to hear the rabbit say to itself, "oh dear! oh dear! I shall be too late!"

> Suddenly a kangaroo hopped past her, saying "Oh dear, oh deary me, I'm late." And the extraordinary thing was that he was [7] white. A white kangaroo!

The other correspondences numbered in Appendix 5 are as follows.

[1] peeped into the book
[1] playing milpatjunangi

In Carroll's original, Alice and her sister are not actually doing anything together. Alice's sister is reading, and Alice is tired of "having nothing to do". Alice does occasionally "peep" into the book her sister is reading, but she is not interested as it has no pictures or conversations. Alitji and her sister, however, have been playing the *milpatjunangi* story telling game and it is during that game that she has started to feel bored and tired. There is thus a loose correspondence between the sister's reading, which leaves Alice bored, with nothing to do, and the *milpatjunangi* game, which tires Alitji out.

There are further correspondences that build on this rather loose and general one. (Note that these do not occur in exactly the same sequence in the English and Pitjantjatjara texts.)

[2] what is the use of a book, thought Alice
[2] very bored

[3] her sister was reading
[3] her sister's voice went on and on

[4] very sleepy and stupid
[4] her eyelids began to droop

Carroll says that Alice was beginning to get "very tired", but he does not use the word "bored". But Alice's dismissive attitude to her sister's book (without pictures), building on previous mention of tiredness, seems to warrant the Pitjantjatjara direct reference to Alitji's becoming "very bored". There is also a kind of parallel in [3] between the sister's reading and the sister's talking: both go on for some time, providing further background to our sense of Alice's (Alitji's) boredom. Finally in this group of comparisons, there is a quite close correspondence in [4] between (feeling) "very sleepy and stupid" and "eyelids beginning to droop", but this is another instance where information is presented in a different sequence in the two texts.

[5] SHE WAS CONSIDERING IN HER OWN MIND
[5] she said to herself

The equation of "considering in her mind" and "said to herself" is relatively uncontroversial, although, yet again, there is a difference in order, for "said to herself" leads directly to Alitji's idea of collecting berries, whereas Carroll has intrusive clauses expanding on Alice's tiredness.

[6] MAKING A DAISY-CHAIN
[6a] collect some tjintjulu berries to decorate my hair
[6b] pierce the berries

In [6] we have another clear example of what is sometimes called "cultural transference", with the substitution of gathering berries to decorate the hair for gathering daisies and making a chain of them. The global correspondence of the two activities is supported by several details, notably the fact that both activities involve gathering a quantity of small plant items, and both involve piercing and threading the items for a decorative purpose.

Thus we can find various points of anchorage, where the translator has matched the English rather closely in the Pitjantjatjara. But these points of anchorage not only keep the text and translation similar, they also provide points from which to launch out adventurously into much looser and more creative similarities. Intriguingly, some of the most adventurous cultural "reinterpretations" (the white kangaroo for the white rabbit, the story telling game for making daisy chains, and suchlike) are relatively easy to identify and establish. We can, so to speak, see the equation clearly, even though we are struck by the difference between the two items being equated, and the equation stands out from the context. More subtle are the kinds of correspondence illustrated by the items numbered [2]-[4]

above. Here, wording such as a question about the use of a book and a reference to reading for some extended period works together to generate conclusions and impressions which then justify (to a greater or lesser extent) different wording, in a different language, about being bored and a voice going on and on.

In fact we are able to talk of some measure of equivalence by appealing to various kinds of similarity. In some instances, we have more or less straightforward correspondences, often based (or so we trust) on a high degree of similarity in human experience, as with being tired or sitting or having a sister. In other instances, we have surprising correspondences, as with rabbit and kangaroo, but even here we can agree to an equivalence *in this context*. There are similarities which we perceive and draw on: both animals jump or hop, both are common and familiar in the relevant environments, and in this context, both are white, and both play the role of running past as Alice (or Alitji) is bored and tired, taking on human characteristics (such as talking), catching her attention and drawing her into the subsequent adventures. In yet other instances, as with the example discussed above, a complex configuration of tiredness and boredom, of a book without pictures and a sister who reads it, and so on, has to be interpreted before we can speak of equivalence between asking what use a book is and being bored, or between a sister's reading and a sister's voice going on and on.

Thus it seems entirely reasonable to say, for example, that in this text *malu* (kangaroo) is equivalent to "rabbit". The translator here has worked creatively to cross a bridge (Firth [Palmer 1968: 197], cf. Gregory 1980) or fashion a likeness (Haas 1962: 228). How successful the translation is can be debated, but no-one, presumably, would argue that the translator was mistaken about the meaning of either "rabbit" or *malu*.

But equivalence is not something permanent and guaranteed. To say that the white rabbit and white kangaroo are equivalent here is not to say that there will be many texts that can sustain this equivalence. We do not want to argue, for example, that a Pitjantjatjara-English dictionary ought to give "rabbit" as the equivalent of *malu*.

5. From similarity to equivalence

As mentioned in section 3 above and argued elswhere in this volume, there is no sharp boundary between paraphrase and adaptation and translation. Various kinds of similarity justify correspondences which, under certain conditions, may reach a point at which many of us are content to speak of equivalence or even identity, even though deeper reflection might cause some misgivings.

To some extent, our ability to sustain a notion of accurate translation or exact equivalence rests on our having shaped a world in which identity seems under control, a world in which science and technology, mass production and standardisation have had enormous impact. Thus, the words for manufactured items like "car, chair, bottle, paperclip, screwdriver" are among the easiest to translate — provided that we ignore any kind of specially contextualised or metaphorical uses, like "the chair of a committee" or "screwdriver" as the name of a cocktail, and provided of course we are dealing with languages which have already taken aboard the technology of paperclips and screwdrivers.

This is by no means just a matter of material objects — machines, tools, manufactured containers, and so on — spreading around the world. What it is now fashionable to call "globalisation" is merely the latest phase in a process of aggressively disseminating internationalised ways of manufacturing, buying, selling, record-keeping, communicating, playing sport, entertaining, and so on and so on. The impact of this internationalisation is enormous and a high proportion of the world's translation work, driven by commerce and technology, is underpinned by it. In effect, the internationalisation of technological culture has surmounted diversity. For, if Britain, Egypt, Germany and Indonesia now share much the same technology of motor vehicles, computers, telecommunications, refrigeration and so on, then texts about such topics are likely to be relatively similar in their linguistic organisation, and it may well be relatively easy for a translator to draw on close parallels of vocabulary, text structure and so on.

The (more or less) universal aspects of human anatomy and behaviour and thinking are likewise reflected in vocabulary that may be relatively easily equated across languages, such as "arm, leg, laugh, cry, cough, stand, sit, say, believe". Again, we should not be too sanguine. Languages differ in how they "construct" the body, for example in how they "divide up" the body into head, face, neck, nape, shoulder, etc., and in how they conceptualise kinds of "sitting" or "standing", and so on, quite apart from the various metaphorical uses of such words.

But our common humanity, across the world's language and cultures, gives us some grounds for confidence in translation (see Gregory, chapter 3 of this volume). Studies of a variety of languages do suggest that there may be broad similarities among all languages, in such aspects as their metafunctions and stratal organisation, in the iconicity of some features of intonation, in the experiential identification of processes and participants. And such aspects of language may reflect both a measure of universality in the world and a tendency for humans to respond to and organise that world in similar ways.

6. The uniqueness of translations

If we move away from the kinds of text that have been strongly (re)shaped by internationalisation, we might turn to, say, personal letters, children's stories, poetry or ceremonial texts, on which internationalisation has had less impact. Here it may be quite impossible to produce a translation that closely resembles any existing text. To put it in concrete terms: the translator who is faced with translating a commercial contract from Indonesian into English knows that there have been many previous commercial contracts in both English and Indonesian, and that there are local and international conventions governing them; but the translator who is faced with translating a uniquely Indonesian text, such as the Pancasila, a philosophical statement of the five principles on which the Indonesian nation is founded, can have much less certainty about appropriate analogies and precedents. The Pancasila has a Sanskrit name and faint echoes of Buddhist vows, but it is an Indonesian text, functioning powerfully in the Indonesian nation. Thus, while other countries have their own political philosophies or constitutional texts, none of them has a Pancasila.

As Steiner suggests (in chapter 6 of this volume), there are grounds for considering translations to constitute a register of their own, a register whose properties are due to the nature of translation. Certainly no translation is identical to the text which served as its starting point. Where internationalisation has yielded some measure of unification, we may be able to *count* a text and its translation as equivalent, even identical, for example in the case of translation of a document such as an invoice or a list of spare parts or a report of trade negotiations. But without such internationalisation, equivalence is much more clearly a construct. A translation of the Pancasila into English, functioning perhaps as information for English-speaking visitors or students, is not the same text as the Pancasila itself, functioning as the official unifying basis of Indonesia. A translation of *Alice in Wonderland*, whether adventurously translated or not, is no longer Lewis Carroll's original text.

7. Conclusion

Where an increasingly global world supports translation — by the existence of the "same" vehicles and telephones and office computers and banks and shopping centres across the world — it is not so difficult to see equivalence as a clear aim of translation. And, without minimising the challenges and difficulties that remain, equivalence can be judged with the help of reference to almost universal objects and procedures and structures.

With texts like *Alice in Wonderland*, the Pancasila, or the Bible, points of anchorage are less obvious, and translation may be highly creative and imaginative. But, as we have seen with *Alitji in the Dreamtime*, it is still possible to produce a translation which remains in some sense faithful to the original, a translation which shows points of correspondence with the original, even if some of those correspondences are unusual, to the point of being unacceptable in other contexts. Serious discussion of the merits of such a translation must draw on a broad understanding of humanity, functionality and context.

In a world in which everything is unique, there is of course no ultimate guarantee of equivalence, whether in the translation of technical manuals, contracts or commercial correspondence, or in the translation of more obviously unique texts. What we encounter are similarities, points in which, as humans, we can discern connections and relationships. Equivalence is not a relationship that is fixed once and for all, and the question is, as always, what kind of similarity we are prepared to accept as equivalence in a particular context for a particular purpose. Equivalence is constructed, not out of absolute identity but out of a rich diversity of similarities.

Acknowledgment

The extracts from *Alitjinya Ngura Tjukurtjarangka: Alitji in the Dreamtime* are reproduced with the kind permission of the publisher, the Department of Adult Education, University of Adelaide.

Appendix

Appendix 1
Lewis Carroll, Alice's Adventures in Wonderland, 1865
First four paragraphs

Alice was beginning to get very tired of sitting by her sister on the bank, and of having nothing to do: once or twice she had peeped into the book her sister was reading, but it had no pictures or conversations in it, "and what is the use of a book," thought Alice, "without pictures or conversations?"

So she was considering in her own mind (as well as she could, for the hot day made her feel very sleepy and stupid) whether the pleasure of making a daisy-chain would be worth the trouble of getting up and picking the daisies, when suddenly a White Rabbit with pink eyes ran close by her.

There was nothing so *very* remarkable in that; nor did Alice think it so *very* much out of the way to hear the Rabbit say to itself, "Oh dear! Oh dear! I shall be too late!" (when she thought it over afterwards, it occurred to her that she ought to have wondered at this, but at the time it all seemed quite natural); but when the Rabbit actually *took a watch out of its waistcoat-pocket*, and looked at it, and then hurried on, Alice started to her feet, for it flashed across her mind that she had never before seen a rabbit with either a waistcoat-pocket, or a watch to take out of it, and burning with curiosity, she ran across the field after it, and fortunately was just in time to see it pop down a large rabbit-hole under the hedge.

In another moment down went Alice after it, never once considering how in the world she was going to get out again.

Appendix 2
Alitjinya Ngura Tjukurtjarangka: Alitji in the Dreamtime, adapted and translated from Lewis Carroll's story Alice's Adventures in Wonderland by Nancy Sheppard, edited by Barbara Ker Wilson, Department of Adult Education, University of Adelaide, 1975
First two paragraphs of Pitjantjatjara text

Alitjinya karungka rawa nyinara pakuringangi. Kangkurura pula nyinara milpatjunangi, ka Alitjinya karkararingu kangkuru rawa wangkanyangka, munu kulingka kunyu pilupiluringangi.

"Awarinatju, wanyunatju puta tjintjulu mantjila," munu kunyu uranu mununku mangkangka tjintjulu wakaningi, ka wati wirtjapakanu malu, watjara, "Awari, awarinatju, malaringuna." Ka wanyu kulila, malu palurua piranpa — piranpa alatjitu. Munu kunyu iluru-ilururira yakutja kali kulu witira ma-tarararira pitingka tjarpangu. Ka tjitji panya kungkangku nyakula urulyarara pakara wananu, munu ma-wanara pitingka tjarpangutu, piruku pakantjikitjangku kulilwiya alatjitu. Munu kunyu tjarpara piti unngu ankula ankula punkanu, munu kunyu rawa punkaningi kulira, "Ngati pulka manti nyangatja, munta, ngati wiya, purkarana punkani." Munu paluru tjaruringkula para-nyangangi, munu walu-nyangangitu, palu putu kunyu nyangangi marungka, piti panya unngu. Ka ngarangilta lau tjukutjuku tjutangka mai kutjupa kutjupa, ka Alitjilu punkara marangku lau kutjunguru mantjinu piti tjanmatatjara, palu mai mulya mulyararira ngalkuwiyangku wantingu, munu marangku kanyiningi punkatjingaliangku anangu kutjupa tjaru nyinantja winyulpungkuntjaku-tawara. Munu kunyu rawa ukalingkula piti malakungku tjunu, lau kutjupangka.

Appendix 3
Alitjinya Ngura Tjukurtjarangka: Alitji in the Dreamtime, adapted and translated from Lewis Carroll's story Alice's Adventures in Wonderland by Nancy Sheppard, edited by Barbara Ker Wilson, Department of Adult Education, University of Adelaide, 1975
First three paragraphs of the English accompanying the Pitjantjatjara text

Alitji was getting very tired of sitting in the creek-bed. She and her sister had been playing milpatjunangi, a story telling game. They each had a stick and a pile of leaves, and took it in turn to tell a story about people in the tribe. The sandy ground was their stage; the leaves were the tribespeople. As they told their stories, each softly tapped her stick in time to the rhythm of her rising and falling voice, and every now and then they would sweep the sand smooth with the backs of their hands.

Alitji had become very bored as her sister's voice went on and on, and her eyelids began to droop. "Well", she said to herself, "perhaps I'll collect some tjintjulu berries to decorate my hair." This she did, and then began to pierce the berries with small sticks, and poke them through the strands of her hair.

244   Colin Yallop

Suddenly a kangaroo hopped past her, saying "Oh dear, oh deary me, I'm late." And the extraordinary thing was that he was white. A white kangaroo! He hurried on anxiously, clutching a dilly-bag and a digging-stick, and disappeared from view down a hole in the ground. In great surprise, Alitji jumped up and followed him, the tjintjulu berries bouncing about her head; down she went into that hole in the ground, never stopping to think how she would get out again.

Appendix 4
Alitjinya Ngura Tjukurtjarangka (see Appendix 2)
Portion of the Pitjantjatjara text with English gloss

Alitjinya karungka rawa nyinara pakuringangi.   Kangkurura pula nyinara
Alitji   in-creek continually sit   become-tired with-older-sister two   sit

milpatjunangi, ka Alitjinya karkararingu kangkuru rawa wangkanyangka,
'story tell'   and   Alitji   become-fed-up older-sister continually talk

munu kulingka kunyu pilupiluringangi.   "Awarinatju, wanyunatju puta
and   in-heat apparently become-quiet   hey   let's   whether

tjintjulu mantjila," munu kunyu uranu mununku mangkangka tjintjulu
gumnut   get   and apparently gather and   in-hair   gumnut

wakaningi, ka wati wirtjapakanu malu, watjara (...)
pierce   and across   run   kangaroo say

Notes to Appendix 4
1. The glosses in the above portion of text are intended to convey to English-speaking readers the meaning of each Pitjantjatjara (orthographic) word, as far as this possible in a word-for-word translation. Pitjantjatjara has an extensive system of suffixing and many of the words in this passage are morphemically complex. While some attempt has been made to represent the semantic consequences of this (for instance in the gloss "in creek" for *karu* "creek" followed by the locative suffix *-ngka*) much of the morphological detail has necessarily been ignored. Note for example that verbs are glossed without any indication of the subtleties of their marking for such categories as tense and aspect. No attempt has been made to differentiate word meanings where Pitjantjatjara makes a distinction that is not relevant in English: for example *ka* (used to link clauses which do not have the same actor) and *munu* (used to link clauses which do share the same actor) are both glossed as "and".
2. The word *milpatjunangi* refers to tapping or striking the ground, but in context refers to a story telling game in which participants tap the ground (as explained in the English version of this text, in Appendix 3).
3. The word *tjintjulu* is commonly translated as "gumnut" but in the English version of this text (see Appendix 3) the Pitjantjatjara form is maintained in the translation "tjintjulu berry".

Appendix 5
Lewis Carroll's Alice in Wonderland (see Appendix 1) and Alitji in the Dreamtime (see Appendix 3)

Portion of the two English texts presented interlinearly

ALICE WAS BEGINNING TO GET VERY TIRED OF SITTING BY HER
Alitji was getting very tired of sitting

SISTER ON THE BANK, AND OF HAVING NOTHING TO DO: ONCE OR
      in the creekbed.   *She and*

TWICE SHE HAD [1] PEEPED INTO THE BOOK [3] HER SISTER WAS
her sister had been [1] playing milpatjunangi (.........)   *Alitji had become*

READING BUT IT HAD NO PICTURES OR CONVERSATIONS IN IT, "AND
[2] WHAT IS THE USE OF A BOOK," THOUGHT ALICE, "WITHOUT
[2] very bored as [3] her sister's voice went on and on, and [4] her eyelids

PICTURES OR CONVERSATIONS?" SO [5] SHE WAS CONSIDERING IN
began to droop.   *"Well," [5] she said to herself, "perhaps I'll*

HER OWN MIND (AS WELL AS SHE COULD, FOR THE HOT DAY MADE
[6a] collect some tjintjulu berries to decorate my hair." This she did and then

HER FEEL [4] VERY SLEEPY AND STUPID) WHETHER THE PLEASURE
began to [6b] pierce the berries with small sticks and poke them through the

OF [6] MAKING A DAISY-CHAIN WOULD BE WORTH THE TROUBLE OF
GETTING UP AND PICKING THE DAISIES, WHEN SUDDENLY A
strands of her hair.   *Suddenly a*

[7] WHITE RABBIT WITH PINK EYES RAN CLOSE BY HER. THERE WAS
kangaroo hopped past her,

NOTHING SO *VERY* REMARKABLE IN THAT; NOR DID ALICE THINK IT
SO *VERY* MUCH OUT OF THE WAY TO HEAR THE RABBIT SAY TO
                                                      saying "Oh dear,

ITSELF, "OH DEAR! OH DEAR! I SHALL BE TOO LATE!"
oh deary me, I'm late." And the extraordinary thing was that he was [7] white.

Notes to Appendix 5:
1. Carroll's text is in CAPITALS, with the back translation of the Pitjantjatjara in italics.
2. Several sentences have been omitted following the word *milpatjunangi* in the back translation. These give an explanation of the game and are additional to the translation of the Pitjantjatjara. They can be found in Appendix 3.
3. The numbers in square brackets are intended to assist in identifying points of correspondence. For example, [5] SHE WAS CONSIDERING IN HER MIND can be judged to correspond to *[5] she said to herself*. The numbers have no other significance: they do not mark clauses or sentences.

References

Gregory, Michael .J.
  1980   "Perspectives on translation from the Firthian tradition", *Meta* 25: 455–66.

Haas, W.
  1962   "The theory of translation", *Philosophy* 37: 208-28.

Halverson, Sandra
  1997   "The concept of equivalence in translation studies: much ado about something", *Target* 9: 207–33.

Palmer, F.R. (ed.)
  1968.   *Selected Papers of J.R.Firth 1952-59*. London: Longman.

Pike, Kenneth L.
  1967   *Language in Relation to a Unified Theory of the Structure of Human Behavior* (revised edition). The Hague: Mouton.

Sheppard, Nancy
  1975   *Alitjinya Ngura Tjukurtjarangka: Alitji in the Dreamtime* (adapted and translated from Lewis Carroll's *Alice's Adventures in Wonderland*). Adelaide: Department of Adult Education, University of Adelaide.

Statham, Nigel
  1997.   "E. Gentzler's critique of Nida: a response", *Current Trends in Scripture Translation, UBS Bulletin* 182/183: 31–38.

Part III
Working with translation and multilingual texts: computational and didactic projects

Teaching translation

Susanna Shore

1. Introduction

Traditionally the teaching of translation in schools and universities has been seen as a means of teaching a foreign language.[1] Texts have been translated in a vacuum — students are given a text and are simply instructed to "translate the following text into English" (or some other language) — and the underlying assumption is that a translation is always a complete and faithful rendering of a SL text. Often the texts that students are asked to translate are representative of genres that are rarely translated (at least in full) into another language, e.g. newspaper columns and reports.

If one sees teaching translation as teaching students to be translators, then it seems to me that an important step in the development of professional awareness is to give students (extracts from) real translation assignments or tasks that simulate real assignments. The use of real translation assignments gives students (1) practical insight into what is actually involved when texts are translated from one language into another and (2) practical experience with diatypic variation in and across languages and cultures. Even if the aim is not to produce professional translators and translation exercises are part of a written skills component in a university syllabus, the use of real translation assignments would seem to be more valid as an exercise in understanding sociocultural and linguistic differences than the translation of texts in a vacuum.[2]

This article is concerned with the practicalities of teaching translation: it discusses the kinds of things involved in a linguistically informed approach to teaching translation illustrating the process with two excerpts from a catalogue of Finnish children's literature (see Appendix 1), the preface and an entry on Mauri Kunnas, one of the authors presented in the catalogue. The Finnish text is accompanied by an English translation, which is the published translation (done by a native speaker of British English). For ease of presentation, I shall quote this translation when I refer to the original Finnish text.

Section 2 will deal with some central concepts in translation studies applicable to the teaching of translation. Sections 3–8 will look at each of the steps in the teaching process in turn. This is intended only as a suggestion and guideline, to be adapted as necessary by the individual teacher. I shall discuss various options and possible alternatives — not exhaustively but to give some indication of other approaches — as it seems to me that it is best to use a variety of approaches, although the approach adopted is often constrained by practical factors such as time allocated to the course etc.

2. Basic concepts

As in the teaching of any other professional skill, the teaching of translation is necessarily evaluative: the aim is not to produce bad translators (or writers or doctors), the aim is to produce good ones. This means that the teaching of translation is — implicitly, at least — based on the notion of a "good translation". And the notion of a good translation depends on at least two factors. Firstly it depends on our views of the way in which the meanings, forms or structures in text A in one language can be related to the meanings, forms or structures in text B in another language, such that text B is considered to be a translation of text A. Secondly it depends on our views of translation and our views of what is involved in translation.

Both of these factors are based on our views of the relationship between a language and the sociocultural and material reality in which it is embedded. According to Grace (1987), one view of language in modern linguistics sees languages as being analogous to different maps of a common reality and, thus, anything that can be expressed in one language can be expressed in another. Another view of language is that not only are the maps different but so too are the socio-cultural realities that are construed through language and ways of saying are also ways of meaning. This latter view underlies the approach taken in systemic-functional linguistics and in the London School of linguistics (e.g. Firth 1957, 1968; Halliday 1978, 1987, 1992; Hasan 1984a, 1984b). Even if we agree that every language and the sociocultural reality in which it is embedded is sui generis, there are nevertheless commonalities based on similarities in human experience and on globalising tendencies (in technology and the media, for example), and the extent to which ways of sayings and ways of meaning approximate each other across languages is an important factor in translation.

A central concept in looking at this approximation of ways of saying and meaning is equivalence, a term which is potentially misleading in that students are likely to see equivalence as a statement to the effect that a particular meaning, form or structure in language A is the same as (or can be equated with) a particular meaning, form or structure in language B. This naïve notion of equivalence also turns up in translation studies. Firstly, it underlies a lot of early theorising about translation within the context of bible translation: the Word of God could not be tampered with and translations of the Bible were based on the assumption that the meaning remained the same in spite of the fact that the forms and structures changed (Chesterman 1998: 18). Secondly a naïve version of equivalence has been attributed to Catford (1965) by Snell-Hornby (1988), whose views have been influential in translation studies.[3] Snell-Hornby's analysis of Catford is clearly based on a misreading and selective reading of Catford and the theoretical framework in which he was working. Catford (1965: 35) explicitly states: "In terms of the theory of meaning that we make use of here — a theory deriving largely from the view of J.R. Firth — the view that SL and TL texts 'have the same meaning' or that 'transference of meaning' occurs in translation is untenable". Catford's theory may be dated, as Snell-Hornby points out, and it may be sketchy, but it is nevertheless the first linguistic theory of translation that attempted to come to terms with "correspondences" or "equivalences" across texts and across systems in two different languages, and as such deserves more than a superficial reading.

Certainly some notion of equivalence or correspondence is needed in talking about what happens when texts are translated from one language to another. A translation of Pinter's *The Caretaker* is not a translation of Stoppard's *Rosencrantz and Guildenstern are Dead*. Moreover, in the teaching of translation, we are invariably involved with judgements about equivalences or correspondences across languages at a very concrete level, as indicated by the following example based on the preface of the catalogue and possible translations of it. The first translation (2) is the published translation; the second translation (3) is a translation that I have invented based on student translations of this particular passage. (The number in square brackets refers to the number of the sentence in Appendix 1.)

(1) *Kaikkiaan valikoimaan sisältyy 26 kirjailijan tuotantoa: kuvakirjoja, lastenrunoja ja -kertomuksia, satuja ja nuortenromaaneja.* [3]

Published translation:
(2) *This issue covers selections from the work of 26 authors: picture books, children's poetry, children's stories, fairy tales and teenage novels.* [3]

Translation based on student translations:
(3) *Taken together the production of 23 novelists is discussed in this select bibliography: illustrated books, nursery rhymes, tales, saga and juvenile novels.*

It would be fairly difficult — if not impossible — to judge, for example, whether *picture books* or *illustrated books* is the more appropriate translation of *kuvakirjoja* in this particular context without recourse to some underlying notion of equivalence or correspondence across languages.

Much of the debate about equivalence has stemmed from the fact that the term as a theoretical label is confused with the everyday term understood in a mathematical sense. For this reason, I have avoided the term "equivalence" in the teaching of translation and have referred to "correspondences" instead. Nevertheless what I would prefer to call textual correspondence is essentially what Catford referred to as "textual translation equivalence". Catford (1965: 27–34) distinguished between formal correspondence, correspondence between categories in any two linguistic systems, and textual translation equivalence, correspondence between (parts of) a text and translations of it. He saw textual equivalents as texts or textual items with "the greatest possible overlap of situational range", acknowledging that situations are not identical across cultures (Catford 1965: 49). To put this in more contemporary systemic-functional terms, texts or parts of a text are equivalent if they can be said to function in the TL in much the same way as the original text or part of a text in the SL.[4] And as Catford suggests by "the greatest possible overlap", the notion of correspondence between a text and a translation of it is a question of degree. As Chesterman (1998: 21–22) points out, however, Catford sees textual equivalence as a de facto relation between a given text (or parts of a text) and a translation of (parts of) it as determined by a competent translator or bilingual. This notion seems to be based on just one translation. My use of the term "(textual) correspondence" is meant to underscore the fact that there can be more than one translation that corresponds to a given SL text (or a part of it).

Formal correspondence, on the other hand, was for Catford a more abstract notion based on similarity between categories in any two linguistic systems. Given the period in which he worked, Catford's categories were defined formally, but there is no reason why they cannot be extended to include functional categories, in which case a more appropriate label for this kind of correspondence would be systemic correspondence. Thus, while formal or systemic correspondence is a relationship between categories in different linguistic systems, textual correspondence (or equivalence) is a relationship that can be postulated across texts, i.e. instantiations of linguistic systems.[5]

As Halliday points out in his chapter in this volume, Catford's notion of equivalence is a stratified one (cf. Koller 1979, who takes a similar approach). As indicated above, Catford defined textual translation equivalence in contextual terms, but he nevertheless recognised that texts or portions of a text could be equivalent at other strata (or levels): there could be restricted translation at the graphological, phonological, grammatical or lexical level. Catford's discussion was also framed within a theory that made explicit reference to ranks and units in language, e.g. textual translation equivalence can occur across units of equal or non-equal rank. Halliday (this volume) introduces a third dimension or vector: a metafunctional one. Thus, for example, a particular text (or a part of a text) in the SL could be regarded as interpersonally equivalent to a TL text, but not ideationally equivalent to it.

One way of building on Catford's work, as Halliday suggests, is to look at translations (textual translation equivalents) in terms of their "equivalence value", or what might also be referred to as their "equivalence weighting", i.e. the weighting of systemic correspondences at a particular level (context, semantics, lexicogrammar, phonology, phonetics), a particular rank or unit (e.g. clause, sentence, tone group, phrase, foot, word, morpheme, syllable), or a particular metafunction (ideational, interpersonal, textual). In other words, a certain type (or certain types) of correspondence may be prioritised in the translation of a particular genre or in a particular type of translation, which would mean that other types of correspondences may be sacrificed. For example, one might expect phonological correspondences to be foregrounded in the translations of songs, interpersonal correspondences to be foregrounded in the translation of fund-raising letters or political pamphlets, and so on. The equivalence value or weighting may also be affected by the status of the SL text and/or its translation, e.g. its literary or legal status. For example, unusual ways of saying and meaning (unusual lexicogrammatical and semantic correspondences) are more likely to be valued, and thus prioritised, in the translation of a literary text than in the translation of instructions for using a video-recorder.

A further perspective on equivalence value or weighting is the degree to which a translated text (either the whole text or parts of it) is oriented either to the SL or to the TL (together with the cultural norms and values of the languages in question), or to use Venuti's (1995) terms the extent to which a translated text is foreignised or domesticated. For ease of reference, I shall refer to this as "the orientation factor". As I understand it, the orientation factor is dependent on a number of other factors, including the translation norms that are valid in a particular community at a particular time in the translation of a particular genre (cf. Toury 1995 esp. Ch. 2, Chesterman 1997).

Within contemporary translation practices in Europe, for example, one would expect a good translation of an advertisement (to the extent to which it is sensible to translate advertisements) to be oriented to the TL and a good translation of a valued literary work to be oriented to the SL. However, even valued literary texts can be translated for various purposes, and the consequent translation may not be a valued literary text in the TL.[6] Moreover, literary texts also vary in their status and function: the translation of children's literature, for example, is more likely to be TL oriented than the translation of adult literature, as the function of children's literature is generally perceived as being different from that of adult literature (cf. Yallop's chapter on the Pitjantjatjara translation of *Alice in Wonderland*, where the White Rabbit becomes a white kangaroo). The orientation factor may also be affected by the relative status of the SL and TL: as Toury (1995: 278) points out, tolerance for deviations from cultural and linguistic norms may increase when a text is being translated from a major world language into a minor language, as is the case with a English text being translated into Finnish. This is evidenced, for example, by the increasing number of calques (e.g. *pitkässä juoksussa* 'in the long run') and translation loans (*tekstuaalinen* 'textual') that have come into Finnish from English.

Tied to the orientation factor is the kind of editing and adaptation that often occurs when a text that was originally written in the SL, and based on assumptions of the source language and culture, is translated into another language. A simple example is from a translated history of the Finnish Ministry for Foreign Affairs that I came across. The text contained at least ten references to years in which something significant had happened, and although the year that Finland became independent is probably the most significant year in the history of Finland and the text made reference to the event, the actual year was not mentioned in the translation. In the Finnish SL text, of course, there is no need to mention this date, as every (adult) Finn knows the date. Sometimes editing needs to be more extensive, and the borders between translation, adaptation and copywriting begin to get blurred.

Constraints on equivalences between a SL text and its TL translation can be more concrete. For example, some texts appear in parallel format in both the SL and target language(s), e.g. tourist brochures in Finland often appear in Finnish, Swedish and English, and the simple fact that the texts appear in parallel may have a constraining effect on the translation and the kinds of correspondences that are established. Translators may, for example, be less likely to introduce changes into a text (additions, explanations) if it can be checked against the original. Moreover, problems may result from restrictions on the amount of space that is available. A Finnish text, for example, is invariably shorter than its English translation: strong agglutinating tendencies in Finnish mean that a Finnish text invariably has fewer words than its English translation.[7]

So far I have assumed that a translation is a full translation, but any discussion of translation also needs to address what Catford (1965: 21) referred to as the extent of the translation. Not all translations are full translations, some are partial translations e.g. selective or summarising (cf. Sager 1993: 179–181). Such translations may also involve the introduction of additional material. For example, a newspaper report on a disaster occurring somewhere else in the world may not only involve a selective translation of a SL text, it may also involve additions to the TL text, e.g. relating the disasters to similar disasters in the TL context etc. As indicated above, partial translation can also be the result of restrictions due to space.

Some translations, which I shall refer to as adapted translations, involve deliberate and explicit generic changes, i.e. changes in the field, tenor or mode. An example is television subtitling, which is often a partial translation as well since there are restrictions on the length of the translation (stemming from the width of the screen and the time that viewers have to read the text). Subtitling involves a change in the channel, from spoken to written, and this may also result in changes (or tensions) in the code, along the continuum between the colloquial (spoken) code and the standardised (written) code. Subtitling of American films screened on Finnish television, for example, sometimes appear to censor the original language: a strong swearword in the original is replaced by a mild one in Finnish, in spite of the fact that strong swearwords are used in Finnish films screened on television. Part of the reason for this may be that since swearwords are typical of the spoken code, they appear even more forceful when written. Film and television subtitling would be one of the most common types of (adapted) translation, at least in northern European countries; other kinds of adapted translation appear to be rare in actual translation practice. An example might be an adapted translation of a SL prose work as a TL play, but my impression is that such adaptations are based on translations of the original prose work.

To sum up, there are different kinds of texts, different kinds of translation, and different kinds of correspondences that can be established between a text and its translation. Given this, the problem of defining translation (in the context of translation teaching) is a tricky one. It is all very well for translation scholars to adopt a post-hoc definition of translation (e.g. Toury 1995: 23–39; Chesterman 1997: 59) and say that a translation is anything that is accepted as a translation in the target culture. In a pedagogical context we at least need to attempt to formulate a working definition of translation, and whether or not this definition is explicitly stated, it cannot but have an effect on how translation is taught. Moreover, as pointed out earlier, such a definition is of necessity evaluative, and would not include bad translations (e.g. translations done by amateurs with little understanding of the SL), which do occur and are accepted as translations.

For the purposes of teaching translation, I think it is useful to have some kind of yardstick, by which different kinds of translation can be measured. Most ordinary, everyday translations (e.g. done in translation agencies) seem to be based on two assumptions: (1) the meanings construed in the translation using the lexicogrammatical resources of the TL are as close as possible to the meanings construed in the SL text and (2) the translation should be fluent and read like a TL text. If these assumptions are in conflict, then it is generally the second that is given precedence: translators need to produce a translation that can be tied to the SL text, but they need to produce a text that can be understood and function effectively as a TL text. Given this as a yardstick, then any deviations, adaptations and changes (of the kinds mentioned above) will need to be motivated by appealing to such factors as SL orientation, lack of correspondence in meaning between SL and TL, lack of correspondence between SL and TL genres (or to the fact that there is nothing that could be considered a corresponding genre in the TL), the status and function of the SL text and its translation, restrictions and constraints related to the type of translation and/or the nature of the commission etc.

3. Preliminaries

In what follows, I shall not be concerned with curriculum design or with the overall organisation of a translation course, e.g. the number of classes and how often the classes are held. I shall assume that the translation course is like most other university courses, meeting once a week (or once every two weeks) over a half-year or full-year period.

If classes are held every week, this means that assignments are handed in and corrected within a week or students are given a week (or more) to complete an assignment and the teacher has a week (or more) to correct it. However, a timetable based on classes meeting once a week can be too restrictive, and some flexibility (e.g. meeting every three or four weeks) would allow the students to work (together) on longer assignments. If classes are held each week and assignments are handed in and corrected over a two-week period, the first few weeks can be devoted to introducing key concepts in translation studies and text analysis, if this is not done in other courses attended by the students. If the students already have a strong theoretical background, the first sessions can be devoted to group work and/or to a practical discussion of the factors that need to be taken into account in different kinds of translation. This can be based on an analysis of translations of a number of different texts or on a comparison of a number of translations of the same text. Alternatively the discussion can be based on translations done by (pairs of) students of very short extracts (1–2 sentences) from texts representing vastly different genres, e.g. an EU directive, a pop song, a highly valued literary text, a television commercial.[8]

4. Choosing and completing the assignment

The first step is to choose the assignment and decide on how it is to be completed. The assignments can either be selected by the teacher or by the students. It seems to me that it is best if the majority of assignments are chosen by the teacher,[9] as this allows the teacher to select a variety of translation tasks representative of a variety of genres and to select SL texts that highlight particular translation problems. The illustrative texts for this article — the catalogue texts — were chosen to focus on two fairly central grammatical problems: differences in (1) the Theme–Rheme organisation of Finnish and English and (2) the Finnish and English passive. They were also chosen to focus on the more general issue of negotiating across cultures: the preface to the Finnish catalogue has certain properties which are not characteristic of similar genres in English.

Related to the selection of the assignment are a number of other practical issues: the length of the assignment and the time given to students to complete the assignment. If students are expected to hand in an assignment each week, then the length of the assignment has to be restricted to short texts (1–2 pages) or extracts from long texts, in which case the whole text can be given and the extracts that are to be translated can be indicated in some way. If there is some flexibility in timetabling, then long full-length assignments can be given to the students. A related consideration is whether assignments are done individually or with pairs or groups of students working either on the same sections or on different sections of the text. Even if the assignments are done individually, it seems to me that students should be encouraged to talk with each other (or e-mail each other) about any problems they may encounter.

It is usually more practicable to give students a reasonable amount of time to complete the assignments (e.g. 1–2 weeks), but it may occasionally be useful to make students work under pressure (3–6 hours completion time): a lot of real translation work needs to be done within a short period of time.

5. Preparing for the assignment

Once the assignment has been chosen, and the students have read through the SL text, the next step is to discuss and prepare for the translation task. The exact nature of the commission should be discussed. The catalogue texts, for example, were accompanied by the following instructions, which, in part, are meant to simulate the instructions given with the original commission:

> *Translate the following texts into good, idiomatic and stylistically appropriate English. The texts are from a publication compiled at regular intervals and sent to international publishers and book fairs.*

Information about the commission is sometimes implicitly or explicitly included in the SL text itself. With the catalogue texts, there is actually a clear statement of the purpose of the catalogue at the end of the preface:

(4) *The Finnish Section of IBBY trusts that enthusiasts of children's books will find much of interest in this catalogue.* [17]

(5) *We also hope that scholars of the field will be able to picture the trends and developments in Finnish literature for the young, and that this catalogue will help those looking for suitable works for translation.* [18]

The instructions given to the students may also need to include information about the actual format of the published translation, e.g. the positioning of diagrams and photographs, particularly if reference is made to these in the body of the text. Of relevance to the translation of the catalogue texts is the fact that the SL text was written to be translated: the publication will appear in English only.

Because the translation courses that I have taught have been part of a university syllabus, students have always been asked to translate into "good, idiomatic English". However, given the discussion in section 2 on the orientation factor, this instruction may need to be discussed and subsequently modified for some translations (or parts of them): e.g. translations of literary works oriented to the original source language and culture may involve ways of meaning and ways of saying that are foreign to the TL language and culture. Another aspect of the quality of the English has to do with the target audience of the translation: the catalogue texts, like many texts translated (from Finnish) into English, are not directed exclusively at native speakers of English. Finnish children's literature has been translated into many languages, including Japanese, and, thus, for some purposes, there is a limit to how idiomatic a translation should be.

A necessary preliminary to many translation tasks given to students is some kind of cross-linguistic genre analysis. This can be done in a number of ways, e.g. (i) a preliminary discussion based on the relevant genres in both languages and/or (ii) using a parallel text in the TL. More often than not students of translation do not have a background in a specific linguistic theory, and many of them do not even have a background in linguistics. They are more likely to have a wide cultural and literary background and a sensitivity to style and linguistic variation. Rather than use the translation class to teach theory or theoretical concepts, it seems to me that it is more expedient — and pedagogically more sound — to use the theory to inform and feed back into a discussion based on the students' knowledge of the features of the SL genre and the features of a corresponding genre in the TL (or if there is nothing that could be said to correspond to the SL genre, then the discussion could focus on features of related genres).

The discussion could be triggered by questions such as the following:

Who wrote the text and why? Who wants it translated and why?
Who is the intended reader? Is the reader a layperson or a specialist in some field?
Is there something that was unclear in the original? Why?
What effect does the SL text have on the reader? What effect is the TL text supposed to have on the reader?
How would you characterise the language in the original? Is it standard Finnish?
Are there any stylistic shifts in the original? Do you think they were intentional?

Many of the answers to these questions will, of course, depend on the kind of text that is being translated and the orientation factor. This is particularly true of questions such as the following:

Is there something in the text that is so culturally specific that it would be difficult to translate? How would you go about tackling the problem?
Is there presupposed information in the text? In other words, does the text presuppose something that every Finn would know but something that may need to be made explicit to a non-Finnish audience?

There are other questions that could be asked (cf. Nord 1991). I am not suggesting that these questions should be presented as a checklist, a discussion of one or two relevant questions is enough. Moreover, students may find it easier to respond to questions that are more open-ended, in which case, it might be more appropriate to ask a vague, general question requiring a subjective response, e.g. "What do you think of the text?" or "How would you feel about translating a text like this?"

The discussion can also be based on parallel texts. I am using the term parallel text to refer to a text representing a similar genre in the TL. (In some branches of corpus studies, this is referred to as a comparative text, and the term parallel text refers to a translation of a text.) A parallel text can either be provided by the teacher or students can be asked to find a parallel text and read it as preparation for the assignment. It is not always easy to find parallel texts, particularly if one is teaching in a country in which the target language is not spoken; in the case of the catalogue texts, however, it is relatively easy for students to find a parallel English text from a bookshop, a library, or the Internet. If students are asked to find a parallel text, it seems to me that the text should be handed in as part of the assignment and used in the follow-up discussion. This is important because the notion of a parallel text in translation studies is a fairly loose notion, often simply based on similarity in the (second-order) field, e.g. medicine, or a similarity in an aspect of mode, e.g. instructional mode.[10] From the point of view of teaching translation, however, the vagueness of the notion has a number of advantages. As indicated above, it is often difficult for practical reasons to find a text that is parallel with respect to each of the contextual variables. Further, the texts that the students do find can be used as a concrete way of investigating generic similarities and differences. Getting students to find parallel texts also means that the students will gradually build up a collection of parallel texts that can be filed and consulted in future assignments (or commissions).

The examination of parallel texts often serves to highlight features of the SL text that are not immediately apparent to the students (or even to the teacher). The preface to the Finnish catalogue is in the form of a letter, which is headed *Lukijalle*, translated as "To the reader". On the basis of the parallel texts that I have come across, this kind of heading is unusual in this context. One is more likely to find a salutation such as "Dear Reader" or "Dear Colleague" or no heading at all (even when there is a signature at the bottom of the page). The heading "To the reader" is more likely to occur in English in a non-promotional context, e.g. as a note written to the reader by the translator of a novel or by the writer of an instruction manual.

A text analysis of the catalogue texts could focus, for example, on the fact that the Finnish texts are directed at two different kinds of reader, researchers and publishers, and the conflicts that may arise from this. The Finnish preface is, in fact, fairly impersonal and factual, and stylistically it is more like a scholarly and informative text than a promotional text. There is, for example, no direct reference to the reader in the form of the second person singular. The epithets used to describe two of the most famous illustrators of children's books in Finland (Kaarina Kaila and Mauri Kunnas) in sentence (8a) are *jo perinteinen* 'well-established, already part of a tradition" and *hyvä* 'good'. In light of the fact that the publication will be sent to international publishers and book fairs, it may be appropriate to change the style so that the TL text is more involving and dynamic.

Another feature of the Finnish text which is in conflict with its promotional function occurs at the beginning of the second paragraph. This particular sentence, reproduced below, is textually significant in that it introduces the main section (sentences 5–16), which is an overview of what has happened in Finnish children's literature during the period the catalogue covers:

(6) *Kolmivuotiskausi 1993–95 alkoi myös kirjallisuuden kohdalla Suomea ahdistelleen laman merkeissä.*[5]

(7) *The three year period 1993–95 began at a time when the economic recession in Finland also took its toll on the literary world...*[5]

In the Finnish, however, the recession is personified as something harassing Finland (the verb *ahdistella* 'harass, pursue' is typically used with a human actor), and in keeping with the style of the Finnish, students are likely to translate this as follows:

(8) *The three year period ... began at a time when Finland was in the grips of a depression ...*

The feature that I am trying to highlight is what I have sometimes referred to as "the Finnish whinge (or whine)". A recurring feature in some of the texts that I have translated is a tendency for the Finnish writer to begin a text that is supposed to be promoting Finland by focusing on the reasons why we Finns are not quite as good as we could be: Finland is a small country, our language is difficult, we do not have many natural resources, we are situated at the northern periphery of Europe, we have long, cold winters etc. etc. When I have come across such features in texts that I have been asked to translate, I have negotiated with the writer of the translation and have suggested changes to the text. The discussion in the translation class could focus on ways of downplaying the original feature. — Conversely, from a Finnish point of view, some texts written in English are so full of self-praise that they echo the sales talk of the proverbial used-car salesman, and undoubtedly there are similar rhetorical incongruencies across other languages and cultures. These incongruencies need to be taken into account if the aim is to make the TL translation function effectively in a TL context, i.e. if the aim is to make the translation TL oriented.

The preliminary discussion can also focus on particular translation problems (e.g. specific terms that need to be translated correctly) and discuss resources that can be used, e.g. bilingual and monolingual dictionaries (either general or field-specific dictionaries), the Internet, and reference books. It may be worth pointing out to students that in real translation work, it is also possible to consult the original writer, who more often than not is also an expert in the terminology in his or her field in English. For some translations, it may be useful for the teacher to play the role of the original writer.

It seems to me that the use of bilingual dictionaries should be discouraged in the translation of texts that are not highly technical or full of specialist vocabulary and, even with technical and specialist texts, students should be critical of translations given in a dictionary. Sometimes the translations are misleading or out-of-date, often no context is given for the use of a term, and most of the bilingual Finnish-English dictionaries have been written by Finns. Moreover, the use of bilingual dictionaries predisposes students to look for correspondences at the rank of word. Another assumption that students make is that meanings are made somewhere else and the SL text simply codes these meanings. For example, one of the problems with the catalogue preface is the categories of children's literature that are referred to:

lastenkirjallisuus (child+ GEN/PL + literature) 'children's literature'
nuortenkirjallisuus (young+ GEN/PL + literature) 'literature for the young'
nuorisokirjallisuus (youth+literature)'literature for young people'
varttuneiden nuorten kirja (grown-up+GEN/PL young + GEN/PL book) '(a) book for older young people'

The problem for the translator is to determine how these are related to each other in the Finnish text. For example, *nuortenkirjallisuus* 'literature for the young' and *nuorisokirjallisuus* 'literature for young people/youth' could be regarded as synonyms, but they are not being used synonymously in this particular text. The answers to problems like this are often to be found in the text itself, not in a dictionary or some other external source. The translator then needs to relate these terms to English categories (*children's literature, teenage literature, young adult literature, literature for young people* etc.).

Before the students actually do the assignment, it is often useful to highlight one or two translation problems in the text, especially recurrent problems that can be approached using some kind of translation strategy, i.e. a way of solving a translation problem or a way of translating something based on similarities and differences between the source and target language.[11] A particularly useful strategy in translating from Finnish into English is related to Theme–Rheme and Given–New patterns in a text. This strategy is important because students tend to translate texts sentence by sentence and overlook the thematic progression in texts. Thematic progression is in many respects similar in Finnish and English, but a major difference is that the unmarked Theme does not necessarily conflate with the grammatical subject in Finnish. This means that the (unmarked) Theme in Finnish can be an adverbial, as in the first paragraph of the preface text (sentences 2–4), which is reproduced below but simplified and glossed for ease of illustration. The Theme appears in boldface type:

(9) ***tähän luetteloon**   on kerätty   nuortenkirjallisuutta*
    to this catalogue   is collected   children's literature

   vuosilta 1993–95 [2]
   from years 93–95

(10) ***valikoimaan**   sisältyy   26 kirjailijan tuotantoa* ...[3]
     to the selection   includes   26 author's works ...

(11) ***luettelossa**   on   kustakin kirjailijasta*
     in the catalogue   is   from each author

   lyhyt tietoisku....[4]
   a short information package

In instances like these, some novice translators are likely to either translate the clause-initial adverbial as an adverbial and leave it at the beginning and introduce a subject (example 12) or look for what would correspond to a subject in English, i.e. the NP at the end of the clause, and change the word order in the translation so that the subject comes first (example 13):

(12) in this selection, we have included the works of 26 authors

(13) *the works of 26 authors are included in this selection*

Translating in either of these ways will result in translations that are textually marked: either (too many) marked clause-initial adverbials or (too many) clause-final adverbials that contain information that is both thematic and given (and thus should be at the beginning of the clause). The strategy for keeping given and thematic information at the beginning in translations from Finnish into English could be expressed as something like "if there is a clause-initial adverbial in Finnish that is related to the Theme–Rheme organisation in the text (or — to put it in everyday terms — to the way in which the subject matter is developed in the text), try translating it as a subject in English and make other changes (e.g. in the verb) to accommodate this change":

(14) *This catalogue includes literature for children and young people published between 1993 and 1995... The selection covers the work of twenty-six authors...*' [cf. 2–4]

This is, in fact, a fairly simple example and many students would automatically translate the adverbial as a subject, however, it is worth focusing on this strategy as there are less obvious instances and it helps students to direct their attention to the thematic progression in the text.[12]

This section has introduced a variety of possible topics for the preliminary discussion; however, it seems to me the analysis of the text should not be exhaustive and should simply focus on a few relevant topics or, at least, the breadth and depth of the discussion should vary from one assignment to the next. Some of the topics mentioned so far can be moved to or picked up again in the follow-up discussion.

6. Completion of the assignments

As mentioned earlier, I am assuming that the students complete the assignment individually, but nevertheless consult with each other about possible problems and work co-operatively on finding solutions to particular translation problems (e.g. technical terms). Alternatively, students could work in pairs or in groups, each translating the same section or translating different sections.

Students need to be reminded to read the text at least twice before attempting to translate it and that time spent reading the text is not time wasted. Before translating the text, it may also be useful for students to mark difficult sections that may need to be unpackaged or complex clauses that may need to be broken up into two clauses. In the first few assignments, it may also be useful for students to plot out the thematic progression in the SL text, i.e. by underlining the Themes (as indicated in sentences 1–3 above), marking given information in some way, and drawing arrows to show the way in which the text progresses.

7. Marking the assignment

When the assignments have been completed, they need to be discussed and/or checked. Again there are a number of alternative ways of doing this: they can be checked and commented on by other students. Even if the assignment is eventually checked by the teacher it may be a good idea to get students to check each others' assignments, as this eliminates obvious mistakes and mistakes due to carelessness, and most teachers are grateful of even minor ways of cutting down on their marking load. It also serves as a reminder that any translation that is done should always be checked by someone else, a procedure that is followed in good translation agencies.

If the translations are checked by the teacher, it seems to me that this should serve two purposes 1) to alert the teacher to recurrent problems in the students' work and 2) to alert students to possible errors and ways of improving their translations. When I mark translations, I jot things down and end up with a summary sheet of consistent errors, infelicities and discussion points in the translations, and these form the basis of the follow-up discussion. The students' papers are not corrected as such (except for obvious spelling and punctuation mistakes etc.), instead I use lines, symbols and abbreviations to indicate my reaction to the translation. This is meant as feedback, and students are invited to disagree — after all, not even professional translators agree on how to translate something.

Appendix 2 gives a list of the shorthand I use in giving feedback on translations. This consists of symbols, e.g. various ways of underlining, and abbreviations used to explain why a particular section has been marked, e.g. T–R for Theme–Rheme organisation. I shall use the published translation to illustrate how I would mark a student's translation. Solid underlining means that I think the translation is clearly inappropriate ("wrong"): there is either a clear grammatical mistake or lack of correspondence between sections of the SL text and its translation. The translation of *toimittajien päivä* as *editors' day* in the Kunnas text (sentence 32) is a clear (minor) mistake. A *toimittaja* in Finnish is a journalist, a *päätoimittaja* [head+journalist] is an editor. As with this translator, students often make mistakes like this out of carelessness and/or lack of time, and unless it is a consistent mistake reflecting an underlying translation problem, it seems to me that it is unnecessary to make an issue of it.

A wavy line means that I think the translation could be improved. Examples of this include a misleading translation: a possible example of this occurs in sentence 25 of the Kunnas text. The word *vanha* in *vanhassa talonpoikaisyhteisössä* is translated as 'an *ancient* farming community'. The Finnish *vanha talonpoikaisyhteisö* is 'an old peasant community', and while it seems to me that the change from "peasant" to "farming" does not make a substantial change in meaning in this context, using "ancient" to describe the way of life 100–300 years ago is misleading. And as the text is directed at adults, not children, exaggeration is unwarranted.

Other sections that would be marked with a wavy line include inappropriate stylistic choices, choices that are (inappropriately) marked in some way, and odd collocations. A possible example is "the recession has begun to abate" in the preface (sentence 6). It seems to me that one is more likely to talk about a recession "easing off" or about "an improvement in the economic situation", but this is perhaps debatable. With students translating from Finnish I tend to mark (perhaps overmark) even minor bumps in the thematic progression in a text, as for example, in sentence 33 of the Kunnas text, which reverses the information structure of the original.

(15) *Toimittajien päivä on värikäs ja vauhdikas. Erityistä kiirettä saa pitää valokuvaaja Timppa ...* [33]

(16) *The editors' day is colourful and action-packed. The photographer, Timppa, is particularly under pressure.* [33]

With the canonical view of word order presented in many grammatical descriptions of English (SV(O)A), translators often forget that English word order is not fixed, and, for example, a complement can precede the subject if it presents given or implicitly given information and the subject presents new information:

(17) *Particularly stressed out ~ overworked is the photographer, Timppa.*

Another common use of a wavy line is to mark a section of a translation that goes against "the end-weight principle": a sentence with a long subject (sometimes preceded by a long adverbial) that ends abruptly with the verb. This is common in translations from Finnish into English. There is not a good example of this in the translated text, but based on the original Finnish text some translators are likely to translate sentence 29 in the Kunnas text as:

(18) *As in the author's two earlier books set in Koiramäki, the historical details in both the text and the pictures have been carefully researched.*[29]

This end-weight principle is, of course, another slant on unmarked information flow: given information is followed by new information, which is often longer and more weighty. Ways to avoid these "front-weighted" clauses could then be discussed in the follow-up session of an assignment that focuses on this particular problem.

The solid and wavy lines used to mark the translations are accompanied whenever possible by an abbreviated explanation, e.g. "T–R" for thematic progression, "col" for collocation, "cor" or "eq" for lack of correspondence or equivalence. In practice, however, it is often difficult to pinpoint the reason why a particular section of a translation sounds odd, in which case I resort to a vague explanation such as "awkward" or "odd". Even without a specific explanation students often agree that what they have written is odd, and if they do not agree then the problem can be discussed in class.

When giving feedback, it is all too easy to focus on what students will inevitably perceive as "mistakes", and forget that students also need positive feedback. Ticks, plus signs and/or short written comments can be used to draw attention to particularly good sections of the translation. It is also a good idea to write at least a short overall comment that focuses on the positive aspects of the translation. Alternatively overall comments can be given to the student on a feedback form with a number of headings or questions, related to such areas as cohesion, thematic progression, stylistic consistency etc.

8. Follow-up discussion

The follow-up session can also be handled in various ways. Often it is more practicable to go through and analyse the translation sentence by sentence, discussing various options and looking at translation problems. This analysis can also be based on a comparison of translations: for example, the published translation can be compared with a translation done by one of the students. However, a step-by-step analysis can become too time-consuming and involve too much detail, in which case the teaching of translation is reduced to a list of ad hoc and unrelated details, and there is the danger that students will not be able to see the wood for the trees. While attention to detail is sometimes unavoidable, it seems to me that it is better to focus on the things that are generalisable. And generalisations can only be based on an explicit lexicogrammatical and textual understanding of both SL and TL and the relevant genres in both languages.

As indicated earlier, these generalisations presuppose an (informal) analysis of the students' translations, e.g. by jotting things down as one is marking the assignments. For example, students translating from Finnish into English often translate the word 'year' in contexts such as the following:

(19) *The catalogue includes the principal titles in Finnish literature for children and young people published from the years 1993 to 1995.* [2]

This is because the word for 'year' invariably occurs in Finnish texts (*vuosilta 1993–95* 'from years 1993–95') because the stem of the word for 'year' is needed so that a circumstantial (locative) case-ending can be attached to it. Case-endings are used in Finnish to express the kinds of meanings expressed by prepositions in English: *vuonna 1998* 'in (the year) 1998', *vuodelta 1998* 'from (the year) 1998' etc.). The word "year" is unnecessary in English because a preposition can stand alone; if it does occur in an English text, it is generally marked or it refers to a year that is special in some sense: "in the year 2000". There are other similar examples in the text e.g. *kirjassa Koiramäen talvi …* (sentence 5), which novice translators sometimes translate as "in the book *Winter in Koiramäki* (Dog/Canine Hill)" rather than as "in *Winter in Koiramäki*".

Another translation problem that can be generalised is the translation of the Finnish passive in the first paragraph of the Kunnas text. This is a subjectless verb form which incorporates a bound morpheme with exophoric reference to non-specified human participants (Shore 1986). It can correspond to an agentless English passive, but it can also be used to refer to what people generally do, in which case its experiential meaning is similar to English personal pronouns used to refer to human activities within a defined context, e.g. *we/they/you drink a lot of coffee in Finland*. The following examples of the Finnish passive occur in sentences 26–28 of the Kunnas text:

valetaan kynttilöitä (make wax candles),
kehrätään (spin yarn),
pestään pyykkiä avannolla (do the washing in a hole in the ice),
työtä tehdään (work is done),
käydään joulukirkossa (go to church at Christmas),
juhlahetkinä riemuitaan (at times of celebration rejoice) etc.

One could discuss various ways of translating these in terms of their stylistic appropriateness and their appropriateness from the point of view of thematic progression: adding a nominal subject such as *people* or *Finns* or a pronoun subject (*people/they wash their clothes in a hole on the ice*), changing the Finnish object into a subject and producing an agentless English passive (*the washing is done in a hole in the ice*), change the structure of the sentence so that a nominalised verb form can be used (*the book describes how they spent their winters: doing the washing in a hole in the ice ...*) etc.

Even specific translation problems are seldom entirely specific. I spend a lot of time checking collocations using the British National Corpus, and the collocations are discussed in class.[13] For example, "juvenile" as an alternative to "young adult" or "teenage" is inappropriate in the preface text because its collocates are often negative (*juvenile delinquents, juvenile crime, juvenile humour, juvenile behaviour*) unless the context is purely legal (*juvenile court*) or scientific (*juvenile diabetes, juvenile crabs*).[14] While each instance is different, the phenomenon itself — the way in which certain words tend to go together in certain contexts — is something that students need to be aware of.

Moreover, the translation of a particular word, phrase or clause in a particular context can always be related to the way in which it might be translated in another context. For example, the translation of *tai* 'or' in the second last paragraph of the preface:

(20) *Children's and teenage books entertain the reader with their bubbling family humour, satire, irony **or** grotesque exaggeration.* [15]

In this context, it would have been more natural to translate Finnish *tai* as *and*, because *or* in English (unlike Finnish *tai*) tends to have an exclusive interpretation, and the implication is that only one of these features (*humour, satire* etc.) applies to all of these books. In a legal text, on the other hand, Finnish *tai* would probably be translated by *or,* and English *and* would correspond to the Finnish *ja*.

9. Concluding remarks

As I have indicated throughout, the teaching of translation always needs to address the issue of what is generalisable and what is not, and make students aware that a translation that is acceptable in one context is not necessarily acceptable in another: there are different types of texts and different kinds of translation. As I see it, the major problem with teaching translation is that there is too much to teach and too many details that could be covered. With experience, however, one learns to use a particular translation assignment to focus on a number of important issues.

Whether or not the approach outlined in this article is effective — whether students can learn to be better translators through explicit instruction — is a moot point. With translation, as with many other language skills, there is a great deal that depends on the individual aptitudes of students and their talent for picking up things and being able to apply them to new (linguistic) situations. From the point of view of the teacher, however, it seems to me that the extent to which translation is teachable is proportionate to the extent to which it is not ad hoc or a matter of finding unique solutions to unique problems. Moreover, as I pointed out in the introduction, not all university-level translation courses are designed to teach students to be translators. If this is the case, a translation course can be used as a practical way of investigating grammatical differences between languages, diatypic variation in and across languages and cultures, and ways of negotiating meanings, and it seems to me that, for the most part, these are things that are teachable and can be learnt.

Appendix 1: The catalogue texts

(1) Lukijalle

(2) Tähän IBBY:n Suomen osaston julkaisemaan kahdeksanteen englanninkieliseen luetteloon on kerätty keskeistä suomalaista lasten- ja nuortenkirjallisuutta vuosilta 1993–95. (3) Kaikkiaan valikoimaan sisältyy 26 kirjailijan tuotantoa: kuvakirjoja, lastenrunoja ja -kertomuksia, satuja ja nuortenromaaneja. (4) Teosten esittelyn lisäksi luettelossa on kustakin kirjailijasta ja tämän käyttämistä aihepiireistä lyhyt tietoisku.

(5) Kolmivuotiskausi 1993–95 alkoi myös kirjallisuuden kohdalla Suomea ahdistelleen laman merkeissä. (6) Parina viimeisenä vuonna alkoi lama hellittää, mutta jätti jälkensä lähinnä vauraina vuosina runsaana kukoistaneeseen kuvakirjatuotantoon. (7) Kuvakirjojen lukumäärä supistui vakiintuakseen vasta myöhemmin kohtuullisena pidettävälle tasolle. (8a) Kaikesta huolimatta on uusia, lahjakkaita kuvittajia (mm. Maija Ranta, Riitta Uusitalo) astunut jo perinteisten, hyvien taiteilijoidemme (esim. Mauri Kunnas, Kaarina Kaila) rinnalle (8b) ja kuvituksen aihepiirit löytäneet uutta ilmettä.

(9) Myös perinteinen suomalainen lastenkertomus väheni ja alkoi samalla muuttua kuvitteellisempaan suuntaan. (10) Vuonna 1995 saatiin kuitenkin toivottu lisäys niin lastenkertomuksiin kuin lastenrunoihin, jotka alkoivat sekä uudistua että monipuolistua.

(11) 1980-luvun loppupuolelta asti hyvin pintansa pitänyt varttuneiden nuorten kirja on laajentanut aiheitaan käsittelemään entistä enemmän nykypäivän ajankohtaisia tapahtumia (esim. Mika Wikström: Sukupolvi X). (12) Suomen historiaa kartoittavaa ainesta esiintyy nuorisokirjallisuudessamme, joukossa myös harvinaiseksi jääneitä suomalaisten merkkihenkilöiden elämäntyön luonnehdintoja (Raili Mikkanen, Anneli Toijala). (13) Jo klassikoiksi

(1) To the Reader

(2a) This is the eighth English language catalogue to be issued by the Finnish section of IBBY. (2b) It includes the principal titles in Finnish literature for children and young people published between 1993 and 1995. (3) This issue covers selections from the work of 26 authors: picture books, children's poetry, children's stories, fairy tales and teenage novels. (4) As well as presenting the books, this catalogue provides some brief factual details about the authors and their work in general.

(5) The three year period 1993–95 began at a time when the economic recession in Finland also took its toll on the literary world. (6) Over the last two years, the recession has begun to abate but it has nevertheless left its mark on a literary output which has thrived largely in periods of affluence. (7) The proportion of picture books initially diminished considerably, and it took some time before this stabilised at an acceptable level. (8) Nevertheless, several new talented illustrators have emerged (e.g. Maija Ranta, Riitta Uusitalo) alongside the many excellent, well-established artists (e.g. Mauri Kunnas, Kaarina Kaila), infusing new expression into the range of book illustrations.

(9) There was also a decrease in traditional children's narrative, which has recently tended towards fantasy. (10) 1995 nonetheless witnessed a very desirable surge in children's stories and poetry, which gained in both vitality and versatility.

(11) The teenage novel, which established a foothold in the late 1980's, has broadened its range by addressing topical issues with increasing frequency (e.g. Mika Wickström's *Generation X*). (12) Finnish history has also inspired teenage literature, which includes some rare portraits of significant Finnish historical figures (Raili Mikkonen, Anneli Toijala). (13) There have been publications of collected works by authors who have become classics of children's literature

muotoutuneiden kirjailijoiden (Kaija Pakkanen, Marjatta Kurenniemi) tuotantoa on kerätty kokoelmiksi, ja lahjakkaat esikoiskirjailijat saaneet tunnustusta (Inka Nousiainen: Kivienkeli). (14) Suomen nuorisokirjallisuuden tyylilajit ovat puolestaan laventuneet ennen muuta erivivahteisen huumorin suuntaan. (15) Niin lasten kuin nuorten kirjat kykenevät hauskuuttamaan lukijoitaan iloisena kuplivan perhehuumorin, satiirin, ironian tai vallattoman liioittelun avulla. (16) Näitä piirteitä tukee usein samaan henkeen viritetty kuvitus.

(17) IBBY:n Suomen osasto toivoo, että lasten ja nuorten kirjojen ystävät löytävät kiinnostavaa tutkittavaa luettelostamme. (18) Toivomme myös, että nuorisokirjallisuuden tutkijat saavat siitä viitteitä Suomen lasten- ja nuortenkirjallisuuden kehitystrendeistä ja että siitä on apua käännettäviksi sopivia kirjoja etsiville.

(19) Helsingissä kesäkuun 30 päivänä 1996

(20) IBBY:n Suomen osasto ...

(21) Mauri Kunnas

(22) Koiramäen talvi

(23) Etusivun juttu

(24) Mauri Kunnas (syntynyt 1950) on graafikko, pilapiirtäjä ja humoristi, joka persoonallisten eläinhahmojensa välityksellä kertoo lapsille elämänmenosta ennen vanhaan, nyt ja tulevaisuudessa. (25) Kirjassa Koiramäen talvi kuvataan talvisia askareita vanhassa talonpoikaisyhteisössä. (26) Valetaan kynttilöitä, kehrätään, pestään pyykkiä avannolla. (27) Käydään myös juhlavassa joulukirkossa. (28) Työtä tehdään olan takaa, mutta juhlahetkinä riemuitaan sydämen kyllyydestä. (29) Kuten kahdessa aiemmassa Koiramäkikirjassa, tässäkin niin runsas kuvallinen kuin sanallinenkin perinneaineisto on tarkoin tutkittua. (30) 4–7 -vuotiaille.

(31) Etusivun juttu kertoo kuinka sanomalehti syntyy. (32) Toimittajien päivä on värikäs ja vauhdikas. (33) Erityistä kiirettä saa pitää valokuvaaja Timppa, jonka on otettava kuvat niin presidentinlinnan hienoista vieraista kuin rallikuskista, joka

Teaching translation 271

(Kaija Pakkanen, Marjatta Kurenniemi), while new writing has also won deserved recognition (Inka Nousiainen: *The Stone Angel*). (14) The stylistic scope of Finnish literature for young people has expanded particularly in its variety of humour. (15) Children's and teenage books entertain the reader with their bubbling family humour, satire, irony or grotesque exaggeration, (16) much of which is enhanced by art work in the same spirit.

(17) The Finnish Section of IBBY trusts that enthusiasts of children's books will find much of interest in this catalogue. (18) We also hope that scholars of the field will be able to picture the trends and developments in Finnish literature for the young, and that this catalogue will help those looking for suitable works for translation.

(19) Helsinki, June 30th 1996.

(20) The Finnish Section of IBBY ...

(21) Mauri Kunnas

(22) Winter in Koiramäki

(23) Front Page Story

(24a) Mauri Kunnas (b. 1950) is a graphic artist, cartoonist and comic writer. (24b) He uses the animal characters he has created to tell children about the way of life in days of old, in present times and in the future. (25) *Winter in Koiramäki* concentrates on the winter activities of an ancient farming community: (26) making wax candles, spinning yarn and doing the washing in a hole in the ice. (27) There is also a solemn Christmas visit to church. (28) Work is a heavy burden but moments of rest are enjoyed to the full. (29) As in the author's two earlier books set in Koiramäki, the wealth of historical detail in both the text and the pictures is the result of careful research work. (30) For ages 4 to 7.

(31) *Front Page Story* is about how a newspaper is created. (32)The editors' day is colourful and action-packed. (33a) The photographer, Timppa, is particularly under pressure. (33b) He has to get shots of the guests at the President's Palace as well as of

törmää munavuoreen. (34) Juttuja puretaan, yhdistellään, kuvitetaan. (35) Ja juuri kun kaikki on valmista, etusivu meneekin uusiksi! (36) Lehden tekeminen Kunnaksen eläinten kanssa on sekä hauskaa että opettavaista. (37) Kuvakirjan välissä on toimittajien päivän työ; pieni mustavalkoinen sanomalehti. (38) 7–11 -vuotiaille.

the rally driver who crashed into the egg mountain. (34) Stories are pulled apart, sewn together and pictures are chosen for them. (35) And just as everything looks ready, the front page has to be changed again! (36) There is a lot of fun, and a lot to learn, in making a newspaper with Kunnas' animal characters. (37) In the middle of the book, there is the result of a day's work in the editors' office: a small, black and white newspaper. (38) For ages 7 to 11.

Appendix 2: Symbols & abbreviations used in marking translations

✓	excellent!
✓✓	brilliant!
═══	double underlining = !!??
───	single underlining = could definitely be improved
~~	wavy underlining = could be improved
....	dotted line = not quite right

These lines can also be drawn vertically to mark a section of the translation.

( )	brackets = this could have been left out
/----/	unnecessary
∧	caret = something seems to be missing
	transpose = it would be better to interchange the positions of these words or phrases
│ 2	= a single, wavy or dotted line alongside a section of the translation and the number 2 means that there is too much information packed into one sentence, and it would be better to divide the sentence into 2 sentences or into two clauses separated by a semicolon.
│ 1	= a single, wavy or dotted line alongside a section of the translation and the number 1 means that 2 or more sentences could have been combined into 1 sentence.

Am.	= typically American usage or spelling, when the rest of the text is British
awk.	= awkward (sometimes combined with other abbreviations but often used a "fall-back" when it is difficult to come up with an explanation)
Br.	= typically British usage or spelling, when the rest of the text is American
cf. PT	= this particular element or feature is not typical of parallel texts in English
coh.	= cohesive link (e.g. either a cohesive link is needed or the one used is inappropriate in this particular context)
col.	= collocation, the words do not collocate (in this context ~ for this genre)
con.	= connotation, the word or expression has the wrong connotations (in/for this context)
cor./eq.	= correspondence (or equivalence), i.e. this word (or section) does not correspond to the Finnish (in this particular context)

end W	= end weight, i.e., this clause goes against the "end weight principle", (often combined with G–N)
G–N	= Given–New, i.e. something wrong with the Given–New organisation (e.g. Given information has been placed at the end of the sentence).
M	= marked, i.e. either (i) something is marked (unusual or contrastive) in the English text but unmarked in the Finnish text or (ii) the grammatical resources of Finnish and English do not correspond and something that is marked in Finnish cannot be translated as a marked item in English.
odd	another "fallback" (see "awk" above)
≠ off.	= not official, i.e. not the recommended official translation (e.g. for the name of a Finnish political party)
st(yle)	= stylistically inappropriate (for this genre)
T–R	= Theme–Rheme, i.e. there is something wrong with the thematic progression at this point in the text
WO	= Word Order, i.e. there is something marked about the word ~ constituent order (e.g. separation of the verb and (a relatively short) object with a Circumstance)

Notes

1. Many of the ideas about translation in this article are based on ideas passed on to me by my colleagues at the University of Helsinki. I am particularly grateful to Andrew Chesterman, Mary Hatakka, and Ritva Leppihalme for comments on earlier versions of this article. I am also indebted to Eva Buchwald for the texts used in this article and for practical advice on translations and translating.
2. The teaching of translation does, in fact, involve a certain amount of language teaching, but this aspect of translation teaching will be ignored in this article. Also ignored is the issue of whether students are translating into the mother tongue or into a foreign language.
3. They are quoted, for example, in a recently published dictionary (Shuttleworth & Cowrie 1997) and an entry on *equivalence* in the *Routledge Encyclopedia of Translation Studies* (1998). A more balanced reading of Catford can be found, for example, in Fawcett (1997: 53–63) and in Chesterman (1998: 21–24).
4. The entry on *equivalence* in the *Routledge Encyclopedia of Translation Studies* (1998), written by Dorothy Kenny, on the other hand, interprets the above definition as saying that a SL text and its TL translation have "approximately the same referents" and, moreover, she understands Catford as having "an essentially referential theory of meaning". Catford relates SL and TL texts to each other by reference to the situations in which the texts function not because his theory of meaning is referential but because meaning is something that is not constant across languages.
5. The distinction made by Catford is not always made in discussions of equivalence, and some non-linguists confuse the issue by failing to clearly distinguish between relationships that can be postulated between linguistic systems and relationships that can be postulated between texts. For example, Bassnett (1991: 16–18) discusses Nida's diagram of the translation process and then exemplifies it with her own diagram, which is used to illustrate the translation of "hello" into French "ça va?"; however, the label "source language text" in Nida's original diagram becomes "source language" in Bassnett's diagram. A text consisting entirely of "hello" (with no response or follow-up) is a highly unusual one and is certainly not a typical text.
6. Moreover, the translation may be affected by more mundane considerations such as the time that a translator is given to complete an assignment (in my experience more often

than not a translation is due the day before yesterday) and the remuneration received by the translator.
7. This is illustrated by the preface texts in the Appendix: the Finnish text has 275 words and the English translation has 410 words. The texts have approximately the same number of letters, but the spacing between words makes the English text longer.
8. As discussed in this chapter, a context needs to be given for these extracts and the exact nature of the commission needs to be made explicit.
9. This means that the teacher needs to build up a collection of real translations and original SL texts. (This also gives the teacher some idea of the kinds of texts that are translated from the SL to the TL.)
10. For a more fine-tuned, systemic-functional approach to text type, see Halliday & Hasan 1989, Martin 1992.
11. The notion of a translation strategy as used above is slightly different from the more ad hoc translation procedures and production strategies discussed in translation studies (e.g. Vinay and Darbelnet 1958, Gile 1995, Chesterman 1997: Ch. 4), although undoubtedly further research on translation procedures and production strategies will eventually produce strategies that will be relevant to the teaching of translation. As I see it, a translation strategy is not a strategy until it has been abstracted from a number of similar instances, and there is not much point in telling students to change the word class, e.g. change a verb into a noun, or to change the unit (e.g. translate a word as a phrase) unless one can specify the kind of (recurrent) translation problem that a particular procedure is likely to solve.
12. With further translations, this strategy would subsequently be amended and extended. For example, some adverbials come before a clause-initial subject, and some of these, e.g. time adverbials, are used cohesively, and should be kept at the beginning of the sentence etc.
13. I have access to this corpus, but unfortunately the students do not. It is, however, possible for students to do a pilot search of the British National Corpus and of the Collins Cobuild Bank of English, and there are also other, more limited corpora available on the Internet.
14. Regardless of how large it is, a corpus nevertheless only represents a fraction of a language, and I do not think it should be regarded as revealing the ultimate truth about language. For example, I have, in fact, come across the term "juvenile literature" in an American literary publication, and I suspect it could also occur in British publications; however, it seems to me that this is a reflection of older usage.

References

Bassnett, Susan
    1991   *Translation studies*. Revised edition. London: Routledge.

Catford, J.C.
    1965   *A linguistic theory of translation*. Oxford: Oxford University Press.

Chesterman, Andrew (ed.)
    1989   *Readings in translation theory*. Helsinki: Finn Lectura.

Chesterman, Andrew
    1997   *Memes of translation: the spread of ideas in translation theory*. Amsterdam: Benjamins.

Chesterman, Andrew
    1998   Communication strategies, learning strategies and translation strategies. In: Kirsten Malmkjær (ed.) *Translation and language teaching: language teaching and translation*, 135–144. Manchester: St Jerome.

Cloran, Carmel, David Butt and Geoff Williams (eds.)
    1996   *Ways of saying: ways of meaning — selected papers of Ruqaiya Hasan*. London: Cassell.

Fawcett, Peter
    1997   *Translation and language: linguistic theories explained*. Manchester: St Jerome.

Firth, J.R.
    1957   *Papers in linguistics 1934–1951*. London: Oxford University Press.

Firth, J.R.
    1968   *Selected papers of J.R. Firth 1952–59*. Edited by F.R. Palmer. London: Longmans.

Grace, George
    1987   *The linguistic construction of reality*. London: Croom Helm.

Gile, Daniel
    1995   *Basic concepts and models for interpreter and translator training*. Amsterdam: Benjamins.

Halliday, M.A.K.
    1978   *Language as social semiotic*. London: Edward Arnold.

Halliday, M.A.K.
    1987   Language and the order of nature. In Nigel Fabb et al. (eds.) *The linguistics of writing*, 135–154. Manchester: Manchester University Press.

Halliday, M.A.K.
    1992   How do you mean? In: Martin Davies & Louise Ravelli (eds.) *Advances in systemic linguistics: recent theory and practice*. 20–35.

Halliday M.A.K. and Ruqaiya Hasan
    1989   *Language, context and text: aspects of language in a social-semiotic perspective*. Oxford: Oxford University Press.

Hasan, Ruqaiya
    1984   What kind of resource is language? In *Australian review of applied linguistics* 1984: 57–85. Reprinted in Carmel Cloran et al. (eds.) 13–36.

Hasan, Ruqaiya
    1985   Ways of saying: ways of meaning. In R. Fawcett, M.A.K. Halliday, S. Lamb & A. Makkai (eds.) *The semiotics of language and culture, Volume 1: Language as social semiotic*, 105–162. London: Frances Pinter. Reprinted in Carmel Cloran et al. (eds.) 191–242.

Koller, W.
    1979   *Einführung in die Übersetzungswissenschaft*. Heidelberg: Quelle und Meyer. (An extract from this entitled "Equivalence in translation theory" has been translated into English in Andrew Chesterman ed. 1989, 99–104.).

Martin, James
1992   *English text*. Amsterdam: Benjamins.

Nord, Christiane
1991   *Text analysis in translation: theory, methodology, and didactic applications of a model for translation-oriented text analysis*. Translated from German by Christiane Nord and Penelope Sparrow. Amsterdam: Rodopi.

Routledge Encyclopedia of Translation Studies.
1998   Edited by Mona Baker (assisted by Kirsten Malmkjær). London: Routledge.

Sager, Juan C.
1993   *Language engineering and translation: consequences of automation*. Amsterdam: Benjamins.

Shore, Susanna
1986   On the so-called Finnish passive. *WORD* 39: 151–176.

Shuttleworth, Mark and Moira Cowrie
1997   *Dictionary of Translation Studies*. Manchester: St. Jerome.

Snell-Hornby, Mary
1988   *Translation studies: an integrated approach*. Amsterdam: Benjamins.

Toury, Gideon
1995   *Descriptive translation studies and beyond*. Amsterdam: Benjamins.

Venuti, Lawrence
1995   *The translator's invisibility: a history of translation*. London: Routledge.

Vinay, Jean-Paul and Jean Darbelnet
1958   *Stylistique comparée du français et de l'anglais*. Paris: Didier.

Computer assisted text analysis and translation: a functional approach in the analysis and translation of advertising texts

Chris Taylor and Anthony Baldry

1. Introduction

Interest in the role that systemic-functional linguistics might play in translation studies has never been feverish, though a number of articles have been written on the subject (Newmark (1988), Ventola (1994), Steiner (1996), (1997), Taylor Torsello (1996), Taylor (1993), (1997)) and seminars have been held and whole sections of conferences given over to the subject (Ghent 1995, Turku 1995, Sydney 1996, Cardiff 1998). Similarly, it has taken some time for translation to find its place in the area of computer assisted learning, as opposed to computerised translation. The two major projects discussed in this article bring together the three fields of (systemic) linguistics, translation and computer studies through the illustration of past, present and future phases in the creation of computer assisted, didactic software involving text analysis and translation. Both projects, but particularly the second, go further and explore the strategies required to analyse and translate multimodal texts, where visual elements, additional sound features and moving pictures are included in complex semiotic "events".

1.1. Linguistics and translation

As regards the role of linguistics in general Catford (in 1965) demonstrated the importance for the translator of isolating a grammatical unit, "a stretch of language activity which is the carrier of a pattern of some kind", and of being aware of the need at times to shift between the hierarchical ranks of word, phrase, clause and sentence when moving from one language to another (Catford 1965: 5). As a functional grammarian, Halliday (1966) also exploited the rank system (morpheme-word-group-clause) in his "stepping-stone" approach to translation from Russian and Chinese, this time advocating a progression from a literal "item-for-item" transcription to reconsiderations based firstly on an understanding of the "context of situation" of the text, and secondly on the grammatical and lexical restrictions of the target language.

The translation scholar Newmark (1981) made the observation that "translation and interpretation have to be based on words, sentences, linguistic meaning, language…"

Later (in 1988) he illustrated his acknowledgement of the usefulness of grammar in the widest sense, by discussing, for example, Fillmore and Tesnières in terms of "case gaps" allowing the translator to account for missing words, groups, clauses, even sentences, but he also acknowledged the importance of functional grammar, by discussing Halliday, particularly in terms of grammatical metaphor and cohesive texture. Newmark's entire chapter on systemic linguistics (1991: 65–77) talks of language as being primarily "…a meaning potential … determining the constituent parts of a source language and its network of relations with its translation."

The "constituent parts of a source language" are what may also be called functional components. A study of the higher order syntactic functions of these components allows translators to construct their target texts without regard to the restricting temptations of the source syntax — they can thematise a verb in Italian or Spanish or move an adverb to the end of the clause in English. They can passivise an Italian active or convert noun strings in English into chains of prepositional and adjectival groups in Italian.

As its very name suggests, systemic-functional linguistics is based on the idea of a "system" showing what people do with language in the light of what they "can do", in the light of meaning potential. Adapting a particularly appropriate Hallidayan concept, translators, like all linguists, should "…pay attention to what is said… and relate it systematically to what might have been said but was not." (Halliday 1973: 67)

It is this notion that should provide the clues as to the options to select in translation, selecting those items that reflect what was actually said and not what might have been or was not said.

1.1.1. *Context of situation*

The Malinowski-inspired concept of the context of situation, further developed by Firth and Halliday, provides an excellent framework for the analysis of a text for translation, and for the selecting of the most suitable linguistic options for the target language version. Basically a text is seen as being created within a particular context which can be described in terms of three parameters — "field", "tenor" and "mode". "Field" refers to the subject matter and the nature of the activity, i.e., what is happening, to whom, when and where, what they know, why they are doing what they are doing, and so on. "Tenor" refers to the social relationships existing between those involved in terms of power and status (e.g., father/son, manager/clerk, boyfriend/girlfriend, etc.) and thus how they feel about each other, whether they know each other well and so on. It refers also to the role structure (questioner/answerer; informer/enquirer, etc.). "Mode" concerns how the language is being used, the organisation of the text, whether it is written (faxed, e-mailed, etc.) or spoken (on the phone, recorded, etc.). Some texts are actually "written to be spoken" (e.g., political speeches) or "spoken to be written" (e.g., dictated letters). "Mode" also refers to whether a text is performative or reflective, spontaneous or well thought out.

These three elements enable the speaker/writer (subconsciously) to construct the context of situation. The translator, transposing a text at a second remove, must strive to maintain the situational and cultural context by matching the three variables in the target language version. By establishing the "field" of text, decisions can be made as to what terminology may or may not be adopted, how information should be presented grammatically (active/passive, stative/dynamic, etc.) and what shared knowledge should be assumed to exist between writer and reader. The "tenor" will inform the translator as to which register to employ, in the sense of formal/informal, technical/non-technical, archaic/modern, etc., and whether the indicative (affirmative or interrogative) or imperative mood should be employed. The "mode" points the way to the organisation of the information in terms of theme and rheme, given and new information, information focus, and so on (Taylor 1998: 79)

As Firth (1968: 87) pointed out "Translation problems can be solved in the mutual assimilation of the languages in similar contexts of situation and in common human experience." Linking the use of language with this notion of "context of situation", Juliane House (1981, 1997) has provided *A Model for Translation Quality Assessment,* which "...provides for the analysis of the linguistic-situational peculiarities of a given source text and its target text." (1981: abstract)

The House approach essentially looks to equate source and target contexts of situation via a series of eight "dimensions", namely geographical origin, social class, time, medium, participation, social role relationship, social attitude, and province.

House's model can also be seen in terms of matching function with function. Translators, in systemic parlance, can be seen (like a speaker) to be constantly selecting from a paradigmatic network, their selections being restricted by a variety of factors, many of which can be traced back to House's dimensions. They do not always select wisely or appropriately however, leading to what House terms mismatches between source and target text, mismatches in function which can then be identified and assessed. In terms of functional grammar, House's approach can be said to deal adequately with the "field" and "tenor" of the context of situation, basically what is happening and who is involved, but this form of assessment would benefit from the integration of a wider "mode" component dealing more directly with how the language is used, and this is where Halliday's form of text analysis (cf. analysis of the "Silver text", (1985); "the Zero Growth Text", (1992)), which is the one principally used in the first project described below, proves to be so useful.

1.2. Computer-assisted Studies

Joint research involving the universities of Trieste and Pavia has made it possible to develop interactive computer applications designed for translation students. These applications integrate the "context of situation" model (see above and Halliday and Hasan (1985: 3–14)), Halliday's systemic-functional grammar analysis (e.g. in Mann and Thompson, eds. (1992)) and Gregory's notion of phase and transition (In press) in an attempt to provide educational instruments to sensitise students to the multi-faceted nature of texts for translation.

The particular authoring system adopted is *HyperContext* (created by Marco Piastra and Roberto Bolognesi, Pavia, Italy), an application which has enabled the designers to integrate linguistic theory, didactic methodology and computer-student interaction. It comprises a working memory, a monitoring system, dynamic links, a parsing method and feedback facilities. It permits the use of images with the high semiotic value that that entails: the combining of text and pictures enables the user to control several information flows; it is thus suitable for university student use where a level of data needs to be combined with one or more metalevels which permit a comment or a theoretical illustration of the data in question. And this combination is dynamic; the correspondences between the levels vary in accordance with the choices made by the user. The student moves through the application opening windows, gaining information, answering questions, and correspondingly advancing or regressing. In other words, the user communicates with the computer, is asked to choose between diverse routes in search of solutions to problems, and moves around the application in search of information or useful hints. He or she can proceed smoothly or make mistakes and be corrected. The computer is the virtual teacher in a learning exercise simulating the inquisitive question/answer format that is the basis of all learning.

HyperContext is in fact an authoring system devised specifically for the creation of advanced educational applications. It is designed to satisfy the six validity criteria for educational software drawn up by Baldry and Crivelli (1994: 5):

1) quality of information
2) clear educational objectives
3) ability to motivate
4) integration of previously acquired and new knowledge
5) capacity to stimulate learning

The project has undergone a number of changes over the years, but as it stands it essentially consists of three parts:

INTRODUCTION: the student/user first learns how to move around (to navigate within) the computer application.

PRE-TRANSLATION TEXT ANALYSIS:
a) the student analyses a text with regard to such factors as the context of situation, thematic structure, cohesion, transitivity, the information system, and mood. He or she then has to perform some language related task such as identifying the linguistic elements that realise structures in the text, in order to proceed; otherwise s/he is given the relevant information or suggestions via a continuous dialogue between man and machine.
b) the student's work is assessed and s/he is advised to proceed or re-do the exercise.

TRANSLATION:
a) the student attempts to translate the text by either responding to a number of suggestions presented in the form of multiple-choice exercises or attempting to actually translate "chunks" of text. The computer responds to both acceptable and less acceptable options with explanations and advice, referring back constantly to the earlier pre-translation text analysis.
b) the student's work is assessed and s/he is advised to proceed or re-do the exercise.

2. The Computer Assisted Text Analysis and Translation Project (CATAT)

Following an initial experiment, using a newspaper article, the text eventually chosen for the first pilot project was an advertisement for the Mitsubishi Pajero car (see below). Subsequently, encouraged by the interest shown by users, the project was extended to include the dynamic texts of TV advertising. In this article, Christopher Taylor (University of Trieste) will illustrate the development of the original pilot project, now fully operational (section 2), while in section 3, Anthony Baldry (University of Pavia) will describe work in progress on the latter objective.

2.1. The Mitsubishi Advert

My mother wanted me to have piano lessons.
My father wanted me to go to Harvard.
My teacher wanted me to become a lawyer.
My wife wants me to stay at home.

Whenever you want to do something somebody expects something else.
And of course, you always satisfy them.
But is the real you always going to take a back seat to the wishes of others.
Aren't your own desires just as important?
For that little voice inside you, **we** build leisure and sports utility vehicles like our highly acclaimed Pajero ("Montero" en España).
Cars that are created to impress only yourself.
Impress yourself.
MITSUBISHI MOTORS CREATING TOGETHER.
So here **I** am.

Figure 1. The text of the Mitsubishi advert (with the picture of the car omitted)

Firstly a Hallidayan functional grammar analysis of the Mitsubishi text (Fig. 1) was programmed into the computer. This type of analysis attempts to strip the text bare, so to speak, in order to find out exactly what is going on, how the text is organised and what it is trying to do. The data regarding the thematic development, the way new information is gradually presented, the way the text hangs together and is related to the visual image behind it, the producer's attitude to what he is saying and the types of processes described, all contribute to determining the text's sociosemiotic value and tell us a lot about the workings of language. Furthermore, it can provide essential guidelines for translators as they attempt to recreate a (target) text that must abide by the same parameters as the source text, if it is to say what was said in the original and not what might have been said but was not. As the translation takes shape, translators can assess a number of factors: whether the topic themes are being adhered to, how far the logic of thematic progression is being respected, whether information focus is being obscured, how grammatical metaphor is being dealt with, whether genre restrictions are being observed. For example, Italian texts often contain a certain degree of redundancy in the form of tautologous adjuncts, and German texts often contain complicated premodifiers and postmodifiers and digressions affecting theme organisation (see Ventola 1994) that have to be dealt with without upsetting target language syntax.

The user should be able to apply the correct grammatical criteria and attempt to match the socio-cultural features (cf. House's "dimensions"), thus providing a target language version that reflects the context of situation in all its guises and at the same time works at a textual level, dealing competently with theme and information structures, grammatical metaphors, comparative syntax and all the relevant elements contained within the text for translation.

2.2. The Text Analysis Phase

The basic theoretical components relating to the linguistic analysis are explained in boxes that the user can call up on the computer screen. Thus, explanations of theme & rheme construction, the concepts of given & new, cohesion, mood and transitivity are available, and can be constantly referred to at any stage of the analysis. For example, the "cohesion" box explains the basic tenets of anaphoric and cataphoric reference, substitution, conjunction and lexical cohesion. Clearly, any didactic use of this instrument would involve a certain amount of background reading in support of these boxed extracts, and the software application therefore includes bibliographical references and important quotations from the major exponents of systemic-functional linguistics and translation studies.

The findings of the macro- and micro-analysis relating to the "car ad" text are then presented. The methodology applied, as mentioned above, is based on Halliday (1992) and thus addresses the following aspects:

1) Theme & Rheme Structure
2) Information Structure
3) Mood and Modality
4) Cohesion
5) Transitivity Structures

These parameters are used both for the macro-analysis (text as a whole) and for the micro-analysis (sentence by sentence).

2.2.1. Macro analysis

THEME & RHEME STRUCTURE: The first part of this highly iconic text consists of four sentences suspended over the aerial view colour photograph of a scene showing a boundless expanse of land crossed by a vehicle making its way at speed towards the foreground. There are four unmarked topical theme/subjects, all subservient to some implied superordinate master theme representing a general authoritative figure.

The main body of the text then comes in with a number of diverse themes (subordinate clause, topical subject, textual themes) preceding the advertiser's target figure "you". In the first sentence the main clause theme (someone) alludes to the four "villains" mentioned in the first part of the advertisement. The "you/your" is found as topical theme in the next three clauses, but later switches to "we" and finally to the subject matter of the text "cars" (the first topical theme in this part of the text to be unencumbered by textual or marked theme types), before the specific "Mitsubishi". Finally the theme "I" wins out in bold letters. Mitsubishi can be seen to have transformed "you" into "I", blending the two virtual figures into one.

Returning to the beginning, the first four sentences are not marked in isolation but in their progression they clearly stand out, as each represents an example of the unmentioned macro theme of the "oppressor" which the reader can easily imagine if not visualise. These are set up against the following series of human themes (you, we, I), concealed behind textual and minor thematic elements, which assert the writer's (and the reader's) authority over the symbolic figures thematised in the first section.

Generally speaking, textual themes such as conjunctions (And, But, for…), and modal adjuncts, have such a high frequency in normal text as not to represent an example of non-casual language. However, in an advertisement every word counts (and costs) and it is reasonable to assume that even the "ands" and the "buts" and the "therefores" play an important role. And in this text they smooth out the discourse so that it ebbs and flows naturally, in a conversation-like way. The adverbial "Whenever", with its intensifying suffix, heightens the sense of frustration felt towards the mother/father/etc. figures above.

The contrastive "But" wakes the reader up to his/her own importance. The preposition "For…" introducing the clause of purpose in the fifth paragraph sets the scene in the reader's favour, as the object of the advertisement then takes information focus position at the end of the clause.

The presentative position of the "I" in the final section, that is the right-shifting of the pronoun towards the information focus position is a typical device for circumventing English syntax and revitalising the bland, but unmarked, "I am here". One can imagine the text continuing now with "I'm heading off on my own now, being my own boss", etc.

The thematic progression is mostly a repetition of the macro theme (you) in constant theme position, with a variation late in the text where the rhematic "yourself" is picked up as the theme in the succeeding imperative command "(you) Impress yourself". There is, however, an interesting example of linear progression where the specific name of vehicle "Pajero" in rheme position provides the theme of the next clause "cars". "Pajero", "Montero" and "cars" are all part of the pre-plan heralding the mention of the key player "Mitsubishi".

INFORMATION STRUCTURE: Information Structure is a function of theme/rheme progression, the placing of information focus, and the concept of Given/New information. In the spoken language, intonation patterns give voice to information structure as the communicative dynamism of theme and rheme and Given/New information (see Firbas 1964) provide an important element of meaning. Advertising is a genre in which the distinctive features of the spoken language (low lexical density, dynamic flow, verbalisation) are transferred to the written variety in an attempt to create a more intimate, friendly rapport with the reader. The advertising text also attempts to provide some of the impact of the spoken language by arranging the words on the page in an arresting manner, by varying font sizes, colours, letter shapes and so on, and by imaginative syntactic structuring.

The first part of the text, unusually, provides new information in theme position in each new clause but provides wholesale repetition in the rheme. However, it can also be argued that the choice of theme in each case is predictable enough to be considered as partially Given information (a series of symbols of authority). The combination of all this semi-Given information contrasted with the really New information at the end of the rhemes is rhythmically and iconically highly effective as a scene-setter.

In the second part of the text, if it is read aloud, it can be appreciated how the stress patterns bring out the topical theme "you" and later "we", "cars", "Mitsubishi", and finally "I". "You" is of course concealed but Given in the early text as "me", and reiterated in the final "I", where the identity of the person in the text and the reader imperceptibly merge.

MOOD AND MODALITY: In terms of mood the succession of declarative indicative clauses is abruptly halted by the interrogative introduced by "But..." which sets the pattern for a second question. Both questions are rhetorical in that they are not answered directly, and this is in keeping with the informal tone of the text. Surprisingly, there is only one example of imperative mood structure in the discourse, which is nonetheless as persuasive (vocative) as any standard, more imperatively oriented advertisement (cf. "Buy Blotso", "Hurry while stocks last", etc.). In this case the imperative mood must be understood by the reader; the sophisticated aura of "Mitsubishi" excludes a list of commands. The only non-finite, moodless clause (Mitsubishi Motors Creating Together) stands out (also unusually) and is fundamental to the coherence of the text. The "together" unites all the participants in the context of situation, setting the scene for the mental passage from "you" to "I".

COHESION: The most instantly observable element of cohesion in the text is that of lexical cohesion. It has already been pointed out that all words count in this type of text and nothing here is left to chance. The semantic field of authority has already been mentioned. The verb/accusative/infinitive combination wanted/me/to... (note the subtle change to "wants" in line 4) is an example of straight repetition and syntactic equivalence, but the differing infinitive phrases that end the four clauses also have something in common — they are predictable in their bourgeois, establishment connotations.

Thereafter the pronoun "you" provides the main cohesive referential link through continual anaphoric linkage. The nominal "wishes" harks back to the much-repeated "want" and points forward to "desires". The motoring synonyms "vehicles", "cars", "motors" are preceded in a part/whole relationship by "back seat" in the idiomatic expression "to take a back seat". This is interesting in that this oblique reference sets up the later specificity. Of course the copywriter can play it this way as he has visual elements to back him up.

The three indefinite pronouns "something", "somebody", "something" constitute a tight little referential bundle which exploits alliteration and repetition to enhance the feeling of antipathy towards outside interference.

TRANSITIVITY: In terms of transitivity structures, the text begins with a series of "want" mental processes plus projection followed by a mental process clause with "expect". Thereafter the text slides into a more material mode though the metaphorical "take a back seat" and the clauses containing "satisfy" and "create" are not concretely material. The text ends with the relational process "So here I am". This balance of abstract material, and mental/relational processes ensure that although the text is dealing with real entities (cars) and real events (driving), there is a lot of thinking and expecting and desiring involved too. The general structure is predominantly paratactic with separate, punchy sentences and clauses linked by conjunctions (And, But). The macro theme & rheme (Fig. 2) and cohesion analyses (Fig. 3) are made available to the user on the computer screen. The user can call up whichever part of the analysis he or she is working on at any time and in whatever order. When the macro-analyses have been studied and understood, the user can progress to the micro-analysis, where each clause is examined individually.

THEME AND RHEME STRUCTURE

The first part of this highly iconic text consists of four sentences suspended over the aerial view colour photograph of a scene showing a boundless expanse of land crossed by a trail wending its way towards the horizon. There are four unmarked topical theme/subjects, all subservient to some implied superordinate master theme representing a general authoritative figure.

The main body of the text then comes in with a series of minor themes preceding the advertiser's target figure "you". In one case the subordinate alludes to the four "villains" mentioned in the first part of the advert. The "you" is then switched to "we" and finally to the subject matter of the text "cars" and then the specific "Mitsubishi". Finally, the theme "I" wins out in bold letters. Mitsubishi can be seen to have transformed "you" into "I", blending the two virtual figures into one.

The first four sentences are not marked in isolation but in their progression they clearly stand out, as each represents an example of an unmentioned macro theme which the reader can easily imagine if not visualise.

These are set up against the following series of human themes (you, we, I), concealed behind minor thematic elements, which assert the writer's (and the reader's) authority over the symbolic figures thematised in the first section.

My mother wanted me to have piano lessons.
My father wanted me to go to Harvard.
My teacher wanted me to become a lawyer.
My wife wants me to stay at home

Whenever you want to do something, somebody expects something else.
And of course, you always satisfy them.
But is the real you always going to take a back seat to the wishes of others. Aren't your own desires just as important?
For that little voice inside you, we build leisure and sports utility vehicles like our highly acclaimed Pajero ('Montero' en Espana).
Cars that are created to impress only yourself.
Impress yourself.
MITSUBISHI MOTORS CREATING TOGETHER.
So here I am.

Figure 2. Theme & Rheme structure

COHESION

The most instantly observable element of cohesion in the text is that of lexical cohesion. It has already been pointed out that all words count in this type of text and nothing here is left to chance. The semantic field of authority has already been mentioned. The verb/accusative combination wanted/me (note the subtle change to 'wants' in line 4) is an example of straight repetition, but the differing infinitive phrases that end the four clauses also have something in common - they are predictable in their bourgeois, establishment connotations.

Thereafter the pronoun 'you' provides the main cohesive referential link through continual anaphoric linkage. The nominal 'wishes' harks back to the much-repeated 'want' and points forward to 'desires'. The motoring synonyms 'vehicles', 'cars', 'motors' are preceded in a part/whole relationship by 'back seat' in the idiomatic expression 'to take a back seat'. This is interesting in that this oblique reference sets up the later specificity. Of course the copywriter can play it this way as he has visual elements to back him up.

The three indefinite pronouns 'something', 'somebody', 'something' constitute a tight little referential bundle which exploits alliteration and repetition to enhance the feeling of antipathy towards outside interference.

Figure 3. Cohesion analysis

288   Chris Taylor and Anthony Baldry

2.2.2. Micro analysis

The analyses of three clauses are illustrated below in the form of a table (Table 1):

Table 1. Micro-analysis

Sentence one	My *mother* wanted me to have *piano* lessons.
Theme	Topical, unmarked + rheme (*verb + accusative + non-finite, infinitive phrase*)
Information	All New (including theme). The info. focus is on what is desired. Graphic emphasis on key words "mother" and "piano".
Cohesion	My mother — exophoric reference to the writer's?/reader's?/ anyone's? mother.
Modality	Indicative, declarative. Past tense for past time state.
Transitivity	Mental process in main finite clause. Human senser, abstract phenomenon.
Sentence two	My *father* wanted me to go to *Harvard.*
Theme	Topical, unmarked + rheme (*verb + accusative + non-finite, infinitive phrase*). Graphic emphasis on key words "father" and "Harvard".
Information	New but partially Given theme: antonymic relation between mother/father and repetition of authoritative figure. The verb "wanted" is also partially Given as a predictable pattern emerges. The information focus remains on what is desired.
Cohesion	Lexical cohesion. Mother/father antonymic reference. Repetition of "wanted" + infinitive construction. Piano lessons/Harvard — same semantic field of education and ambition.
Modality	Indicative, declarative. Past tense for past time state.
Transitivity	Mental process in main finite clause. Human senser, abstract phenomenon.
Sentence five	(a) Whenever you want to do something, (b) somebody expects something else.
Theme	(a) subordinate clause: "Whenever" — marked; "you" — topical + rheme (*verb + infinitive phrase*) (b) main clause: Topical, unmarked + rheme. *or subordinate clause is considered as theme of whole sentence.
Information	(a) Topical theme Given — the "me" in the first four sentences is, in effect, the "you" thereafter. The verb "want" has earned full Given status within this text. The infinitive phrase is New, albeit generic. The information focus remains on what is desired, even though the subject is now "you". (b) Theme indirectly Given: the "someone" is the mother/father, etc. Now the rather vague but New element "something else" has information focus.

Table 1. Micro-analysis (Continued)

Cohesion	My mother — exophoric reference to the writer's?/readers?/anyone's? mother.
Modality	Indicative, declarative. Past tense for past time state
Transitivity	Mental process in main finite clause. Human senser, abstract phenomenon.

2.3. The translation phase

As explained above, the translation component is largely based on the preceding text analyses. After the user has completed the detailed analysis of the text and answered a few questions based upon it (the questions appear at regular intervals along the route), the hypermedia module moves on to the guided translation.

Table 2. The translation phase

My *mother* wanted me to have *piano* lessons. **Mia madre voleva che prendessi lezioni di piano**		T(heme)	R(heme)
		semi G(iven)	N(ew)
Mood:	declarative + subjunctive		
Cohesion:	zero; it is the beginning of the text		
Transitivity:	mental process (with embedded material process)		
Note:	accusative/infinitive pattern must be transformed to "che" + subjunctive		
Alternatives	… che io prendessi lezioni di piano … che suonassi il pianoforte … mi voleva a lezioni di piano		
My father wanted me to go to Harvard. **Mio padre voleva che studiassi a Harvard**		T	R
		semi G	N
Mood	declarative + subjunctive		
Cohesion	(lexical)semantic field of family (mia madre/mio padre); semantic field of bourgeois ambition (piano/Harvard); semantic field of effort (prendessi lezioni/studiassi)		
Transitivity	mental process (with embedded material process)		
Note	accusative/infinitive pattern must be transformed to "che" + subjunctive		
Alternatives	… andassi a Harvard … che io studiassi … mi voleva a Harvard		

Table 2. The translation phase (Continued)

Il mio insegnante voleva che diventassi avvocato		T	R
		semi G	N
Mood	declarative + subjunctive Cohesion (lexical)		
Cohesion	semantic field of figures of authority (mia madre/mio padre/il mio insegnante); semantic field of bourgeois ambition (piano/Harvard/avvocato);		
Transitivity	mental process (with embedded relational process)		
Note	accusative/infinitive pattern must be transformed to "che" + subjunctive lawyer = avvocato (generic terms)		
Alternatives	Il mio maestro/a… Il mio docente… La mia insegnante… …mi voleva avvocato		
Mia moglie vuole che stia a casa		T	R
		semi G Mood	N
Mood	declarative + subjunctive		
Cohesion (lexical)	semantic field of figures of (mock) authority (mia madre/mio padre/il mio insegnante/mia moglie);		
Transitivity	mental process (with embedded material process)		
Note:	accusative/infinitive pattern must be transformed to "che" + subjunctive but tense change		
So here I am **Per questo Eccomi qui**		T	R
		G	semi-N
Mood	declarative, presentational		
Cohesion	"questo" — anaphora/substitution; "mi" — anaphora		
Transitivity	relational process		
Alternatives	E dunque … … Io sono qui		

The user is required, in the first part of the text, to type his or her proposed translation in the space provided, and in the second part, to choose the most suitable option from a series of four multiple choice alternatives. As it is almost impossible to dictate what is a definitive translation of any clause, the software application authors pooled the combined efforts of a group of advanced Italian translation students at the Translation and Interpreting School of the University of Trieste, in an attempt to find the "best" possible translation. This standard version can be seen below in Table 2 in which a sample clause-by-clause presentation is given, accompanied by annotations based on the previous analysis.

In order to assist the user as he or she progresses with the translation, the computer module picks up on the previously programmed information, as represented in the above exposition, and comments on the users' responses in relation to whether they have or have not given due consideration to the relevant findings of the analyses. In the first part of the text where the user is asked to actually provide a target language version in the space provided by clicking on the word "translation", the computer is prepared, through a pattern cascade system (see Fig. 4) for a series of possible alternatives of varying degrees of "appropriateness".

The alternatives are all possible, and in this sense correct, but inappropriate in some way. Any deviations from the "Trieste" model are therefore commented on in terms of errors or misjudgements in, for example, theme choice, mood choice, register, use of lexis, cohesive ties. Any versions which are definitely incorrect, either grammatically or semantically, receive the invitation to "Try again!" A selection of responses can be seen below. An important aspect of the software application is that at all points during the text analysis and subsequent translation phases, the user is either encouraged to continue or advised to consolidate his or her progress via a process of revision and repetition, until such time as he or she successfully completes the circuit. In addition, the user can be assessed throughout the translation phase and can check out his or her score by clicking on a button called "your score".

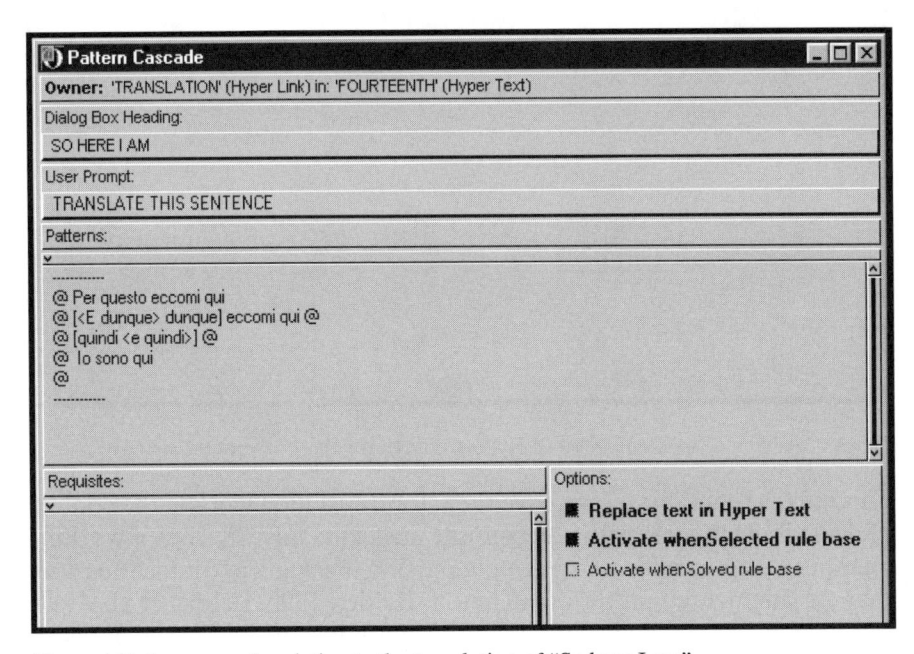

Pattern Cascade		
Owner: 'TRANSLATION' (Hyper Link) in: 'FOURTEENTH' (Hyper Text)		
Dialog Box Heading:		
SO HERE I AM		
User Prompt:		
TRANSLATE THIS SENTENCE		
Patterns:		
@ Per questo eccomi qui @ [<E dunque> dunque] eccomi qui @ @ [quindi <e quindi>] @ @ Io sono qui @		
Requisites:	Options:	
	■ Replace text in Hyper Text ■ Activate whenSelected rule base ☐ Activate whenSolved rule base	

Figure 4. Pattern cascade relative to the translation of "So here I am"

3. Analysing TV advertising with a view to translation potential

In the first part of this project the focus was on the construction of an interactive computer application relating to a magazine advert in which the focus was on sentence-by-sentence translation guided by the parameters outlined by Halliday (1992,1994[1985]). This application is currently operative in our respective universities and other Universities in Northern Italy where translation is taught. The application has been instrumental in demonstrating the effectiveness of hypertext tools which differ somewhat from those available commercially. Unlike many commercial hypertext tools *HyperContext* (Baldry et al. 1994) has, since its inception, incorporated a working memory (Fig. 5) able to check a student's current response for its compatibility with the set of previous responses given by the student and a rule base that allows a set of "if-then" rules to be associated with each link.

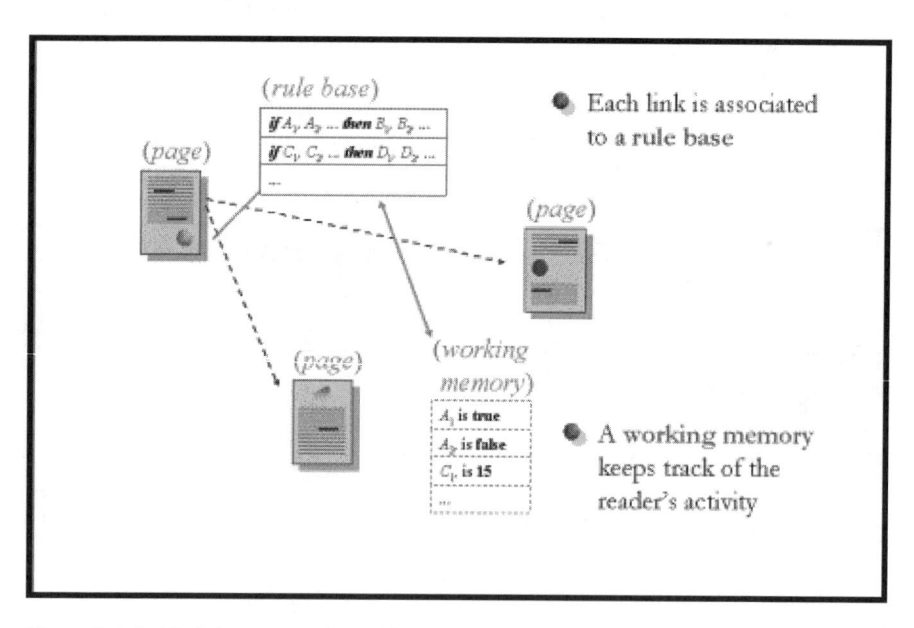

Figure 5. A behind-the-scenes view of HyperContext: rule base + working memory

This makes it suitable, as we have seen, for translation work in the context of *static* images such as the Mitsubishi magazine advert. Thus a working memory, coupled with a very simple parsing mechanism (in fact no more than an augmented pattern matcher cf. Baldry, 1990, Baldry et al., 1994, see also Fig. 4) and an architecture consisting of rule-based links, is enough to allow many different potential translations to be taken into account. But *HyperContext,* conceived of some ten years ago, was never designed to take into account the very different needs of translation in the context of *dynamic* images. Thus, in the second part of this paper the focus will instead be on TV commercials and the need for much more advanced software tools than *HyperContext* if we are to be able to carry out the appropriate analysis within the framework delineated above. In this respect, this part of the paper describes some of the features associated with the *HyperContext Web Project* which is currently being developed in Pavia. Specifically, it relates to research in progress to integrate conceptual and software tools capable of making translation students aware of the "translation potential" of a genre such as TV commercials. With respect to the first project it is, so far, restricted to the first two phases, namely: 1) "Introduction Phase"and 2) "Pre-translation Text Analysis Phase". Moreover, the first phase, the Introduction Phase, is the more extensive including many of the features previously included in the second phase. The main function of the first phase is to look at the translation potential of a text (macro analysis) before moving on to a more detailed frame-by-frame/utterance-by-utterance analysis (micro analysis).

3.1. Introduction Phase

A number of points need, however, to be borne in mind in developing new software that meets these needs. The first relates to the translation potential alluded to above: what is this potential and how can we measure it? Firstly, all advertising can be subsumed under the general heading of creative writing and it therefore offers a challenge to the translator, while TV advertising adds the further characteristic that additional semiotic modalities come into play: sound, music, speech, colour, movement, gesture and so on. These aspects too need "translating" but not in the same way as the purely static text. As has been pointed out in the first part of this paper a magazine advert is a careful integration of various semiotic modalities: visual and spatial as well as verbal. Complex and highly creative meanings can be made precisely as a result of this integration. In TV advertising, precisely because of the presence of the additional resources mentioned above, and in particular the fact that the text is a dynamic text that changes in time, and therefore in meaning, this creativity can become far more complex.
Take for example an advert in which two primary schoolchildren are passing a message behind their teacher's back. One, a boy, passes a note to the second, a girl: the note reads "Do you love me?" and contains "Yes" "No" check boxes. When the girl checks the "No" box and hands the text back, the boy, far from being discouraged, modifies the note by eliminating the

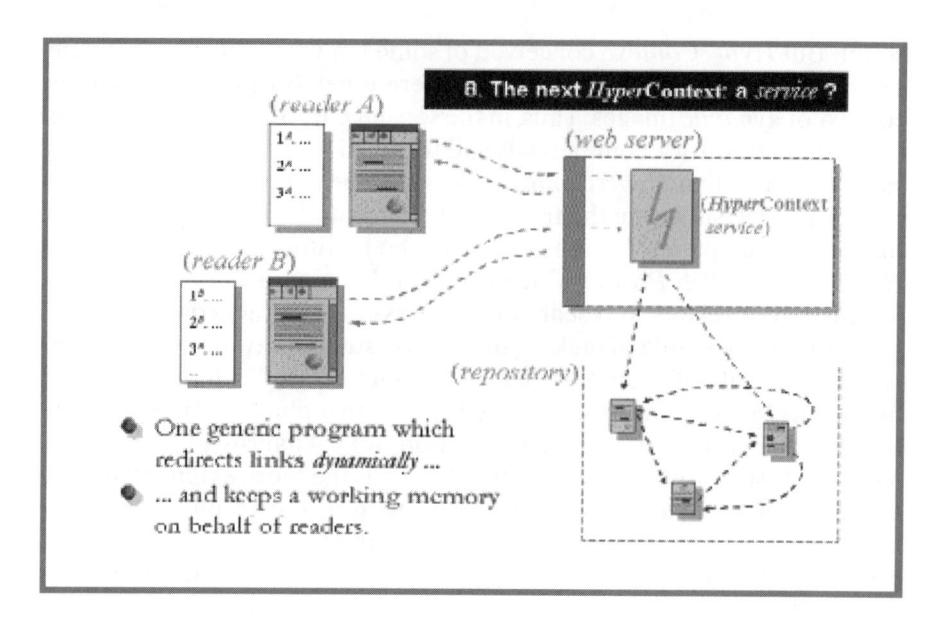

Figure 6. Towards a dynamic control of a dynamic text

"No" box leaving the "Yes" box to be checked by the girl. This first text (the schoolroom scene) takes on a completely different meaning when the comment "You're never too young to learn about recycling?" appears on the screen — so that what appeared to be transgressive behaviour ("you can't pass love letters in class behind the teacher's back") comes to be reconstrued as highly sociable behaviour ("kids need to experiment all kinds of communication and need to be aware of ecological problems which is why teachers are sometimes right to turn a blind eye as to what is going on behind their backs"). Clearly, without the first part of the advert, the second part is difficult if not impossible to interpret. Texts as Halliday says (Halliday (1985)) are always embedded in a context but the same text can, of course, take on a different meaning in a different context and TV adverts can be, and often are, made more effective by the process of recontextualisation of texts. Such a process itself relies crucially on intertextuality taken as the active process on the part of the reader, listener and, in our case, the viewer of creating associations between (parts of) texts (cf. Lemke (1985, 1989, 1990), Thibault (1989, 1994)). Such a process is not absent, of course, in magazine advertising but in TV advertising it takes on a new dimension often creating, for example, effective punchlines as in the example quoted above. The complex visual+verbal integrations of TV advertising (cf. Thibault (1990)) represent a good training ground for future translators as regards their understanding of the translation potential of texts. We can take the principle of recontextualisation a step further and invent a rather special form of intertextuality in which the trainee is faced with the problem of a dynamic source text and a dynamic target text: that is we can ask the student to look at different *states* of the "same" text. We can, for example, take a text such as the public service advert described above and using appropriate software (e.g. *Adobe Premiere*) postproduce it so that it exists in various forms (for example a black and white version, a version in which all or parts of the written text are removed, a "slow-motion" version in which a selection of frames is shown for a few seconds, various translated versions and so on). The differing states will correspond to differences in the realisation of, for example, theme & rheme structure, information structure, mood and modality, cohesion, transitivity structures. The goal of the activity in this preliminary phase is thus a *comparative* awareness of text states. Such a mechanism becomes possible when we alter the way that Internet works as indicated in Fig. 6 by introducing the principles of a working memory and dynamic control of hypertext links (a matter which is easy to conceive of but less easy to achieve in practice in software applications).

3.2. The text analysis phase

Time in secs.	Visual Frame	Linguistic resources
1		OK, I want the scrambled ...
2		... brown rice...
3		... sweet pickled...
4		... toma-toes...
5		
6		Easy on the...

Non-linguistic resources

PHASE 1 (1-6)

Experiential function
- Participants: human participants; American customers and food servers
- Circumstances: fast food restaurant in New York
- Processes: request of goods and services

Interpersonal function
Visual modality: low; black and white represents realism or naturalism; interpersonal distance close – head/shoulders; horizontal angle level reflects audience and participants in relation of equality

Textual function
Oral discourse; the customers are very demanding

Figure 7. First phase of the Chrysler Neon ad

A second point that needs to be made relates to the careful reflection required regarding the *conceptual* tools available to us. Such reflection needs to take place before any consideration can be made of the *software* tools required in the creation of an interactive computer application that extends what has already been done with magazine advertising to TV advertising. While the public service advert quoted above uses no oral discourse, this is not normally the case with most TV advertising. Car com-

Computer assisted text analysis   297

Time in secs.	Visual Frame	Linguistic resources	Non-linguistic resources
7		... Dijon, kosher veal [*fade*]...	**PHASE 2A (7-12)** *Experiential function* ❏ Participants: car ❏ Circumstances: country scene ❏ Processes: non-transactional narrative *Interpersonal function:* Visual modality: high; dominance of red represents sensuality and contrasts with the above black and white; the car is seen from the top since it does not belong to the real world and represents the object of our desire *Textual function:* Written discourse provides concrete technical information and contrasts with the visual information of the top. Visual resources build up the theme and rheme structure of the text: the car, which is the new element, is located on the right
8		*The two litre Chrysler Neon LX*	
9		*The two litre Chrysler Neon LX*	
10		*The two litre Chrysler Neon LX*	
11		*The two litre Chrysler Neon LX*	
12			*TRANSITION*

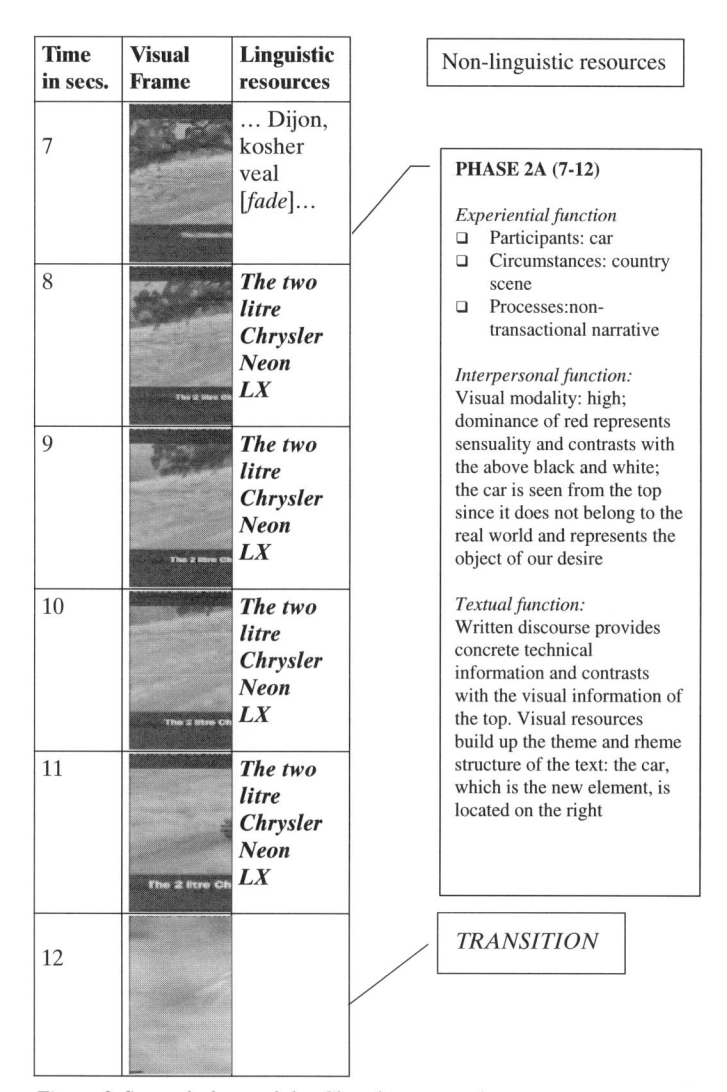

Figure 8. Second phase of the Chrysler neon ad

mercials for example usually deploy a very complex interplay of semiotic resources, that often includes music, song, jingles, and special uses of voice quality. This complexity is determined, on the one hand, by the highly specialised quality and quantity of information that such a commercial must provide, and on the other hand by the need to compress meaning in a very short time.

Two analytical tools seem particularly appropriate when analysing such texts, namely Halliday's notion of metafunctions (1985) and Gregory's notion of phase and transition (In press), both of which were originally

298 Chris Taylor and Anthony Baldry

Time in secs.	Visual Frame	Linguistic resources	Non-linguistic resources
58		The Chrysler Neon *The Chrysler Neon LX £ 13,755 on the road*	**PHASE 6 (58-64)** *Experiential function* ☐ Participants: car; British speaker ☐ Circumstances: country scene ☐ Processes: non-transactive action narrative *Interpersonal function* Visual modality: high; final central view of the car *Textual function* Written text introduces further technical information Oral text by a British speaker; recontextualisation of the American brand in a British context The term "demanding" retrospectively recontextualizes the specialised requests of the American customers and reflects the capability of the car to satisfy the needs of the potential British buyer
59		built for the most *The Chrysler Neon LX £ 13,755 on the road*	
60		Demanding *The Chrysler Neon LX £ 13,755 on the road*	
61		Country *The Chrysler Neon LX £ 13,755 on the road*	
62		In the world *The Chrysler Neon LX £ 13,755 on the road*	
63		*The Chrysler Neon LX £ 13,755 on the road*	
64			

Figure 9. Final phase of the Chrysler Neon ad

applied to language but which are assumed here to be extendable to other semiotic modalities in the manner indicated by various scholars (Kress, van Leeuwen (1996), Thibault (1997)). In so doing it is appropriate to recall that this second part of the research has entailed a shift away from the notions of "field", "tenor" and "mode" towards a systematic use of the metafunctions.

As Figs. 7, 8, 9 demonstrate, a multimodal transcription can apply these two tools to TV commercials by virtue of "exploding" a video sequence into a series of frames, each providing a detailed description of both the linguistic and non-linguistic resources deployed. Future translators can thus see that the visual and the verbal are not simply added to each other but that the two systems are specialised to make the meanings they do in different ways and that the multimodal integration of the two produces a multiplying effect, such that the one contextualises the other to produce an overall text meaning (Thibault 1997, 1998). Figures 7, 8, 9, in fact, give excerpts from a Chrysler Neon LX commercial, designed to advertise an American car for a British audience by combining linguistic and non-linguistic resources. In the first phase of the commercial, the attention of the audience is caught by the exploitation of the black and white, which contrasts with the typical use of colour in commercials. The ad is structured around 2 apparently disjoined situations which are in fact cohesively tied to each other by means of both linguistic and visual elements. We can distinguish 3 phases, each consisting of two micro sequences with a black and white microsequence preceding a full colour scene. The two sequences in each phase are opposed in several ways: situation (a fast food restaurant in New York, a British country road), participants, modality. Eventually the contrasts are resolved by the semantics of the word "demanding", which acts as a unifying/cohesive element. Thus the word "demanding" spoken by the British presenter in the final phase takes on a retroactive recontextualising function. It ties together the fast-talking customers in the restaurant scenes with all their highly individualistic demands to the again highly specific demands which the various characteristics of the Chrysler also claim to meet.

The text thus combines two opposed social registers which both reflect the highly specialised needs of the American fast food consumers and the potential users of the car. In the voice prosodics of the speakers in the fast food scenes, we hear very rapid, quick fire speech using the rhythms and other prosodic features typical of New York city speakers. But the verbal text is also interesting from the point of view of its register-specific lexis: again the highly demanding customers are heard to use extremely specialised lexis to indicate their rather individualistic demands and requirements. By the same token the written text that accompanies the visual image of the car also presents the viewer with a register specific lexis deriving from the contextual domain of cars and in particular the highly specialised characteristics of the Chrysler Neon, which are intended to meet the particular needs of potential buyers of the car.

A multimodal transcription of the type shown in Figures 7, 8, 9, with its analytical description constitutes a first important stage in the development of computer assisted translation tools for dynamic texts. But it is not enough for translation work with translation trainees in which different *states* of the same text are presented — the specific state shown on the computer screen depending on the student's performance in answering questions posed previously in the computer application. Significantly, a particular multimodal transcription can be derived from a relational database, that is, a particular multimodal text can be created on the fly (dynamically) with reference to frame numbers, with reference to phases, transitions, circumstances, processes and so on in a way that meets the requirement of relating text states to *actual* student performance. There are many ways in which this can be done but in working out the most appropriate software procedures a feature that we will need to retain is the capacity to constantly broaden the comparative framework to embrace an ever wider set of texts and text states as the student's performance improves. In this way translation students will be properly aware that the co-deployment of semiotic resources (Thibault 1997) is a basic principle that needs to be taken to heart by all those who study human communication.

4. Conclusion

This paper has taken a few steps towards defining the adjustments that need to be made vis-à-vis traditional translation courses in order to accommodate the translation of multimodal texts, of which car advertisements are a small, albeit significant, example. The paper is set against a background of thinking which views translation as part of the wider process of understanding and adaptation of texts to different cultural systems. Increasingly, it is the case that software programs are "localised" (rather than translated), that advertising companies make commercials which attempt to take a "pluricultural" "transnational" society into account and that the day-to-day work of many translators involves texts that, as well as being multimodal, are also multigeneric and often multilinguistic. This is the case with both the Mitsubishi and Chrysler adverts which contain explicit references to more than one society, to more than one genre, to more than one language system apparently in an effort to bridge cultural differences, and, where possible, to turn them to the advertiser's own advantage. They are based on the assumption that in a "pluricultural" "transnational" society many viewers by definition have a detailed knowledge of more than one culture and more than one language and can thus easily grasp references to different systems. This assumption appears to lie behind many other adverts such as the recent Honda advert on Italian TV which perfects the principle described in the Chrysler advert relating to the Am./Br. voice contrast: it uses a single voice which speaks both in English and Italian, the words in English being associated with the "ideal" world of image and power and the words in Italian being associated with the "real" world of technical specification. The ideal/real contrast is, of course, typical of much advertising (Baldry 1999: 21–25) and we can see how a translator would need to learn that in the context of an advert for Italian clothes for an English-speaking society the same principle might apply but with the English/ideal and Italian/real distribution reversed. The CATAT project's analysis of the adverts discussed above will help translation students to understand that the ideal/real contrast can be expressed not only in terms of language but also in terms of such resources as colour, voice prosodics and spatial disposition.

With its concern with multimodal texts that are the expression of increasingly integrated cultural systems, this paper has also attempted, albeit very tentatively, to define the elusive notion of the "translation potential" of a text in terms of a knowledge of cultural systems. The focus has been on arguing that translation studies need to include the conceptual tools that provide a basis for developing a working definition of, for example, advertising texts in the contemporary culture of North America, Britain and many other cultures where English is used and that as such it should also be an exercise for translators to understand translation not in terms of the language semiotic *tout court* but rather in terms of a text where the language semiotic has to be translated bearing in mind the entire meaning-making activity of the text. The conceptual tools required to train students in this kind of translation clearly exist within systemic-functional linguistics. Missing are the instruments that allow us to apply these notions with the same facility that, for example, a bilingual dictionary can be used. Such instruments need to be dynamic in nature so as to bring the trainee translator up against changes in the translation potential of a text (e.g. as suggested above, by modifying one of the meaning-making parameters in the original or the target text). Whereas the commercial market has provided many translation software packages and many electronic dictionaries, little has been done to develop packages that are capable of applying translation/linguistic theory to texts — almost as if there were no need for such tools! As work to date within the CATAT project has clearly demonstrated, this does not mean that we have to start from scratch. Far from it. Time and again, research suggests that we need to take what already exists and modify it to suit our needs. Internet is, after all, a development of Arpanet, itself an interpretation of previous thinking. The step being taken in the CATAT project (and indeed in many other educational applications) is to modify Internet to fit in more effectively with teaching/learning needs. A small step it may be, but it is one that may well influence the way that translation studies are conceived of within universities, in an age in which, after all, distance learning techniques will increasingly hold sway.

Acknowledgements

We gratefully acknowledge the advice and assistance given by Prof. Paul Thibault, Associate Professor of English Linguistics, University of Venice with an earlier draft of this paper. Dr. Marco Piastra, Artificial Vision Laboratory, University of Pavia and Dr. Roberto Bolognesi are also thanked for permissions relating to *HyperContext* and *HyperContext Web,* the former in particular for permission to use diagrams relating to the latter project.

We are grateful to Chrysler Jeep UK for granting permission to reproduce elements of the 1996 launch TV commercial for the Chrysler Neon entitled 'Deli'.

References

Baldry, Anthony
    1990   *Research into self-access study for advanced learners: computer-assisted studies of English*, Udine, Campanotto.

Baldry, Anthony
    1999   ESP, Multimodality and Multimediality. In: M. Karagevrekis (ed.) *Compelling Learning Techniques in ESP/EAP, Proceedings of the 3rd ESP Conference,* Thessaloniki, English Language Unit, University of Macedonia/Zefyros Publications, pp. 5–32.

Baldry, Anthony and E. Crivelli
    1994   Il documento ipertestuale: problemi di pianificazione, creazione, sperimentazione e valutazione. In: A. P. Baldry and E. Crivelli (eds.) *Dialogare con il computer: strumenti e percorsi didattici e linguistici nell'apprendimento delle lingue straniere*, Udine, Campanotto Editore.

Baldry, Anthony, M. Piastra and R. Bolognesi
    1994   Retraction with face saving: modelling conversational interaction through dynamic hypermedia. *Association for Learning Technology Journal 2/2*, pp. 249–270.

Catford, John
    1965   *A Linguistic Theory of Translation*, Oxford, OUP.

Firbas, Jan
  1964   On defining the theme in functional sentence analysis, TLP, 1.

Firth, J. R.
  1968   Linguistic Analysis and Translation. In: Palmer 1968.

Gregory, Michael
  In press. Phasal analysis within communication linguistics: two contrastive discourses. In: Peter Fries, Michael Cummings, David Lockwood and Wm. Sprueill (eds.), *Relations and Functions in Language and Discourse,* London, Cassell.

Halliday, Michael
  1966   Linguistics and Machine Translation. In: A. McIntosh and M.A.K. Halliday (eds.) *Patterns of Language,* London, Longman.

Halliday, Michael
  1973   *Explorations in the Functions of Language.* Edward Arnold, London.

Halliday, Michael
  1978   *Language as social semiotic: the social interpretation of language and meaning,* London, Arnold.

Halliday, Michael
  1994 [1985] *An Introduction to Functional Grammar,* London and Melbourne, Arnold.

Halliday, Michael
  1992   Some Lexicographical Features of the Zero Growth Text. In: W. Mann and S. Thompson (eds.) *Discourse Description,* Amsterdam, John Benjamins.

Halliday, Michael and R. Hasan
  1985   *Language, context, and text: Aspects of language in a social-semiotic perspective.* Geelong, Victoria, Deakin University Press.

House, Juliane
  1981, 1997 *A Model for Translation Quality Assessment,* Gunter Narr Verlag, Tübingen.

Kress, Gunther and Th. Van Leeuwen
  1996   *Reading Images. the grammar of visual design.* London and New York, Routledge.

Lemke, Jay
  1985   Ideology, intertexuality, and the notion of register. In: J. D. Benson, W. S. Greaves (eds.) *Systemic Perspectives on Discourse, Vol 1. Selected Theoretical Papers from the 9th International Systemic Workshop,* Norwood, NJ, Ablex, pp. 275–294.

Lemke, Jay
  1989   Semantics & Social Values. In: J. D. Benson et al. (eds.) *Systems, Structures, and Discourse, Word* Vol 40 nos. 1–2, pp. 37–50.

Lemke, Jay
  1990   Technical discourse and technocratic ideology. In: M.A.K. Halliday, John Gibbons, and Howard Nicholas, (eds.), *Learning keeping and using language,* Vol. II Selected papers from the 8th World Congress of Applied Linguistics, Sydney, 16–21 August 1987, Amsterdam and Philadelphia: John Benjamins, pp. 435–460.

Newmark, Peter
1981 *Approaches to Translation*, Prentice Hall, Oxford.

Newmark, Peter
1988 *A Text-book of Translation*, Prentice Hall, London.

Newmark, Peter
1991 *About Translation*, Clevedon, Multilingual Matters.

Palmer, Frank (ed.)
1968 *Selected Papers of J. R. Firth 1952–59*, Bloomington: Indiana University Press.

Steiner, Erich
1996 An Introduction to Linguistics and Translation Studies — Opening Remarks of a Lecture for Beginning Students: In: Angelika Lauer, Heidrun Gerzymisch-Arbogast, Johann Haller, and Erich Steiner (eds.), *Übersetzungswissenschaft im Umbruch. Festschrift für Wolfram Wilss zum 70. Geburtstag*, Tübingen: Gunter Narr Verlag pp. 53–58.

Steiner, Erich
1997 An extended register analysis as a form of text analysis for translation. In: Gerd Wotjak and H. Schmidt (eds.), *Modelle der Translation — Models of Translation. Festschrift für Albrecht Neubert*. Bd. 2. Leipziger Schriften zur Kultur-, Literatur-, Sprach- und Übersetzungswissenschaft. Frankfurt/Main: Verfuert-Verlag pp. 235–256.

Taylor, Christopher
1993 Systemic Linguistics and Translation. In: T. Gibson and C. Stainton (eds.), *Occasional Papers in Systemic Linguistics* No. 7, Nottingham, University of Nottingham.

Taylor, Christopher
1997 Il ruolo della linguistica sistemico-funzionale nella traduzione. In: *Tradurre: Un approccio multidisciplinare*, (a cura di M. Ulrych), Torino, UTET Libreria.

Taylor, Christopher
1998 *Language to Language*, Cambridge, Cambridge University Press.

Taylor Torsello, Carol
1996 Grammatica e Traduzione. In: G. Cortese (ed.), *Tradurre i linguaggi settoriali*, Torino, edizioni libreria Cortina.

Thibault, Paul
1989 Semantic variation, social heteroglossia, intertexuality: thematic and axiological meaning in spoken discourse. In: *Critical Studies*, Vol. 1, No. 2, pp. 181–209.

Thibault, Paul
1990 Questions of genre and intertextuality in some Australian television advertisements. In: R. Favretti Rossini (ed.), *The Televised Text*, Patròn, Bologna pp. 89–131.

Thibault, Paul
1994 Intertextuality. In: R. E. Asher and J. M. Y. Simpson (eds.), *The Encyclopedia of Language and Linguistics,* Vol. 4, pp. 1751–1754.

Thibault, Paul
- 1997 *Re-reading Saussure: The dynamics of signs in social life.* London and New York, Routledge.

Thibault, Paul
- 1998 Graphology and Visual Semiosis. Dept. di Studi linguistici e letterari, europei postcoloniali, University of Venice: Mimeo.

Ventola, Eija
- 1994 Thematic Development and Translation. In: M. Ghadessy (ed.), *Thematic Development in English Texts*, London, Pinter.

Translation, controlled languages, generation

Anthony Hartley and Cécile Paris

1. Introduction

1.1. Overview

In this chapter we explore the relationship between translation and *controlled languages*. These are stringent sets of writing rules or guidelines designed to prevent authors from introducing ambiguities into their texts, and they are increasingly used in the commercial world for authoring technical documents such as maintenance and user manuals. Very often, these documents then serve as the source from which translations are produced into a large number of target languages.[1]

We further explore the relationship between controlled languages and *generation*, by which we mean natural language generation — the production by computer of texts in human languages, such as English, French and German. At first sight, it looks as if natural language generation has much to gain from work on controlled languages, by adopting rules designed for human writers as the basis of its computer programs. However, on closer examination it becomes apparent that controlled language research can benefit as much, if not more, from work in natural language generation. In building natural language generation systems it is good practice to clearly distinguish rules concerned with pragmatic and semantic function from rules concerned with syntactic form, and then to specify appropriate mappings between them.

1.2. Translators and controlled languages

If we turn our attention from the process of translation to its agents, the translators, we can identify a number of roles that they may play in their professional contacts with controlled languages.

- *Translating from a controlled language source text*: In this era of globalisation, the need to publish product documentation and instructions in multiple languages has become pressing. Correspondingly, the introduction of controlled languages is becoming more widespread as companies attempt to reduce time-to-market by using translation memories and machine translation. The effectiveness of translation memories—bilingual databases of phrases and sentences aligned with their translated equivalent—is impaired if their contents are inconsistent. Similarly, the quality of machine translation output can be notoriously degraded if the input is ambiguous. Since controlled languages aim to pre-empt both inconsistency and ambiguity, translators will increasingly find themselves working from a controlled language source, whether they are using machine aids or not. In principle, this will spare them the frustration of having to interpret wordy and imprecise texts.

- *Translating into a controlled language target text*: Complex installations, whether software or hardware in the most general sense, often comprise subassemblies made by different suppliers, possibly from several countries and each with its own documentation. The client nevertheless expects the end-user documentation to be coherent and consistent and so, in such a situation, the translator must adhere to any controlled language standard imposed by the prime contractor. These constraints on the nature of the target text could mean that the translation differs significantly in form from the source text.

- *Authoring a controlled language source text*: As "companies are finding that documentation and translation are two aspects of the same requirement for efficient information flow" (Lockwood et al. 1995: 63), the distinction between the roles of translators and technical authors becomes blurred, a trend reflected in the new currency of designations like *language mediator, langagier* and *Sprachvermittler*. Translators' multilingual sensitivity suits them for the task of writing for an international audience. But they need to extend their competencies: a shift from translating to authoring emphasises information design skills over reliance on the structures provided by a source text.

- *Designing a controlled language*: The fast-growing interest in controlled languages over recent years is due in large part to two factors: their use in conjunction with translation tools, and the development of controlled languages for human languages other than English. The multilingual dimension of both these activities invites an appraisal of the state of the art from a fresh perspective. Once again, those most apt to take up the challenge to design improved controlled languages are those with translation skills.

It is clear, then, that the use and nature of controlled languages are issues which concern translators in a number of capacities, and which call for their active involvement in future developments.

2. Motivation and background for controlled languages

The principal goal of requiring authors to adhere to a controlled language is to increase the consistency and readability of the texts that they produce. Typically, these texts are intended to enable their readers to operate or maintain equipment, and are written by a team of authors rather than by a single person. Often the readers will be non-native speakers, who are less able to correctly interpret poor writing. When it is known at the outset that the documentation will be published in multiple languages, there is typically an additional goal of making the source version easier to translate.

Underlying these goals is the commercial motivation of producing better quality and timely documentation at a lower cost. Quality reduces, among other things, the risk of litigation, while timeliness means that products can be shipped in all language versions simultaneously to domestic and foreign markets, avoiding loss of revenue through delays (Hartley and Paris 1997b: 112). The re-use of text through the use of author memory (Murphy, Mason and Sklair. 1998; Allen 1999) and translation memory is essential for producing rapidly rising volumes of text without extending lead times. Savings of up to 70% have been claimed for authoring and translation costs alone, thanks to the use of a controlled language in conjunction with machine translation (e.g., Pym 1991).

The means of achieving these goals is, in general terms, to devise guidelines which preclude any ambiguity of expression. More specifically, a controlled language prescribes the grammatical constructions, the common vocabulary and the specialised terminology that authors are allowed to use. In so doing it proscribes, either implicitly or explicitly, other constructions and lexical items that form part of the overall resources of the corresponding human language. Thus, a controlled language is a restricted variety of a human language, which is geared to the authoring and communication needs of a particular field or even of a particular company.

Historically, the general notion of controlled language derives from that of simplified English proposed in the 1930's (Ogden 1932) and was first introduced into a commercial setting in the 1970's by the Caterpillar Tractor Company in Illinois. Nowadays, various controlled languages are widely used in the engineering, telecommunications, automotive and office technology sectors. Perhaps the best known controlled language is AECMA Simplified English (AECMA 1995), whose use in the authoring of aircraft maintenance manuals was made mandatory by the Air Transport Association of America in 1987.

Although the majority of controlled languages are based on English, they also exist or are under development for other human languages, including Swedish, German and French (Almqvist and Sågval Hein 1996; Sågval Hein, 1997; Janssen, Marks and Dobbert 1996; Schachtl 1996; Barthe 1997, 1998). Among these is the Guide du Français Rationalisé (GIFAS 1996), proposed as a French counterpart to the AECMA standard for English documentation.

3. Typical controlled language rules

Since most controlled languages are proprietary, a complete description of them is not in the public domain. However, partial descriptions that are available for English-based controlled languages—for example, Perkins Approved Clear English (Pym 1991) and Bull Controlled English (Lee 1993)—encapsulate their rule sets in some ten higher-level rules which appear virtually identical. Moreover, these are consistent with AECMA Simplified English, a fully-specified industry-wide standard which is commercially available. For this reason, we base this section on (AECMA 1995).

To illustrate the fact that controlled languages are indeed meeting a genuine need, we quote these three extracts (1–3) from a published engine maintenance manual.

(1) *Water pump drive belt loose.*

(3) *Fit timing tool to engine in fuel pump position ensuring firstly that splined shaft with master spline is fully located in pump drive shaft and then that register of tool is seated in fuel pump locating aperture.*

(3) *The heavy duty oil bath air cleaners are usually fitted with a centrifugal pre-cleaner mounted on top of the main cleaner, this should be removed and the air inlet vanes in the bottom plate of the assembly, the ejection slots on the side of the cone and the vanes in the outlet tube, cleaned of dust and dirt.*

Each of these examples is clearly flawed in a number of respects; we shall see more precisely what the flaws are in the following sections.

3.1. Rules at the lexical level

We can summarise the lexical rules by the instruction to use only the approved entries in the controlled language dictionary, in the sense defined and the part of speech given. A significant proportion of the time spent on creating a controlled language is expended, therefore, on defining the lexicon. Its size will reflect the complexity of the domain to be documented; for example, Caterpillar Technical English has about 70,000 terms of narrow semantic scope (Kamprath et al. 1998).

However many entries there may be, each one is defined with a single sense and each one has a unique form, thus eliminating both polysemy and homography as sources of potential ambiguity. The selected AECMA entries in Table 1 illustrate this, the approved uses being given in upper case and disapproved uses in lower case. Thus, "support" can be used only as a technical name (TN) with a specific, countable sense; it cannot be used in a generic, non-countable sense or as a verb. The sense of "moor" as an expanse of heath has no place in this dictionary. Even function words are included: "about" is permitted only as a preposition and in a single sense.

Another lexical rule that appears to be common across English-based controlled languages is one that bans the use of clusters of more than three nouns. Example (4) from (Farrington 1996: 14) illustrates how a text can be revised to respect this rule.

(4) a. *Inspect the forward strut rear angled needle roller bearing housing.*
    b. *Inspect the housing of the rear-angled needle-roller bearing on the forward strut.*

What the rewritten version (4c) does is to isolate the subconstituents of the cluster and make explicit the relations between them. The same remedy can be applied to Example (1) and also within (2) and (3).

Table 1. AECMA dictionary entries

KEYWORD (part of speech)	Assigned meaning/ USE	APPROVED EXAMPLE	Not Acceptable
ABOUT (pre)	"Concerned" with NOTE: For other meanings, USE: APPROXIMATELY	FOR DATA ABOUT THE LOCATION OF CIRCUIT BREAKERS, REFER TO THE WIRING LIST.	
MOOR (v), MOORS, MOORED, MOORED	To attach something to the ground	YOU MUST MOOR THE AIRCRAFT.	
support (n)	HOLD (v), SUPPORT (TN)	MAKE SURE A PERSON HOLDS THE ITEM WHILE YOU DISCONNECT IT. PUT A SUPPORT BELOW THE ITEM BEFORE YOU DISCONNECT IT.	Make sure there is adequate support for the item before disconnecting it.

3.2. Rules at other levels

We present in Table 2 a selection of writing rules from the AECMA guide, which justifies each one and exemplifies them at length. Their statement in this brief form is nonetheless sufficient for judging Examples (2) and (3) above.

- The limit on the number of topics in rule 4.1 is clearly broken in Example (3), but (2) arguably respects it, if "fitting" is taken to be the topic.

- The omission of determiners in (2), while characteristic of much technical writing in English, infringes rule 4.2.

- Both examples use connecting words, as prescribed by rule 4.4, but within rather than between sentences.

- If we consider both examples as procedures, neither respects rules 5.1, 5.2 or 5.3 relating sentence length to the number of instructions. Moreover, (2) flouts rule 5.4 in not using the imperative.

- Example (3) appears to comply with rule 5.5, although the description is not a dependent clause. But the full explanation in the guide refers only to situations where the dependent clause describes a condition to be met before the action in the instruction is done, which is not the case here.

Table 2. AECMA writing rules

Sentences	4.1	Keep to one topic per sentence.
	4.2	Do not omit words to make your sentences shorter.
	4.3	Use tabular layout (vertical layout) for complex texts.
	4.4	Use connecting words to join connecting sentences that contain related thoughts.
Procedures	5.1	Keep procedural sentences as short as possible (20 words maximum).
	5.2	Write only one instruction per sentence.
	5.3	Write more than one instruction per sentence only when more than one action is done at the same time.
	5.4	In an instruction, write the verb in the imperative ("commanding") form.

Table 2. AECMA writing rules (Continued)

	5.5	If you start an instruction with a descriptive statement (dependent clause), you must separate that statement from the rest of the instruction with a comma.
Descriptive writing	6.1	Keep sentences in descriptive writing as short a possible (25 words maximum).
	6.4	Each paragraph must have only one topic.

It is by no means incidental that these various collections of controlled language rules — from AECMA, Bull and Perkins, among others — call themselves *guides*. They are all documents which rely on the intelligence and experience of human authors for their sensible interpretation and application to their writing tasks. As such, their purpose is essentially didactic; they serve to train new staff and provide a common, prescriptive reference within the company. But they also assume — and therefore do not make explicit — a great deal of knowledge about technical authoring in general.

4. Challenges for the development of controlled languages

For a writers' guide, it is a sensible strategy to leave implicit information that can be assumed known to the reader. But if we want to conduct a critical review of an existing controlled language (Hartley and Paris 1997a) or develop a new controlled language from first principles, we need not only a precise but also a complete specification of the object of our attention. We outline three challenges for this enterprise.

4.1. Distinguishing between linguistic levels

We can "unpack" some of the rules in Table 2 to reveal the linguistic levels at which they apply.

- *Pragmatics*: The *communicative goal* of the writer towards the reader is in the realm of pragmatics. Differences of intention are reflected in the categorisation of rules as applying to *procedures*, where the goal is to instruct, or to *descriptions*, where the goal is to inform. Rules applying to sentences can be assumed to hold generally, whatever the communicative intention of that piece of text. Rules 5.2 and 5.3 relate pragmatic concerns (instructions) to semantic concerns (actions), while 5.4 links pragmatics to syntax.

- *Semantics*: The domain of semantics is relation of language to the state of the world. The applicability of rules 4.1 and 6.4 appeals to a notion of semantic uniqueness. The logical conclusion that we draw from them is paragraphs will never be more than one sentence in length. However, we have already seen in Example (2) that there may be difficulties in circumscribing "a topic". And our intuitions tell us that the scope of "topic" envisaged in 4.1 is narrower than in 6.4. Rule 5.3 likewise relies on knowledge of events in the world.

- *Syntax*: All the rules have a syntactic dimension. What is interesting is to see whether the source of the constraints on the syntax is pragmatic, semantic or both. Another noteworthy observation is the range of syntactic phenomena that are subject to constraints: sentence constituents (4.2), conjunction and clause complexity (4.4), voice (5.4) and clause ordering (5.5).

- *Punctuation*: In rule 5.5, punctuation is governed by a cluster of pragmatic and syntactic factors.

- *Layout*: Rule 4.3 links layout to semantics. The full explanation in the guide makes it clear that "complexity" is here an inherently semantic notion — a reference to complex actions and events — rather than a syntactic one. However, the definition of "complex" is left tacit. The notion of "paragraph" mentioned in 6.4 also belongs to this level.

Even this cursory analysis shows the reduction of controlled languages to "a limited set of syntactic constructions" to be a simplistic characterisation. An understanding of the interaction of factors at all these linguistic levels is a prerequisite for advancing the development of controlled languages on a principled basis.

4.2. Introducing greater context sensitivity

As we have just seen, the applicability of some controlled languages is explicitly localised to a certain section of a document, such as a procedure, description, caution or warning. Other rules are not restricted in this way and can be assumed to be valid in any and every section. One example of a global rule is the prohibition — widespread in English-based controlled languages — of the "-ing" form, in part because of the kind of ambiguity illustrated in Example (5).

(5) a. *Moving safety cage is dangerous.*

b. *It is dangerous to move the safety cage.*
c. *The safety cage is dangerous when it moves.*

However, in software manuals, for example, the form is commonly used in the body of instructions (6)

(6) *Insert the text by pressing Command + V.*

and in headings (7)

(7) *Creating files*

where the nominalisation "creation of files" would be highly unusual.

The prohibition appears to be motivated more by a wish to palliate the failings of a machine translation system than by a wish to improve readability for a human audience. As Lux (1998b) observes, one objective in designing writing rules is to "encourage the use of already frequent structures [and]…respect the writers' styles and habits." To this we can add the objective of meeting the readers' expectations.

In her analysis of a large corpus of controlled language-compliant documents, Lux (1998a, 1998b) distinguishes *generic* writing rules, which apply to all document types, and *specific* writing rules, which differ from one document type to another. She concludes with a recommendation to increase the number of specific rules, which has the effect of locally approving or even imposing forms previously outlawed. For example, modals remain prohibited in procedures but are permitted in warnings; and passives — generally strongly disapproved — are in fact required, with "shall", in specifications (8).

(8) *Adequate space shall be allocated so that system installation can be completed easily.*

We can expect this trend towards context-specific rules to accelerate. We can also expect that machine translation systems will be enabled to take context into account, since they will be able to identify the context from the mark-up tags — SGML or XML — defining the structure of the document.

4.3. Increasing portability to other human languages

A great deal of effort is currently being put into developing controlled languages for human languages other than English, as we noted in Section in Section 2. Given the predominance of English-based controlled languages, it is understandable that developers have taken them as models to be "ported" to a new language. The best-documented instance of this is GIFAS (1996) *Français Rationalisé* (FR), which has been subject to the particular constraint of being "equivalent to" the AECMA standard.

The developers of FR chose to achieve this equivalence by translating the English rules into French (Barthe 1997, 1998), a strategy that encountered numerous obstacles, which we can characterise by Example (9) involving the verb *empêcher*.

(9) a. *Empêcher le mouvement des volets.*
'Prevent the movement of the flaps.'
b. *Empêcher les volets de bouger.*
'Prevent the flaps from moving.'
c. *Empêcher que les volets ne bougent.*
'Prevent that the flaps move.'

Of these three syntactically correct wordings, (9c) is prohibited in FR because the subjunctive is prohibited and *empêcher* requires the dependent verb to be in the subjunctive; (9b) is prohibited because the direct translation into English contains the prohibited "-ing" form. Thus only (9a) is allowed, even though not all actions may be expressible by a noun in French, and (9b) is the simplest wording.

This example illustrates the problems inherent in trying to impose equivalence at the level of linguistic form, particularly when the forms are not functionally equivalent — as is the case with the simple past tenses in English and French, for example.

The AECMA/GIFAS pair is a special case where direct translation may be defended on the grounds of practical expediency. But we must not forget that the restrictions that English-based controlled languages place on linguistic form reflect the particular structural properties of English. AECMA rule 4.2, for instance, which proscribes the omission of determiners, is directly motivated by the impoverished morphology of English which results in the verb-noun and verb-adjective homography seen in Example (1). A telegraphic style of French that omitted articles would be unlikely to lead to word-class confusions, even if this style is rarely seen in fact in French technical writing. In the general case, then, the wisdom of calquing English rules is open to question.

4.4. Summary

From the technical author's perspective, controlled languages are perceived as tightly-specified—sometimes too much so. From the designer's perspective, in contrast, controlled languages appear greatly underspecified. While some constraints on syntactic form may be quite clear, the link to syntax from semantics and the pragmatic context are tenuous and ill-defined. Similarly, while the need for context-sensitive rules is acknowledged, our understanding of what constitutes a context is hazy. Finally, language-specific rules are not differentiated from rules which are valid across languages.

We call this hiatus between form and function the "controlled language gap". It is possible that work on controlled languages can benefit from the ideas in natural language generation research for using pragmatic context and semantics to guide text production.

5. Natural language generation as a reference model

Natural language generation involves a computer system constructing an appropriate text in response to some communicative goal.[2] As we saw in Section 4.1, communicative goals are rather abstract, whereas text is concrete. The task in natural language generation is to bridge this divide; and the principal question is one of choice, since human languages offer so many ways of structuring a text or expressing a particular idea. A natural language generation system must be capable of making the right choices for the communicative situation in which it is to be used.

5.1. Architecture of a natural language generation system

A natural language generation system's decision-making process is embedded in its overall organisation, or architecture, which we now describe.

It needs to exploit different types of *knowledge*, which we can exemplify here by reference to an imaginary system designed to generate instructions to make a cup of instant coffee.

- *Semantic information*: The system needs access to concepts for ingredients (e.g., coffee, water), utensils (e.g., cup, spoon), agents (e.g., consumer) and actions (e.g., pour, stir). It also needs to "know" how all of these are associated in a task plan which will result in the efficient and successful performance of the task. This information is represented in a *domain knowledge base*.

- *Linguistic resources*: The system needs access to representations of appropriate *text types*; in this instance, recipes are the most obvious model. It also needs a *lexico-grammar* with the appropriate coverage, including, in this case, the necessary lexical items and the ability to generate imperatives.

The system must then be capable of applying these sources of knowledge to the task of generating the instructions. A typical natural language generation system breaks this down into a number of subtasks, each being the responsibility of a particular program *module*. In a simple architecture the output of one module is the input to the next, pipeline fashion.

- *Document planner*: Given a communicative goal to fulfil, this module has to determine the content of the document and decide how chunks of information should be distributed over the document structure. This is the first step in the process of mapping from function to linguistic form. For this, it needs access to both the domain knowledge base and the models of text types. Its output is a document plan, which specifies units of information corresponding to sections and paragraphs and the rhetorical relations between them.

- *Microplanner*: Given a document plan, this module has the job of selecting words and structures from the lexico-grammar and of deciding whether to refer to a concept as, for example, "the coffee jar", "the jar" or "it" at any given mention. It also has to determine the scope of individual sentences. It can require access to all of the knowledge sources we have identified. Its output is a text specification; by this point, the choices have been made. These decisions must be sensitive to their local context within the plan.

- *Surface realiser*: The job of this module is to follow the text specification, converting it into a grammatically correct text with the required word forms, punctuation and layout. To do this, it calls on the lexico-grammatical resources.

A multilingual generation (MLG) system proceeds in the same manner. It needs lexicons, grammars and surface realisers for each of its languages. But in technical domains, the knowledge base is commonly a language-neutral resource shared by all the realisers. Document planning likewise tends to be language-neutral, and it is only at the microplanning stage that language-specific variations may appear.[3]

5.2. Locating the "controlled language gap"

We do not claim that this natural language generation architecture represents all the tasks that human technical authors perform when creating a document. However, it can provide a useful model of how to progressively transform the functional specification of the text into a "concretisation" in paragraphs, sentences and words. We can take it as a reference model for exercising explicit control over the linguistic characteristics of a document. Since natural language generation systems and controlled languages share this common purpose, we can view the challenges for controlled language development in terms of some achievements in the field of the former.

In what corresponds to producing resources for natural language generation, controlled language developers are very successful in defining the specific grammatical constructions and lexicon needed within the field of application. Classically, the construction of new controlled languages is grounded in the analysis of an existing sublanguage, represented by a corpus of documents (van der Eijk, de Koning and van der Steen 1996). A few leading companies have terminological databases which represent in an abstract way the sequence of steps necessary to perform this or that task, which is tantamount to building a domain knowledge base of the kind just decribed (Schütz 1999). As for text types, any company using a controlled language will have developed *Document Type Descriptions* — usually defined in SGML or XML — which define the macrostructure of the documents that it produces.

By analogy with natural language generation processes, document type descriptions make the "top" end of document planning quite clear, insofar as they specify the overall shape of a document and the distribution of content. But it is at what corresponds to the "bottom" end of document planning and in microplanning that the gap appears, as we saw in Sections 4.1 and 4.2.

This is not to say that technical authors have special difficulties with these tasks, assuming, that is, that humans work broadly along these lines. Professional authors excel at realising surface texts that achieve the set communicative goal. The gap comes rather from the difficulty of capturing their expertise and making their working principles explicit.

6. Plugging the gap

A good way to uncover the motivation behind writers' decisions is to undertake a detailed analysis of the texts they produce. We outline below two analyses carried out in order to provide adequate linguistic resources and planning mechanisms for a natural language generation system. Although different in scope, they have in common the ambition of mapping syntactic features of the surface text to underlying semantic and pragmatic factors. The second analysis also tries to address the challenge of making these mappings context sensitive.

6.1. Generation and enablement

As we have said, controlled languages are widely used in the authoring of manuals that detail procedures to be performed, hence rules like 5.3 above that govern how actions are described in words. This issue is of equal interest in natural language generation. Using a corpus of naturally-occurring French and English instructional texts, Delin, Hartley and Scott (1996) looked at the expressions available in each language for conveying certain relations between pairs of actions. The relations on which they focused were the semantic relations of GENERATION and EN-ABLEMENT.

Informally, in the case of GENERATION, performing action α automatically results in the occurrence of action β, as in Example (10).

(10) a. *Turn on the light (β) by pressing the switch (α).*
b. **Press the switch (α) before turning on the light (β).*
c. *Press the switch (α) to turn on the light (β).*

In the case of ENABLEMENT, performing action α brings about a set of conditions that are necessary but not necessarily sufficient for performing action β, as in Example (11).

(11) a. Unplug the device (α) before cleaning it (β).
b. *Clean the device (β) by unplugging it (α).
c. Unplug the device (α) to clean it (β).

The wordings of (10a) and (11a) unambiguously express the respective semantic relation — as the unacceptability of (10b) and (11b) attest. In (10c) and (11c), however, the wording gives no such clear signal; correct interpretation relies on the reader's knowledge of the semantics, that is, knowing whether completing the task necessitates a subsequent action (11b) or not (11a).

One goal of this analysis was to identify the range of permissible expressions of each relation, the preferred expressions, those that are ambiguous and those which are not. This is consistent with the aim of controlled languages to avoid ambiguity while trying to preserve established forms of expression. Interestingly, the two languages differed in their preferred mappings from semantics to syntax, even where they both had syntactically similar structures available. In the expression of ENABLEMENT, for example, the preferred wordings were *by* doing and *pour faire*. This is further evidence that the translation approach adopted by GIFAS (1996) encounters obstacles when structural similarity and functional equivalence diverge across languages.

Another goal was to find explanations for expressions of ENABLEMENT where the expression of β preceded the expression of α, the reverse of events in the world, as in (12).

(12) a. *Before cleaning the device (β) unplug it (α).*
   b. *To clean the device (β) unplug it (α).*

This ordering seems to be chosen either to prevent the user from making a mistake in performing a task prematurely (12a), or to present the purpose (β) of action (α) and to indicate to the reader that the goal named in this purpose is either optional or contrastive. Insights like these, linking syntax to semantics and pragmatics in a precise way, can be exploited by the developers of controlled languages, as can the methods for gaining them.

6.2. Task structure and genre

Going beyond pairs of actions to consider whole tasks, it is useful to establish whether there are any significant correlations between a semantic model of the user's tasks and linguistic features of their expression in a manual. If so, these correlations might be used to control the choices of a natural language generation system. Equally, for controlled language developers they might provide a useful bridge between relatively coarse-grained document type descriptions and fine-grained syntactic constraints.

In this vein, Hartley and Paris (1996) examined sections of a French software manual, using a larger number of semantic units than Delin, Hartley and Scott (1996) but adopting a similar approach in establishing the range of expressions of each unit. The semantic model comprised the elements of the underlying task structure, which would be represented in a natural language generation system's domain knowledge base as a procedural plan for performing the task. The following task structure elements were used.

– *Goals*: actions that users can adopt as goals and which motivate the use of a plan;

– *Functions*: actions that represent the functionality of an interface object—such as a button;

– *Constraints and preconditions*: states which must hold before a plan can be employed successfully;

- *Results*: states which arise as planned or unplanned effects of executing a plan;

- *Substeps*: actions which contribute to the execution of a plan.

They coded the corpus for a large number of syntactic features, including clause complexity, agency, modality and polarity. While certain features or clusters of features tended to co-occur with certain task structure elements, overall the correlations were not strong enough to constrain a natural language generation system to generate texts of the desired form.

Their next step was to establish the mappings between the same set of grammatical features and sections of text with a distinctive communicative goal, notably procedures and ready-reference. These sections were termed *genres*, and they correspond to what Lux (1998b) called *textual modules* defined by different document type descriptions. Again, certain features tended to be more present in one genre than in another, but no clear patterns emerged.

However, when the task and genre analyses were overlaid to show, for example, which grammatical features co-occurred with goals in procedures or with results in ready reference, strong or even absolute preferences for the form of expression became apparent.

So this approach offers not only prospects of control over the output of a natural language generation system, but also a possible answer to the challenge of formulating context sensitive controlled language rules.

7. Prospects for future research

We have outlined some analytical approaches that have been used in the service of natural language generation, a process which entails making choices every step of the way from the starting point — a communicative goal — to the final destination — a text. The results have helped to establish a useful mapping between formal — syntactic — features on the one hand and functional — semantic and pragmatic — features on the other, which can provide the basis for making these choices.

As far as controlled language research is concerned, we believe that the corresponding middle territory between document type descriptions and sentence rules — the controlled language gap — is under-explored. Charting it would advance our current explicit understanding of controlled languages and further enhance their commercial utility. In particular, we believe that applying some of the analyses and mappings tested in natural language generation can provide guidance in bridging this gap.

As regards translation, we hope first to have explained the reasons behind the current intense interest in controlled languages for multilingual documentation. Moreover, we have introduced a framework which — for instructional texts at least — offers a means of capturing the functional equivalence of formally different expressions across languages, at the same time as functional distinctions between formally cognate expressions.

Notes

1. For a concise state of the art in controlled languages, see (Wojcik and Hoard 1997). The proceedings of two international workshops on controlled languages are contained in (CLAW96 1996; CLAW98 1998). These publications also discuss automated checkers that help writers conform to a standard, a topic not addressed in this chapter.
2. Reiter and Dale (2000) offers a comprehensive overview of natural language generation. We adopt their terminology in our description of the architecture of systems.
3. The generation by computer of parallel, multilingual texts—multilingual generation (MLG)—is an emerging technology whose potential to compete with machine-aided translation is considered by Hartley and Paris (1997b).

References

AECMA
    1995   *A Guide for the Preparation of Aircraft Maintenance Documents in the Aerospace Maintenance Language AECMA Simplified English. AECMA Document: PSC-85–16598, Change 5*. Paris: AECMA.

Allen, J.
    1999   Adapting the concept of "translation memory" to "authoring memory" for a controlled language writing environment. In: *Proceedings of Translating and the Computer 20*. London: Aslib.

Almqvist, I. and A. Sågval Hein
    1996   Defining Scania Swedish: a controlled language for truck maintenance. In: *CLAW96*, 159–165.

Barthe, K.
    1997   Le français rationalisé GIFAS. In: E. Pascual, J.-L. Nespoulous and J. Virbel (eds.), 73–79.

Barthe, K.
    1998   GIFAS rationalised French: designing one controlled language to match another. In: *CLAW98*, 96–102.

CLAW96
    1996   *Proceedings of the First International Workshop on Controlled Language Applications CLAW96*. Leuven: CLL, Katholieke Universiteit.

CLAW98
1998   *Proceedings of the Second International Workshop on Controlled Language Applications CLAW98*. Pittsburgh: ILT, Carnegie Mellon University.

Delin, J., A. Hartley and D. Scott
1996   Towards a contrastive pragmatics: syntactic choice in English and French instructions. *Language Sciences* 18 (3–4): 897–931.

Farrington, G.
1996   AECMA Simplified English: an overview of the international aircraft maintenance language. In: *CLAW96*, 1–21.

GIFAS
1996   *Guide du Rédacteur*. Paris: GIFAS.

Hartley, A and C. Paris
1996   Two sources of control over the generation of software instructions. In: *Proceedings of the 34th Annual Meeting of the Association for Computational Linguistics, Santa Cruz, CA, USA*. 192–199.

Hartley, A and C. Paris
1997a   Une analyse fonctionnelle de textes procéduraux. In: E. Pascual, J.-L. Nespoulous and J. Virbel (eds.), 211–222.

Hartley, A and C. Paris
1997b   Multilingual document production: from support for translating to support for authoring. *Machine Translation* 12: 109–128.

Janssen, G., G. Marks and B. Dobbert
1996   Simplified German: a practical approach to documentation and translation. In: *CLAW96*, 150–158.

Kamprath, C., E. Adolphson, T. Mitamura and E. Nyberg
1998   Controlled English for multilingual document production: experience with Caterpillar Technical English. In: *CLAW98*, 51–61.

Lee, A.
1993   Controlled English with and without machine translation. In: *Proceedings of Translating and the Computer 15*. London: Aslib.

Lockwood, R. et al.
1995   *Globalisation: Creating New Markets with Translation Technology*. London: Ovum Reports.

Lux, V.
1998a   Elaboration d'un Français Rationalisé Etendu Modulaire (FREM) pour les manuels de maintenance d'aéronefs. Ph.D. dissertation, Université de Paris7.

Lux, V.
1998b   Modular controlled language design. In: *CLAW98*.

Murphy, D., J. Mason and S. Sklair
1998   Improving translation at the source. In: *Proceedings of Translating and the Computer 20*. London: Aslib.

Ogden, C.K.
1932   *Basic English: a Basic Introduction with Rules and Grammar.* London: Paul Treber.

Pascual, E., J.-L. Nespoulous and J. Virbel (eds.)
1997   *Le Texte Procédural: Langage, Action, Cognition.* Toulouse: PRESCOT, Université Paul Sabatier.

Pym, P.
1991   Simplified English and machine translation. *Professional Translator and Interpreter* 2: 5–9.

Reiter, E. and R. Dale
2000   *Building Natural Language Generation Systems.* Cambridge: Cambridge University Press.

Sågval Hein, A.
1997   Scania controlled Swedish. In: *Proceedings of Translating and the Computer 19.* London: Aslib.

Schachtl, S.
1996   Requirements for controlled German in industrial applications. In: *CLAW96,* 143–149.

Schütz, J.
1998   Multilingual human language technology in automotive documentation workflows. In: *Proceedings of Translating and the Computer 20.* London: Aslib.

van der Eijk, P., M. de Koning and G. van der Steen
1996   Controlled language correction and translation. In: *CLAW96,* 64–73.

Varile, G.B. and A. Zampolli (eds.)
1997   *Survey of the State of the Art in Human Language Technology.* Cambridge: Cambridge University Press.

Wojcik, R.H. and J.E. Hoard
1997   Controlled languages in industry. In: G.B. Varile and A. Zampolli (eds.), 238–243.

Author Index

Abelen, E.   94, 96, 118
Adolphson, E.   324
Adorni, Giovanni   225f.
Åhlander, Lars   118
Allen, J.   309, 323
Almqvist, I.   309, 323
Anwyl, Phyllis   112f., 118
Arndt, W. F.   28, 38
Asp, Elissa   24, 38, 119, 226, 303
Atkinson, Paul   70, 118

Baker, Mona   42, 78, 97, 99, 106, 109, 133, 159, 162, 173, 183, 187, 193, 224, 276
Baldry, Anthony   4, 9f., 277, 280, 282, 292, 294, 296, 298, 301f., 304
Barthe, K.   309, 316, 323
Bassnett, Susan   273f.
Bateman, John A.   73, 86, 88, 110, 113, 116, 118, 194, 197, 208, 219, 224-226
Bauer, W.   28, 38
Beekman, John   23, 38
Bell, Roger T.   13, 18, 42, 44, 48, 51, 117f., 133, 159, 162, 187, 192, 194, 225
Bernstein, Basil   21, 38, 118
Biber, Douglas   138, 148, 159, 162, 187, 225
Bickerton, Derek   66, 118
Black, B.   123
Blanc, E.   113, 118
Böll, Heinrich   106
Bolognesi, Roberto   280, 302
Bowen, John   23, 38
Brandt, Margareta   109, 118
Buchwald, Eva   273
Bühler, Axel   128, 159
Butt, David   18, 122, 275
Buxton, Thomas Falwell   61

Caffarel, Alice   97, 118, 194, 217, 225
Callow, John   23, 38
Carbonell, Jaime G.   112, 118
Carroll, John   129, 159
Carroll, Lewis   8, 232f., 235-238, 241-246
Catford, John C.   15, 18f., 32, 38, 43, 69, 76, 78f., 89, 116-118, 133, 135, 159, 162, 185, 187, 194, 210, 225, 251-254, 273f., 277, 302
Cha, Jin Soon   38f.
Chaucer, Geoffrey   69

Chesterman, Andrew   251-253, 255, 273-275
Chomsky, Noam   7, 10, 24, 38, 42
Churchward, Maxwell C.   103, 119
Cloran, Carmel   18, 122, 275
Conrad, Joseph   109
Coogan, Michael D.   40
Cowan, David   110, 119
Cowrie, Moira   273, 276
Crivelli, E.   280, 302
Cross, Marilyn   122
Crystal, David   134, 136, 159

Dale, R.   323, 325
Damasio, A. R.   66, 119
Damasio, H.   66, 119
Darbelnet, Jean-Paul   171, 190, 192, 211, 214, 224, 227, 274, 276
Davy, Derek   134, 136, 159
Degand, Liesbeth   197, 225f.
de Koning, M.   319, 325
Delin, J.   320f., 324
Dobbert, B.   309, 324
Dodgson, Charles   232
Doherty, Monika   133, 159, 162, 174f., 187, 224

Edmondson, Willis   140, 159
Ellis, J.   14f., 18
Ellmann, J.   123
Emond, Ingrid   41, 79, 117
Emond, Martin   61-64, 117
Emond, Tryggve   41, 109, 117
Emond, Vibeke   41, 117
Estival, D.   113, 119

Farrington, G.   311, 324
Fawcett, Peter   133, 159, 173, 187, 273, 275
Fawcett, Robin   22, 24, 39, 275
Fillmore, C. J.   278
Finegan, Edward   225
Firbas, Jan   285, 303
Firth, J. R.   14, 19-21, 39f., 145, 239, 246, 250f., 275, 278f., 303
Fleming, Ilah   23, 39
Fries, C. C.   20
Fries, Peter   38f., 303
Fujita, Katsuhiko   118

Author Index

Gentzler, Edwin 42, 119, 132, 159, 246
Gerzymisch-Arbogast, Heidrun 133, 159, 304
Ghadessy, Mohsen 122, 225, 305
Gibson, T. 304
Gilardoni, L. 123
Gile, Daniel 274f.
Gingrich, F.W. 28, 38
Goetchius, Eugene Van Ness 27, 39
Grace, George 67, 250, 275
Greenbaum, Sidney 226
Gregory, Michael J. 4, 7, 10, 19, 22, 24, 38f.,42, 69, 119, 185, 239f., 246, 280, 297, 303
Guillaume, P. 113, 118

Haas, W. 239, 246
Halliday, M. A. K. 4-7, 9, 13, 18, 20, 22, 39f., 47-49, 51, 64-70, 75, 79f., 83, 85, 89, 91, 93f., 96-98, 103, 106, 115f., 119f., 122, 134, 136f., 159, 162f., 166, 172, 174, 178, 181, 183, 185-188, 193, 200, 218, 224f., 250, 252f., 274f., 277f., 280, 282f., 292, 294, 297, 303
Halverson, Sandra 231, 246
Hansen, Silvia 182, 188
Hartley, Anthony 4, 9f., 93, 113, 184, 231, 307, 309, 313, 320f., 323f.
Hasan, Ruqaiya 16, 18, 22, 39, 79, 82, 106, 120, 122, 162f., 188, 250, 274f., 280, 303
Hatakka, Mary 273
Hatim, Basil 42, 91, 99, 111, 120, 133, 159, 162, 188, 192, 194, 225
Hawkins, John A. 162, 174, 188, 200f., 204, 225
Hoard, J. E. 323, 325
House, Juliane 4, 7, 10, 127, 134, 143, 154, 159f., 162f., 169, 188, 231, 279, 283, 303
Hudson, Richard 24, 39, 121

Iedema, Rick 49, 121
Ivir, Vladimir 135, 160

Jackendoff, Ray 51
Jakobson, Roman 51, 68, 73, 160
Janssen, G. 309, 324
Johansson, Mats 109
Johansson, Stig 88, 95f., 109, 116, 120
Johnston, Trevor 89, 120

Kaila, Kaarina 260, 270
Kameda, Masayuki 118

Kamprath, C. 310, 324
Keener, Craig S. 27f., 39
Kenny, Dorothy 273
Kittredge, Richard 93, 120f.
Kobayashi, Ichiro 66, 121f.
Koller, Werner 133, 160, 162, 185, 188, 252, 275
Kopesec, Mark 23, 38
Kress, Gunther 49, 53, 62, 64, 121, 299, 303
Kugel, James L. 31, 39
Kunnas, Mauri 249, 260, 265f., 268, 270-272

Labov, W. 70f.
Lager, T. 123
Lamb, S. 275
Lavelli, A. 119
Lavinosa, Sara 183, 188
Lee, A. 310, 324
Leech, Geoffrey 226
Lehrberger, L. 93, 120
Lemke, Jay 294, 303
Leppihalme, Ritva 273
Levy, Jiry 135, 160
Li, Charles 105, 121
Lloyd, Michael 61, 121
Lockwood, R. 308, 324
Lux, V. 315, 322, 324

Makkai, Adam 275
Malinowski, Bronislaw 161, 188, 278
Malmkjær, Kirsten 276
Mann, William C. (Bill) 50, 69, 96, 121, 280, 303
Marks, G. 309, 324
Marshall, Alfred 25, 27-30, 40
Martin, Catherine A. 49, 121
Martin, James Robert 49, 64, 70, 97, 99, 103f., 116, 118, 120f., 138, 160, 162, 165, 174, 178, 181, 186, 188, 225, 274-276
Mason, Ian 42, 91, 99, 111, 120, 133, 159, 162, 188, 192, 194, 225
Mason, J. 309, 324
Matsuda, Toru 118
Matthiessen, Christian M. I. M. 4, 7, 10, 20, 41, 48-51, 54, 66-70, 73,'85, 103f., 106f., 111, 113, 118, 120-122, 162f., 172, 174, 185f., 188, 200, 207, 218f., 224-226, 231
McInnes, David 49, 122

McIntosh, Angus   18, 20, 40, 119f., 163, 188, 225, 303
Mel'cuk, Igor   23, 40
Metzger, Bruce M.   40
Middleton, Christopher   106
Mitamura, T.   324
Mohan, Bernard A.   52, 122
Mudersbach, Klaus   133, 159
Mukařovský   80
Multari, A.   123
Munday, Jeremy   162, 189
Murphy, D.   309, 324
Murphy, Jill   145, 157f.

Nanri, Keizo   118, 122, 224
Nash, Robert J. Jr   25-28, 40
Nesbitt, Christopher   111, 122
Nespoulous, J.-L.   323-325
Netter, K.   119
Neubert, Albrecht   162, 185, 189, 304
Newnham, R.   117
Newmark, Peter   177, 189, 277f., 304
Nida, Eugene   26, 32, 42, 129, 160, 211, 226, 231, 246, 273
Nirenburg, Sergei   118, 121
Nivre, J.   123
Nord, Christiane   184, 189, 259, 276
Nyberg, E.   324

Ogden, C. K.   309, 325
O'Hagan, Minako   113, 122
O'Toole, Michael   49, 52, 62, 64, 122

Palmer, F. R.   19, 23, 40, 102, 123, 239, 246, 275, 303f.
Paris, Cécile   4, 9f., 93, 113, 184, 231, 309, 313, 321, 323f.
Pascual, E.   323-325
Patten, Terry   83, 93, 123
Paul of Tarsus   23
Pawley, Andrew   67f., 123
Payne, John R.   103, 123
Persson, Ingemar   118
Pertsov, Nikolaj   23, 40
Pianesi, F.   119
Piastra, Marco   280, 302
Pike, Kenneth L.   22, 40, 231, 246
Pike, Evelyn   22, 40
Plenker, Birgit   163, 189
Pym, P.   309f., 325

Quirk, Randolph   192, 226

Ramm, Wiebke   94, 123, 174, 189, 200f., 224, 226
Redeker, Gisele   94, 96, 118
Reiss, Katharina   130f., 133, 136, 160, 184, 189, 192, 226
Reiter, E.   323, 325
Robinson, Douglas   132, 160
Rogers A.   123
Rose, David   97, 123, 251
Rosengren, Inger   118
Rothkegel, Annely   174, 189
Ruskin, John   52-58, 61, 63, 65, 116

Sager, Juan C.   192, 211, 226, 254, 276
Sågval Hein, A.   309, 323, 325
Schachtl, S.   309, 325
Schleiermacher, Friedrich   139
Schmidt, Paul   226
Schneider Adams, Laurie   54, 61, 123
Schütz, J.   319, 325
Scott, D.   320f., 324
Shakespeare, William   22, 63, 69, 230
Sheeley, Steven M.   25-28, 40
Sheppard, Nancy   232-235, 243, 246
Shore, Susanna   4, 8-10, 231, 249, 268, 276
Shuttleworth, Mark   273, 276
Sklair, S.   309, 324
Snell-Hornby, Mary   99, 123, 191, 226, 251, 276
Somers, H.   113, 123
Spence, Robert   162, 187, 189
Statham, Nigel   231, 246
Steele, James   23, 40
Steiner, Erich   3f., 6-8, 10, 18, 20, 49, 55, 93f., 104, 116, 123, 134, 160-162, 164, 166, 170, 174, 178, 189, 200f., 215, 218f., 224, 226, 231, 241, 277, 304
Steiner, George   162, 190
Stolze, Radegundis   128, 160
Strevens, Peter   20, 40, 163, 188, 225
Strong, James   28, 30, 40, 146
Sugeno, Michio   66, 121
Svartvik, Jan   226

Taber, Charles   129, 160
Taylor, Christopher   4, 9f., 162, 190, 277, 279, 281, 304
Taylor, Kenneth N.   32
Taylor-Torsello, Carol   162, 190, 277, 304

Author Index

Teich, Elke   4, 8, 10, 73, 82, 88, 91, 95, 108, 116, 162f., 172, 174, 185, 187, 191, 194, 197, 200, 224, 226, 231
Teruya, Kazuhiro   76, 85, 93, 97, 106, 116, 122f.
Tesnières   278
Thibault, Paul   294, 299f., 302, 304f.
Thompson, Sandra A.   50, 94, 96, 105, 118, 121, 280, 303
Toury, Gideon   129f., 160, 173, 190, 253-255, 276
Tomita, M.   112, 118
Turner, William   52-55, 61, 121

Unger, Merrill F.   40

van der Eijk, P.   319, 325
van der Steen, G.   319, 325
van Leeuwen, Theo   49, 53, 62, 64, 121, 299, 303
Varile, G. B.   325
Ventola, Eija   189, 277, 283, 305
Venuti, Lawrence   42, 44, 112, 117, 123, 131, 160, 177, 190, 253, 276
Vermeer, Hans J.   130f., 160, 184, 189, 192, 226

Villiger, Claudia   174, 189
Vinay, Jean-Paul   171, 190, 192, 211, 214, 224, 227, 274, 276
Vine, W. E.   28, 30, 40
Virbel, J.   323-325

Webber, David   69
Weixelbaumer, Ingrid   158
White, William Jr.   40
Williams, Geoff(rey)   18, 275
Wilss, Wolfram   162, 190, 192, 210, 227, 304
Wojcik, R. H.   323, 325
Wu Canzhong   93, 116, 122, 124

Yallop, Colin   3f., 8, 10, 18, 68, 116f., 184, 187, 218f., 227, 229, 254
Yoshimoto, Banana   117

Zadeh, Lotfi A.   79, 124
Zampolli, A.   325
Zeisler, John   30, 40
Zeng Licheng   73, 86, 116, 118, 122, 124, 224
Zock, Michael   225f.

Subject Index

adapted translation 255
AECMA 309-313, 316, 323f.
agency 150, 164, 203f., 207, 322
agnation 80, 82-84, 89
Alice in Wonderland 8, 18, 232, 234, 236, 241-244, 246, 254
Alitji in the Dreamtime 8, 232-234, 236, 242-244, 246
American Bible Society 26
anaphoric reference 283, 286
applied translation studies 191f.
Arabic 41, 110, 119
Aramaic 22
author, technical 316, 318f.
authoring 280, 307-309, 313, 320, 323f.
automatized translation 80, 89, 109
axiality 195, 197f., 214
axis, hierarchy of 76

BEV = Black English Vernacular 70f.
Bible 7, 18, 22, 24-32, 34-40, 144, 230, 242, 251
Bible Society, American 26
Bible Society, Canadian 24f,. 37f.
Bible Societies, United 22
biological system 49
biosemiotic system 51
Black English Vernacular 70f.

Canadian Bible Society 24f., 37f.
Catalan 102
cataphoric reference 283
CATAT = Computer Assisted Text Analysis and Translation 281, 301f.
Chinese 68, 85, 93f., 104-106, 116f., 120f., 277
class 9, 22, 79, 85, 100, 105, 117, 137f., 140, 147, 163f., 185, 187, 192, 207f., 210-212, 214f., 256, 258, 261, 266, 268, 270, 274, 279, 294, 316
cline of delicacy 76, 106
cline of instantiation 74, 80, 87-91, 94, 99, 115f.
code, elaborated 21
code, restricted 21
cohesion 9, 99, 145f., 153, 165, 267, 281, 283, 286f., 288-290, 295
colligation 27

collocation 19, 27, 29, 78, 145, 151, 153, 175, 265f., 268, 272
comparative linguistics 10, 42f., 88
comparison, language 41, 88f., 184f., 187, 196
Computer Assisted Text Analysis and Translation 281, 301f.
concept as a theoretical postulate 23
congruent realization 101, 207-209
content 3, 6, 14f., 49, 64, 89, 96, 98, 103, 106, 122, 128, 133, 137f., 143, 153, 161, 207, 209, 239, 308, 318f.
contrastive linguistics 8, 42, 88, 135, 191, 193f., 196, 199, 212, 214-216, 218f.
controlled language 9, 184, 307-311, 313-325
convergence zone 66
corpora 10, 88, 120, 193, 274
corpus 43, 47, 88, 95, 109, 120, 134, 138, 153f., 224, 259, 268, 274, 315, 319f., 322
correspondence, formal 252
covert translation 136, 139-145, 154-156
covert version 142f., 145
creative translation 10, 19
cultural filter 140-143, 145, 154

Danish 69
de-automatized translation 80
deconstruction 131, 231
delicacy 22, 65, 76, 79, 106, 145, 163, 185, 195, 197f., 214-216
delicacy, cline of 76, 106
descriptive translation studies 129f.
dialect 19, 69, 142, 165
diatype 19
dictionary 23, 89, 120, 230, 239, 262, 273, 301, 310f.
Document Type Description 319
documentation 9f., 307-310, 323-325
documentation, multilingual 9f., 323
Dutch 21, 94, 96, 118, 225
dynamic equivalence 23-26, 129, 211-213, 231

elaborated code 21
enablement 320f.
English 7-10, 15f., 19-21, 24-35, 38-41, 43-48, 50-54, 60-62, 65, 67-71, 73-76, 82-86,

88f., 93-97, 99-110, 119-123, 127, 143, 145, 147, 149, 151-154, 159, 161f., 166-178, 182f., 188, 191f., 194f., 197-205, 207f., 210, 215-217, 219, 222, 224-227, 230, 232-239, 241, 243-245, 249, 254, 257f., 260-263, 266-270, 272-276, 278, 284, 301f., 305, 307-312, 314-316, 320, 323-325
English, Black ~ Vernacular   70f.
English, simplified   309
equivalence   6f., 15-19, 23-27, 29, 31f., 48, 73-76, 78f., 87, 97, 99, 104-106, 109f., 115, 117, 129-131, 134-136, 141f., 152, 156, 187, 191, 210-214, 216-218, 227, 229, 231, 233, 235-237, 239-243, 245f., 250-254, 266, 272f., 286, 316, 320, 323
equivalence value   17, 253
equivalence weighting   253
equivalence, dynamic   23-26, 129, 211-213, 231
equivalence, formal   7, 23-27, 29, 152, 211f.
equivalence, functional   32, 104f., 141f., 156, 212f., 320, 323
equivalence, grammatical   212f.
equivalence, translation   15-17, 19, 32, 48, 73, 76, 78f., 87, 97, 99, 115, 117, 130, 134f., 231, 252f.
evaluation of translation   127-145, 155f.
evaluation, functionalistic   130f.
evaluation, functional-pragmatic   134-139
evaluation, linguistically oriented   133f.
evaluation, neo-hermeneutic   128
evaluation, response-based behavioural   129
exponence   22

field (of discourse)   94, 111, 134, 137-139, 145f., 149-151, 153, 163f., 169f., 278f., 299
Finnish   9, 106, 249, 254f., 257-263, 265-274, 276
focus, information   279, 282, 284f., 288
foreignizing translation   177, 186
formal correspondence   252
formal equivalence   7, 23-27, 29, 152, 211f.
FR = Français Rationalisé   310, 316, 323
fractal types   103
Français Rationalisé   310, 316, 323
free translation   23, 66, 79, 81, 89, 112, 115, 117, 183, 185, 192, 210-213
French   20f., 41, 46, 60, 68, 75f., 85f., 93, 101f., 183, 227, 273, 307, 309f., 316, 320f., 323f.

function   5, 7, 10, 14-18, 20, 22-26, 29, 31f., 38f., 41, 48f., 64f., 67f., 78-80, 84-86, 94, 96f., 99, 101-106, 109f., 116-118, 120-124, 127, 129-131, 133-144, 149-151, 153, 155f., 163, 175f., 178, 183-186, 189, 192-195, 197f., 200, 204, 207, 212-214, 216f., 224, 229, 240-242, 250, 252-254, 256, 260f., 273f., 277-280, 282f., 285, 293, 296-299, 301, 303, 307, 311, 316-323
function-rank matrix   97-100, 105
functional equivalence   32, 104f., 141f., 156, 212f., 320, 323
functional roles   22
functional typology   118, 194
functional-pragmatic evaluation   134-139
functionalistic evaluation   130f.
fuzzy theory   73, 78

generation, multilingual   4, 8f., 42, 73, 111, 113, 116, 161, 166, 184, 194, 224-226, 318, 323
generation, natural language   118, 225, 307, 317-323
genre   43, 47, 91, 128, 130, 138, 141, 149f., 153-156, 177, 224, 249, 253, 256-259, 267, 272f., 282, 285, 293, 300, 304, 321f.
German   7f., 10, 20, 41, 46, 68, 73, 83f., 88f., 94f., 102, 106-109, 117f., 123, 127, 134, 142f., 145, 149-154, 159, 161f., 166-168, 170-178, 181-183, 188f., 191, 194, 197-210, 215-217, 221f., 224-226, 240, 276, 282, 307, 309, 324f.
GIFAS = Guide du Français Rationalisé   310, 316, 320, 323f.
given and new information   53, 197, 262, 266, 273, 279, 283, 285, 288
grammatical equivalence   212f.
grammatical metaphor   70, 174, 181, 183, 186, 194, 199f., 207-210, 214f., 224, 278, 282f.
Greek   20, 22-25, 27-33, 38, 40
Guide du Français Rationalisé   310, 316, 320, 323f.

Hebrew   22, 28, 30-32, 46
hierarchy of axis   76
hierarchy of rank   74, 80, 117
hierarchy of stratification   74, 79f., 87-89
HyperContext   280, 292f., 302

imperative theory   13, 15
inclusive translation   30

indicative theory 13, 15
information focus 279, 282, 284f., 288
information structure 53, 64, 99, 265, 283, 285, 295
information, given and new 53, 197, 262, 266, 273, 279, 283, 285, 288
instantiation 74, 79f., 87-92, 94, 96-99, 115f., 185, 187, 193, 198f., 212, 214, 216, 218f., 252
instantiation-stratification matrix 87, 91f., 96
instantiation, cline of 74, 80, 87-91, 94, 99, 115f.
interlingua approach to machine translation 73, 87
interlingual translation 51f., 66f.
interlingual version 7, 161, 170, 179
intersemiotic translation 51f., 66f., 69, 73, 115
intertextual relationships 181
intralingual translation 68
intralingual version 7, 161-163, 169, 179
Italian 75, 79, 117, 278, 282, 290, 301

Japanese 41, 68, 76, 85, 93, 97, 106, 116f., 120f., 123, 258

Kalam 67f., 70, 101, 104, 123
KPML = Komet Penman MultiLingual 194

language comparison 41, 88f., 184f., 187, 196
Latin 20
Leipzig School 133
lexical metaphor 174, 177, 181, 224
lexicogrammar 15f., 43, 45, 47-50, 64-66, 74, 76, 79, 82, 85, 88f., 96-98, 103, 106, 163, 172, 174, 184-186, 195, 253, 317f.
linguistically oriented evaluation 133f.
literal translation 23, 66, 76, 79-81, 89, 112, 115, 117, 171, 174f., 177f., 181, 184f., 210-212, 214, 216, 218
local semantics 186
logogenesis 115f.
London School 250

machine translation 4, 6, 15f., 18f., 41f., 47, 72, 85, 87f., 112, 118, 194, 196, 203, 207, 209, 217, 307-309, 315, 324f.

machine translation, interlingua approach to 73, 87
machine translation, transfer approach to 73, 86
material model of translation 45-48
material process 175f., 200, 203-205, 208, 289f.
meaning 3, 7, 14, 19, 21f., 24, 26, 30-32, 35f., 43, 46f., 49, 51, 54, 64-67, 69f., 73, 76, 78-80, 89, 93f., 96, 98f., 103, 105, 110, 113, 115f., 119f., 124, 128, 133, 136f., 140, 164f., 174f., 181-184, 186, 189, 196, 214, 224, 233, 235, 239, 244, 250f., 253, 256, 258, 262, 265, 267-269, 273, 275, 278, 285, 293f., 297, 299, 301, 303f., 311
mental process 200, 203-205, 286, 289f.
metacontext of translation 111f.
metafunction 15-17, 49, 64f., 67f., 79, 94, 96f., 99, 101-106, 109f., 122, 195, 197f., 214, 216, 240, 253, 297, 299
metaphor, grammatical 70, 174, 181, 183, 186, 194, 199f., 207-210, 214f., 224, 278, 282f.
metaphor, lexical 174, 177, 181, 224
MLG = multilingual generation 4, 8f., 42, 73, 111, 113, 116, 161, 166, 184, 194, 224-226, 318, 323
modality 42, 64, 73, 102f., 121, 123, 164f., 295-299, 302, 322
mode (of discourse) 94, 112, 134, 137-139, 145, 148-150, 153, 163-165, 169f., 278-280, 299
model of translation, material 45-48
model of translation, relational 45-48
modes of description 19
modulation 83, 103, 117, 192, 211, 213-216
mood 73, 76, 95, 110, 121, 145, 164f., 195, 197f., 224, 279, 281, 283, 285f., 291, 295
motifs, semantic 85, 116
MT = machine translation 4, 6, 15f., 18f., 41f., 47, 72, 85, 87f., 112, 118, 194, 196, 203, 207, 209, 217, 307-309, 315, 324f.
Multex 113, 122
multifunctional paraphrase 185
multilingual communication 5, 42
multilingual documentation 9f., 323
multilingual (text) generation 4, 8f., 42, 73, 111, 113, 116, 161, 166, 184, 194, 224-226, 318, 323
multimodal semantic system 66
multimodal texts 277, 300f.

334 Subject Index

natural language generation   118, 225, 307, 317-323
neo-hermeneutic evaluation   128
new information   53, 197, 262, 266, 273, 279, 282f., 285, 288
New Testament   7, 24f., 28, 30, 37-40
noncongruent realization   207-209
Norwegian   95f., 109, 120

official translation   19, 273
overt translation   136, 139-145, 154-156
overt version   142-145

Papua New Guinea   67
parallel texts   93, 99, 135, 259f., 272
paraphrase   7, 23f., 26, 28-32, 37, 162, 179, 181, 184f., 192, 200, 207, 212, 231, 239
paraphrase, multifunctional   185
partial translation   69, 91, 112, 254f.
pedagogy   4, 8-10, 120, 216, 249f., 256-269
physical system   48f.
Pitjantjatjara   8, 18, 68, 97, 232-239, 243-245, 254
postmodernism   131f.
pragmatics   133f., 145, 313, 321, 324
Prague School   42
predicated theme   106-109, 200
predication, theme   94, 107, 109, 201
process type   44f., 54, 82f., 100, 110, 175, 200, 203f., 206f., 209
process, material   175f., 200, 203-205, 208, 289f.
process, mental   200, 203-205, 286, 289f.
process, relational   175f., 203-205, 208, 286, 290
process, verbal   203-205
profile, textual   137f., 145
projection   101-104, 286
properties of translated texts   162, 173f.
protolanguage   64f.

Quechua   69
Qur'an   230

rank   15-17, 22, 40, 49, 52-54, 62, 70, 74-76, 78-80, 84f., 88f., 97-101, 104-106, 109, 117, 158, 164, 182f., 185f., 189, 195, 197f., 207f., 210, 213f., 216, 253, 262, 277, 304
rank scale   16, 74f., 78, 88, 98f., 104-106, 182, 185
rank, function-~ matrix   97-100, 105

rank, hierarchy of   74, 80, 117
reference, anaphoric   283
reference, cataphoric   283
register   7f., 14, 18f., 43, 60, 69f., 73, 80, 84, 87, 91, 93f., 96, 98, 116, 122, 134, 138, 141, 156, 161-163, 165-167, 169, 171f., 177-182, 184-187, 189, 207, 212f., 216, 218, 225f., 241, 279, 291, 299, 303f., 310
registerial variation   69, 161f., 178-181, 184, 207
relational model of translation   45-48
relational process   175f., 203-205, 208, 286, 290
response-based behavioural evaluation   129
restricted code   21
restricted language   19, 21
rheme   146, 279, 283, 285f., 288, 295, 297
Rhetorical Structure Theory   96, 121
roles, functional   22
Russian   15f., 85, 183, 230, 277

Sanskrit   241
scale and category linguistics   19
schematic representations   65
search space   83, 89
semantically based translation   178
semantic motifs   85, 116
semantic system, multimodal   66
semantics   3, 15, 17, 19, 49, 64, 66, 69, 74, 79f., 82, 86, 89, 96, 98f., 103, 116, 172-174, 176, 179, 184-186, 195, 212, 218, 231, 253, 299, 314, 317, 320f.
semantics, local   186
semiotic system   42f., 47-52, 55, 59f., 63-66, 72f., 91, 97, 111, 116, 123, 138
shadow texts   83
simplified English   309
skopos   130f.
SL = source language   3, 17, 23, 33, 48, 79, 83, 113, 135f., 140, 165, 181, 191, 202, 210f., 214-218, 254, 258, 273, 278
social system   49, 121
sociocognitive linguistics   24, 38
source language   3, 17, 23, 33, 48, 79, 83, 113, 135f., 140, 165, 181, 191, 202, 210f., 214-218, 254, 258, 273, 278
Spanish   46, 83, 102, 107, 278
stratification   3, 15, 74, 78-80, 87-89, 91f., 96, 195, 197f., 212, 214, 216
stratification-instantiation matrix   96-98

stratification, hierarchy of 74, 79f., 87-89
stratum 15-17, 74, 79f., 89, 91, 115f., 195, 212f.
structure 3, 9, 22, 24, 31f., 34, 42, 53, 62, 64, 76, 80, 82, 89, 99, 109, 118, 121, 123, 127, 133, 138, 140, 146, 150f., 163f., 167, 171, 175-177, 183, 185, 201, 219, 222, 240f., 250f., 265, 268, 279, 281, 283, 285-287, 295, 297, 299, 308, 315, 318-322
structure, information 53, 64, 99, 265, 285, 295
sublanguage 69, 93, 121, 319
Summer Institute of Linguistics 32, 38-40
Swedish 41, 62, 69, 79, 94, 109, 117, 254, 309, 323, 325
syntax 278, 283f., 313f., 317, 320f.
system 5-8, 14-16, 22, 24, 28, 41-43, 47-52, 55, 59f., 63-68, 72-74, 76, 79f., 82-89, 91, 93-99, 101-113, 115-117, 121-123, 129f., 132, 134, 136-138, 144, 161-166, 171f., 177, 181, 183, 185, 187, 189, 193-195, 197-207, 210, 212f., 215-219, 224f., 244, 250-253, 273-275, 277-281, 283, 291, 299-301, 307, 315, 317-319, 321-323
system network 82f., 88, 195, 224
system, biological 49
system, biosemiotic 51
system, multimodal semantic 66
system, physical 48f.
system, semiotic 42f., 47-52, 55, 59f., 63-66, 72f., 91, 97, 111, 116, 123, 138
system, social 49, 121
systemic functional linguistics 5, 7f., 24, 39, 122, 134, 162, 177, 182, 193-195, 198, 217, 219, 250, 278, 283
SYSTRAN 8, 224

Tagalog 103, 121
target language 3, 16f., 19, 23, 48, 79f., 83, 135-137, 140, 177f., 183, 202, 208, 210-212, 214-218, 254, 259, 262, 277-279, 283, 291, 307
task structure 321f.
teaching translation 4, 8-10, 120, 216, 249f., 256-269
technical writing 312, 316
tenor (of discourse) 94, 111, 134, 137-139, 142, 145, 147f., 149-154, 163-165, 169f., 182, 278f., 299
text 3-11, 13-18, 20, 22, 24-27, 29, 31-33, 37, 39-43, 48, 52-55, 59, 61f., 64, 67-70, 73-76, 78-80, 82-84, 86-89, 91, 93-102, 104, 106-109, 111-113, 115-117, 119, 121-124, 127-138, 140-156, 160-189, 191-199, 201-203, 206-208, 210-226, 229-231, 233-245, 247, 249-305, 307-309, 311-315, 317-320, 322-324
text type 14, 43, 91, 98, 133, 198, 212f., 219, 274, 317-319
texts, multimodal 277, 300f.
texts, parallel 93, 99, 135, 259f., 272
texts, properties of translated 162, 173
texts, shadow 83
textual modules 322
textual profile 137f., 145
theme 39, 97, 106-109, 123, 145f., 165, 194, 199-202, 210, 224, 226, 279, 282-286, 288, 291, 295, 297, 303
theme predication 94, 107-109, 201
theme, predicated 106-109, 200
theoretical translation studies 191-193
theory, imperative 13, 15
theory, indicative 13, 15
thesaurus 83, 89, 119
TL = target language 3, 16f., 19, 23, 48, 79f., 83, 135-137, 140, 177f., 183, 202, 208, 210-212, 214-218, 254, 259, 262, 277-279, 283, 291, 307
Tongan 103, 119
transfer approach to machine translation 73, 86
transitivity 30, 39, 46, 76, 84, 104-106, 110, 164, 194, 199, 203-205, 210, 281, 283, 286f., 295
translated texts, properties of 162, 173f.
translation criticism 127, 129, 134f., 139, 141, 143f., 155f.
translation difference 68f., 76, 116
translation equivalence 15-17, 19, 32, 48, 73, 76, 78f., 87, 97, 99, 115, 117, 130, 134f., 231, 252f.
translation memory 309, 323
translation potential 53, 292-294, 301
translation procedure 8, 171, 177, 191-194, 208, 210, 212-216, 274
translation quality 133-136, 156, 163
translation shift 48, 68, 74, 78f., 87, 99, 102-104, 107, 109, 115
translation strategy 174, 176, 191-194, 212-214, 216, 262, 274
translation studies 4-8, 10, 42, 79, 86, 88, 91, 99, 128-130, 132f., 143, 162, 187, 189,

191-194, 210, 217-219, 224, 231, 246, 249-251, 256, 260, 274, 276f., 283, 301f.
translation studies, applied   191f.
translation studies, descriptive   129f.
translation studies, theoretical   191-193
translation, adapted   255
translation, automatized   80, 89, 109
translation, covert   136, 139-145, 154-156
translation, creative   10, 19
translation, de-automatized   80
translation, evaluation of   127-145, 155f.
translation, foreignizing   177, 186
translation, free   23, 66, 79, 81, 89, 112, 115, 117, 183, 185, 192, 210-213
translation, inclusive   30
translation, interlingua approach to machine   73, 87
translation, interlingual   51f., 66f.
translation, intersemiotic   51f., 66f., 69, 73, 115
translation, intralingual   68
translation, literal   23, 66, 76, 79-81, 89, 112, 115, 117, 171, 174f., 177f., 181, 184f., 210-212, 214, 216, 218
translation, machine   4, 6, 15f., 18f., 41f., 47, 72, 85, 87f., 112, 118, 194, 196, 203, 207, 209, 217, 307-309, 315, 324f.
translation, material model of   45-48
translation, metacontext of   111f.
translation, official   19, 273
translation, overt   136, 139-145, 154-156
translation, partial   69, 91, 112, 254f.
translation, relational model of   45-48
translation, semantically based   178
translation, teaching   4, 8-10, 120, 216, 249f., 256-269

translation, transfer approach to machine   73, 86
translation, word-for-word   117, 210
transposition   71, 192, 208, 211, 213-216
TREE   113, 123
typology   10, 15, 41, 43, 48-50, 67, 73, 87f., 115, 118, 123, 133, 162, 185, 187, 194, 217, 219, 225
typology, functional   118, 194

unit   4, 16f., 19, 22, 25, 41, 53, 63, 74-76, 78-80, 85, 88, 94, 99f., 116f., 120, 135, 138, 140-143, 153, 164, 181, 185, 187, 189, 193, 198, 210, 212, 222, 253, 265, 271, 274, 277, 286, 318, 321
United Bible Societies   22

value, equivalence   17, 253
variation   8, 14, 16-18, 20, 63, 67-69, 73, 79, 85, 91, 94, 96f., 99, 105, 119, 161-163, 165f., 169, 171, 177-181, 184, 187, 189, 197-199, 207, 210, 214, 225, 229, 249, 258, 269, 284, 304, 318
variation, registerial   69, 161f., 178-181, 184, 207
verbal process   203-205
version, covert   142f., 145
version, interlingual   7, 161, 170, 179
version, intralingual   7, 161-163, 169, 179
version, overt   142-145
Vietnamese   68, 106
Vorfeld   201

weighting, equivalence   253
word-for-word translation   117, 210

New publications from Mouton de Gruyter

Language, Text and Knowledge
Mental Models of Expert Communication
Edited by Lita Lundquist and Robert J. Jarvella
2000. viii, 326 pages. Cloth. DM 168,– / approx. US$ 84.00 / from 1.1.02: € 84
• ISBN 3-11-016724-7
(Text, Translation, Computational Processing 2)

Casting light on the interplay between language and domain-specific knowledge, this new book brings together ideas and approaches from cognitive linguistics and psychology which aim at explaining how language works, and how people combine their knowledge from a variety of sources as they make sense of and draw inferences from text.

Text- und Gesprächslinguistik / Linguistics of Text and Conversation
Ein internationales Handbuch zeitgenössischer Forschung / An International Handbook of Contemporary Research
Klaus Brinker, Gerd Antos, Wolfgang Heinemann, Sven Frederik Sager (Editors)
Two Volumes

Volume 1: 2000. 27 x 19 cm. xxviii, 884 pages; 103 figures.
Cloth. DM 698,– / approx. US$ 349.00 / from 1.1.02: € 348
• ISBN 3-11-013559-0
Volume 2: 2001. 27 x 19 cm. Approx. 750 pages.
Cloth. Approx. DM 598,– / US $ 299 / from 1.1.02: € 298
• ISBN 3-11-016918-5
(Handbücher zur Sprach- und Kommunikationswissenschaft / Handbooks of Linguistics and Communication Science 16)

The main goals of the handbook are to represent recent international research as well as the historical development of research on this complex subject, to explain the basis of both textual and conversational methods of analysis, to analyze the crucial aspects of the constitution and typology of texts and conversations, and to present the dialogue between textual and conversational linguistics with other disciplines and specific areas of practice.

Prices are subject to change.

WALTER DE GRUYTER GMBH & CO. KG
Genthiner Straße 13 · 10785 Berlin
Telefon +49-(0)30-2 60 05-0
Fax +49-(0)30-2 60 05-251
www.deGruyter.de

de Gruyter
Berlin · New York

A Mouton de Gruyter Journal

TEXT
an interdisciplinary journal for the study of discourse

Editors: Srikant Sarangi and John Wilson

Four issues per year (approx. 600 pages per volume).
ISSN 0165-4888

Text aims:
- to challenge through critique and debate the tenets of discourse research across disciplinary boundaries, both in terms of theoretical output and practical outcomes
- to encourage dissemination of scholarly work in under-represented domains (e.g. communication science, artificial intelligence, forensic linguistics, rhetoric and composition, stylistics, narratives, institutional ethnography, sociology of science)
- to remain independent of any individual or group ideology, while encouraging in equal measure the use of discourse to challenge discourse orthodoxy
- to maintain a revitalized specialist board and an expanded advisory board consisting of well-known discourse scholars
- to produce annual *Text* review issues to consolidate discourse-related research publications, including book series.

Text online
Online access is now available to all institutional subscribers of the print version at no extra charge. To register for free online access or for more information, please contact us at wdg-info@deGruyter.de

Subscription rates for Volume 21 (2001):
Institutions / Libraries: DM 390,– / € 199,40 / öS 2847,– (RRP) / sFr 335,– / *US$ 210.00
(Price includes online access at no extra charge)
Individuals: DM 78,– / € 39,88 / *US$ 45.00
Single Issues: DM 98,– / € 50,11 / öS 715,– (RRP) / sFr 86,– / *US$ 53.00

Individual rate not available for residents of Germany, Austria and Switzerland.
*US Dollar prices apply only to orders placed in North America

Prices are subject to change

WALTER DE GRUYTER GMBH & CO. KG
Genthiner Straße 13 · 10785 Berlin
Telefon +49-(0)30-2 60 05-0
Fax +49-(0)30-2 60 05-251
www.deGruyter.de

de Gruyter
Berlin · New York